THE ART OF ·COLOUR· PHOTOGRAPHY

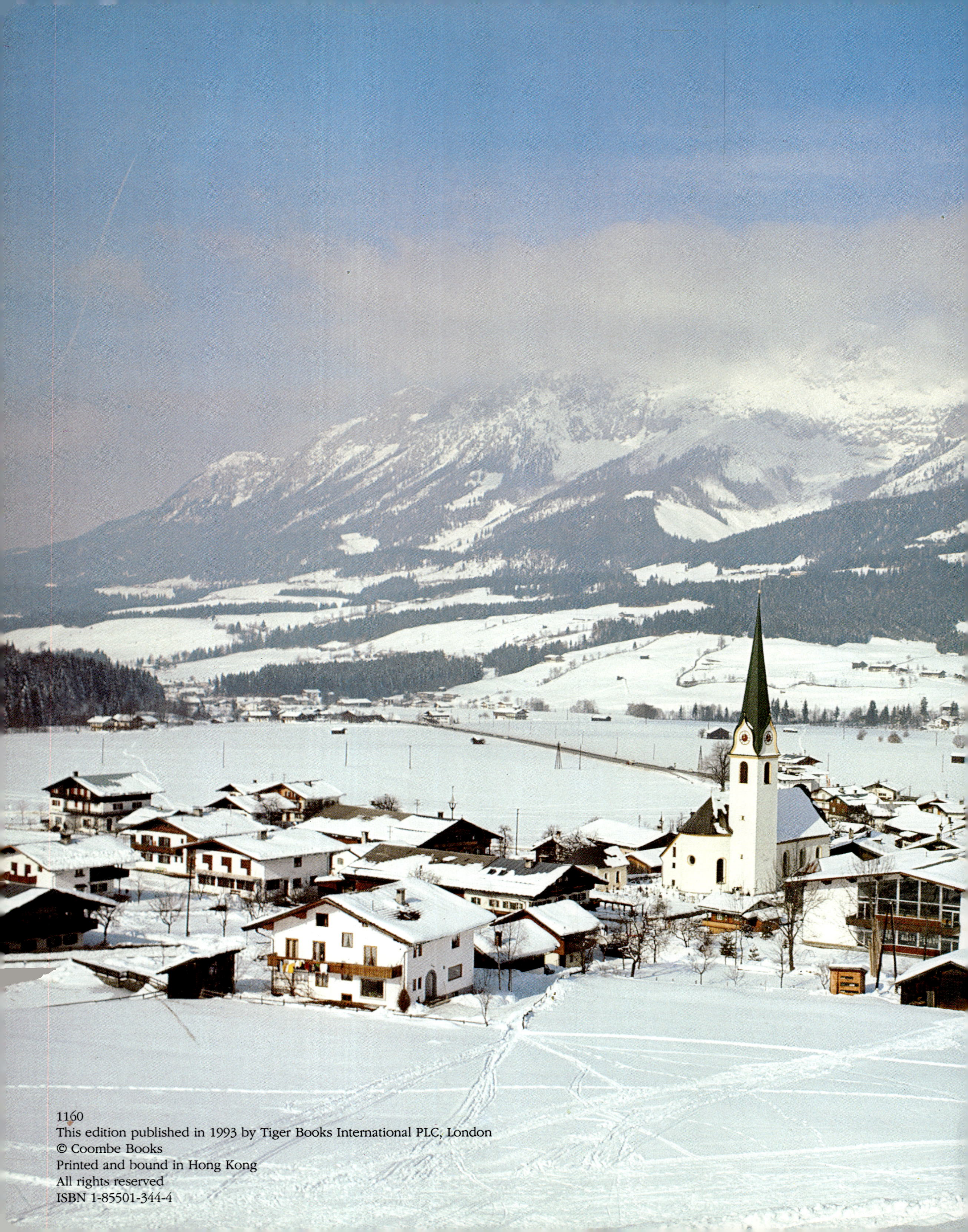

1160
This edition published in 1993 by Tiger Books International PLC, London

Printed and bound in Hong Kong

ISBN 1-85501-344-4

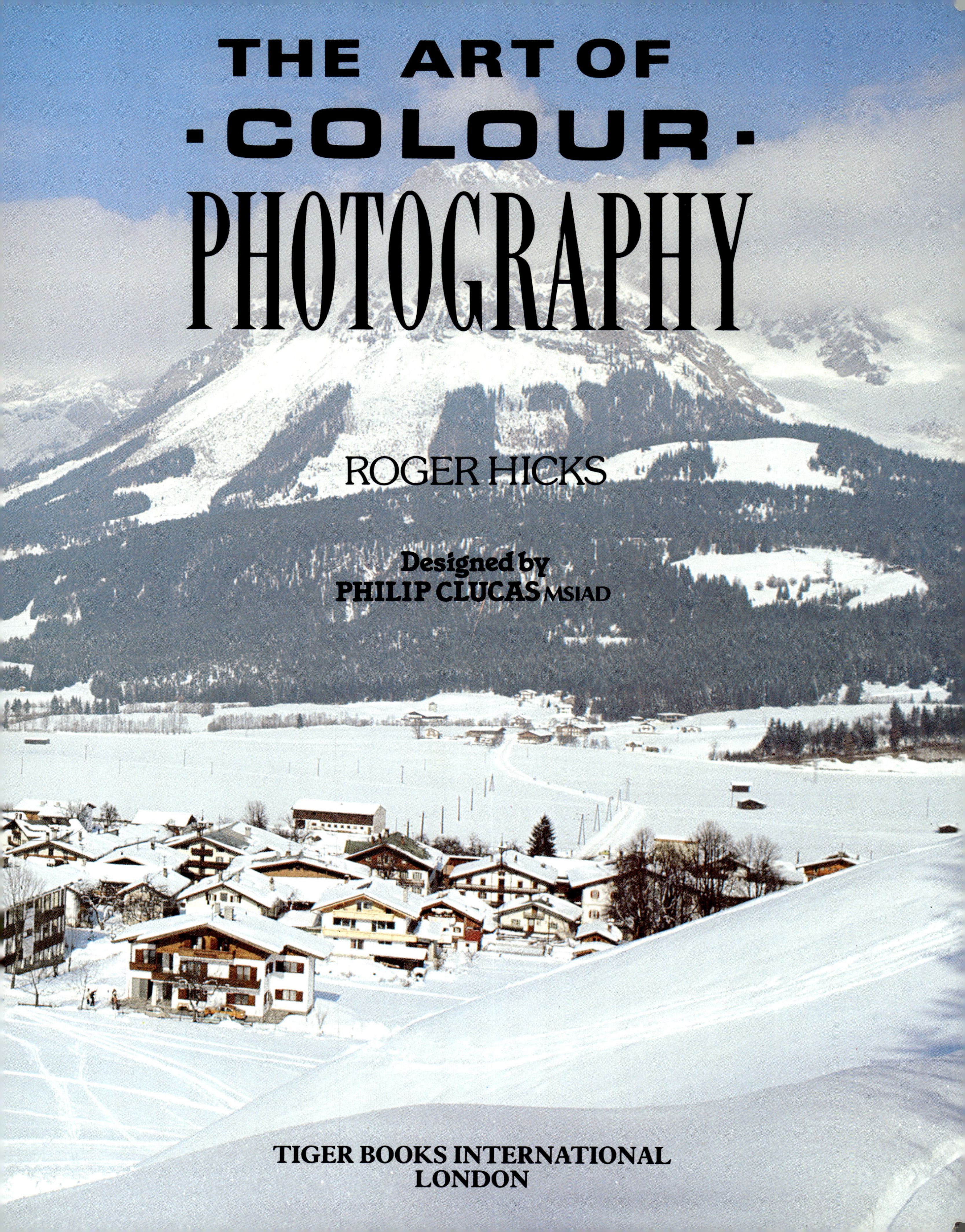

THE ART OF ·COLOUR· PHOTOGRAPHY

ROGER HICKS

Designed by
PHILIP CLUCAS MSIAD

TIGER BOOKS INTERNATIONAL
LONDON

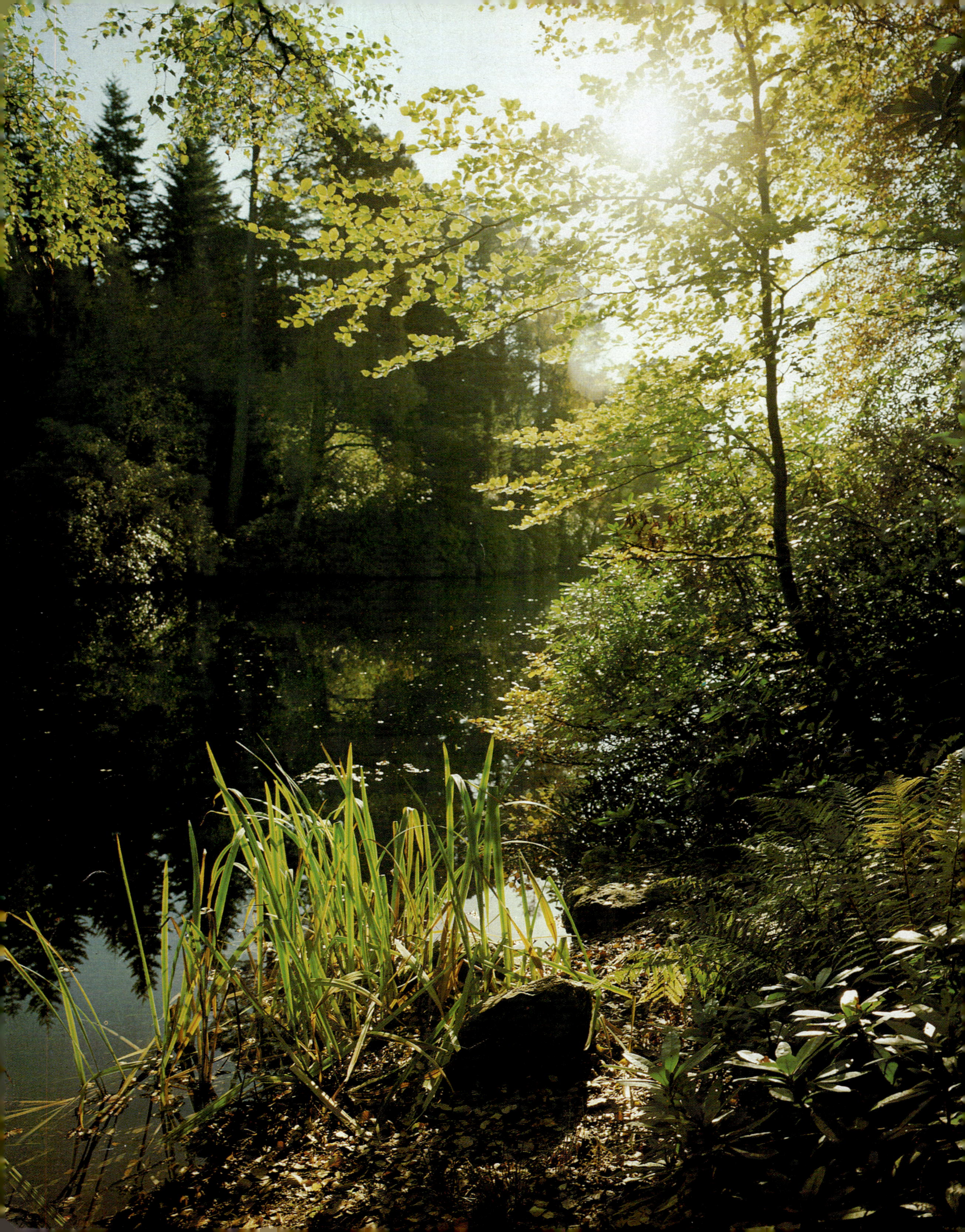

CONTENTS

INTRODUCTION

***Creativity is an approach as** well as a way of seeing. Two of the pictures: **right and below,** were taken with tripod-mounted medium format cameras to preserve richness of detail and gradation: one concentrates on the profusion of nature, and the other on its variety-in-repetition. The picture **far right** was inspired by the contrast in scale between the mountainside and the buildings; it was shot across the valley using a hand-held 35mm camera with standard lens. A larger camera would have been much harder work to carry – but the difference in quality is visible even in reproduction.*

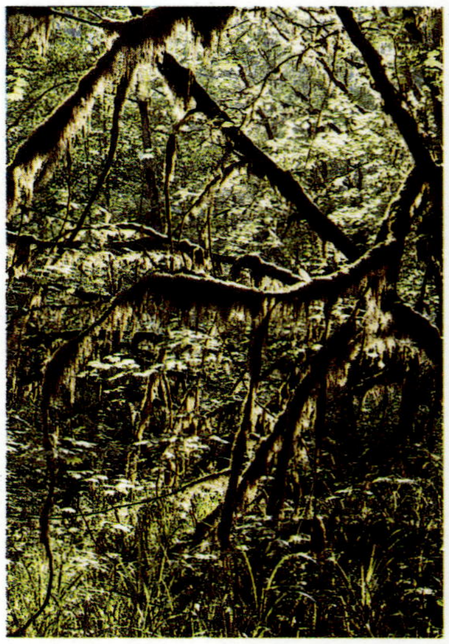

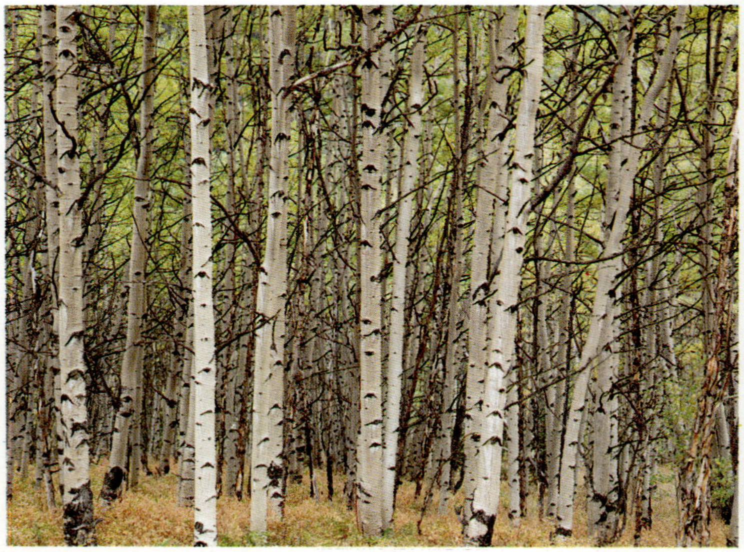

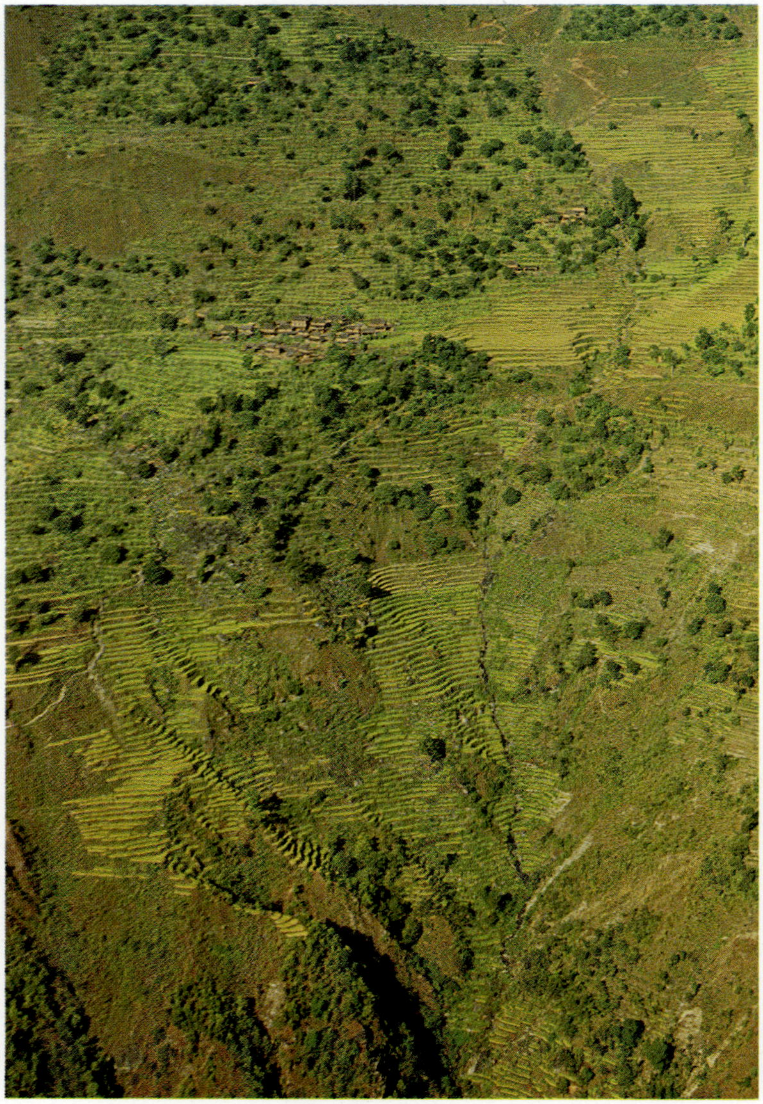

Nowadays, colour photography is arguably the easiest type of photography available – at least, from the user's point of view. The immense and complex technology behind the image need hardly affect the photographer at all: George Eastman's old boast, "You press the button and we do the rest," has never been more true.

What, then, is the need for this book? The answer is twofold. First, there is a world of difference between a photograph which is a thing of beauty in its own right and a simple record shot. The difference may be a matter of luck, but more often it is a matter of creativity. Secondly, the photographer who understands the photographic process has the creative edge over one who blindly follows the meter's settings and the manufacturers' instructions.

Consequently, this book functions on two levels. The pictures are examples of creative photography – of making something more than just a record. The text tells you how to achieve these effects. Of course, some of the pictures could have been taken with the simplest equipment, because there is no substitute for the creative eye. Equally, all the technical expertise in the world can be insufficient to lift a really boring shot into the realms of creativity, but it is a fair comment that more potentially beautiful pictures are spoilt by a lack of technical ability than by an excess.

Before we go on, though, there is another very important point to remember. Not every picture needs to be creative.

Some people spend so much time agonising about creativity that they never take any pictures. Photography is fun. Simply enjoy it, and you will probably find that creativity will come even when you are not looking for it.

A good place to start on the technicalities of colour photography is a brief history; this not only introduces some of the terms you will hear used but also shows the diversity of processes available.

The first colour picture, taken in 1861, involved exposing three separate plates through three separate filters, one for each of the primary colours. The resulting lantern slides were projected (using three projectors) through the same three filters. When all three were in register, the red, green, and blue light combined to recreate the original colours. Because the process involved adding together the different colours, it was known as additive colour.

Subtractive processes, on the other hand, start off with white light and filter out the colours that are not wanted. All conventional modern methods are of this type. For example, a green field is represented by an area which transmits (on a transparency) or reflects (on a print) green, but absorbs all other colours. A white cloud is shown by an area which absorbs no light, and a black doorway by an area which absorbs all light equally.

The theoretical groundwork for these processes was laid in

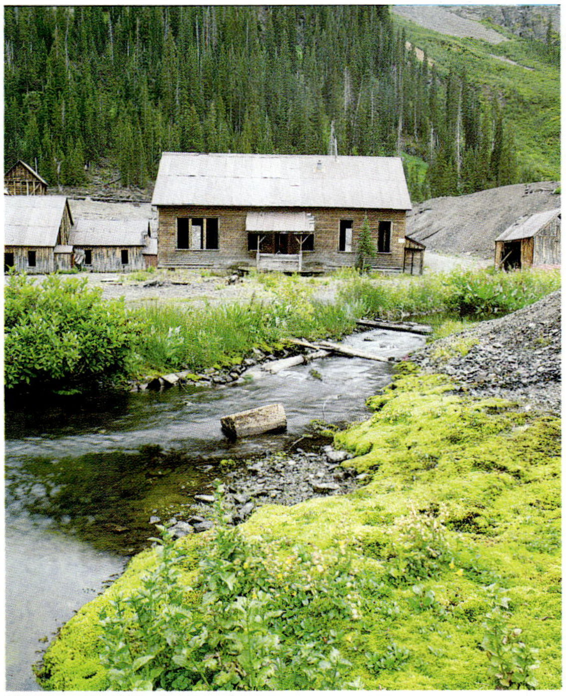

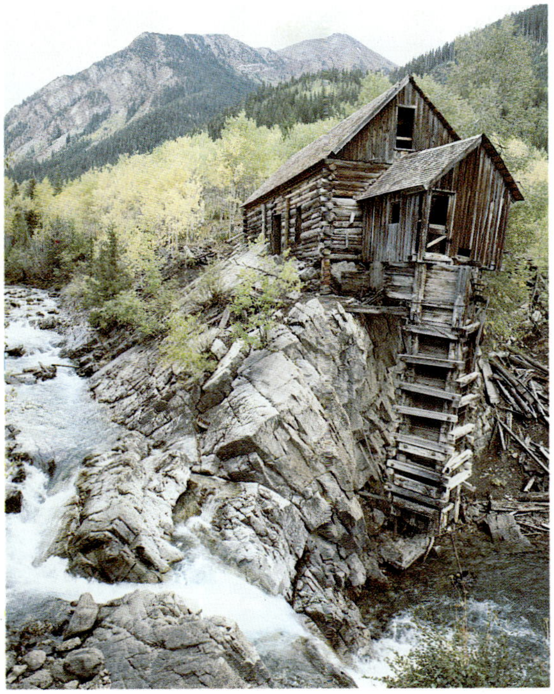

In colour photography, *restraint is often more effective than prodigality. In each of these three pictures, a single predominant hue sets the mood. On the far left, the yellowish green of the grass suggests spring or early summer; the water and the pine trees echo the look of cool freshness. On the left, the bluish tint (typical of high altitudes on an overcast day) emphasises the coldness of the water and the mountains: the impression is definitely cold and bleak rather than fresh and welcoming. The blue of the mist in the picture* ***below*** *suggests scale, by means of aerial perspective, and captures the rainswept grandeur of the Scottish coast; the grey-blue cloud also balances the mass of the land, adding interest to what would otherwise be a blank grey sky.*

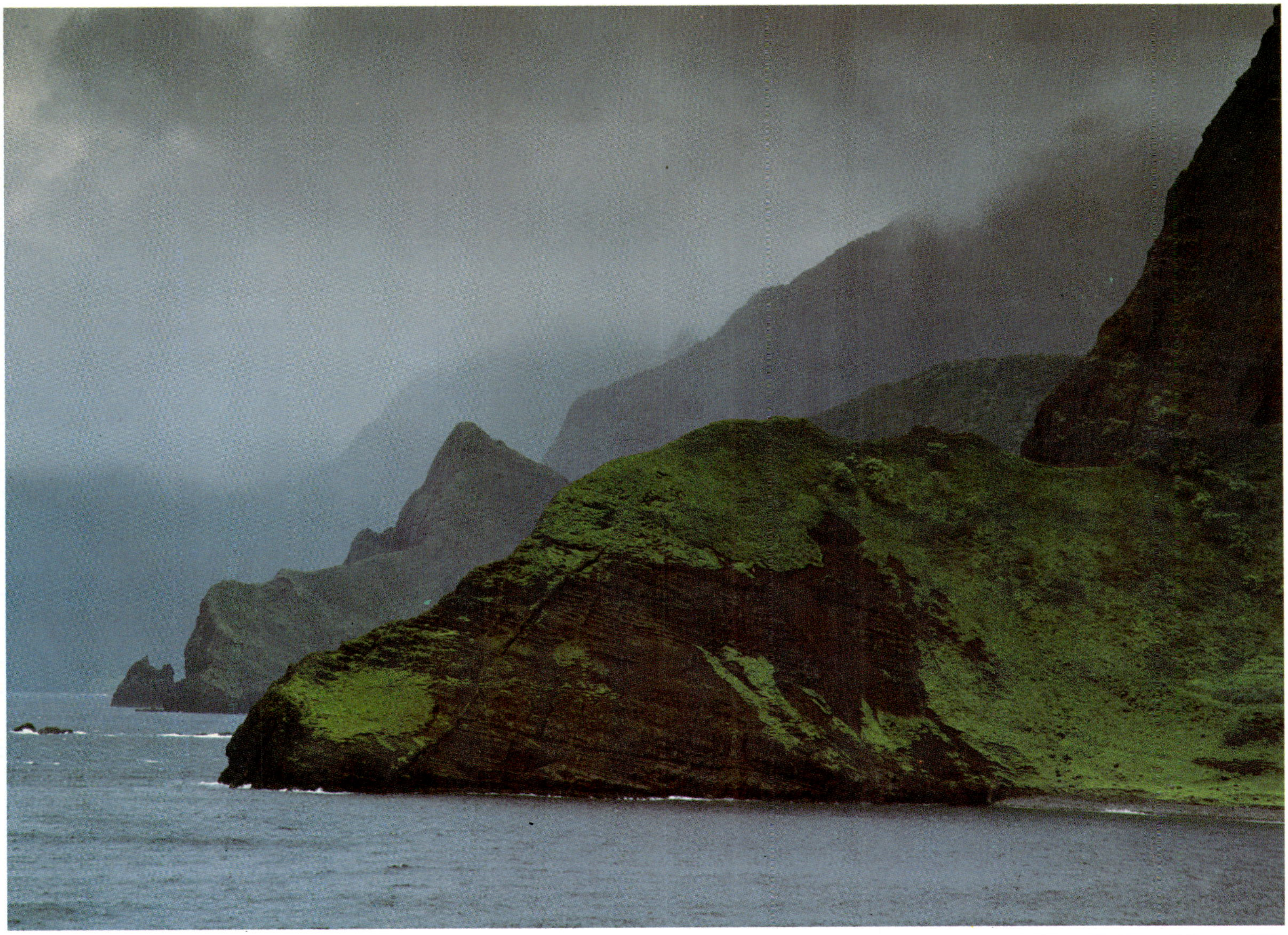

the late 19th century, but it was not until 1907 that the Lumière brothers introduced the Autochrome, the first commercial application of the process. They used dyed potato starch grains as filters, and (hardly surprisingly) a lot of light was lost just trying to get through the *kartoffelsuppe* on the surface: the same objection also applied to the Finlay and Dufaycolor processes, which used mechanically ruled masks. In addition, the mask (or grain) structure became embarrassingly obvious at any more than the most modest magnifications.

In the second decade of the twentieth century, various people were working on the possibility of using dyes instead of masks to filter the colours, and of combining the three dye layers (again, one for each primary colour) in an 'integral tripack'. The technical difficulties were enormous, and they were not solved until the 1930s by Godowski and Mannes; even then, they had to rely on an enormously complex processing sequence in which, in effect, each of the three layers was processed separately one after the other. Their film, Kodachrome, was known as a non-substantive integral tripack, because the dyes were added during processing.

This approach has several advantages, though. The layers can be thinner than in films incorporating the dye couplers in the emulsion, which makes for increased sharpness; there is no danger of the dye couplers migrating to other layers before processing (which is what accounts for colour casts in badly-stored substantive films); and because user-processing is impossible, the manufacturer's quality control can be top-notch. These are the main reasons why Kodachrome continues to be the favourite of most professional photographers working in 35mm. It is also more stable than other slide films; modern Kodachromes will not exhibit detectable fading for 90 years or more, whilst some substantive films will begin to fade in as little as twenty years.

On the other hand, ease of processing means faster access to the finished image, and this is why such films as Agfa's Agfachrome (derived from the 1936 Agfacolor) and Kodak's Ektachrome (1946) are now so popular. Furthermore, because of processing difficulties, Kodachrome is not made in sizes wider than 35mm, so rollfilm and large-format users have to use substantive films. A good processing laboratory can deliver high-quality processed Ektachromes within two hours, and if the film has been properly stored before and after exposure results will be very nearly as good as Kodachrome; in the larger formats, the slight loss of sharpness is more than outweighed by the increased size.

At this point, a note on user-processing is very relevant. Professional processing is so cheap and fast (provided you have access to a laboratory) that it is scarcely ever worth considering doing your own processing. Furthermore, a good processing laboratory may make the occasional mistake, but you will probably make far more. In any case, their quality control and solution monitoring is vastly better than is readily attainable in any part-time set-up.

Choosing a lab is usually a matter of finding who the local professionals use; after all, their livelihood depends upon the quality of the processing. A few professional labs refuse to accept amateur work; some say that it is because they do not like to lower their standards (which is meaningless) but others do have a valid reason. If a professional's films exhibit some fault, he usually knows why. If an amateur's films have something wrong with them, he is less likely to accept that it is his own fault, and may want to argue with the lab. After a couple of bad experiences of this kind, the lab will refuse to accept any more amateur work.

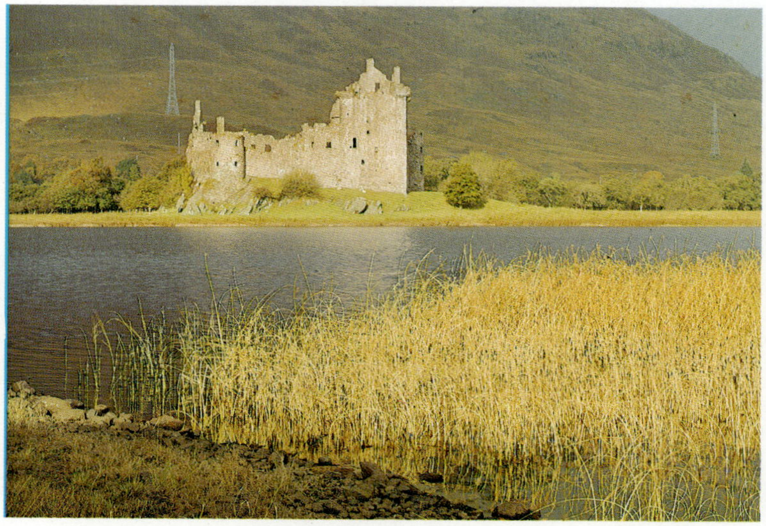

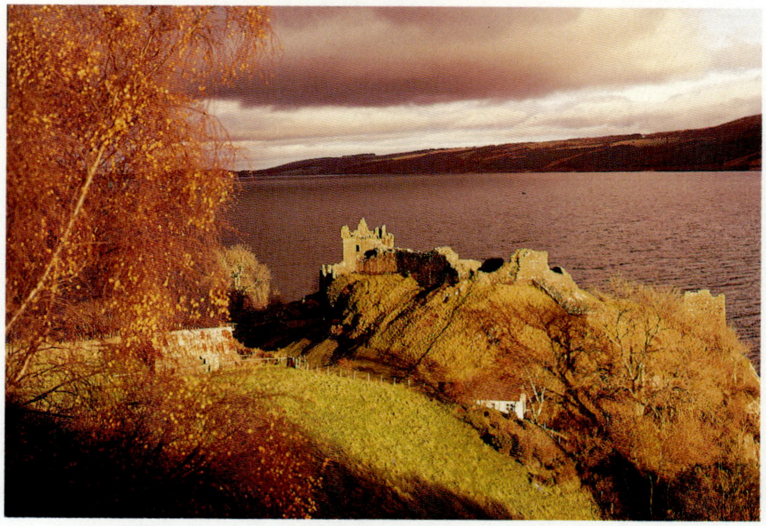

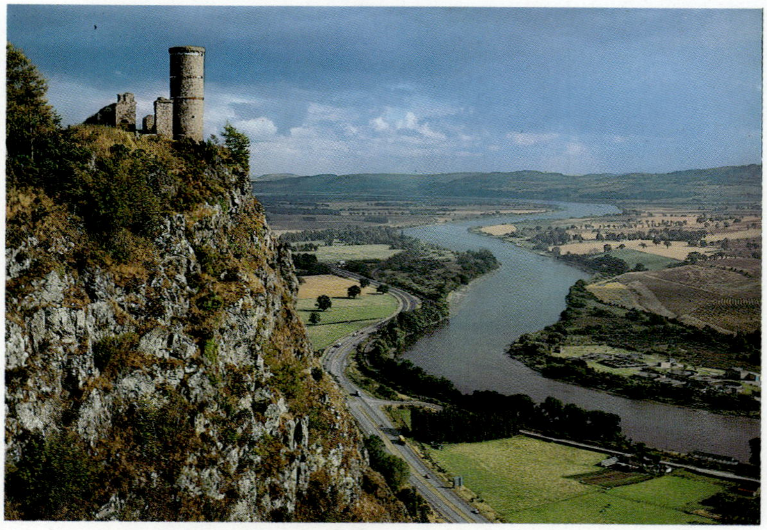

These five pictures illustrate *the effect of film choice on subject rendition. Some films deliver more saturated colours than others, and each reacts differently to over- and under-exposure; in the picture* ***right,*** *the underexposure chosen to saturate the colours has turned the water blue-black. Each, too, has its own colour cast – though the red of the picture* ***above centre*** *is a result of the creative use of filtration.*

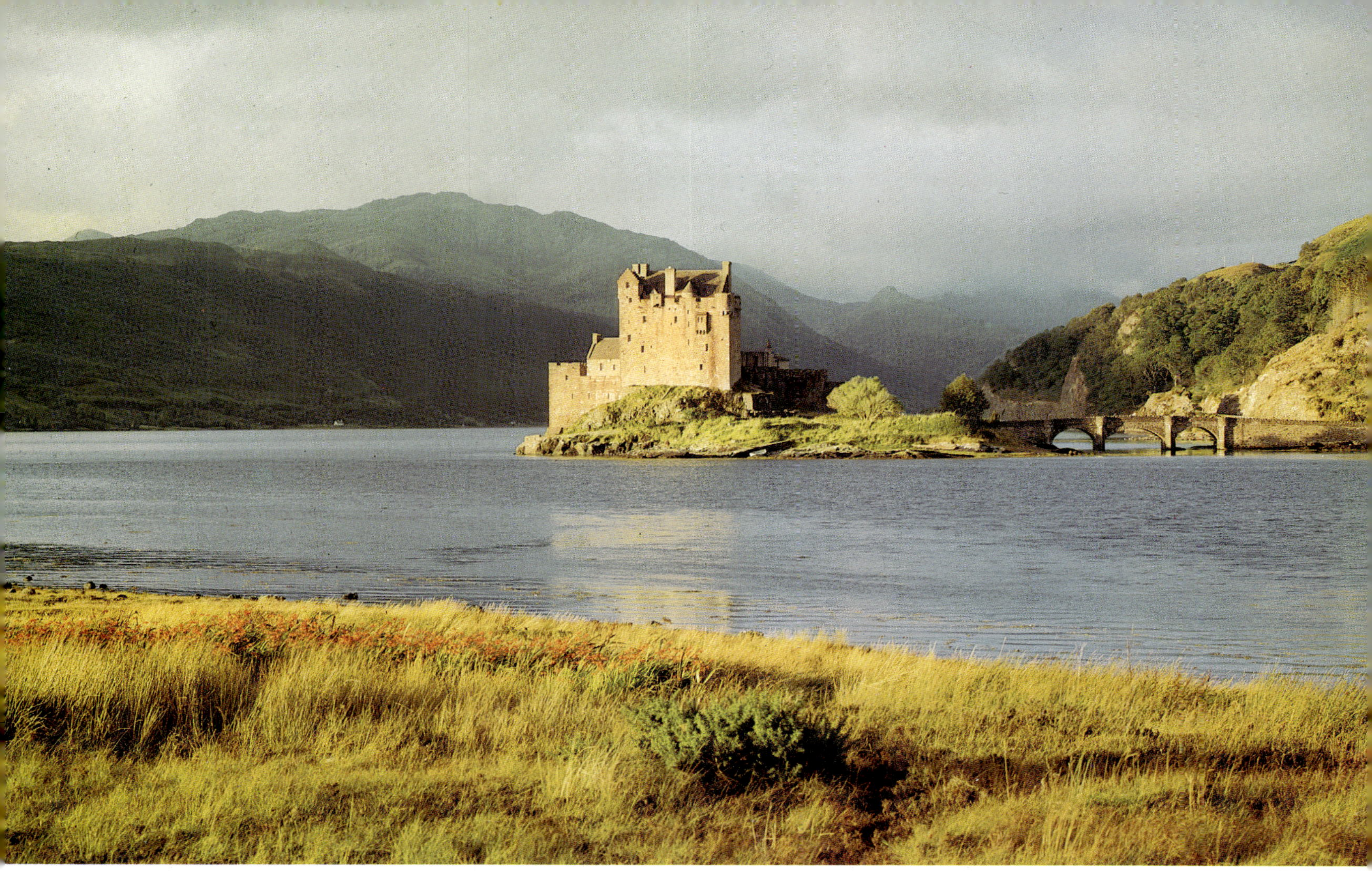

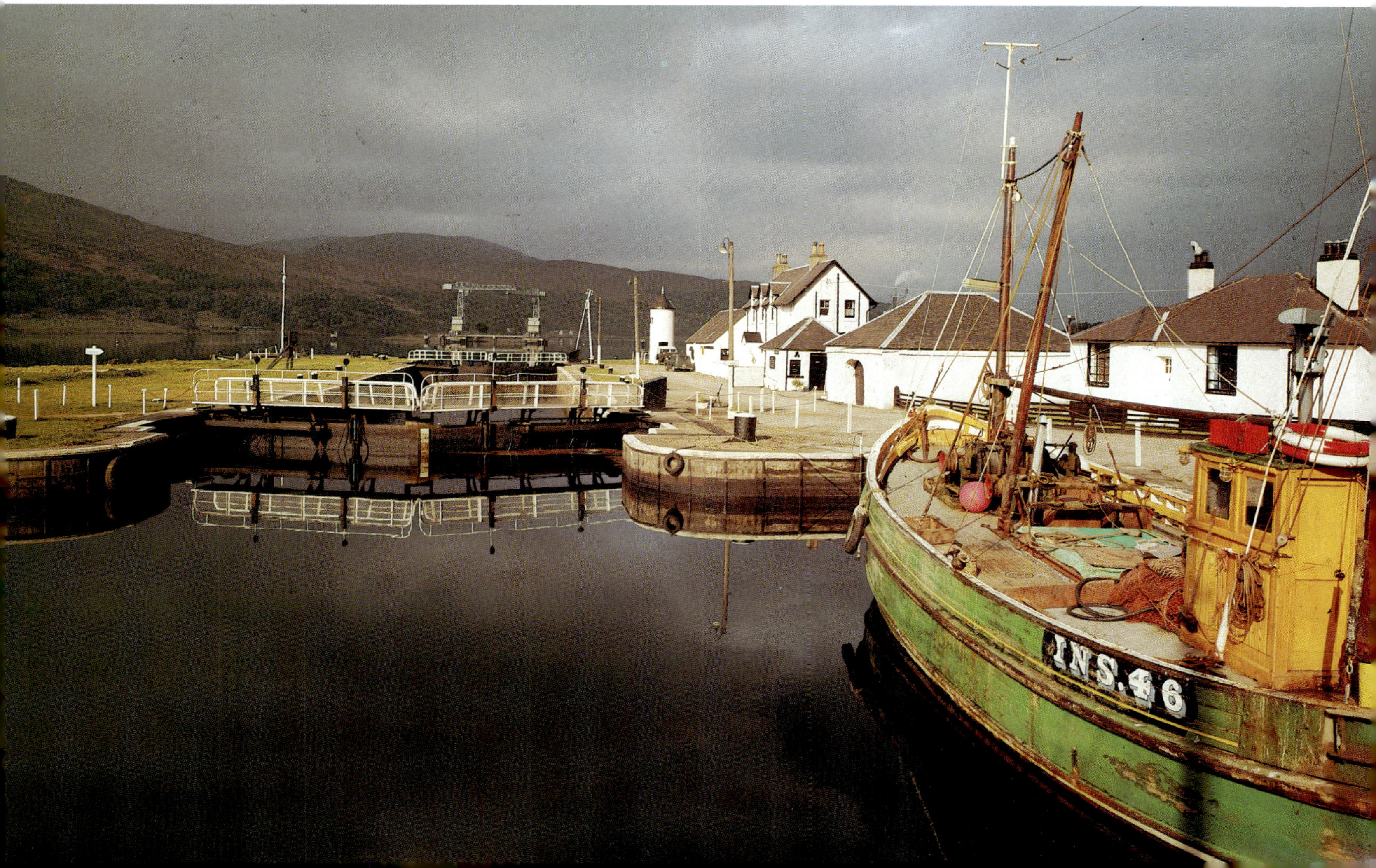
INS.46

INTRODUCTION

Some cheap, amateur-only labs may scratch films (the cardinal sin) or deliver off-colour results as a consequence of less-careful solution monitoring, so the small amount you save compared with professional processing is hardly worth the effort.

So far, we have only looked at slide (reversal or transparency) films. Negative films are a more recent development (Agfa, 1940: Kodak, 1942) and use a similar dye technology to slide films. Tones are reversed (as in a black-and-white negative) and colours are also complementary: a green field reproduces as orange. A similar emulsion (or rather, set of emulsions – once again, the films are integral tripacks) is coated onto a paper base to make prints.

Although colour negative film can produce results of very high quality, the vast majority of colour negative users are snapshotters – and it shows. Machine printing varies from the acceptable to the horrendous, and high-quality hand printing costs the earth. Furthermore, for reproduction (in books, etc.) slide film delivers vastly better quality. The only professionals who use much colour negative film are those whose customers want a print as the final result; essentially, wedding photographers and portrait photographers. For amateur use, you will either have to reconcile yourself to variable quality or do your own printing (though for film processing the professional labs are fine). Life really gets interesting when the subject varies much from the standard which automatic printing machines are designed to handle; black backgrounds go a vile mouldering green, colours are washed out, whites go yellow . . . .

On the other hand, prints do have the advantage of being easily displayed, so it may be unrealistic to urge all serious photographers to use only slide film. One solution, as already mentioned, is to do your own printing. Another is to shoot reversal film, and to have an internegative made (or make it yourself) for printing; this is only feasible if you very rarely want prints. A third possibility, and the one which I use myself, is to use reversal printing materials.

These allow prints to be made direct from slides, with the

Colour saturation, or purity of *hue, is a very important aspect of creative colour photography. Polarising filters reduce white-light glare, and contrasty lenses reduce flare. A lens hood is of course essential. The picture* ***right*** *was taken with a long telephoto lens without polariser or hood; the difference is obvious.*

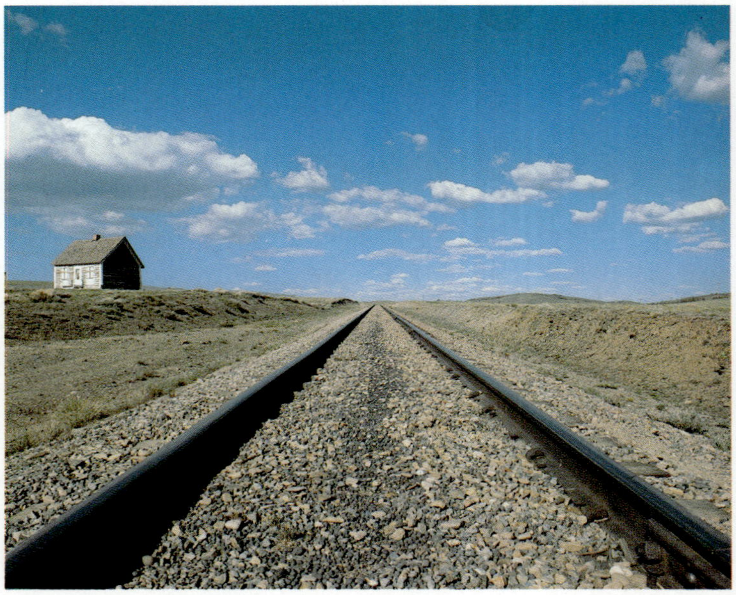

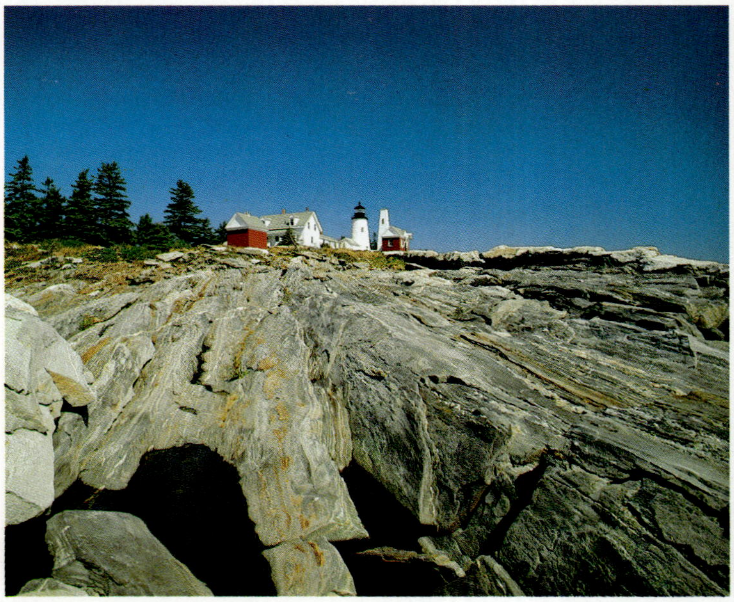

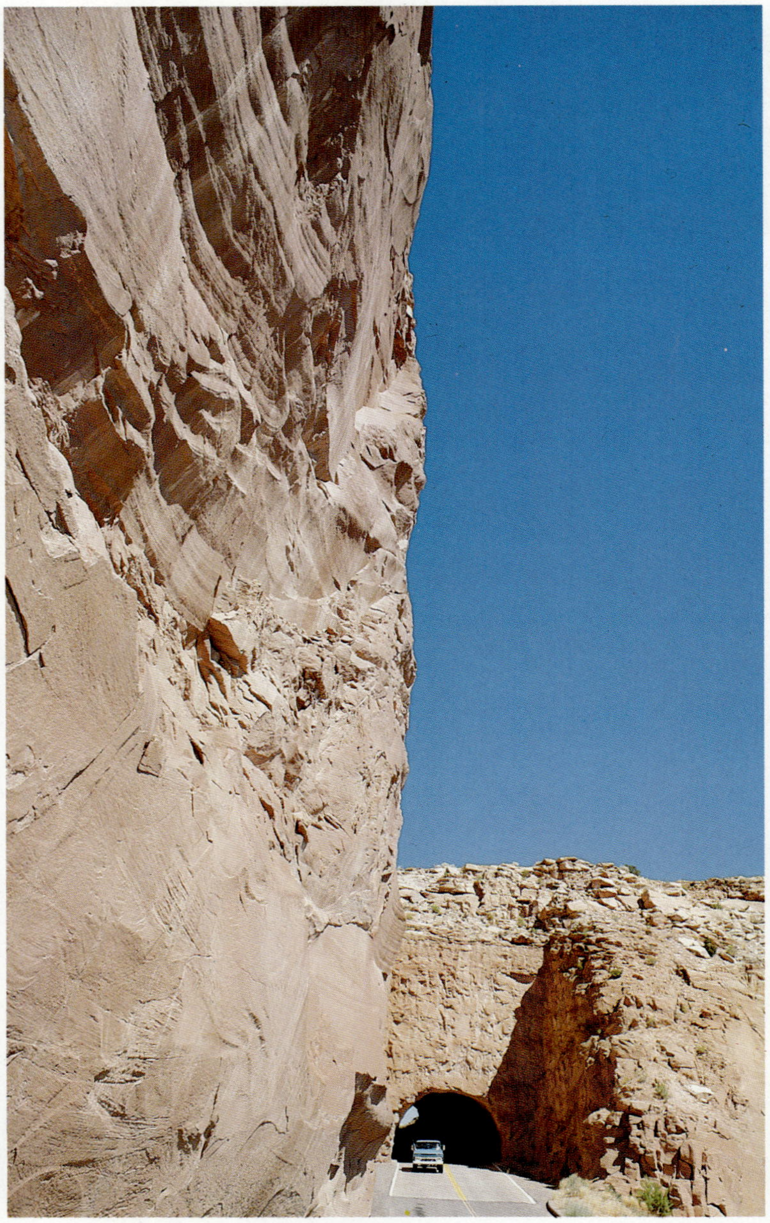

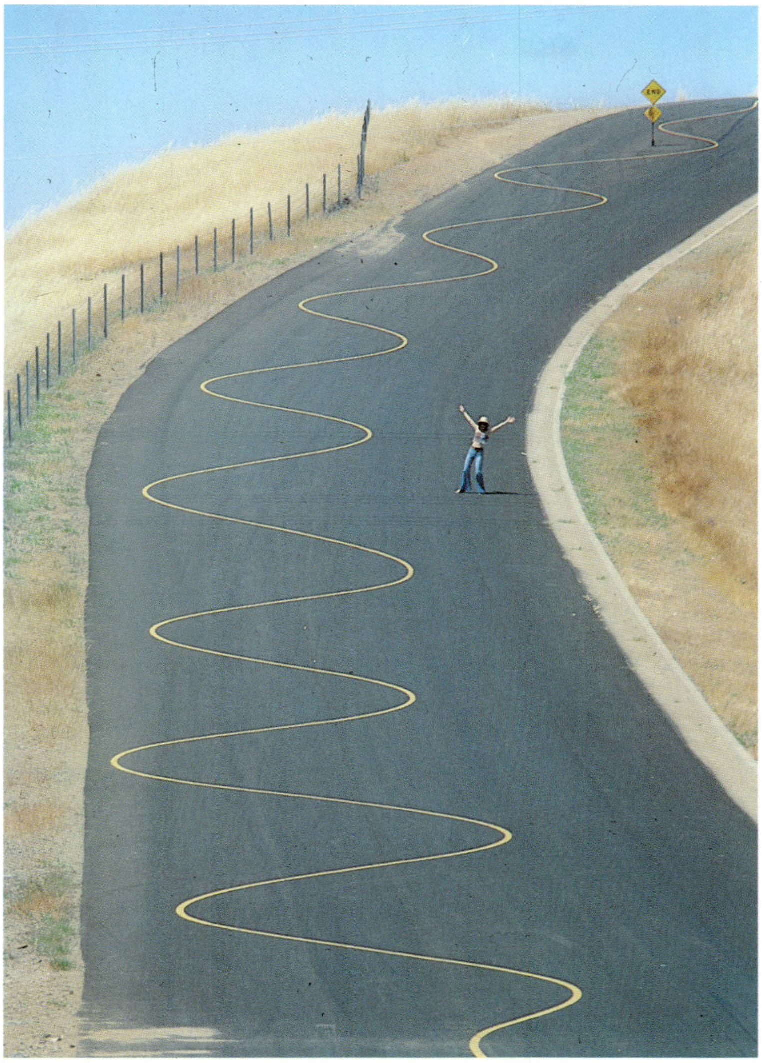

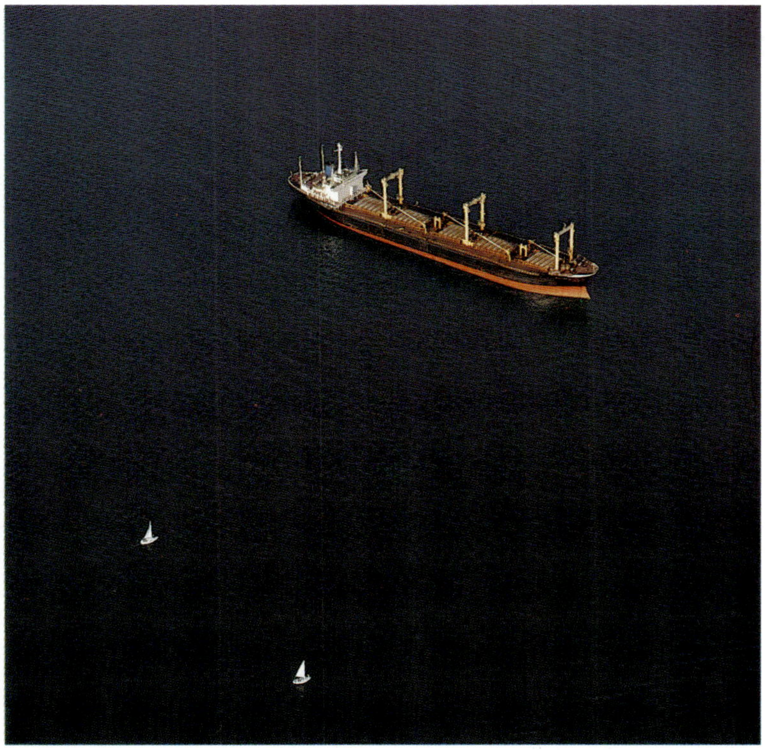

great advantage that you can use slide film and keep the benefits of cheapness, easy judging of results, and suitability for reproduction, whilst retaining the option of having prints. Commercial reversal prints are no worse than machine colour prints, and the best of them are at least as good as the best neg/pos prints. If in addition they are made using dye-destruction materials (notably Cibachrome) they are also considerably more permanent than other types of prints, with a life several times as long. In the dye-destruction process, the dyes are already present in the tripack and are destroyed during development in proportion to their exposure, which allows the use of very much more stable dyes than are found in most colour processes.

These are not the only colour processes. One of the most commonly encountered is the Land system used in Polaroid colour films. This involves migratory dyes that also act as developers, but are immobilised in so doing. The unexposed dyes continue to migrate until they reach the print surface, so the result is a positive (reversal) image.

Others, less frequently met with, include dye transfer (which involves separation negatives and three-colour matrices), trichrome carbro (a similar process), and Fresson (another offshoot of the same process).

Two other contenders, which were relatively new at the time of writing, are Ektaflex and Lasercolor. Ektaflex (from Kodak) is a simple-to-use system which can work with either negative or positive film; it involves an intermediate stage, something between positive and negative, in which a sheet of transfer film is exposed in the enlarger and then squeegeed into close contact with a piece of paper which will become the final print. It owes quite a lot to instant-picture technology, and results seem to be very good. It is especially convenient if used in association with slides, as mentioned above.

Lasercolor is the very antithesis of simplicity, requiring an enormous capital outlay on equipment and thus (for obvious reasons) is not suitable for the amateur. The transparency is laser-scanned to produce a 70mm negative and then printed conventionally. The quality is very high indeed, as is the permanence, and once again it works from transparencies – perhaps the ideal approach for someone who only wants the occasional print.

When it comes to choosing a colour film, a lot will depend on personal preferences and on the trade-offs you are prepared to make. Slide film is the accepted choice if you want to reproduce the picture in a book or something similar, but if you want prints you can choose the neg/pos or pos/pos routes.

Choosing between brands is even more personal. Kodachrome is the standard professional choice in 35mm, as mentioned, but you might also choose to use Ektachrome 200 or 400 ASA when the 25 or 64 ASA of Kodachrome is insufficient; ORWO, for its contrasty and saturated colours; Agfa 50S for its neutrality and absence of colour bias; and so forth. The choice in larger formats is similar, though (unfortunately) Kodachrome is not available.

Some manufacturers offer special 'professional' films. These can offer fractionally better (and more predictable) results than the standard variety, but they must be stored in a refrigerator and processed as soon as possible after exposure; if they are treated like 'ordinary' films, results may actually be worse than usual.

Finally, remember that just as there is no need for every picture to be creative, there is no need for every picture to be of the utmost quality. For snapshots, an ordinary amateur-only lab can be fine. It may not deliver the quality of the professional lab, but it is so much cheaper that you may decide that you are not worried. Keep a sense of proportion – and enjoy yourself.

THE RELEVANCE OF EQUIPMENT

I am not of that school which argues that everyone would do better if they were restricted to using Box Brownies. I firmly believe that in order to get the very best results, you need not only to know your equipment but also to have the right equipment.

The question of what is the right equipment is a vexed one, and in any case depends as much upon the user as on the type of photography he or she want to undertake.

The first and most important thing is always to use good fresh film and have it processed by a reputable laboratory (or, of course, process it yourself). Only fresh film will behave predictably: outdated film varies in speed and colour balance, and poor processing can make even fresh film behave like the worst old stock. Experiment if you like, but for serious work choose a single film and stick with it – or at least, work with a set of films matched to the conditions. I use Kodachrome for quality and its ability to withstand appalling conditions, and Kodak's EL 400 when I need the speed. On rollfilm, I use Agfa's R100S E6-compatible film instead.

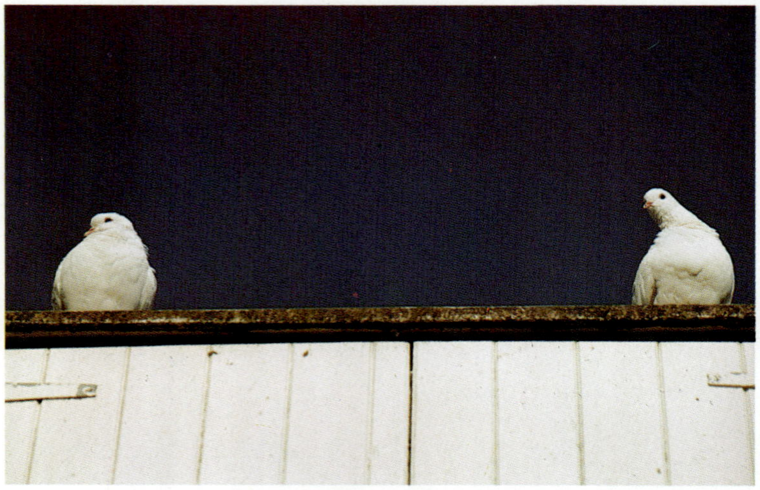

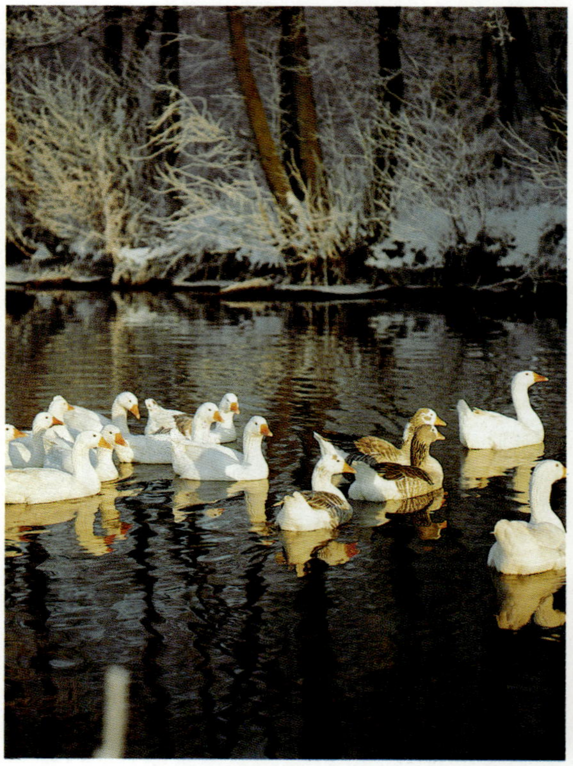

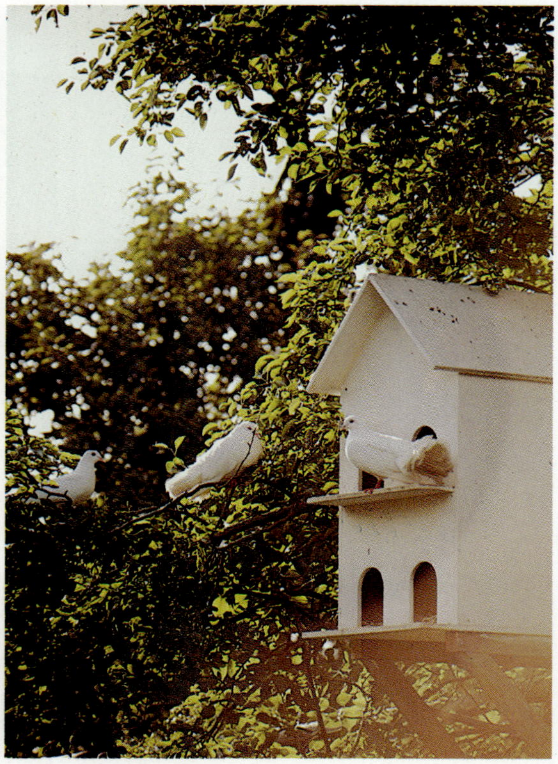

Once again, attention to *colour saturation is vital. These pictures also show how to use the tonal range of the film creatively: 'correct' exposure for the white doves and doors means that the blue sky records as indigo. The soft light on the horse and foal* ***facing page bottom right*** *allows the photographer to record all the tones present; a white wall furnished the reflector which was needed to stop the two white horses* ***bottom left*** *from recording as white blobs in a black hole, whilst in the other two pictures* ***facing page*** *the exposure was determined for the subject of principal interest. The picture of the dovecote shows the effect of not using an adequate lens hood: the flare, sharp-edged from the edge of a lens element, draws the eye away from the subject. Flare can be used, however, to soften the image if desired.*

Whilst it is possible to get great colour pictures using the simplest of cameras, it does make life appreciably more difficult. There is no doubt that 35mm is the best all-rounder, though you will need full manual control if you want to get the very best pictures in anything but ideal conditions; this effectively means buying an SLR or a system rangefinder camera. There is equally no doubt that rollfilm, or even larger formats, will *ceteris paribus* deliver better quality – at a price, in size, weight, versatility, and convenience as well as in money. It is quite possible, though, to use old Rolleiflexes and similar TLRs (available at very low prices second-hand) to give superb results.

Interchangeable lenses are desirable, but bring their own problems. Complex lenses with lots of glasses, like wide-angles of retrofocus design and zooms, can lead to contrast problems as well as reduced definition and increased distortion when compared with the standard lens. Even with standard lenses, the contrast and 'bite' is less on the faster lenses: to choose examples from three formats, I use a 55/3.5 Micro Nikkor unless I need the speed of the f/1.2; a 100/3.5 Planar (Hasselblad) instead of the 80/2.8; and a 105/4.5 Apo Lanthar (Linhof) instead of a 100/2.8 Planar.

Whatever the lens, an efficient lenshood is essential for maximum colour saturation: I would rather use a normally-coated lens with a good lenshood than a multi-coated one without (though, of course, the best choice is multi-coating and a lens-hood). For maximum saturation, a polarising filter can bring surprising benefits by cutting out the white reflected light which scatters off any coloured surface and hence degrades the colour. Of course, if you want soft, degraded colour, leave the hood and filter off, and make sure that the front of the lens is covered with a good layer of dust: if you are after this effect deliberately, a dirty filter on the front of the lens is easier to clean (and less traumatic to smear with petroleum jelly!) than the front element.

With slow lenses and polarising filters, possibly combined with Kodachrome, exposure times are going to be long – so a tripod is a worth-while investment. The sort that extends to five feet from one is uselessly spindly: a good solid tripod is extremely unlikely to weigh less than 5lb, and twice that is not out of the way.

Accurate and controllable metering is essential, and you may wish to consider using a separate hand-held meter, even if you already have a built-in meter in the camera. There are some circumstances in which a built-in meter is far better – close-ups being an example – but there are also many where the ability to measure specific areas of the subject, or the light falling upon it (incident light), is a boon.

The two standard professional meters are the Gossen Lunasix (in both its incarnations) and the Weston Master (in all its avatars). The Lunasix allows you to measure ludicrously low light levels, such as 1 sec. at f/1.4 with 64 ASA film, with ease; with add-on accessories, such as the TELE semi-spot attachment which allows you to target a 15° or 7½° area in the meter's own viewfinder and measure that, it is even more versatile. The Weston Master is more favoured for incident light metering, using the Invercone; this, together with an understanding of the admittedly complicated dial, allows you to place exposures exactly as you wish. Even if used with no understanding whatsoever, the incident light method will lead to a higher percentage of correct exposures than almost any other.

One thing which you must do is establish a personal rating for films. If your results are consistently a little lighter or darker than you would like, simply reset the ASA dial on your meter. Both meters and cameras vary: with a Hasselblad and a Weston Master, I find that my ratings agree exactly with the makers', but with Nikon and Lunasix they come out ⅓ stop darker than I like – so I rate Kodachrome 25 at 20 ASA. For reproduction, a slightly dark transparency is in any case desirable, so I suppose that for many people's taste I am rating it at 16 ASA; but it works for me, which is all that matters.

For really critical work, some people also use a colour

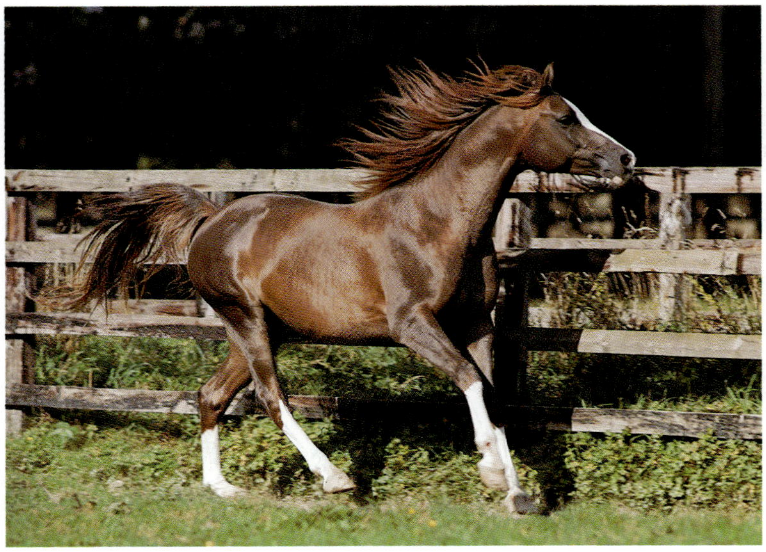

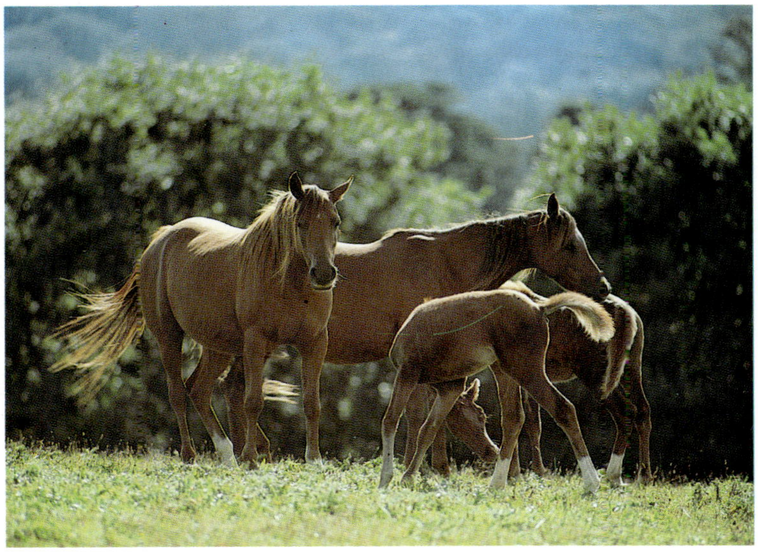

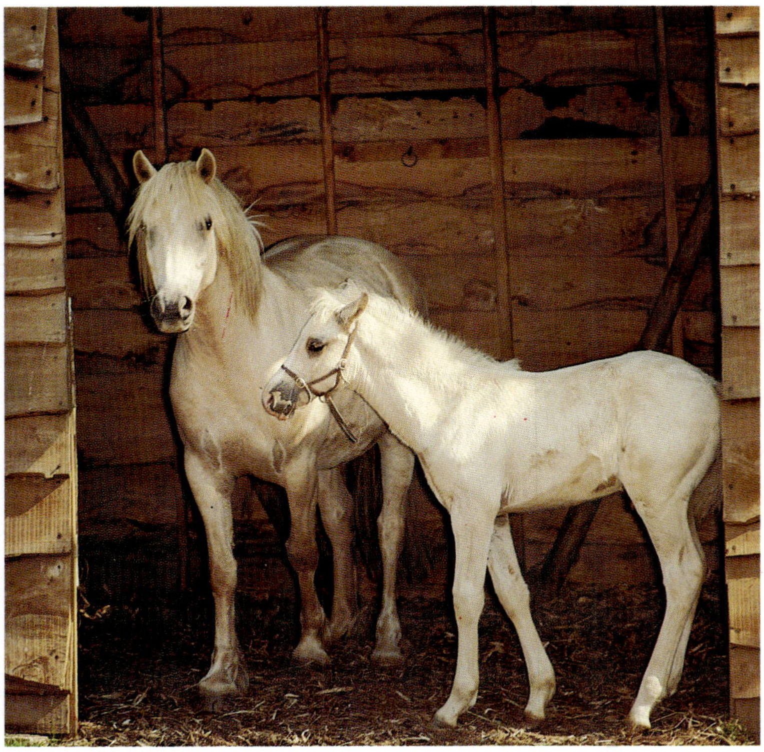

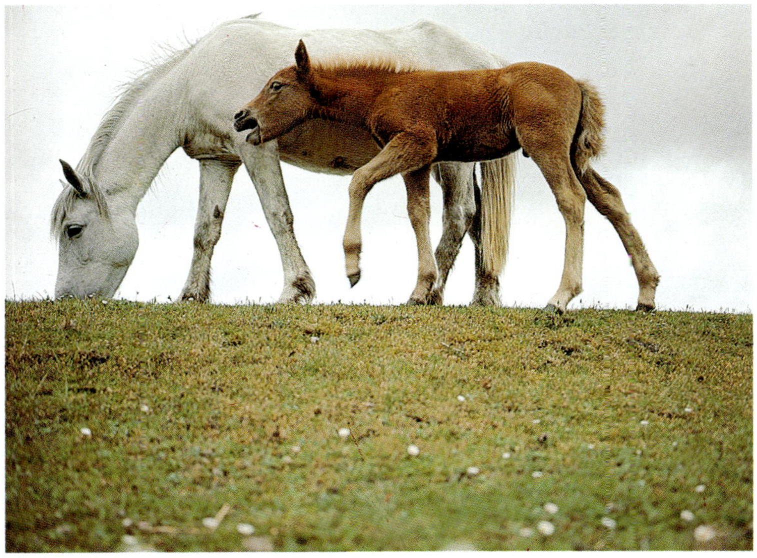

temperature meter. This indicates which filters to use to match the colour sensitivity of the film to the colour of the prevailing light; the filters in question are usually gelatine sheets, very easily marked, which come in tiny colour correction (CC) steps in both primary colours (red, green, blue), and subtractive primaries (yellow, magenta, cyan). They are distinguished by their initials

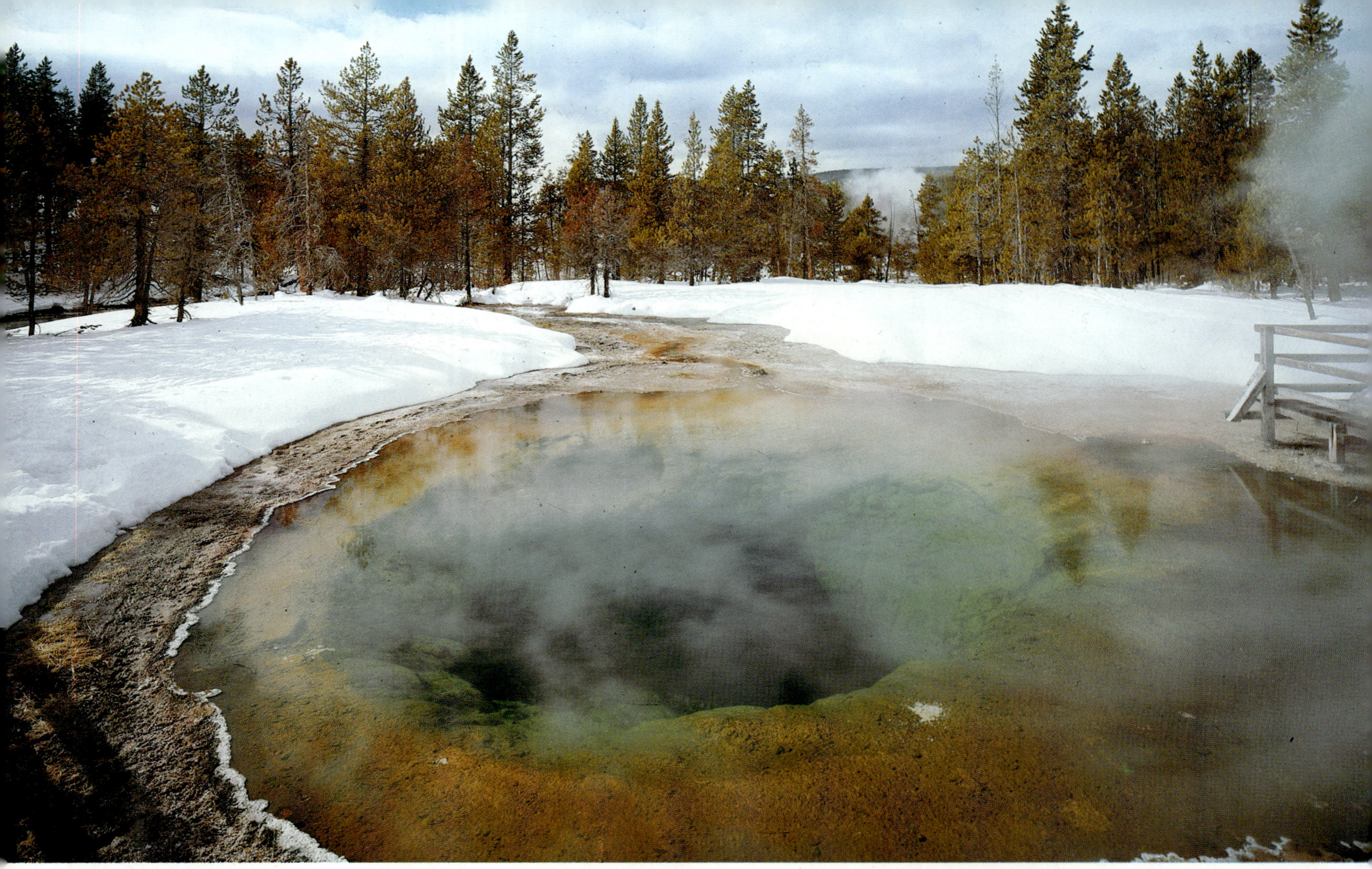

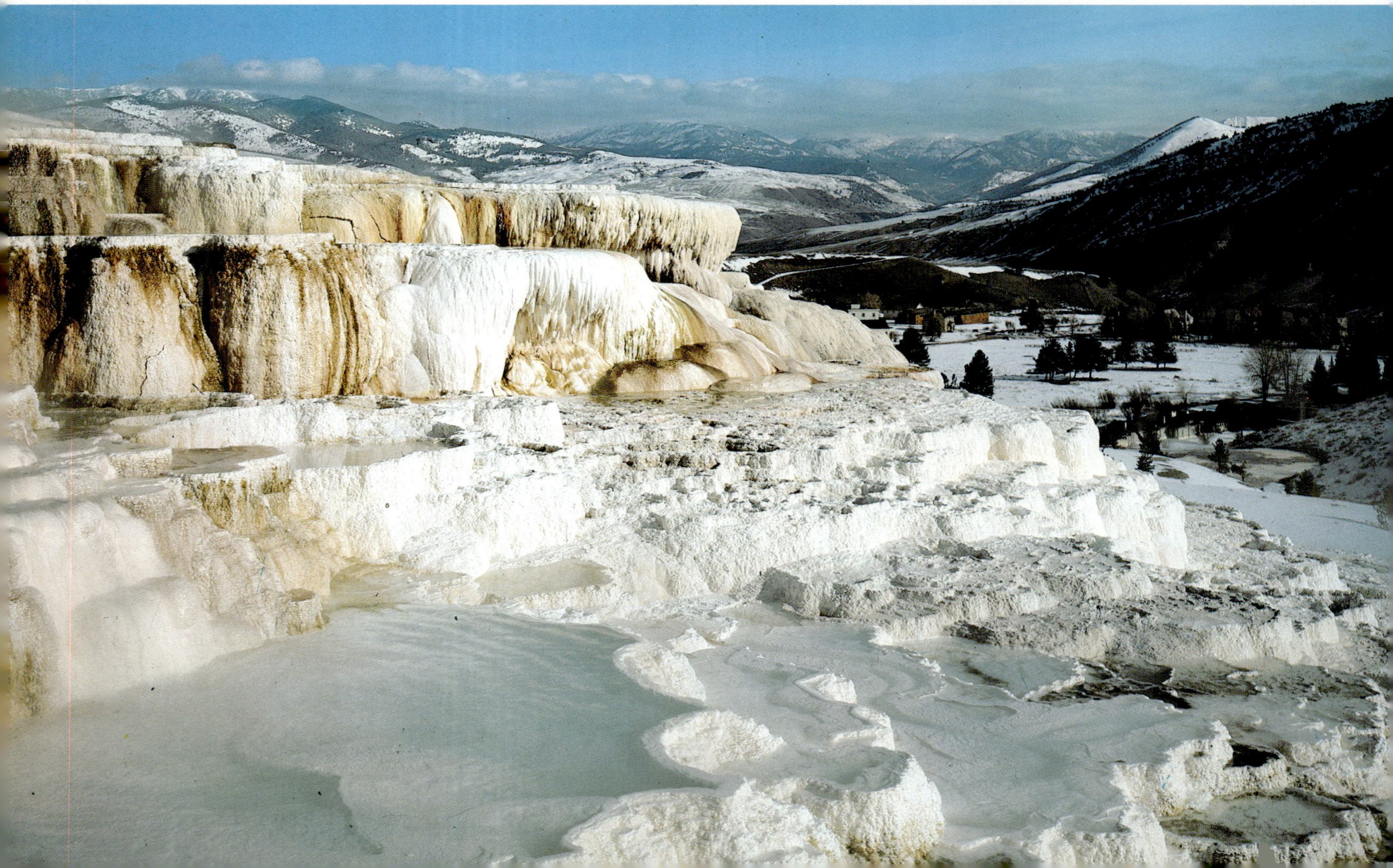

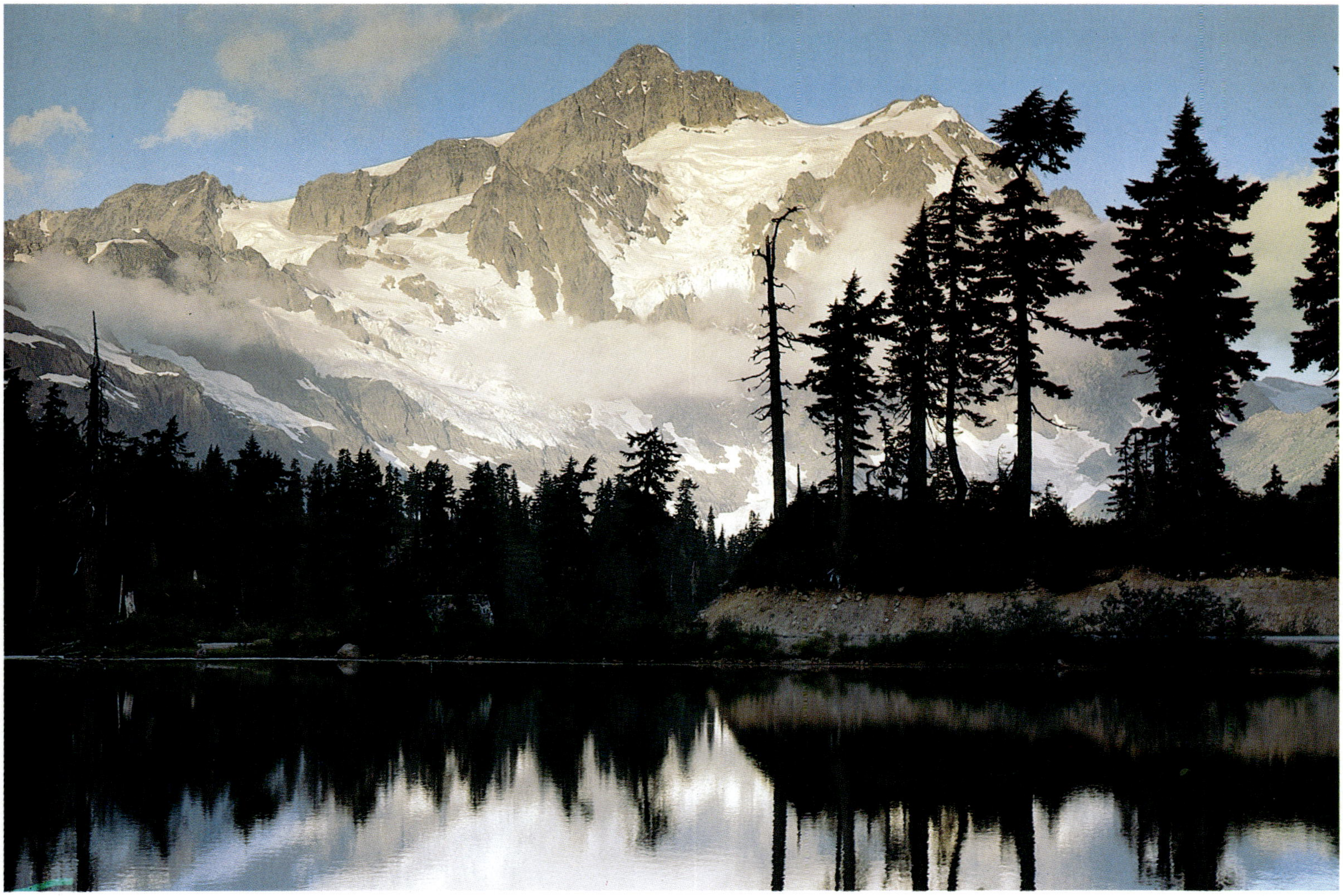

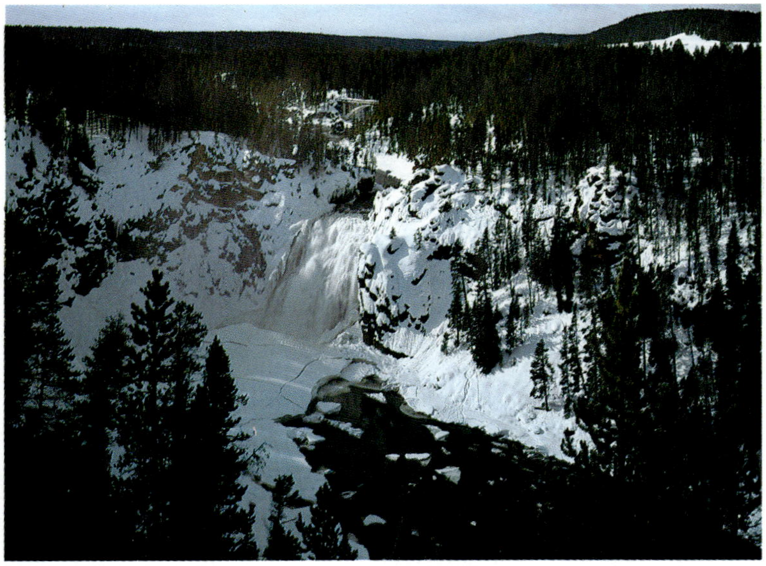

'Straight' pictures of the right *subjects are always more successful than attempts to liven up basically dull pictures with technical pizzaz. It is a fair comment on these pictures that not everyone has access to this sort of scenery, but the same is certainly not true of many of the other pictures in this book; the secret is in looking, not in travelling.*

and a number which indicated their density: thus, a CC05Y is a very faint (barely perceptible) yellow, and a CC50M is very magenta indeed.

The question of correcting for lighting is further considered later but the so-called 'effects filters' can properly be mentioned here.

First, they are no substitute for real creativity. Use them to get a previsualised effect, or experiment with them until you get an effect that you like – but do not confuse the unusual with the attractive.

Having said that, there are literally millions of ways you can use these filters, either singly or in combination. For example, I once wanted to emphasise both the sparkle and the grossness of a commercial Christmas, so I photographed an illuminated city shopping centre at night with a 5-face prism and a 6-point star filter. The effect was at once excessive and magical – exactly what I was trying to achieve.

You need not restrict yourself to commercial filters, either. Pieces of lighting gel, old-fashioned multi-coloured cellophane sweet wrappers, nylon stockings with holes in them (produced with a hot matchtip or cigarette) – all can be grist to your mill.

In creative colour photography, there is no doubt that equipment has its place. Indeed, there are some things which simply cannot be attempted without more-or-less sophisticated attachments: creative darkroom techniques are an example. But in the majority of cases, it is the photographer's eye – your eye – that makes the picture.

SEEING COLOUR

Some people see colour and black and white photography as rivals; but they are the same sort of people who see men and women as rivals, which is about as realistic as considering a knife and a fork as rivals, or a pair of chopsticks. There are some things which colour suits better, and others which black and white suits better – and yet others which may be photographed in either medium, equally well, but differently.

It is a matter for speculation what sort of conditioning makes us react to different pictures in different ways. It is probably as old as Man himself to associate blue with cold and reds and yellows with heat, but the association of coarse grain with immediacy and news is a much more recent phenomenon. 'Reading' blur as action is probably learned, too, from the cartoon movies of our childhood. Whatever the origins of our reactions, they exist, and the wise photographer will be able to use a little psychology (and even a little physiology) in creating a colour picture.

As with much of the rest of this book, you cannot learn from words alone; you have to look at the pictures. The secret of learning is simple: look, and think.

Whilst you are looking at a picture, consider the emotions and associations it conjures up in you. Ask how it achieves that effect. Could you duplicate that effect? Not necessarily the literal effect, by standing in the same place and pressing the same button on the same camera, but the same feeling, the same atmosphere? It is very tempting to say, 'of course', but have you tried it? I always thought that it would be easy to imitate a

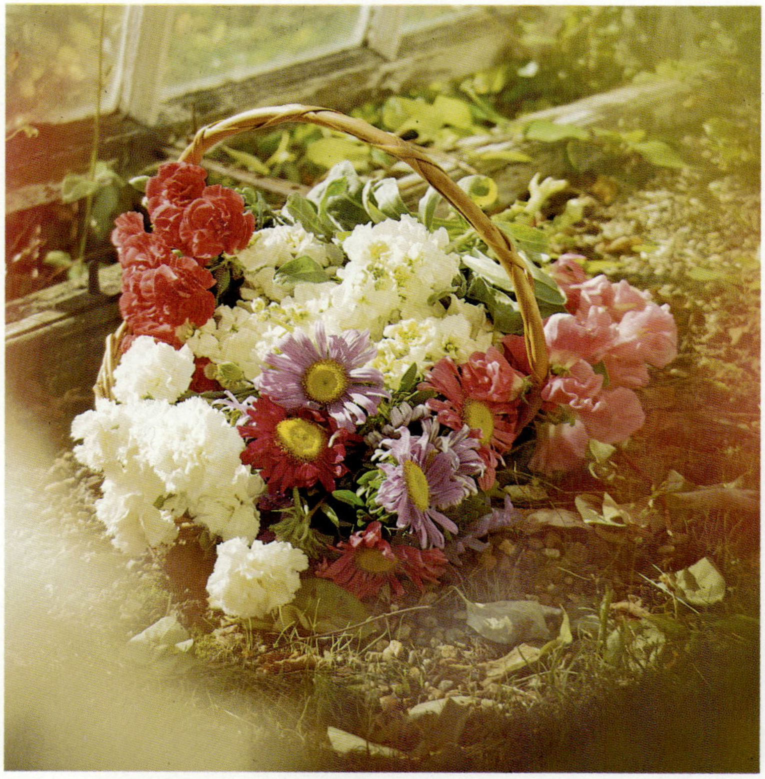

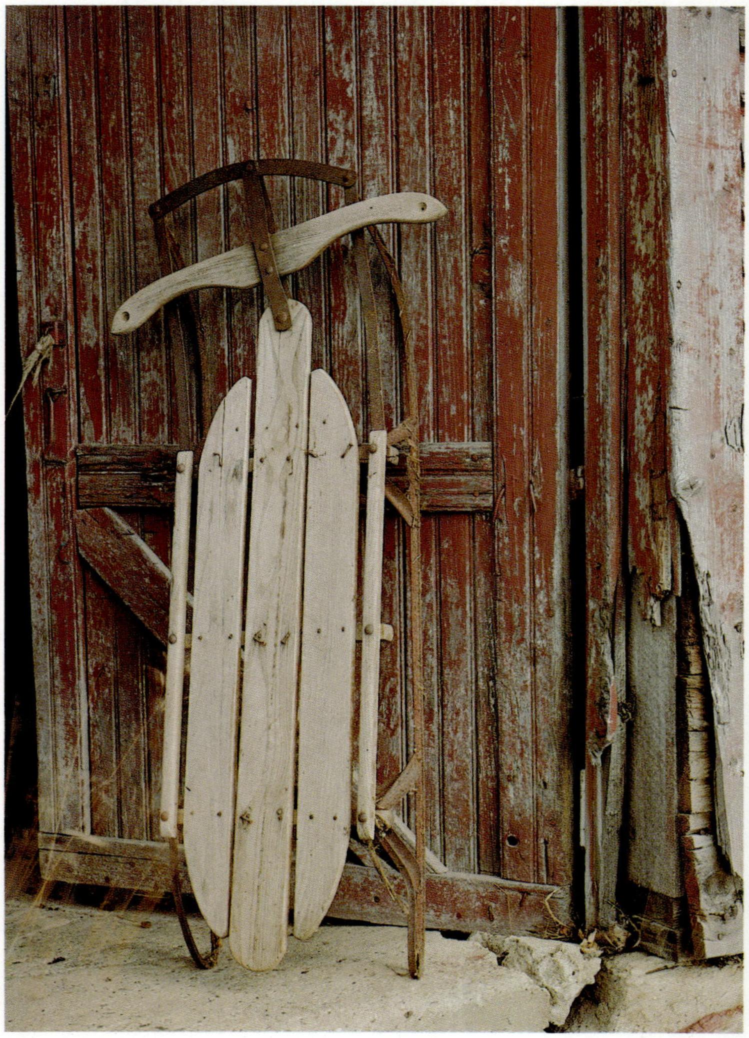

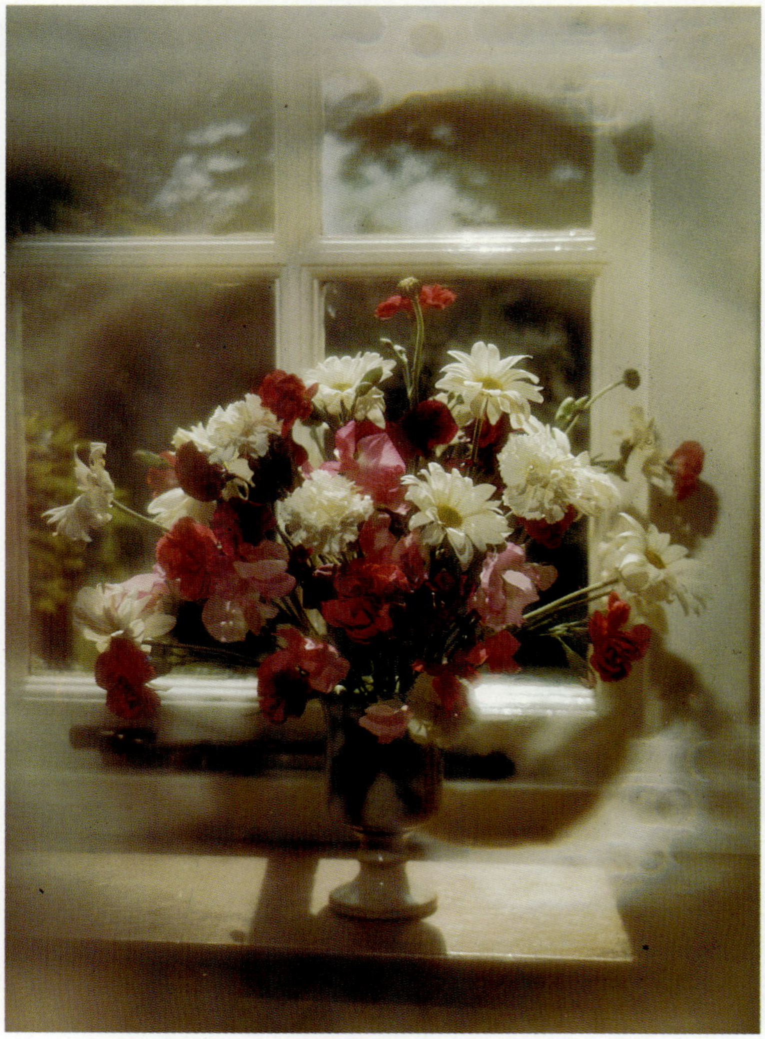

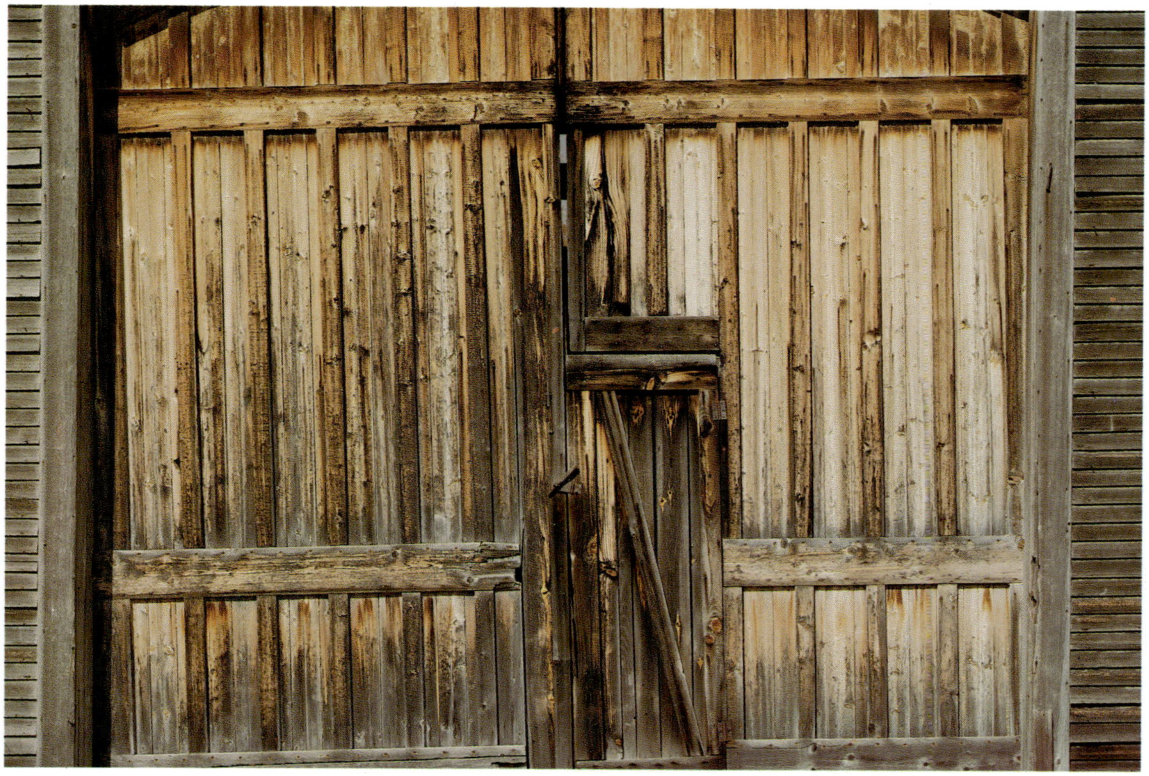

It is interesting to consider *how the pictures on these two pages might be treated in black and white. In the three flower pictures you would need a very different approach: the subject would blend in with the background and the soft-focus would merely look muddy. With the other three pictures, the range of tones and textures would allow you to treat the subjects in a similar way in black and white, though you might use more directional lighting to emphasise form and surface texture. Most photographers find that sometimes they 'see' subjects in colour, and other times in black and white. What you 'see' – line, tone, colour, broad shapes, fine detail – also varies. By being alive to this variation, you can make the best use of your perception; you can also learn to cultivate a way of seeing which produces the results you like.*

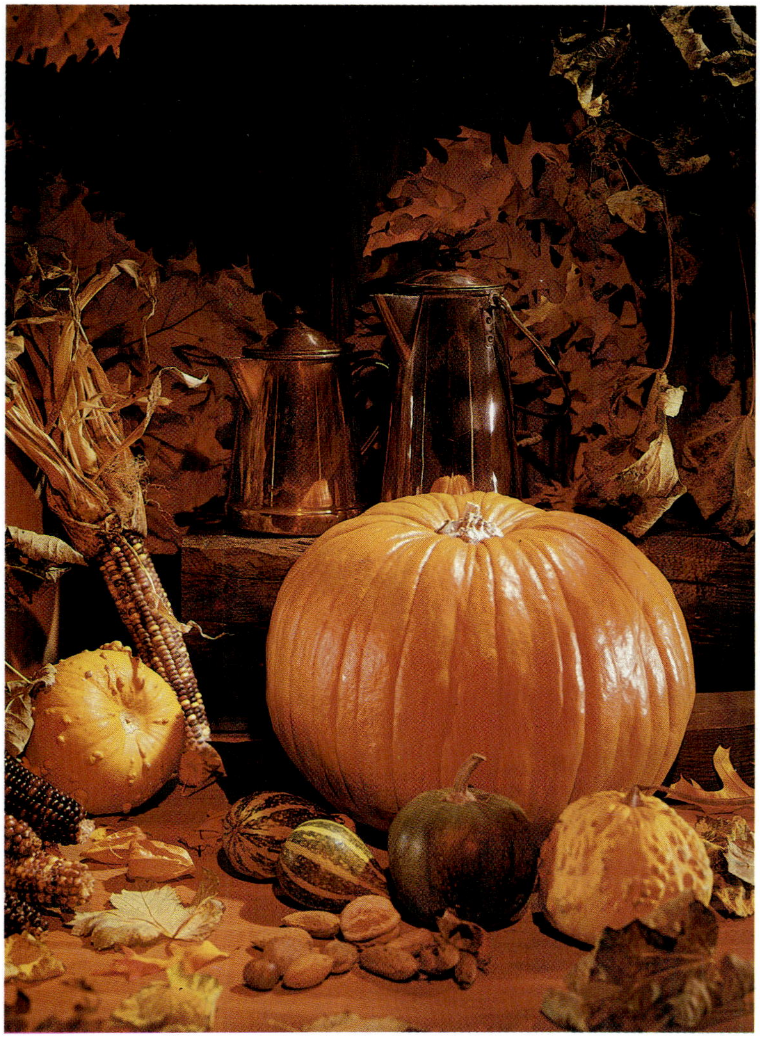

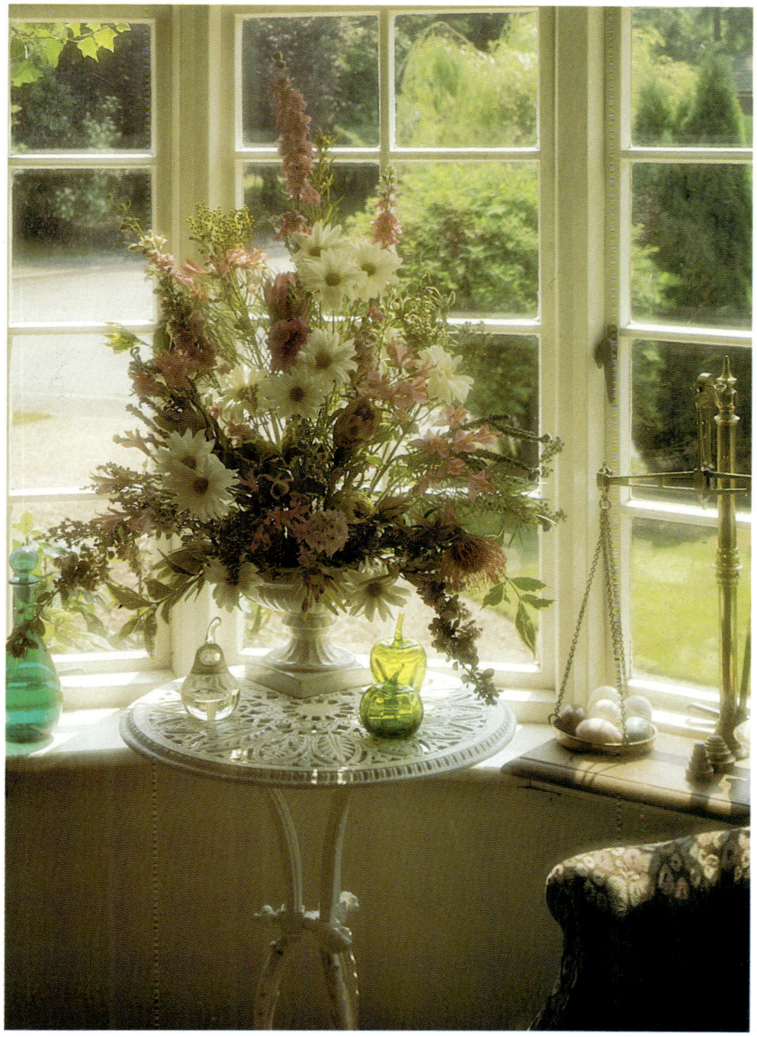

SEEING COLOUR

Weston picture of a pepper – until I tried it. Unfortunately, armchair expertise is all too easy to acquire in photography: if you read the right books, and back up your opinions with an armoury of expensive equipment, many people forget the fact that they have never seen one of your pictures and tend to believe that what you say is true.

Of course, there are warm and cold colours. There are also 'advancing' colours, like most of the reds, which fairly leap out at you from the page, and 'retreating' colours (such as blue, with its suggestions of haze and distance) which suggest recession and expansiveness. Bright, vivid colours promote a feeling of liveliness: soft, pastel colours are often restful. Brighter colours in

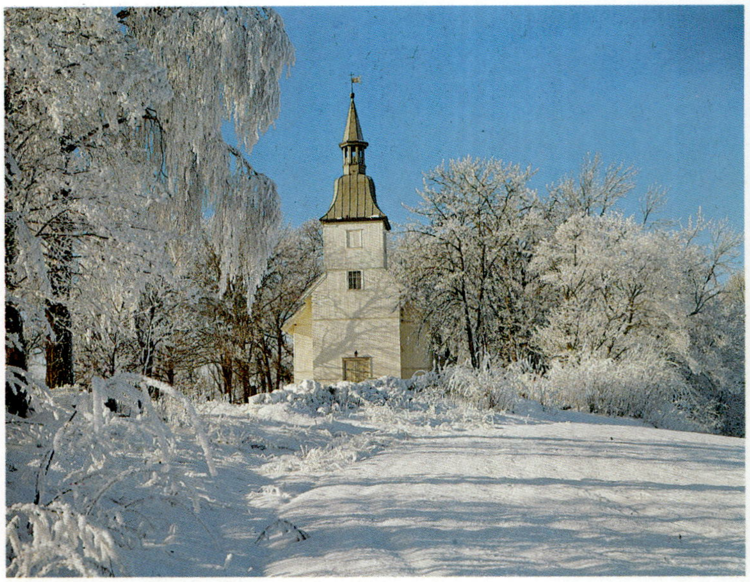

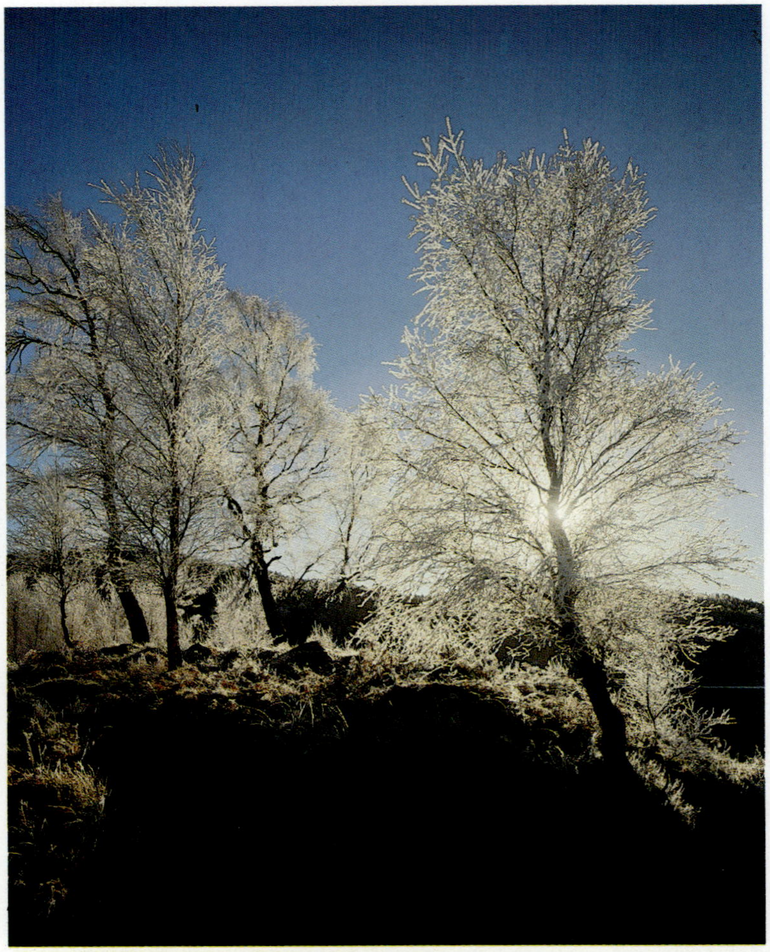

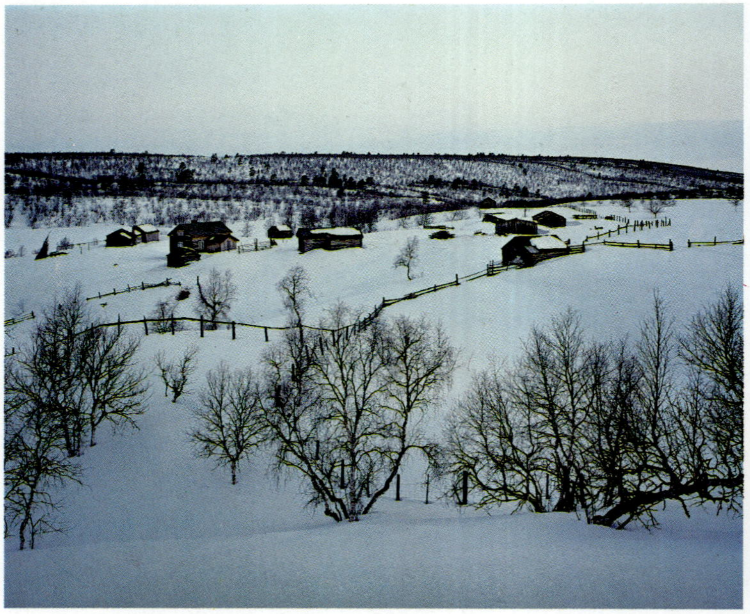

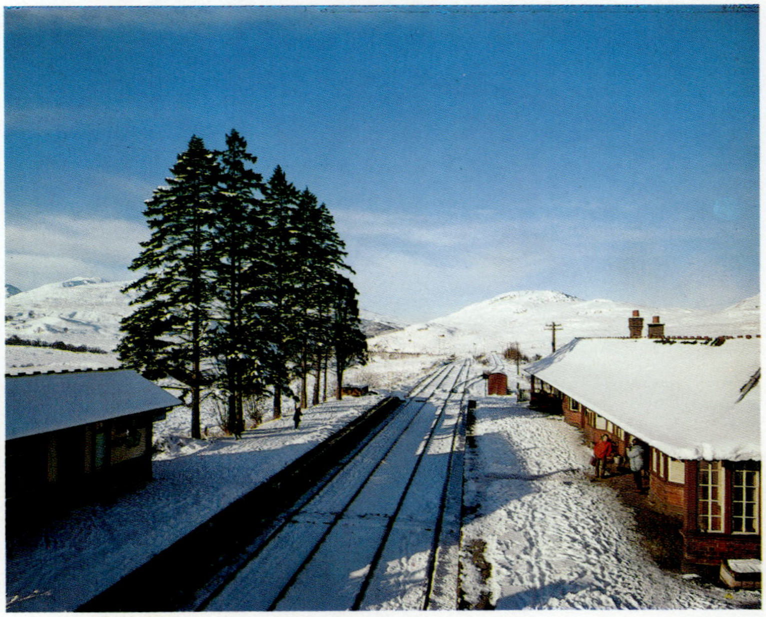

the foreground, fading with distance, give the effect of aerial perspective. Vivid backgrounds with dull foregrounds, on the other hand, can promote a feeling of safety and security, as if the viewer is inside a room looking out on the big bright dangerous world.

Some of the most effective colour pictures are almost monochromatic – a dusty hot yellow landscape, for example, or the cool blue of a lakeside evening. Others rely on vivid contrasts

***Snow is blue; this simple but** often unpalatable fact is a result of its reflecting the blue of the sky. It can also (and simultaneously) be pink, as illustrated by the river scene, when the rays of the dawning or setting sun strike it. By looking at colours as they are, instead of as we expect them to be, we can take very much better pictures. Technical expertise, such as using a polarising filter or underexposing slightly, adds another layer of perception.*

– instead of matching hues, jarring combinations of brilliant colours grab the attention. Whilst it can be very effective to introduce a colour 'note' into a picture – an orange jacket in a green-grey moor, for example – a picture which tries to get everything in is often unsuccessful; this is why so many garden and flower pictures fail to work; they are a jazzy mess of small areas of colour, none of them important enough to capture the eye. By contrast, a small patch of bright colour can draw the attention in quite a disproportionate manner compared with its size.

There are also some visual elements which are stronger than others. For example, a tiny figure in a huge landscape will catch the eye much quicker than anything else, such as a tree or motor-car, even if that is much bigger: again, one could cite evolutionary reasons, or simply accept it.

At this point, we are beginning to move into the realms of composition. In many circles, this is a rude word because of the sterile academicism which used to surround it. An example was the 'rule of thirds': divide a picture into thirds, vertically and horizontally, and the 'centre of interest' must lie on the intersection of a pair of dividing lines. Another was the S-curve, to 'lead the eye into the picture'. A lot of nonsense was talked and written about these and many other rules, until club photography became like the Chinese eight-legged essay: as long as it was formally correct, the fact that it was utterly tedious or even completely meaningless was politely ignored.

In practice, if you analyse successful pictures, quite a lot of them accord with these so-called 'rules' – even more if you permit yourself the kind of freedom of interpretation arrogated by some judges – but quite a lot do not.

The best approach to learning about composition that I have ever heard came from a painter, Senggye Tombs Curtis. Take a piece of blue paper about 20 x 30". Cut out a number of pieces of orange card, in various shapes – circles, rectangles, irregular, smooth, jagged. Just sit down and play with them. See which combinations of shapes and placings please you. Carry on until you lose interest, then stop. Repeat the process a few times, and it will do wonders for your sense of composition. His other piece of advice was to consider the main subject, and to ask if that pleased you; and then to blank it out, either mentally or by putting your hand over it, and ask if the background pleased you. Move things around (or change your viewpoint) until the answer to both questions is yes.

Although it may seem at first that such a considered approach is too long-winded for most types of photography, it very rapidly becomes second nature, and you do it automatically; you just don't take pictures which aren't pleasing.

Alternatively, you may care to try Henri Cartier-Bresson's

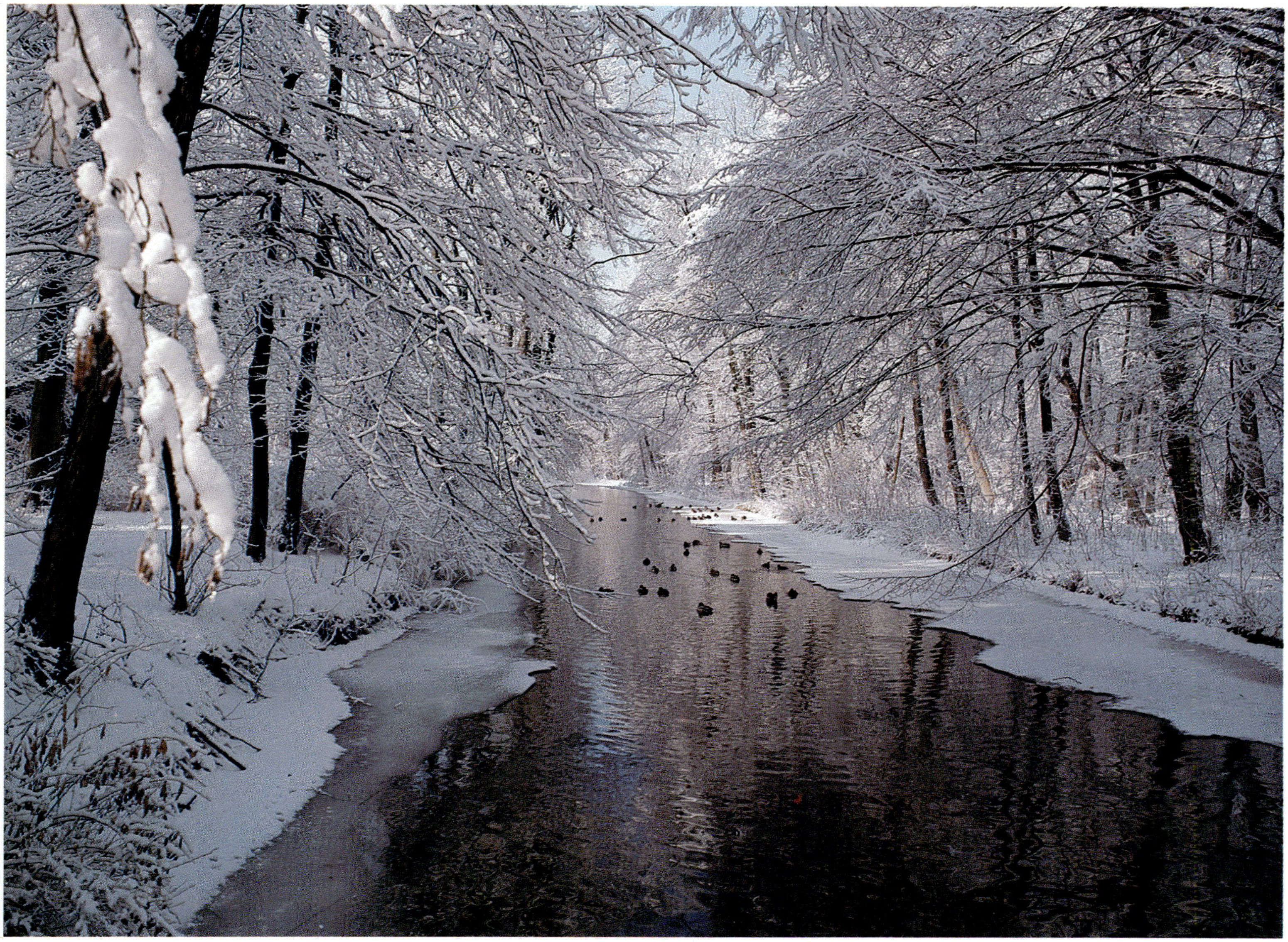

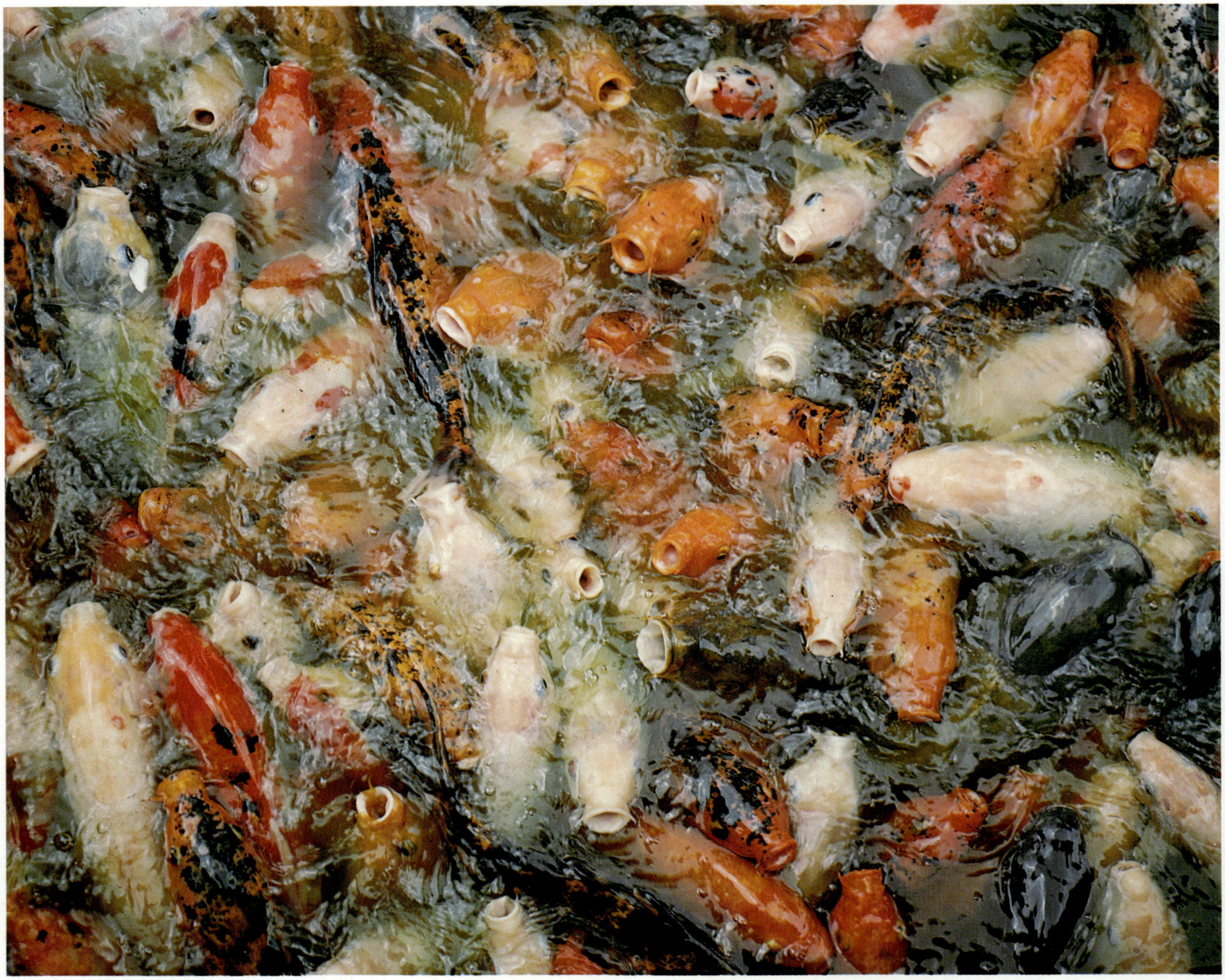

approach. He looks through the viewfinder for a pattern; and when the shape is right (not the subject's expression, or any other detail, but the general shape) he presses the button. In lesser mortals than HCB, this may lead at first to a higher rejection rate of pictures which are unsharp, or in which the people are not doing anything very interesting, but (as with the Senggye system outlined above), it can rapidly grow on you.

The last approach I will suggest comes via David Gibbon, a photographer whose work I hold in the highest regard; he in turn heard it from another painter. It goes like this:

Imagine that you are wearing four pairs of sunglasses at once. With them all on, all you can see is the vaguest outlines. Sketch those. Take off the first pair: a little more detail is visible. This has a line running that way; this is much darker than that. Sketch that in. Take off another pair, and repeat the process; by the time you have taken off the last pair; you will have correctly observed all the details of the original.

Admittedly there is no parallel to sketches in photography (unless it be Polaroid test pictures!), but the application is obvious: as I said at the beginning of the chapter, look, and think.

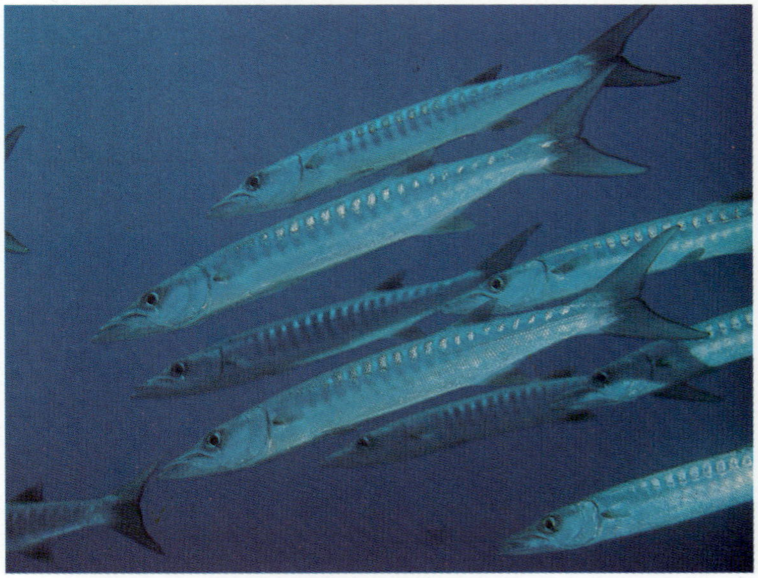

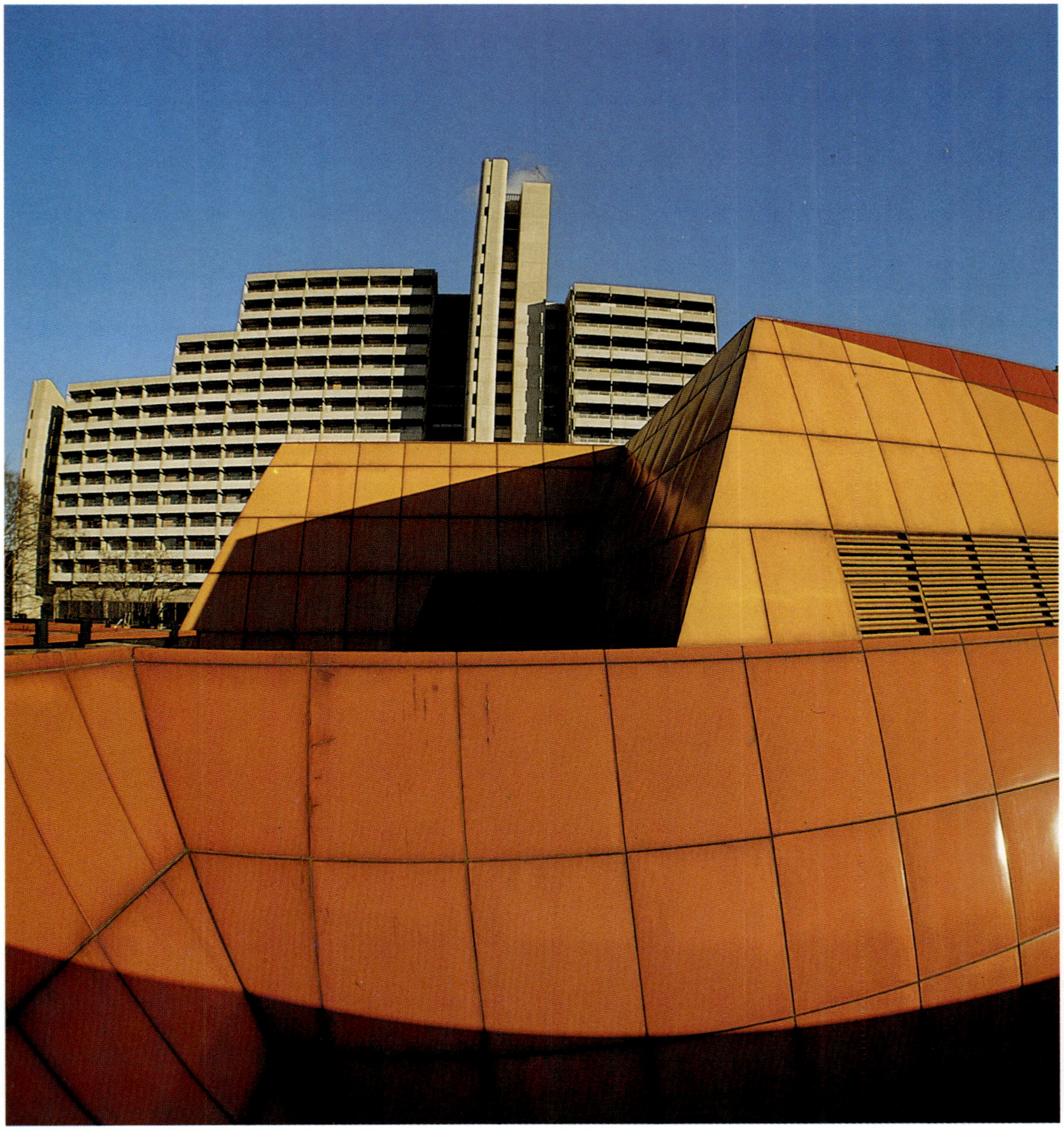

If we appreciate the *photographic process, we can use camera and film to see colour in ways which are alien to us. The blue underwater scene is far more blue than we would remember it – our brain automatically compensates for the blueness, which the film cannot – and the slithering, sliding mass of fish waiting to be fed is frozen by a fast shutter speed. In all of the photographs on this page, a polarising filter has cut glare and saturated colours, either in a way we can readily recognise* ***left and below*** *or in strange and fascinating ways* ***bottom.***

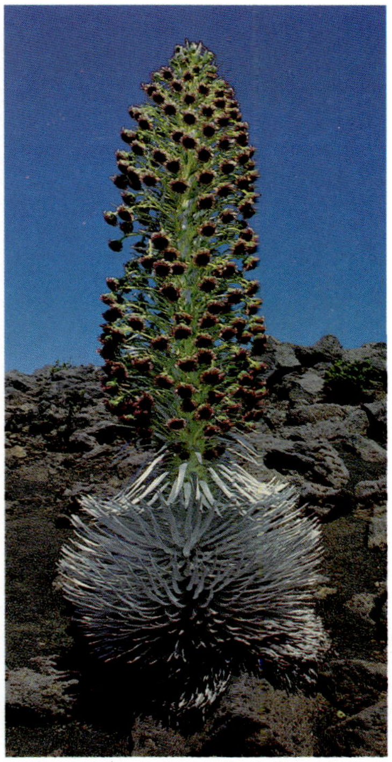

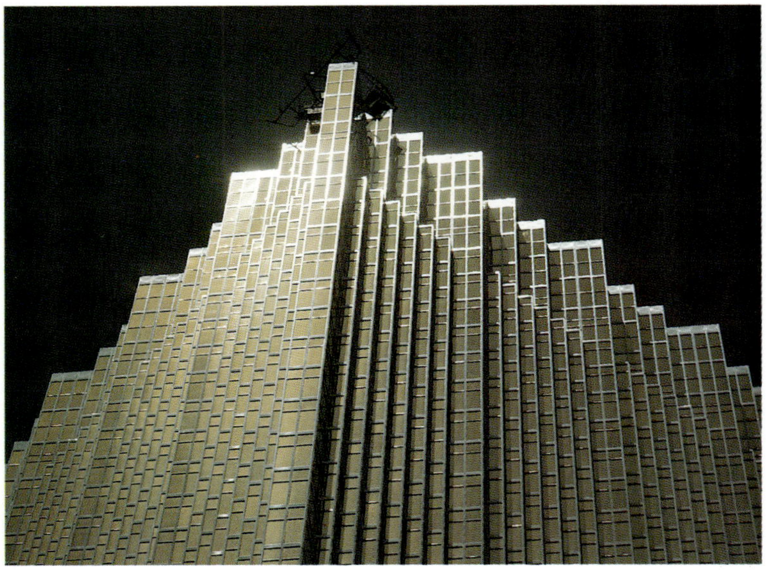

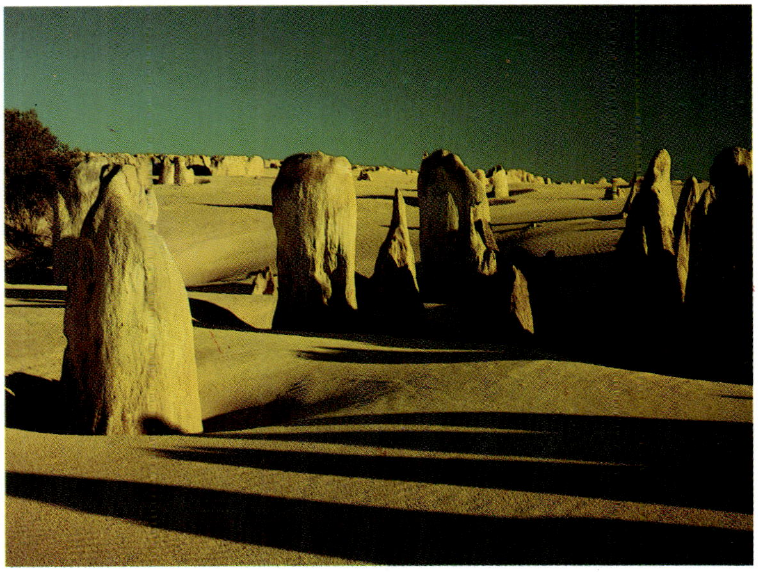

ABSTRACTS

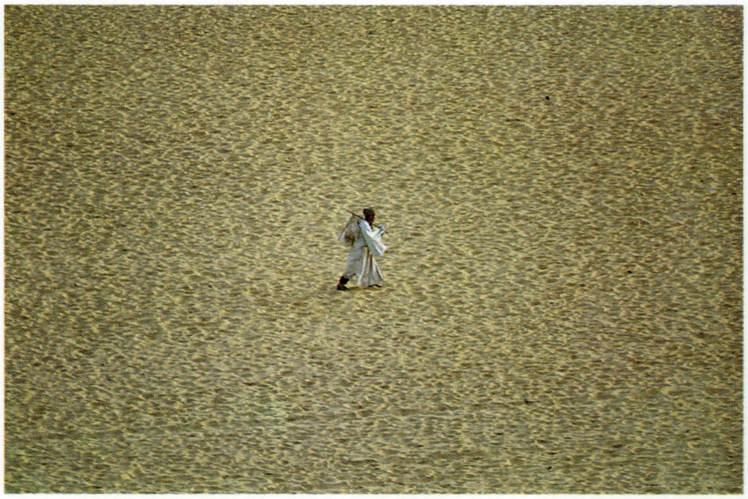

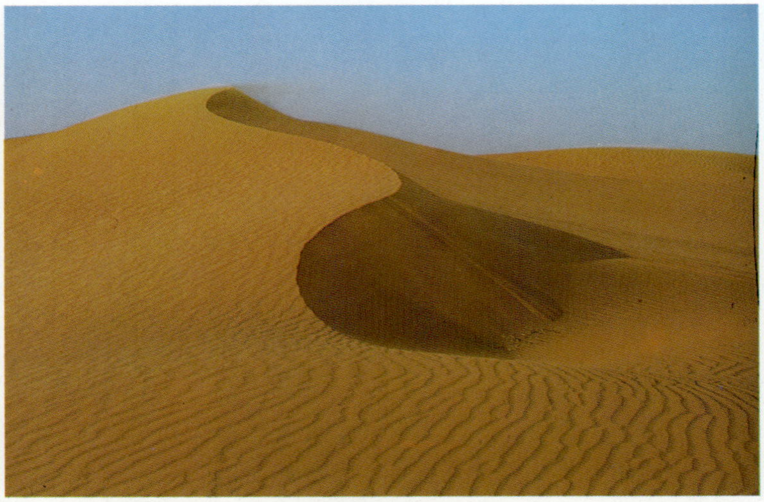

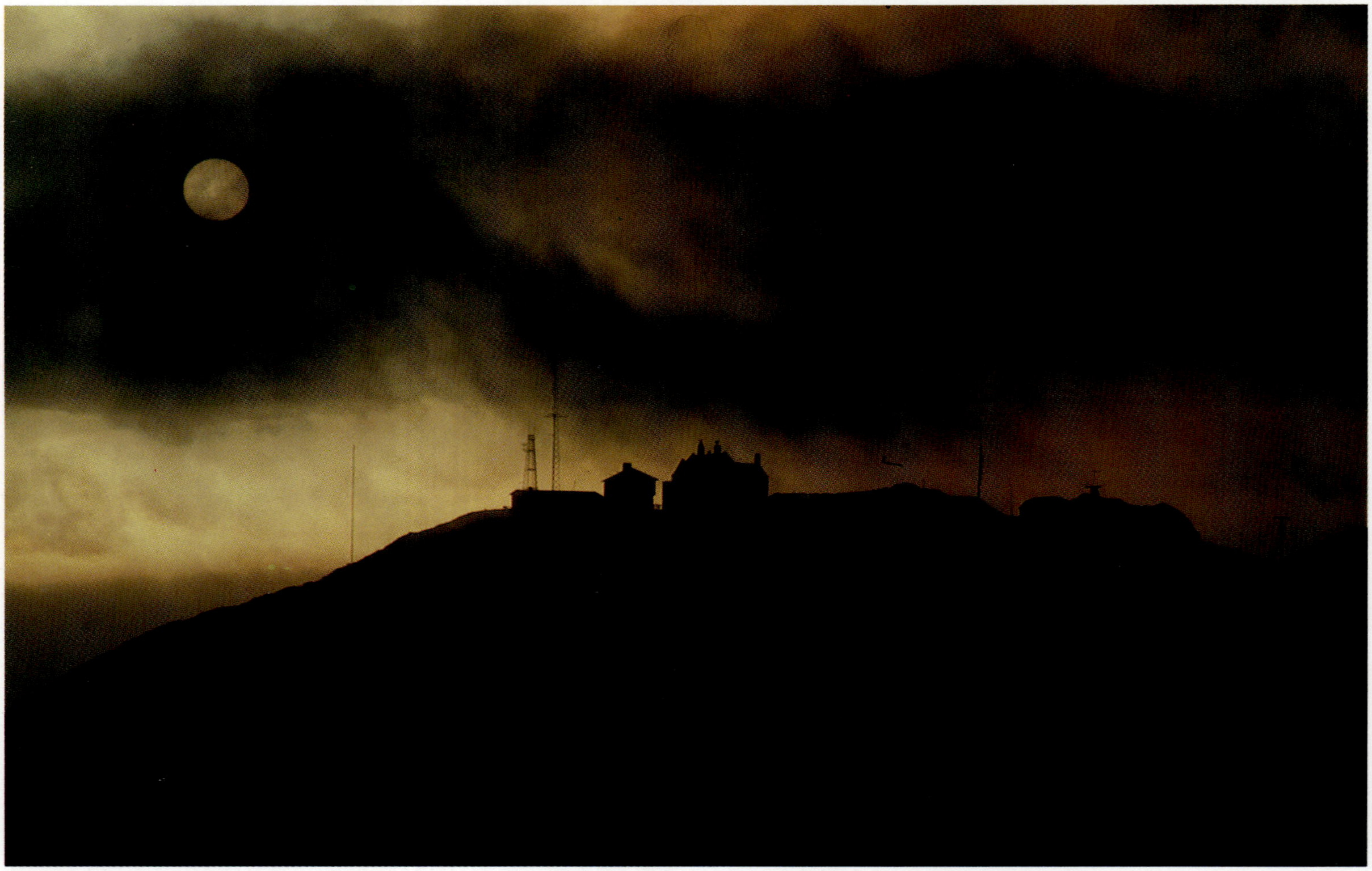

The classical analysis of a painting or photograph breaks it down into four components: line, tone, colour, and form. The four are fairly self-explanatory, though 'form' is sometimes called 'modelling' or 'chiaroscuro', and is to do with the play of light and shade which gives something its roundness or three-dimensionality.

In black-and-white photography, abstraction begins with line and tone; in colour, colour itself precedes tone. It is easy to see why, considering the composition exercise described in the last chapter; the cut-outs could be made of identical tones, but they would still be readily distinguishable by colour.

It is instructive to analyse the *relationship of line, tone, colour, and form in each of the six pictures on this page. In a sense, they are very intellectual pictures: it is possible to work out how each one achieves its impact. Nevertheless, it is also impossible to deny their emotional effect. All of these pictures were taken with 35mm cameras: the lack of detail, particularly in the three figures (figures always draw the eye) is noticeable. It is also substantially irrelevant, as the viewer supplies his own details. Only in the two abstract pictures, in which there is no sign of humanity, do we look more closely at the textures and shapes.*

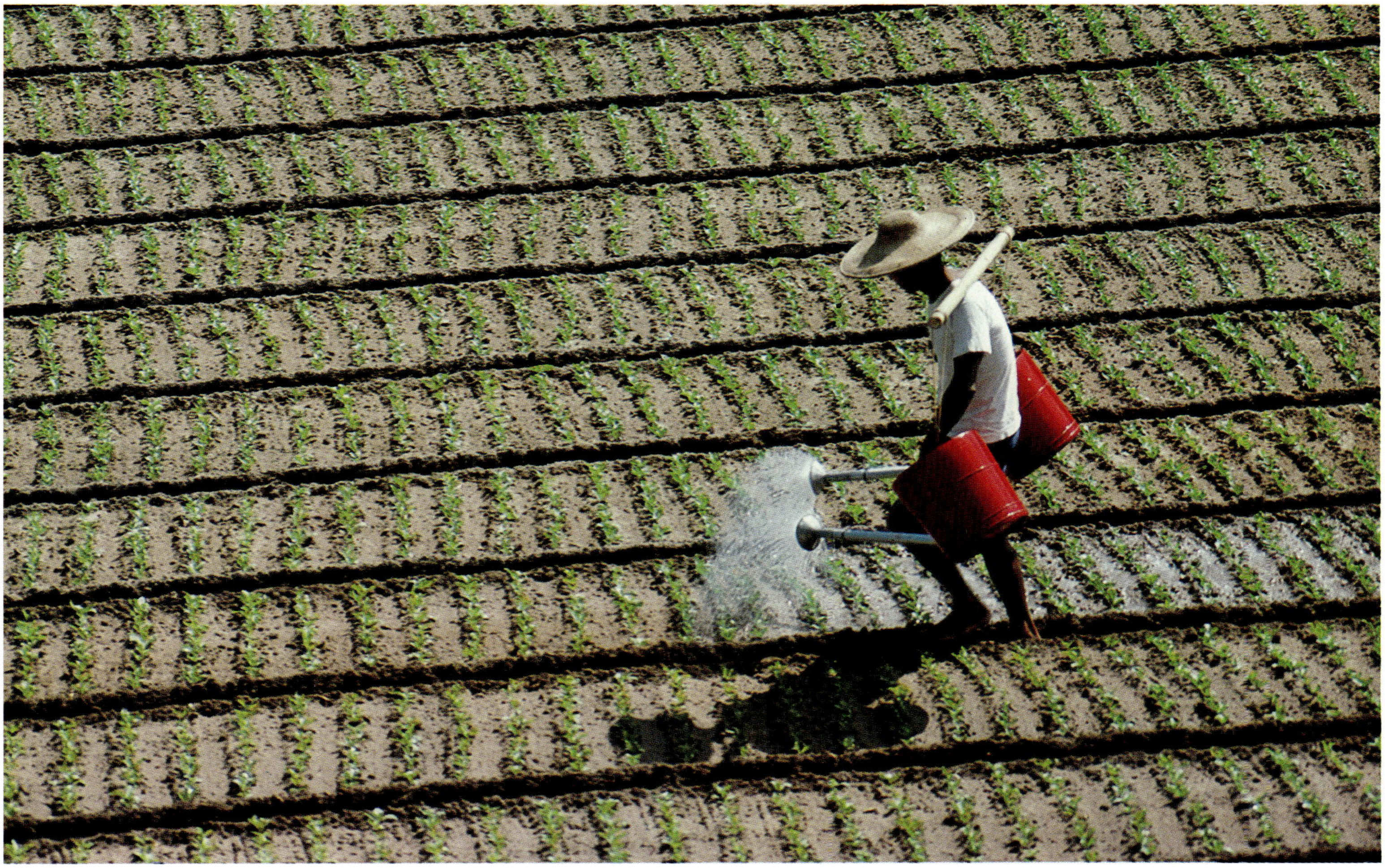

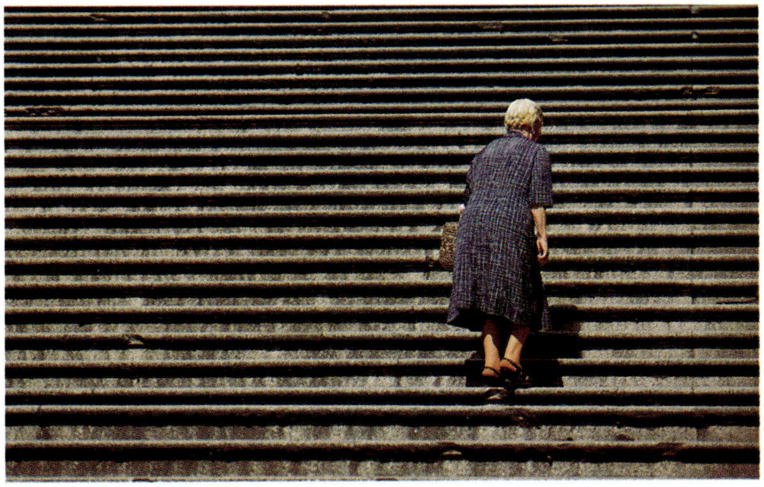

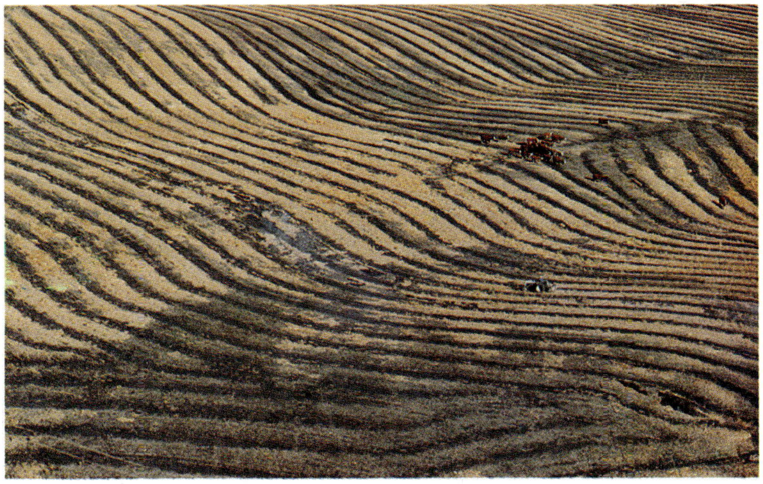

Alternatively, the abstract can work in different tones of the same colour – though now, we have introduced the third variable. Finally, we introduce form; but unless the picture is cleverly composed so that we do not immediately recognise the subject (or rather, so that subject is subjugated to the abstracted elements), it can scarcely be called an abstract. After all, 'abstraction' is by definition the art of taking a part, not all; and a recognisable picture can cease to be an 'abstraction'.

In practice, any one or more of the analytical categories can be the subject of the abstraction. In a picture consisting of a monochrome and black, it is almost possible to reduce it to pure line, and even taking so palpably real a subject as a nude, we can use very flat lighting to reduce the colour to a series of barely separated tones, so that the composition is again reduced almost to pure line.

Abstraction is a way of seeing, and it varies from person to person. Because of the posturings of some *avant-garde* artists, the word 'abstract' has become synonymous in some circles with incompetence; in others, there is the reverent attitude which holds: 'I don't understand it, so it must be art.' But think back to Senggye's lesson on composition: some ways of arranging things are pleasing, some are not. You would not expect everything

ABSTRACTS

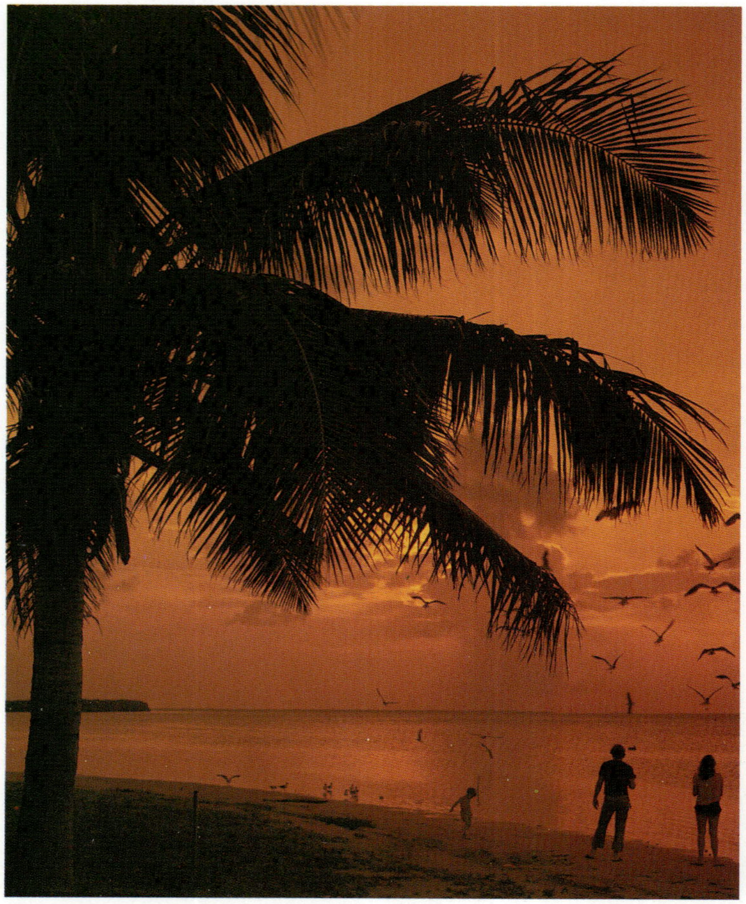

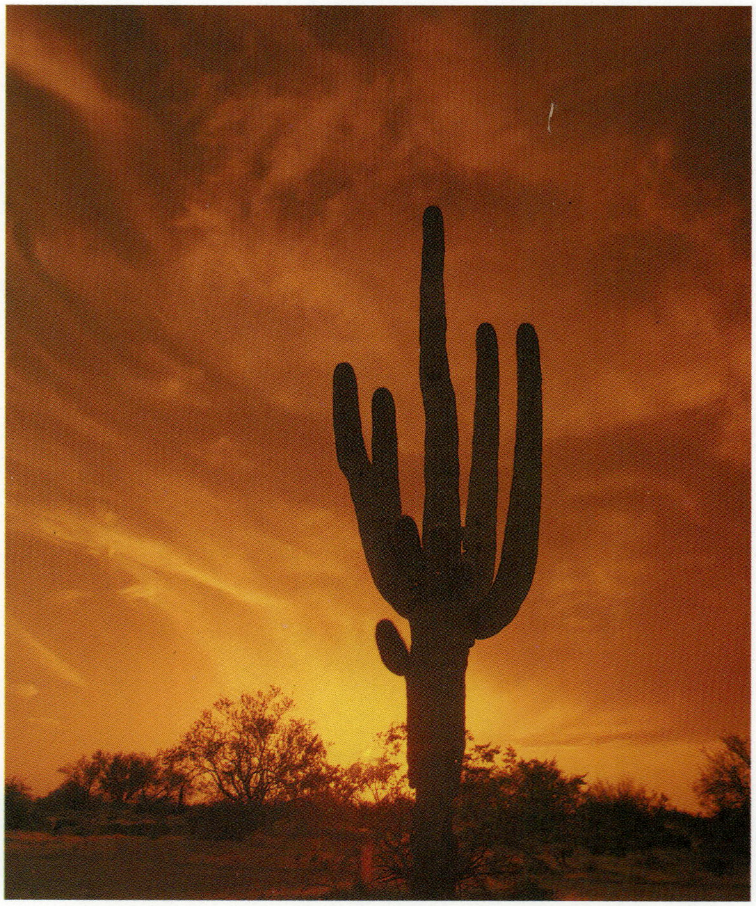

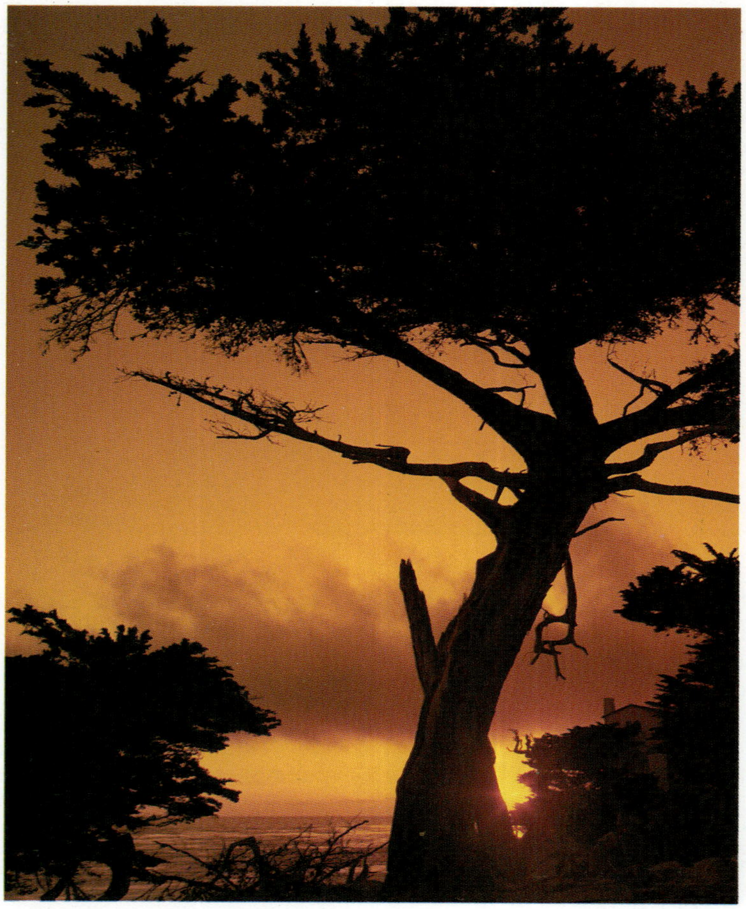

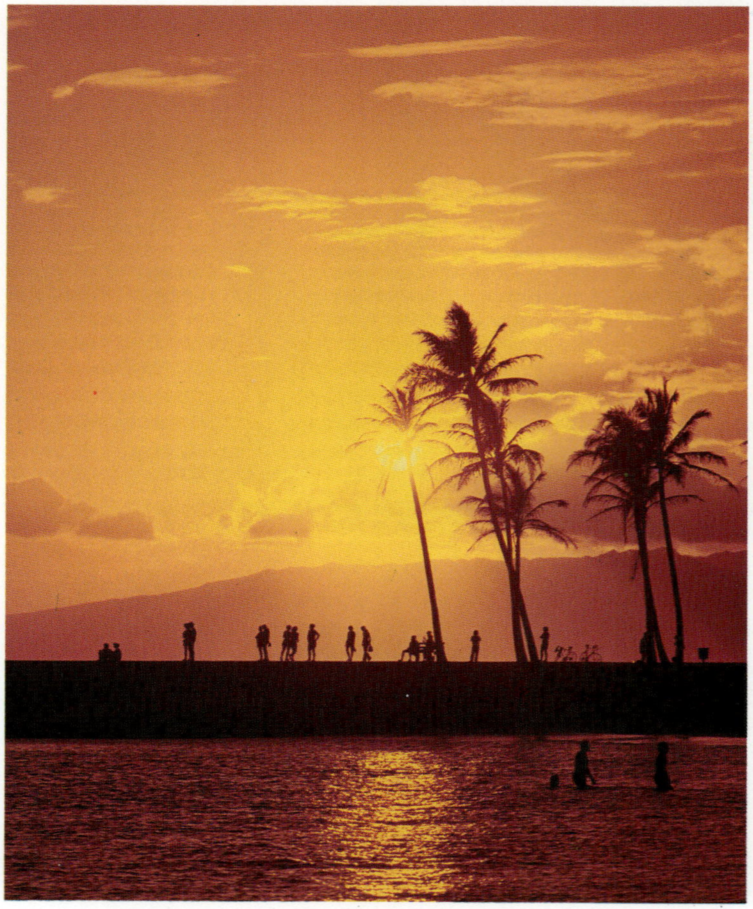

which pleased you to please everyone else, so do not expect their abstractions to please you, or yours to please them. Rather, please yourself – and if your inward eye is good enough, you will please yourself more and more, as well as finding that you can please other people.

Throughout our experience there are examples of abstractions: abstract nudes, abstract still-lifes, abstract landscapes, abstracts culled from city life, to name but a few. The reason for according them a separate chapter here, though, is that they are in many ways the purest form of colour photography, colour for its own sake.

Although the golden rule for understanding the abstract compositions of others, and for spotting your own, is still the same 'look and think', there are a couple of techniques – tricks, if you like – for seeing them. One is to select unfamiliar parts of the whole; a good way of doing this is to move in close, to around eighteen inches or so, or even closer if your lens can manage it.

By isolating things in this way, you can see them for themselves instead of in their everyday functional terms. Another good trick is to look for bright colours; at the intersection of two bright colours, you can get some really vivid colour abstracts.

Motor cars are a particularly good source of brilliant colour, and so is plastic kitchen ware. It sometimes helps to put your eyes slightly out of focus; that way, colours seem to become much, much more vivid in contrast with dull backgrounds.

Although anything can provide the inspiration for an abstract picture, there is often a lot to be gained from rubbish and decay. The higgledy-piggledy juxtaposition of discarded wrappings, toys, fruit peel, and so forth can furnish some excellent abstracts, though it is as well to use a slightly longer than usual lens to keep from getting too close! Cracked and peeling paint, on the other hand, is a lot more hygienic, and I find that I often prefer the aleatory hand of nature to the allegedly more skilled hand of Jackson Pollock.

Closely related to the abstract from a photographic point of view (though the artistic connection is more arguable) is the unfamiliar picture. 'Trick' pictures, from unusual angles, are not uncommon, but we can go beyond this and show something in a genuinely novel way. This is particularly true of close-ups; a common electronic circuit board can look like a surreal science-fiction landscape when carefully photographed. Close-up techniques are further described later.

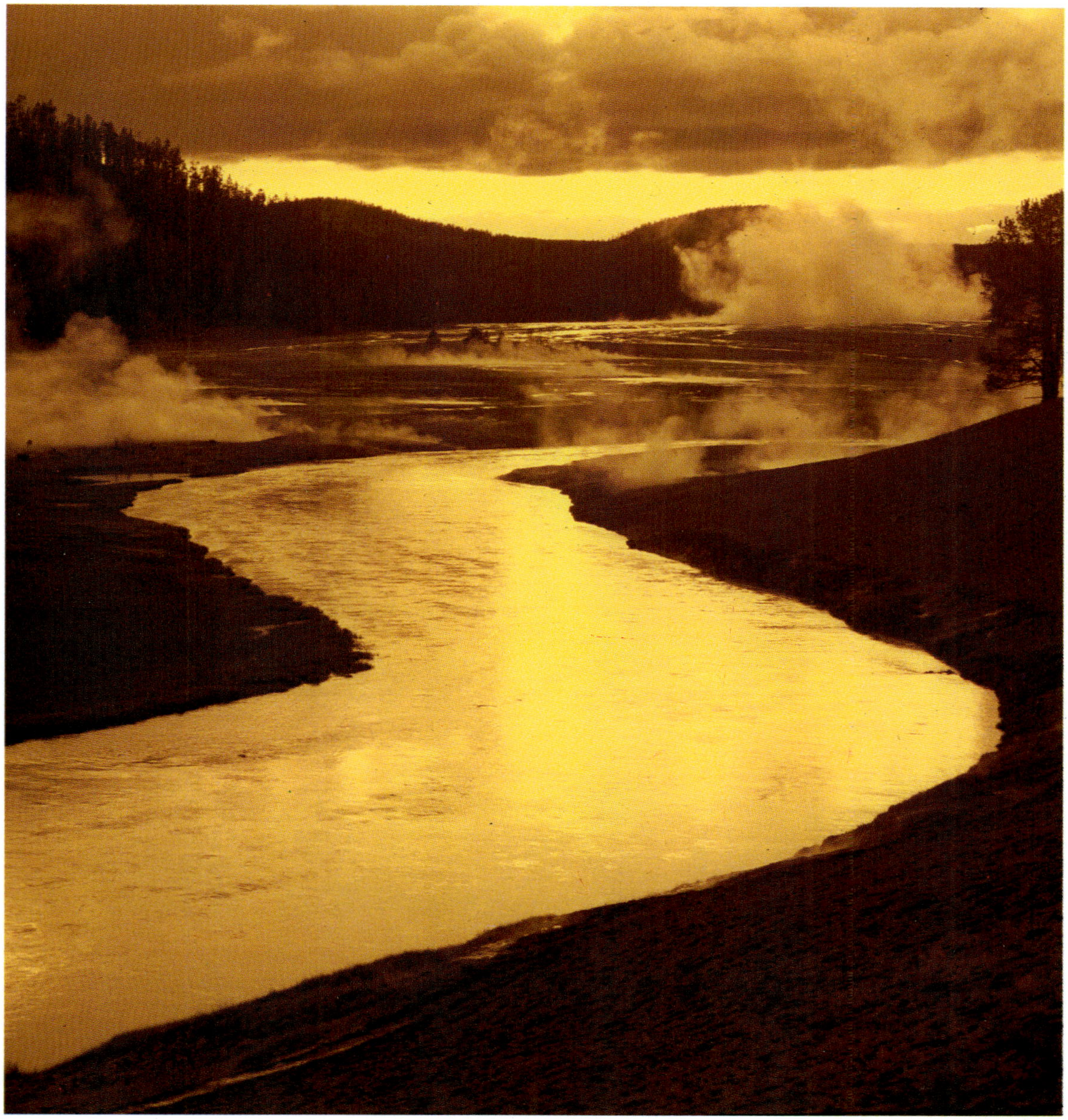

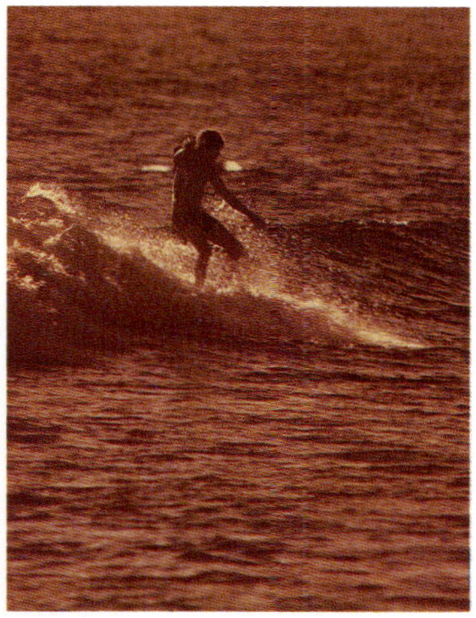

***These pictures are all** exercises in tone. Colour variation and colour contrast have been almost entirely removed, and the use of silhouette techniques minimises modelling, so that form becomes line. The effects which result from using strong monochrome filters on colour film are hard to previsualise, because our eyes can compensate for colour casts to quite an extraordinary degree. The only way to learn about them is to use up some film. Try for strong, clear shapes, and underexpose quite dramatically: try two stops as a starting point (or quadruple your ASA setting). It may seem that reducing colour to monochrome removes the point of using colour film, but the simple question is whether the results justify the means.*

LIGHT

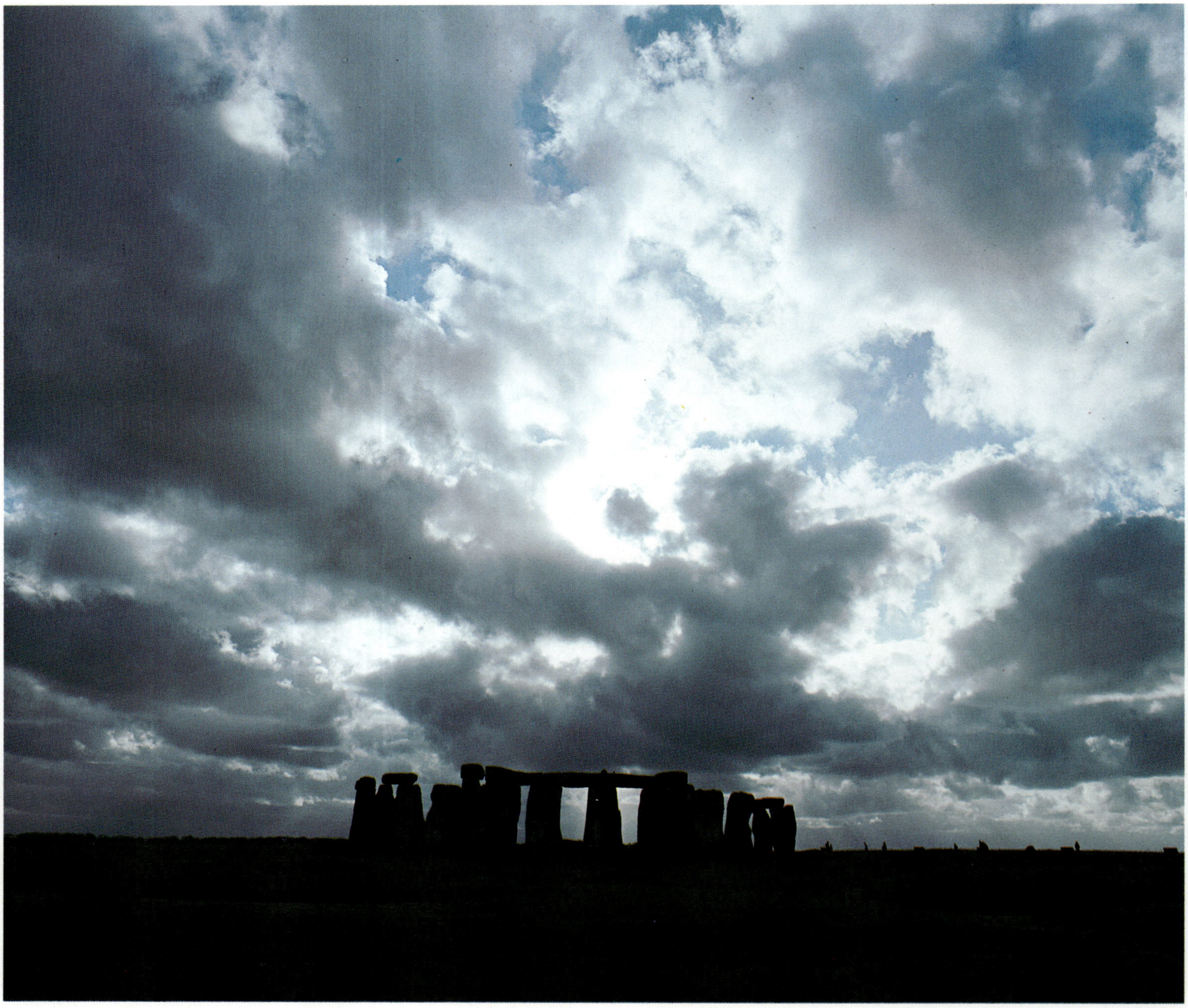

Light is the basis of photography; the word photography comes from the Greek words for light and writing. Despite its pre-eminence, however, few photographers bother to study it that much, or even to think about it at all.

From a photographic point of view, the first important distinction is between available light and controlled light. Available light is the light as we find it. It is free, it requires no setting-up on our part, and most important of all it preserves the atmosphere of a place. Its drawbacks, though, are that it may not be as strong as we would like, it may come from the wrong direction, and it may be of the wrong colour. Controlled light comes from supplementary lamps under our control.

For some kinds of photography, the atmosphere is everything; to change the lighting in any way would ruin the picture. Admittedly, there is a kind of half-way house in which the available light is recreated (and modified) using studio lighting. There are also a couple of useful tricks such as using reflectors out of shot to get a bit more light where you need it, or even

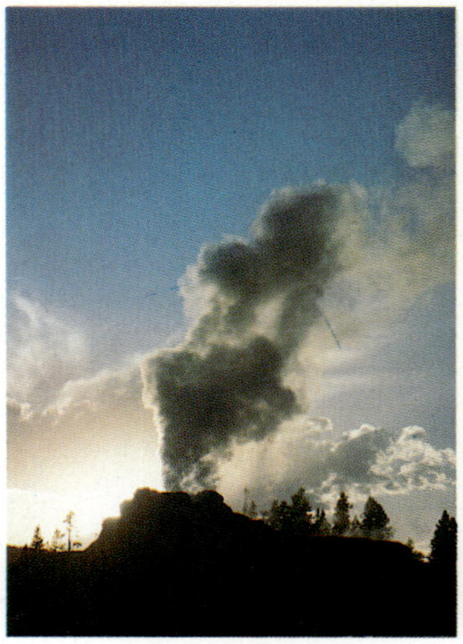

We can, perhaps, best *appreciate the changing nature of light by watching clouds in the sky – especially if there is blue sky and sunlight to set them off. The way in which brightness and shadow, modelling and silhouette, tone and line vary as we watch, is enormously instructive. If we look at a sunset as well, we can see the incredible range of colours contained in an apparently monochrome subject. Even without taking a single picture, cloud-watching is time well spent; and if we can capture the clouds, we have really accomplished something.*

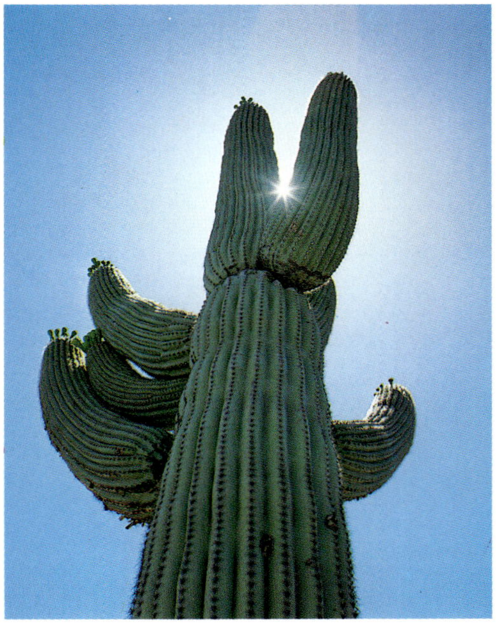
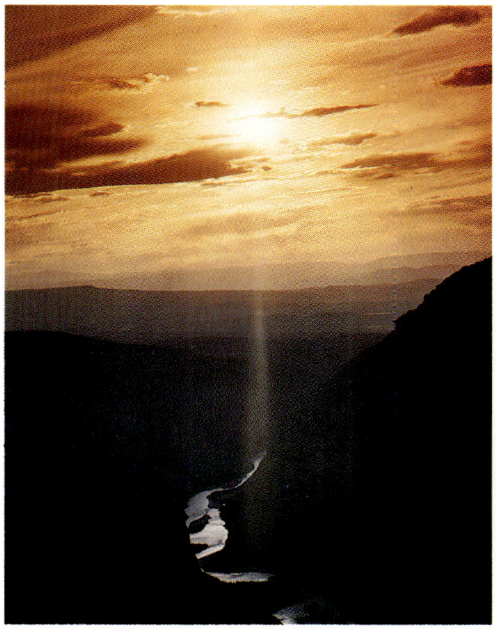
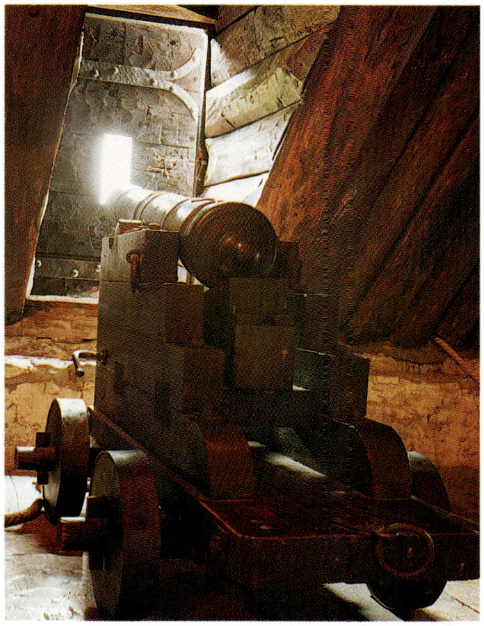
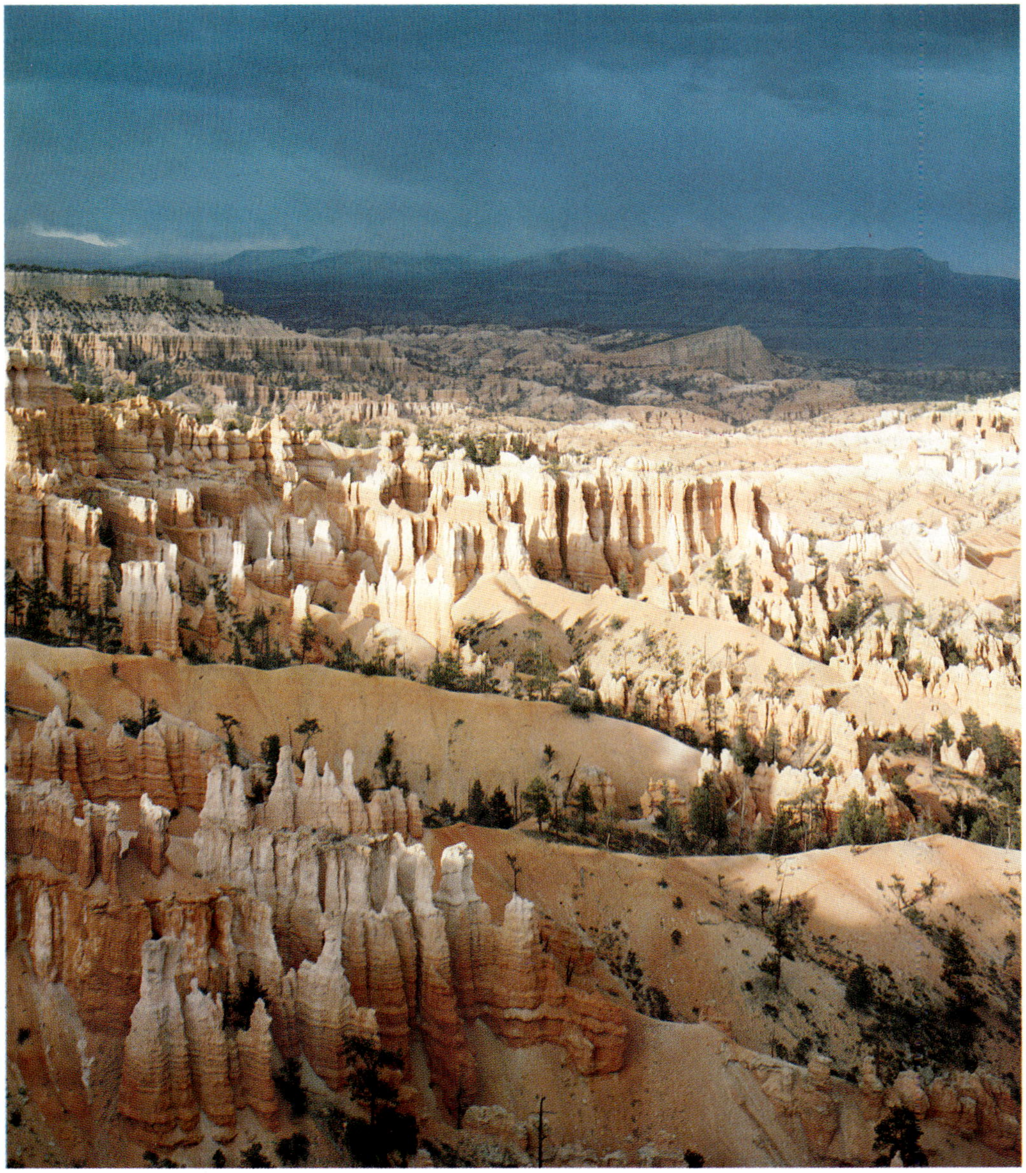
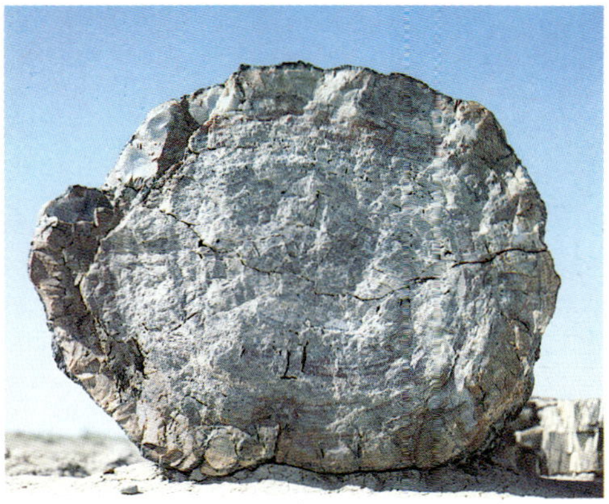
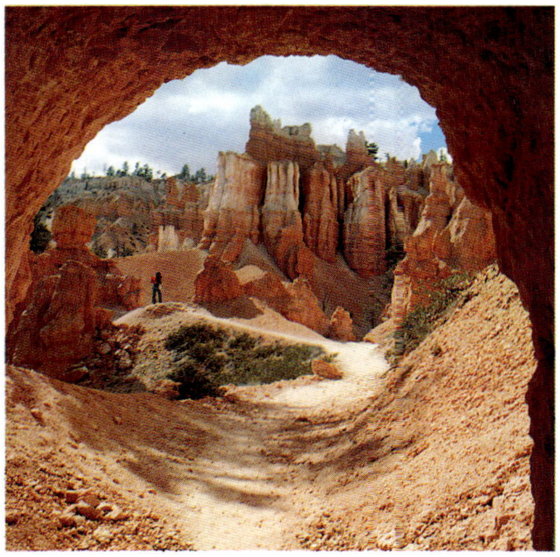

Always be on the lookout for lighting *effects: if you cannot find them by moving around,* ***top right and top left,*** *then try waiting,* ***left and top centre.*** *A patch of sun breaking through clouds often makes for an attractive landscape, whether in Arizona or Hampshire.*

replacing domestic 100 watt bulbs with 275 watt photofloods (which increases heat output as well as light, so watch out for lampshades and furnishings). Generally, though, controlled lighting implies a fairly significant change to the existing light; and it can be achieved in a number of ways.

The quality of light can vary in three main ways, direction, harshness, and colour. Each of these can be controlled.

Direction is the most obvious; the only physical difficulty in controlling it lies in getting the lamp to stay where we want it, and solutions to this range from having assistants to hold each lamp to buying various forms of lamp-stand. Accustomed as we are to the light of the sun, we expect the light to come from more-or-less above and from a single source. Apart from this, we have a free hand.

Harshness is more subtle. Basically, a point source (like the sun in a cloudless sky) casts very clear sharp shadows, whereas a diffuse source (like a cloudy sky) casts no shadows and gives a much softer effect. A small flashgun, or an unshielded bulb, casts strong shadows: for diffusion we can 'bounce' the light off a wall or ceiling or other flat surface, or diffuse it through some translucent material – one photographer of my acquaintance swears by stapling a huge sheet of tracing paper across a doorway and shining a light through that.

Colour is the trickiest of all. We can accept daylight as white, or the light of an electric lamp as white; but if we compare the two side-by-side, we see that the electric lamp is much yellower. Still worse are fluorescent lamps: we may see them as 'white', but on film they often record a sickly green. The problem is that we can adapt mentally; the film cannot.

The consequence of this is that if we use film in illumination for which it was not designed, we must either put up with colour casts or use filters. The easiest way to understand this is via a brief excursion into the theory of colour temperature.

If a perfectly black body is heated, it begins to glow as it gets hot. The hotter it gets, the more blue the light; this is illustrated by the fact that 'white-hot' iron is hotter than 'red-hot'.

Although perfect black bodies are rare, the behaviour of most things when they are heated gets pretty close; a candle, burning at about 1500°C, is redder than a domestic lamp running at about 2500°C and this in turn is redder than the sun (say 5000°C). Furthermore, even light which is not obviously produced by heating (such as the light from a discharge tube in an electronic flashgun) can be assigned a colour temperature. In practice, colour temperatures are given in degrees Kelvin (°K), which represent the same temperature increments as °C but start from 'absolute zero', about −273°C. Typical colour temperatures are, therefore:

Candle	1750°K
Domestic lamp	2600-2800°K (depending on wattage)
Nitraphot lamp	3200°K
Clear flashbulb	4000°K
Sunlight	5000°K
Overcast daylight	7500°K
Blue north sky	10,000-20,000°K

Small differences are more easily visible further down the scale, with a 3200°K lamp detectably different from a 3400°K lamp, and a domestic lamp noticeably much yellower than either. In the higher regions, beyond about 6000°K, it takes about a 500°K difference to be really noticeable.

Films may in theory be sensitised to suit any colour temperature, but they are usually 'Daylight type' (5800 or 6000°K) or 'Artificial Light' (3400°K or more rarely 3200°K). Light source and film can be matched by using warming (brown-orange) or cooling (blue) filters, either according to tables or with the use of a colour temperature meter.

Whilst it does not much matter what sort of film and light we use, provided they match (or can be made to match), the difficulty comes when light from two different kinds of sources are mixed. Daylight and electronic flash are of the same colour temperature, and can be mixed with impunity, but daylight and tungsten light, or electronic flash and tungsten light, cannot. Electronic flash can be made to match tungsten by filtering the flash head itself with a piece of gel or acetate filter; if used in front of tungsten lamps these will often melt, and the only

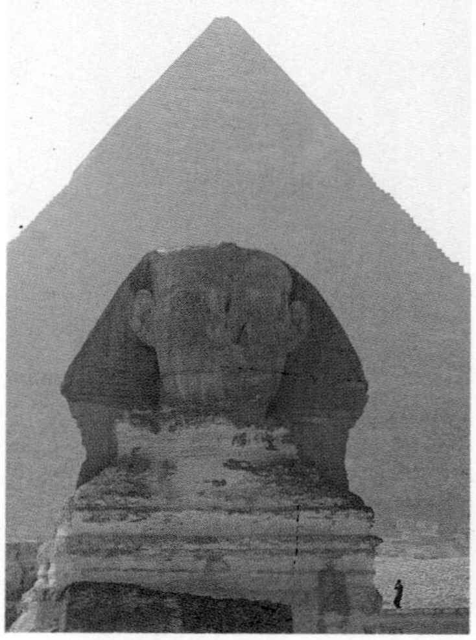

Haze, sun on water, the *darkening sky: each kind of light has its own flavour, its own feeling. Do not be afraid to emphasise the feeling of the light, either by using filters or by colour contrasts within the picture, but be wary of changing it dramatically unless you want a deliberately unnatural or contrived picture. Even if you do want special effects, an awareness of the existing light is essential. Open-awareness – looking, and seeing – must remain the core of successful photography.*

Colour temperature conversions

To obtain 3200 K from:	To obtain 3400 K from:	WRATTEN Filter	Exposure Increase in stops*	Filter Colour
2490 K	2610 K	82C+82C	1⅓	Bluish
2570 K	2700 K	82C+82B	1⅓	
2650 K	2780 K	82C+82A	1	
2720 K	2870 K	82C+82	1	
2800 K	2950 K	82C	⅔	
2900 K	3060 K	82B	⅔	
3000 K	3180 K	82A	⅓	
3100 K	3290 K	82	⅓	
3200 K	3400 K	*No filter necessary*		
3300 K	3510 K	81	⅓	Yellowish
3400 K	3630 K	81A	⅓	
3500 K	3740 K	81B	⅓	
3600 K	3850 K	81C	⅔	
3850 K	4140 K	81EF	⅔	

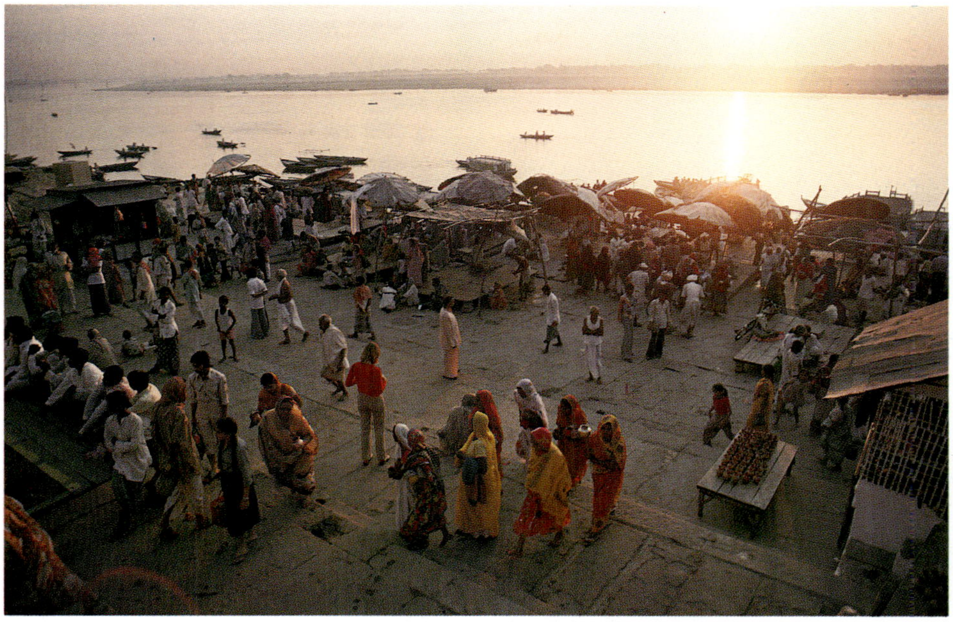

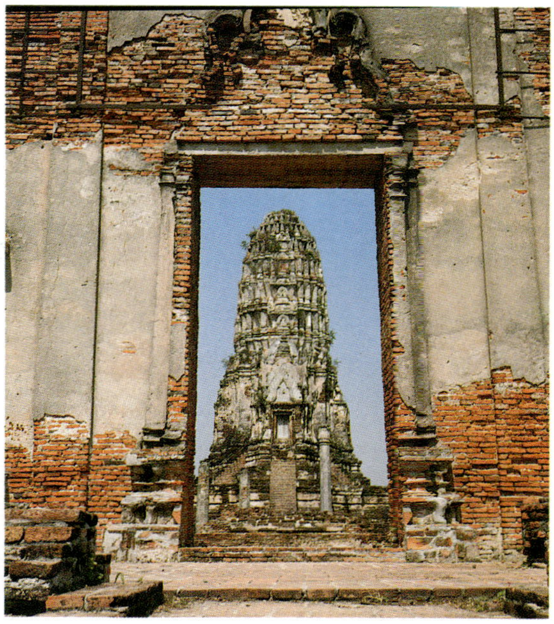

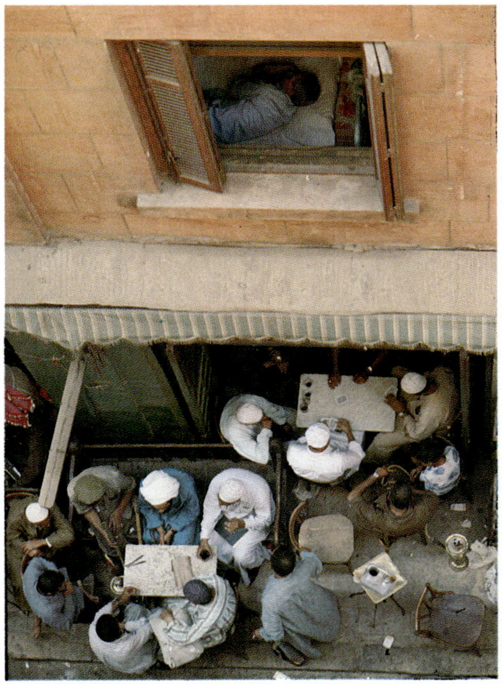

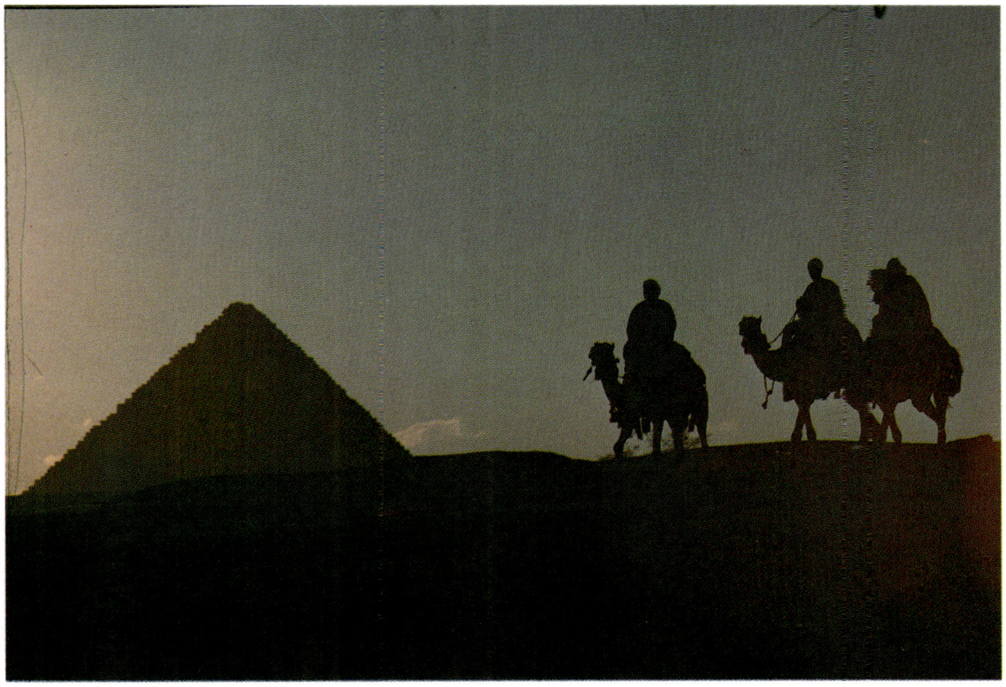

practical approach is to use expensive dichroic glass filters – or to exclude all other light. Fluorescent tubes are in a class by themselves, as they do not emit a continuous spectrum and thus cannot be assigned a colour temperature; the best you can do is to try a CC20M filter and hope for the best.

In unavoidably mixed lighting, such as an office lit partly by daylight, partly by fluorescents, and partly by tungsten-filament draughtsman's lamps, it is flatly impossible to accommodate everything on one film. The best bet is to use Ektachrome 400, which appears to handle this sort of thing acceptably.

Given the three variables of direction, harshness, and colour, we can begin to choose types of supplementary lighting. Once again, there are three divisions: the small on-camera flashgun, tungsten lighting, and studio electronic flash.

The small on-camera flashgun is normally only suitable for snapshots; the harsh shadows behind the subject, the fixed and rather unnatural direction, and the danger of 'flashback' or direct reflection of the light back into the camera ensure this. The dreaded 'red-eye' is a variation of the last, and is caused by the light being reflected straight back from the eyes; the blood vessels of the eye give the characteristic demonic look. In addition, burned-out foregrounds frequently result either from miscalculation or from trusting an automatic flashgun against a dark background.

A certain amount can be achieved by 'bouncing' the light, as described before, but this relies on a powerful gun and a handy reflective surface; low-powered guns often lose too much light by absorption at the reflective surface, and in any case the flash-to-subject distance is the distance from the gun to the reflector and then on to the subject, which may be out of the gun's range. Coloured reflectors add their own tinge to the light as well as absorbing still more of what is available.

One other point which has already been made is that additional lighting can destroy the atmosphere, but there is one

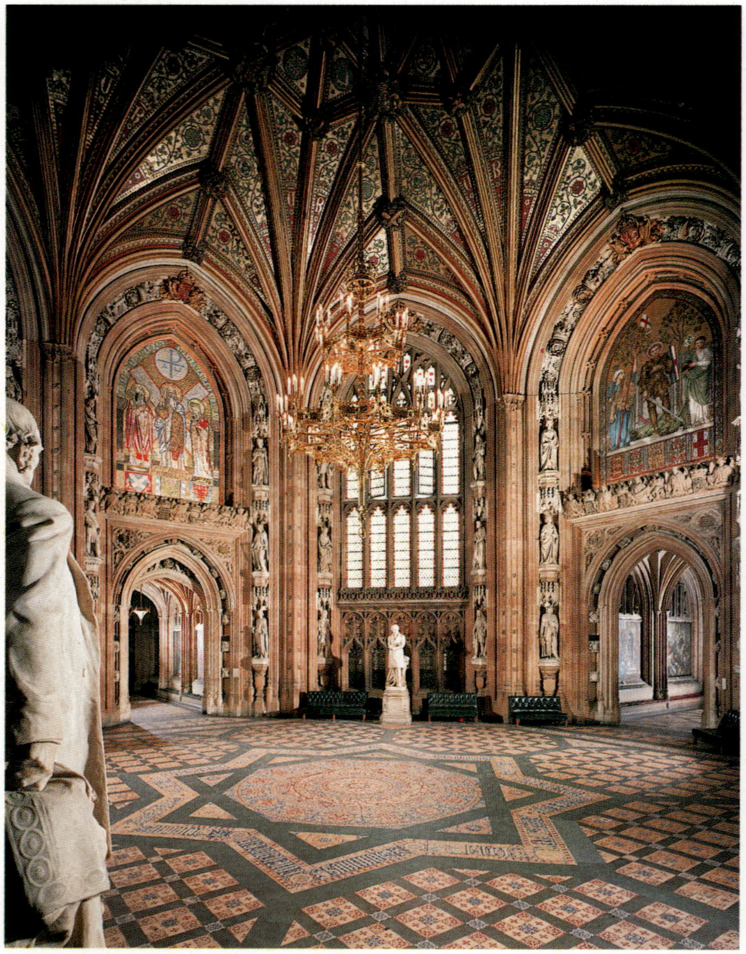

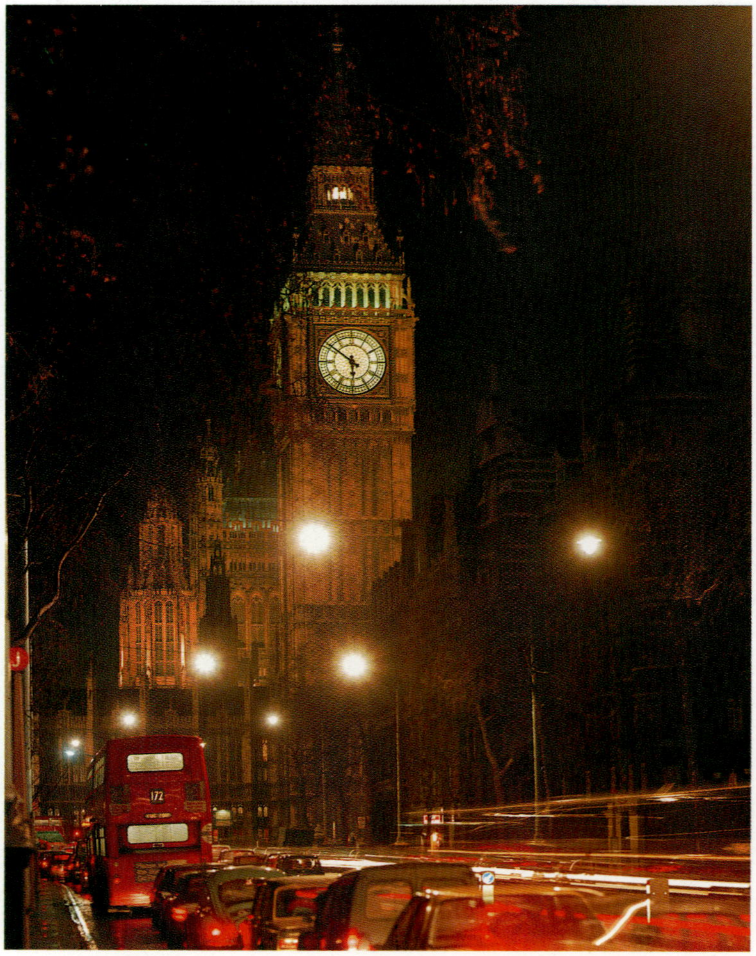

Pictures incorporating light *sources (including windows) require extreme care if these are not to 'burn in' to featureless areas of white. If in addition there is both daylight and artificial light, the problems are even more acute. Three possibilities are (1) multiple electronic flash fired simultaneously, (2) 'painting' dark areas with multiple flashes, and (3) relying on existing lighting as in the interiors on these pages.*

case in which the atmosphere (literally) has its revenge and destroys the picture. A thick, smoky, hazy atmosphere reflects on-camera flash straight back into the lens, giving a flat and degraded picture – and the effect with bounce flash is not much better. 'Snooting' the flash to give a spotlight effect (use a cone of black paper) improves matters, but drastically cuts down on the amount of light available.

On-camera flashguns have other uses than providing straight-forward illumination, though. Fill-in flash, also known as 'synchro-sunlight', is used to fill shadows or to illuminate a subject against a bright background – a simple example is a girl against a sunset. The film cannot handle the contrast range involved, so normally the choice would be between a correctly-exposed sunset (and a silhouette of the girl) or a correctly-exposed girl (and a washed-out sunset). With the flash, you can expose for the sunset (with conventional metering) and light the girl to even things up.

Automatic flashguns are usually useless for fill-in flash, as you need to know the amount of light being emitted. Set them on manual, and use a guide number 50-100% higher than normal: for example, with a gun rated at GN 100 (feet) at 100 ASA, use a GN of 150-200. If the available light exposure is (say) 1/60 at f/8 (and you must remember to use a shutter speed at which your camera can synchronise), then you would need to be about twenty feet away ($180 \div 8 = 22.5$). If you want to be closer, try a folded handkerchief over the flash head: you can gauge how much light it is likely to absorb by metering 'through' it with a conventional meter. Alternatively, if you have a gun with switchable power, turn it down. You may even wish to consider a cheap small gun if you already own a large one, merely to use for fill-in. By playing with the balance between the flash and the available light, you can achieve a variety of effects, including *'nuite Americaine,'* in which the daylight is underexposed and gives the effect of twilight or even moonlight.

You can also filter the light passing through a flash-head. Used out of doors, as balance flash, the filtration will only affect foreground objects: this gives some weird effects. Alternatively, by using filters of complementary colours over the flash head and the camera lens, you can get some quite extraordinary effects. Something similar is sold as 'Color Back' by Cokin.

Most amateurs who want something more versatile than a single flash-head buy lighting stands which accept photofloods. Whilst these have the drawbacks already mentioned of being of a low colour temperature (and furthermore of not being compatible with daylight), they are much less expensive and much less complicated than big studio flash units. They run very hot, and can get through bulbs at quite a rate: because the bulbs are 'overrun' for maximum light, their life is only a few hours, though gas-filled bulbs of the Argophot or Nitrophot type last longer at the expense of lower efficiency (less light for a given wattage) and a slightly lower colour temperature (3200°K instead of 3400°K).

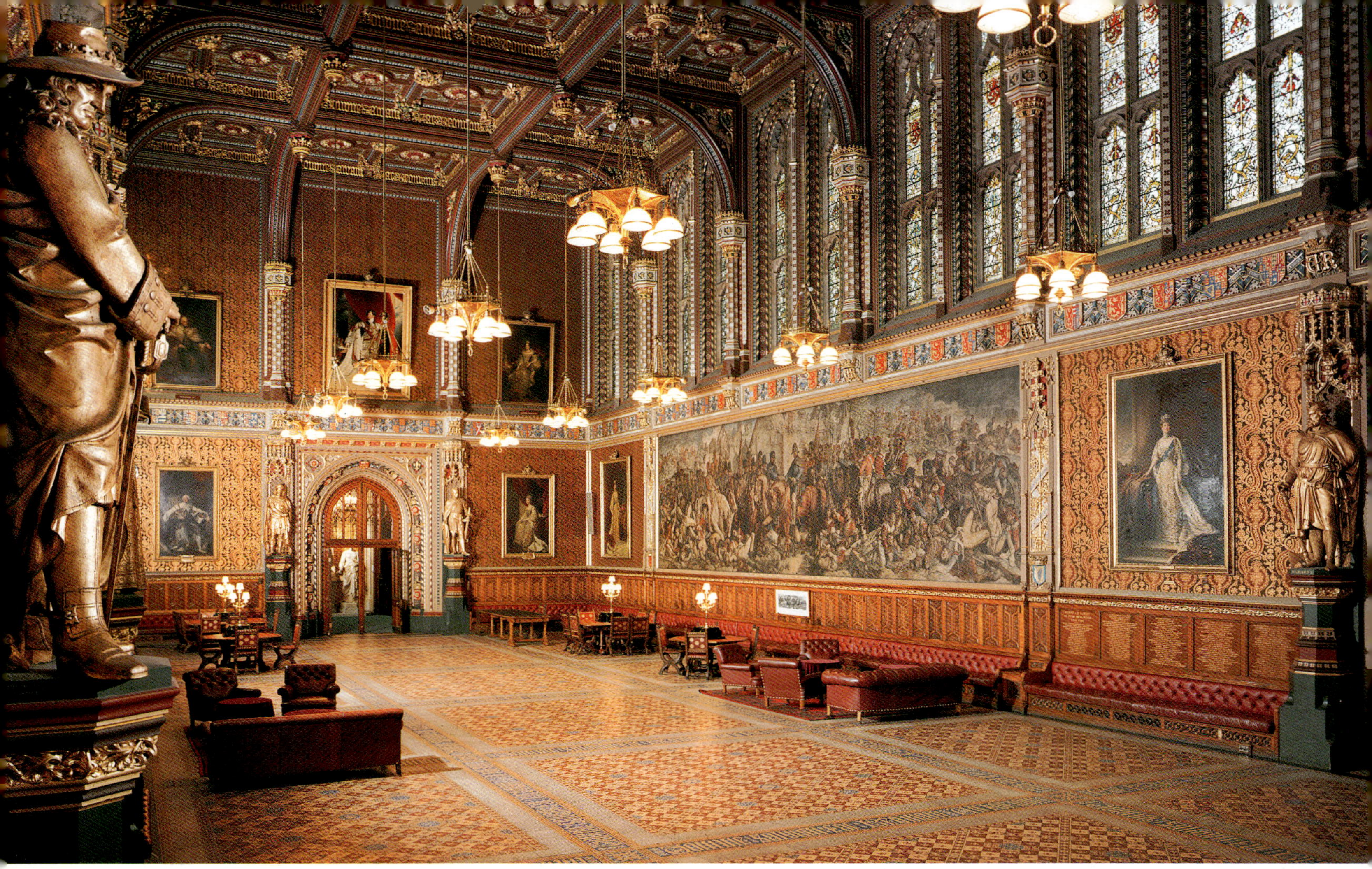

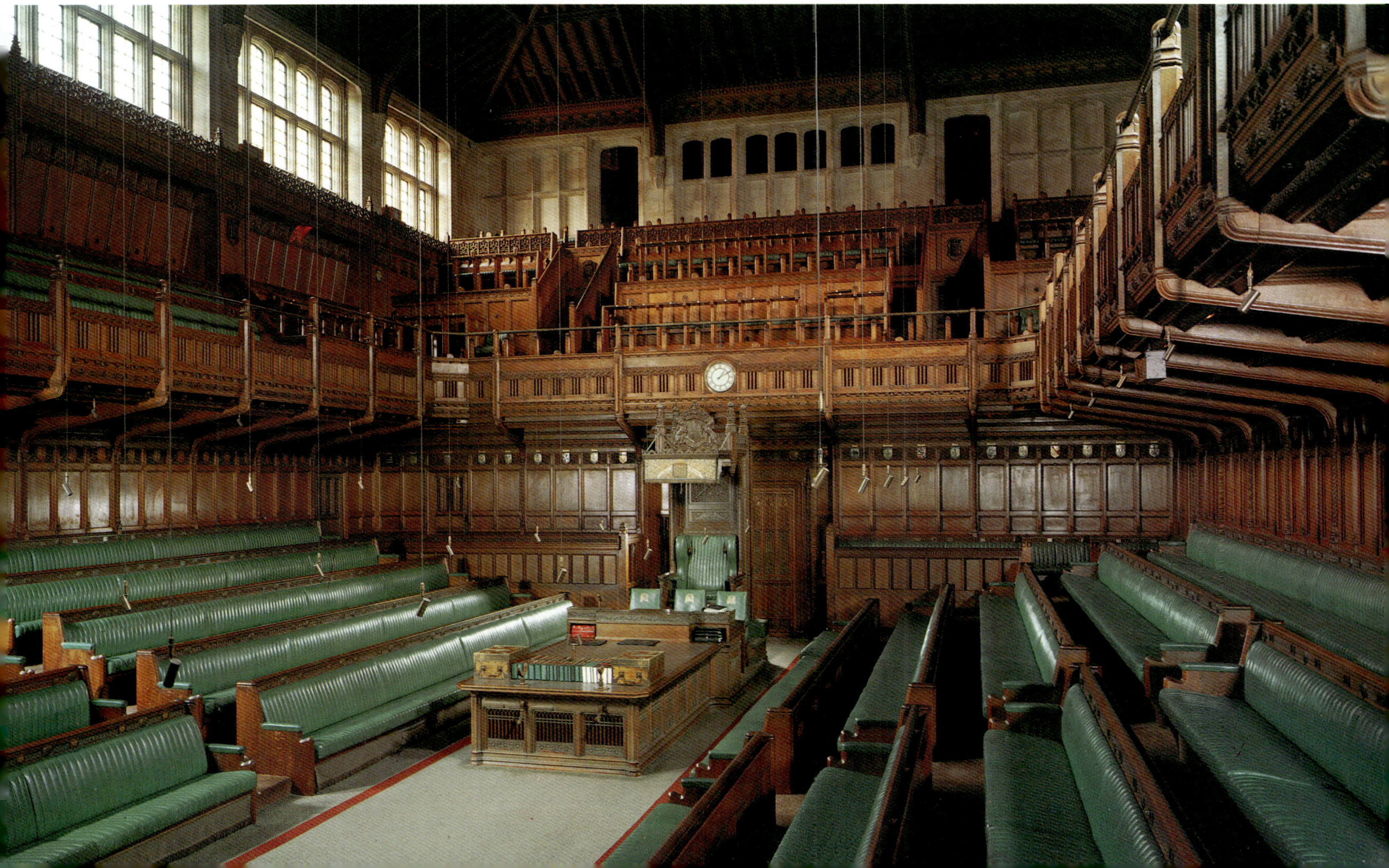

LIGHT

Daylight is often rather *bluish, especially at twilight: in the picture of the trees* ***right*** *the photographer has emphasised this with a weak blue filter. In the small picture* ***below,*** *the blue tinge is due to an overcast sky. A brown graduated filter was used to add 'interest' to the sky.*

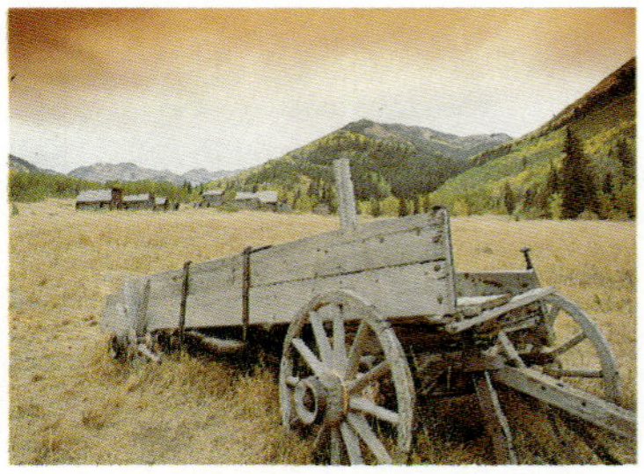

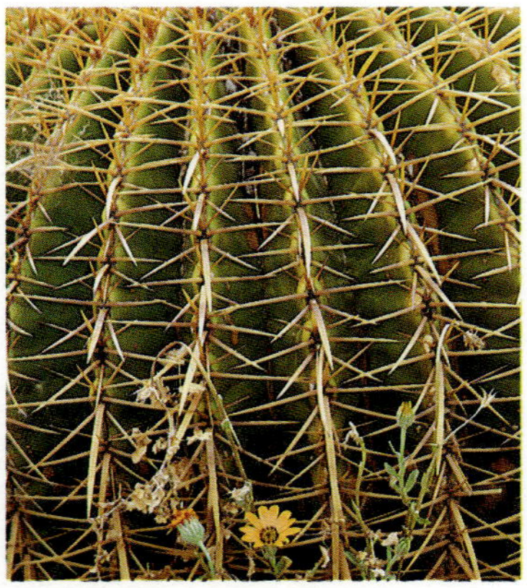

On the opposite page, the *picture on the* ***top left*** *shows an intelligent use of a tobacco graduated filter. Combined with the very red light of the setting sun, the effect is surreal and fascinating. Frequently, of course, the sky produces even more fascinating effects quite naturally. When you look at a picture, try to work out whether the pre-dominant colour cast adds to or detracts from the overall effect.* ***Opposite page: lower left,*** *the misty blue is emphasised; the grass is almost cyan. On the* ***lower right,*** *the warm light complements the brown of the wood. If you have time, it is often worth trying three pictures of one subject: one without filtration, one with a filter which accentuates the colour of the light, and one which is complementary and so reduces it. An 81A (brownish) and an 82 (light blue) are all that is normally required.*

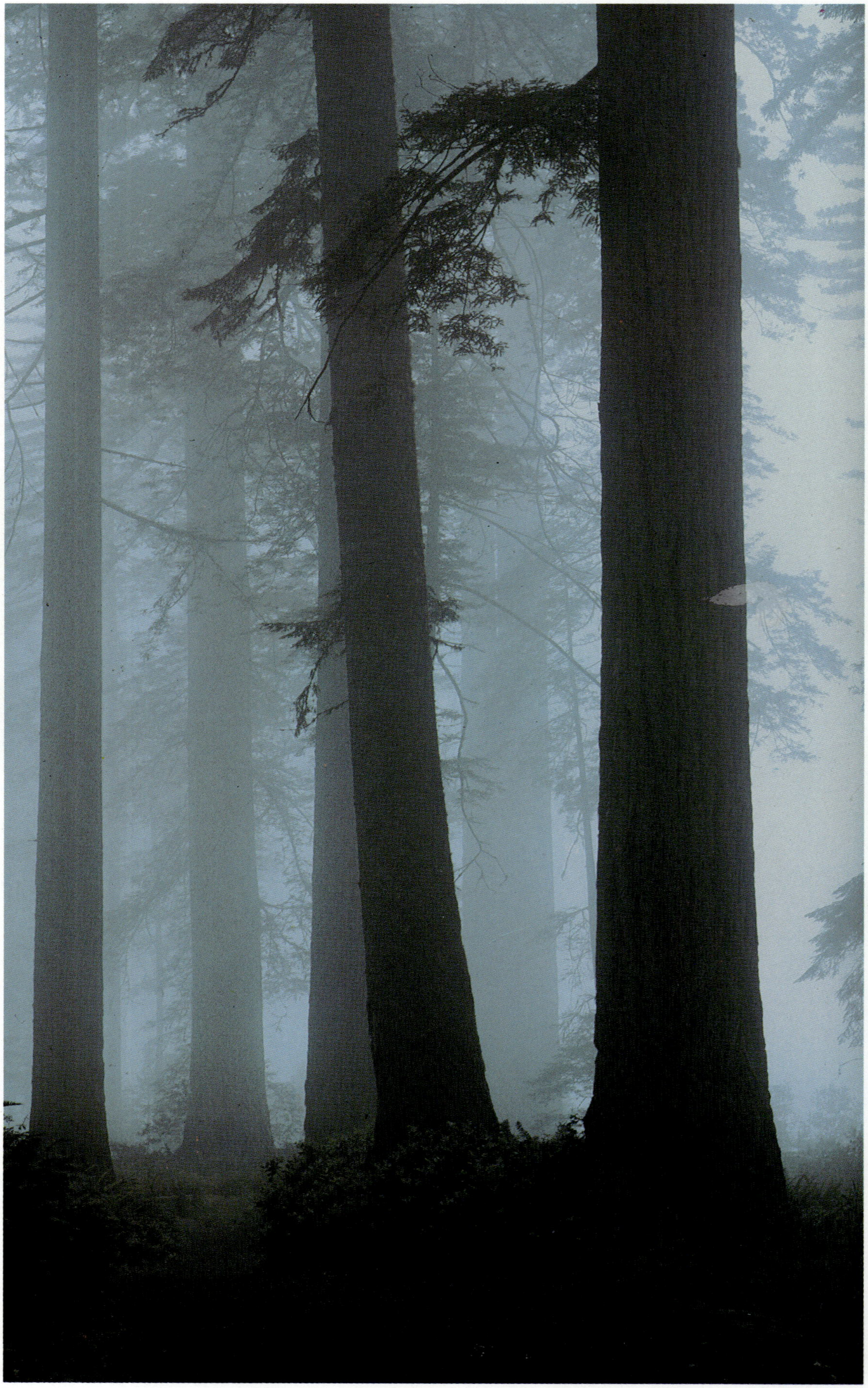

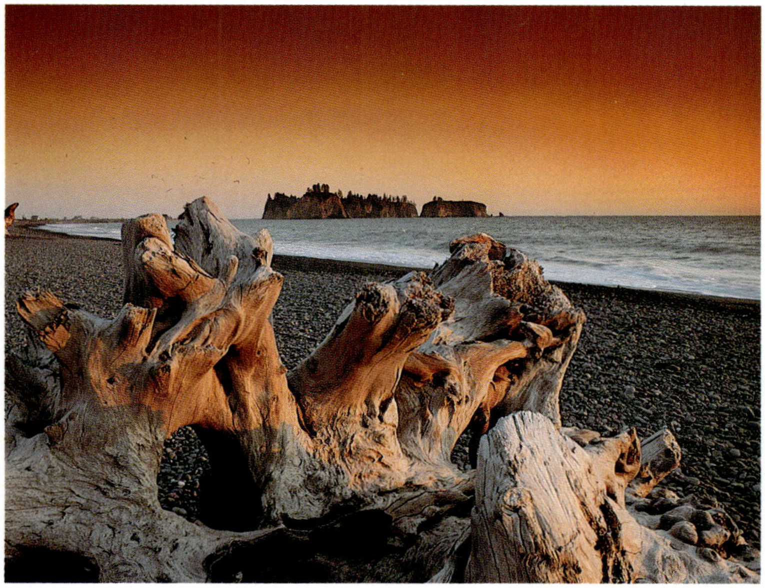

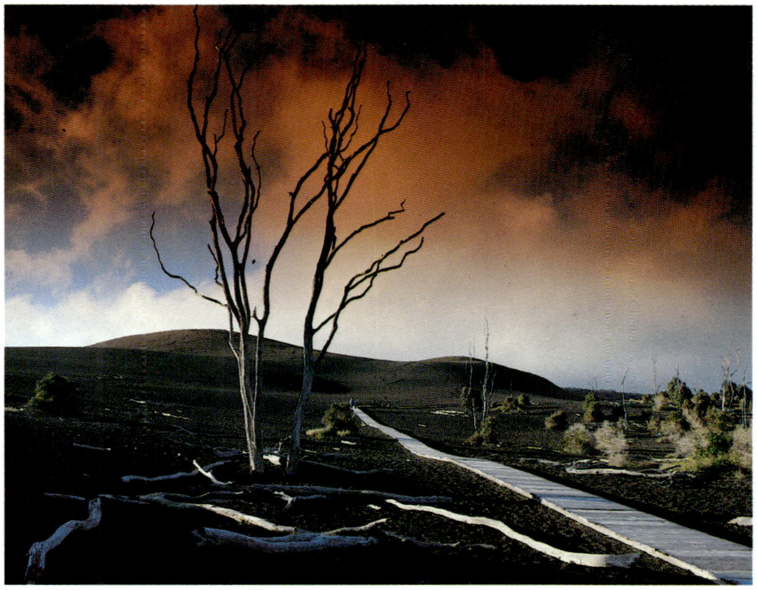

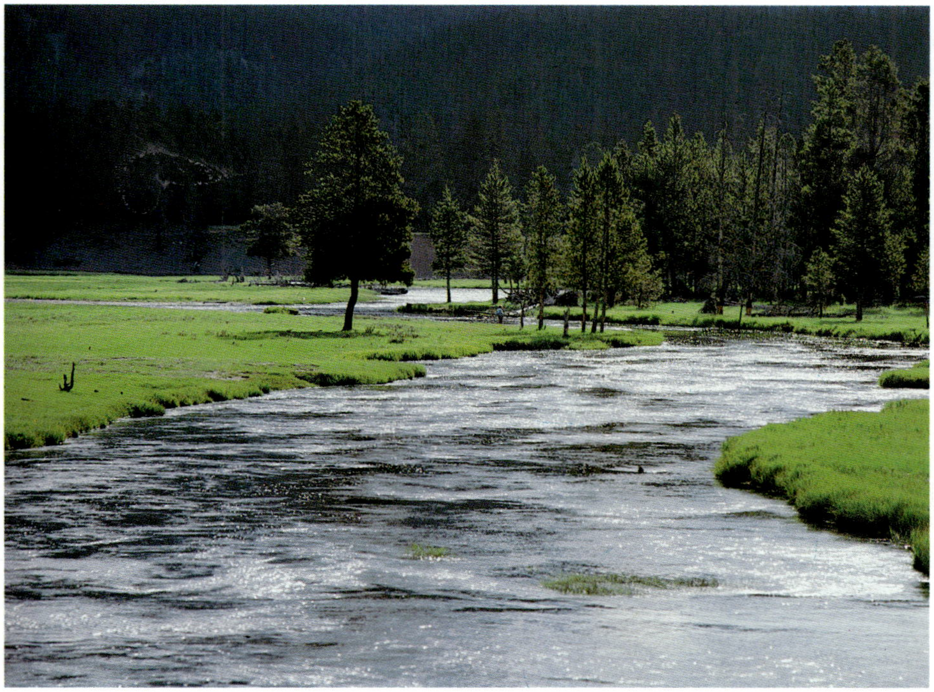

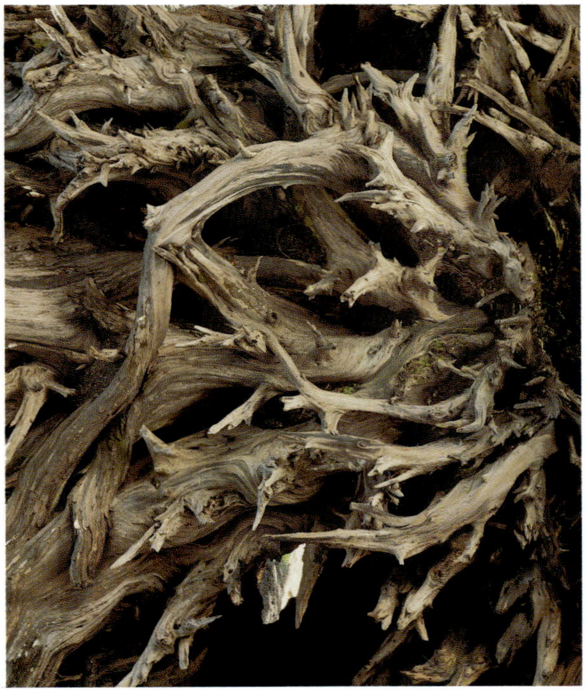

The advantages of tungsten lighting are its relative cheapness (apart from the bulb and power bills) and the fact that no special metering techniques are needed; the cheapest flash meter is about the same price as an expensive ordinary meter. In professional use, tungsten is only considered where other light can be excluded entirely, and where a tremendous amount of light is required. An example is car photography in a studio, where I have seen 28Kw in use – the equivalent, perhaps, of a thousand 100w domestic lamps.

A very much more useful and versatile approach is to adopt the third option and use studio electronic flash. This runs cool, uses little power, does not 'eat' bulbs, and matches daylight in colour temperature. On the other hand, it has three main drawbacks. First, it is expensive – up to ten times as much as comparable tungsten lighting. Secondly, although it is reliable it cannot be repaired by an amateur, especially in view of the lethal voltages stored in the capacitor. Thirdly, a flash meter is a virtual necessity.

All professional units use modelling lights, which are usually switched in proportion to the flash tube, so that you can gauge the lighting without strenuous previsualisation or Polaroid tests. They offer 'system' adaptability with 'brollies' or umbrellas for soft lighting, snoots for spot effects, and (with the bigger packs) a range of large diffuse sources ranging from the 'swimming pool' or 'northlight' (up to 6 x 4′) down to the 18″ square 'fish fryer.'

Whether you use flash or continuous lighting, or even if you rely on available light, you can greatly increase your scope by using reflectors and 'flags.' Reflectors can be anything from a sheet of white paper to an 8 x 4′ 'flat' made of painted wood or (light but bulky) expanded polystyrene. Flags, also known as 'donkeys,' are pieces of black card, wood, or metal attached to stands and used to shade or mask the subject from direct lighting; by having them bright on one side and dark on the other you can also use them as small reflectors.

PEOPLE

People are one of the trickiest subjects to photograph creatively. Over millions of years, we have evolved to recognise people, to wonder what they are doing, and generally to take an interest in them. The drawing power of a figure in a landscape is well known; everything operates on the level of monkey curiosity. If we are to get beyond this, we need more than a sharp, well-exposed picture.

One school of thought maintains that any picture tells us more about the photographer than about the subject, and this is perhaps more true when photographing people than when photographing any other subject. For instance, one girl might be photographed in many different ways.

One photographer might see her as a classical nude, depersonalised and reduced to abstraction. Another might want to

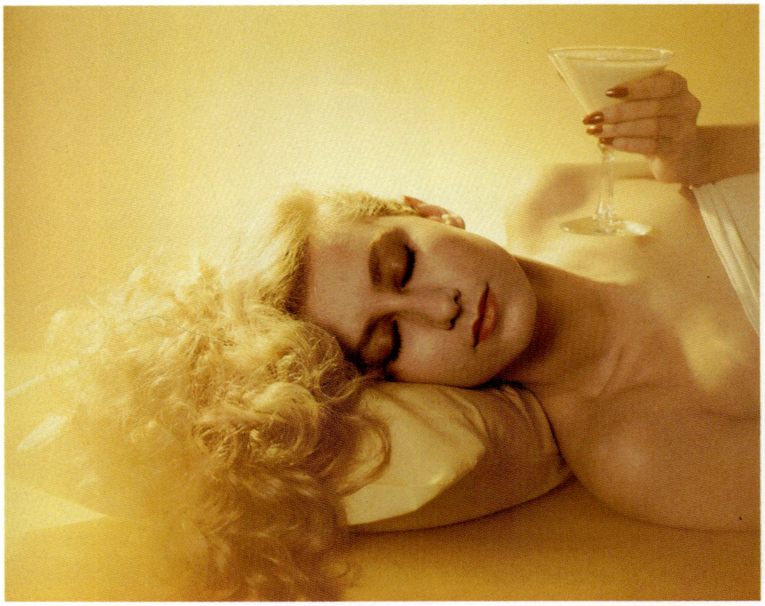

Fantasy pictures can be *tremendous fun for both photographer and model. These were set up as part of a set of pictures for a book on cocktails, but the choice of costumes, props, and lighting is a textbook in its own right. You can use these pictures in two ways: either try to duplicate them, or devise other ways of illustrating the same theme.*

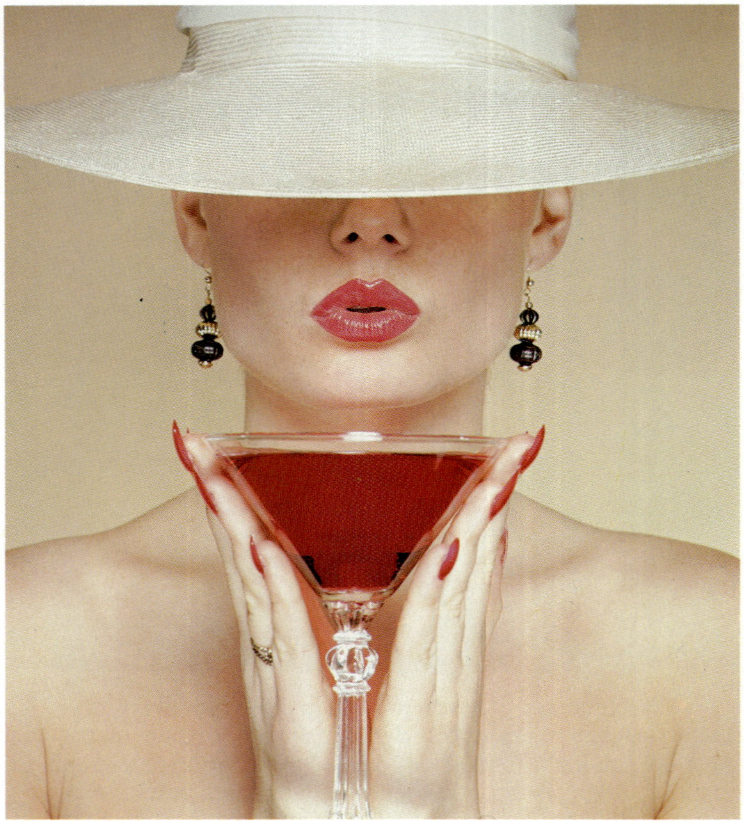

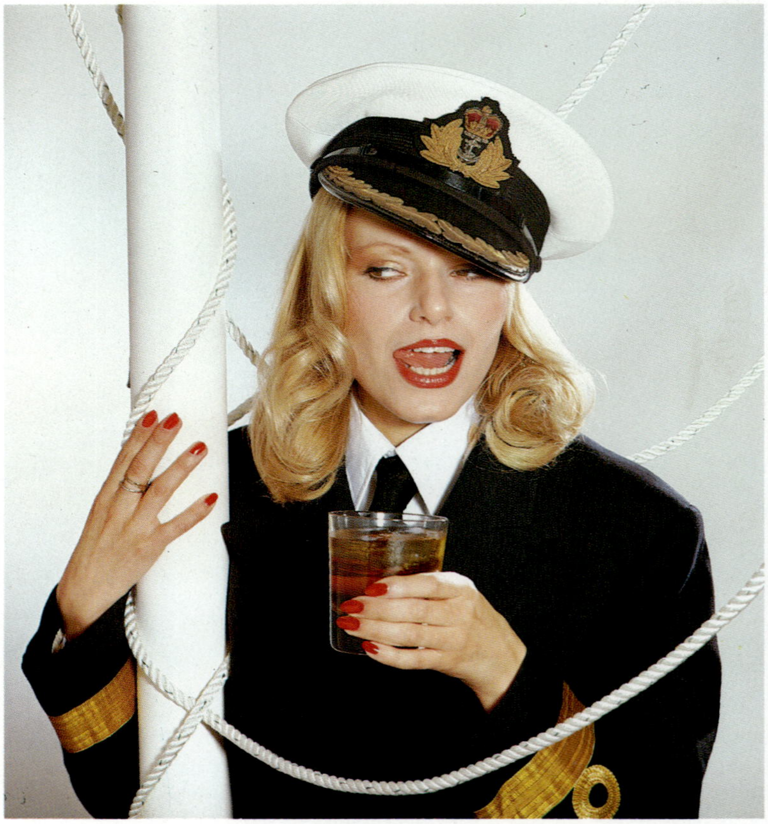

photograph her as a pin-up – no less depersonalised, but changed from an abstraction into a symbol, a focus. An advertising photographer might direct her like an actress, until she behaved the way he wanted in order to convey (say) a typical clothes-buying teenager. Yet a fourth might attempt an 'in-depth' picture, trying to show something of her feelings or emotions (at least as he perceived them), whilst a fifth might say that he was a passive mirror and photograph her without preconceptions.

Because all these techniques are essentially different, and employ different aspects of creativity, they are worth considering separately. Before that, though, there are a few observations about general techniques which may be useful.

Equipment is not critical. You can use whatever you have – although inevitably some types are going to be more useful than others. The 35mm SLR is (as usual) the best all-rounder, but for candid and unplanned work the rangefinder camera may be more appropriate. For better image quality, a larger format is obviously desirable – anything from an old Rollei through a Hasselblad to a 10 x 8″ studio monorail (some people use them for photographing nudes).

Exposure and colour, on the other hand, are extremely critical. We can judge flesh tones better than anything else, and pictures which are too light or too dark or exhibit colour casts (unless any of these effects is obviously deliberate) will be extremely obvious. Use fresh material, correctly exposed, and

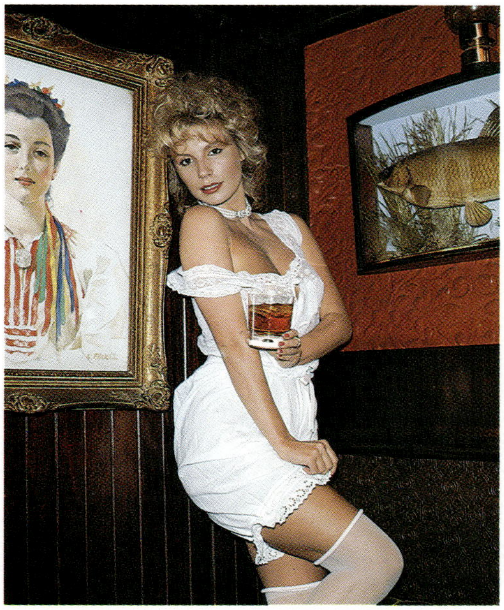
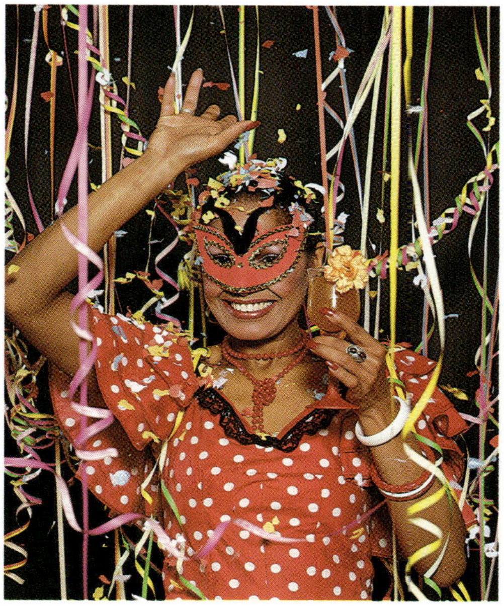
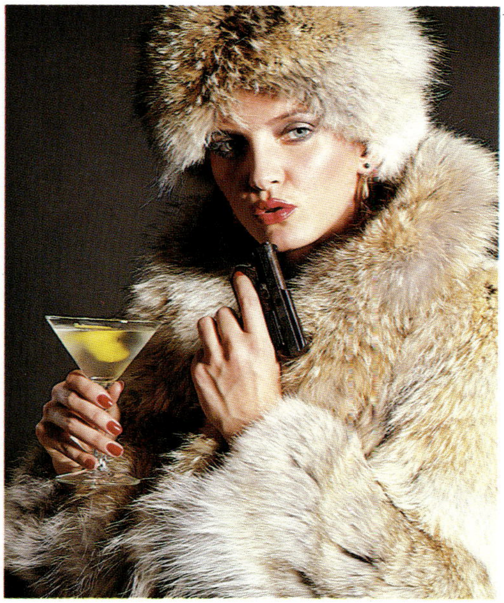
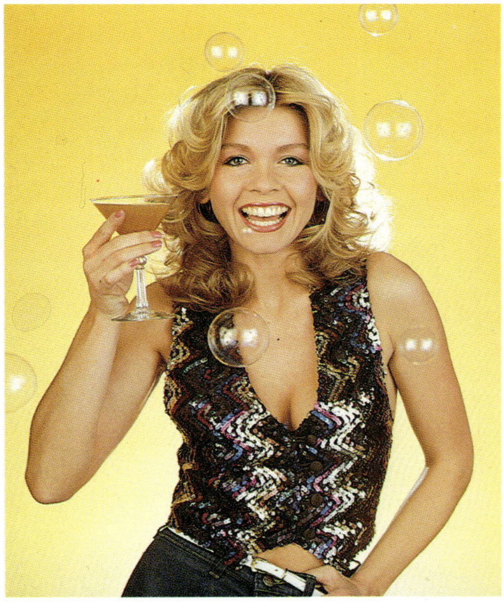
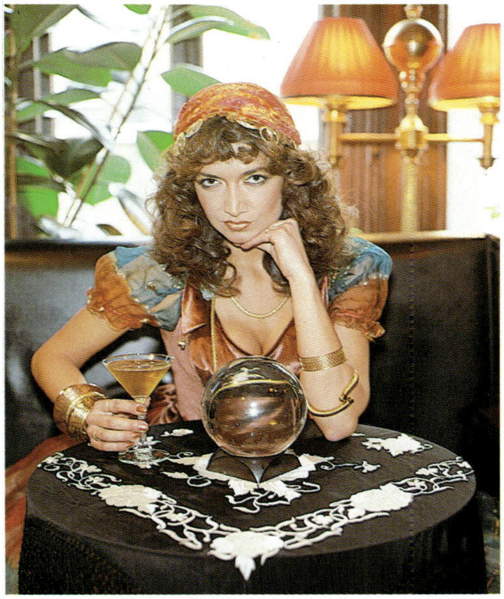
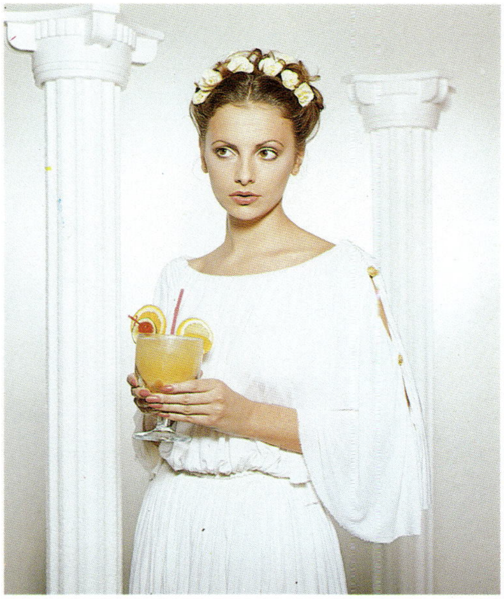
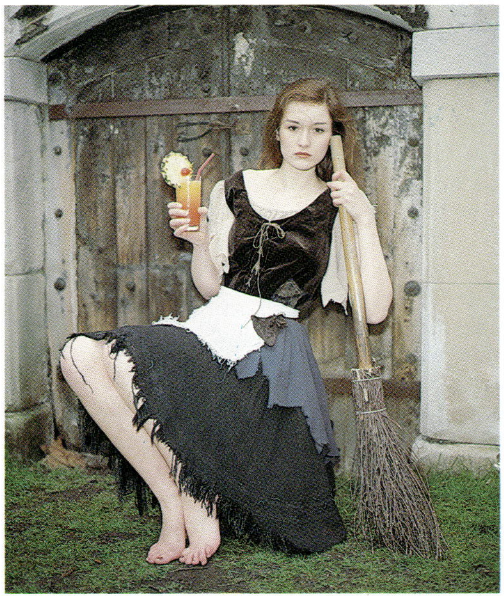
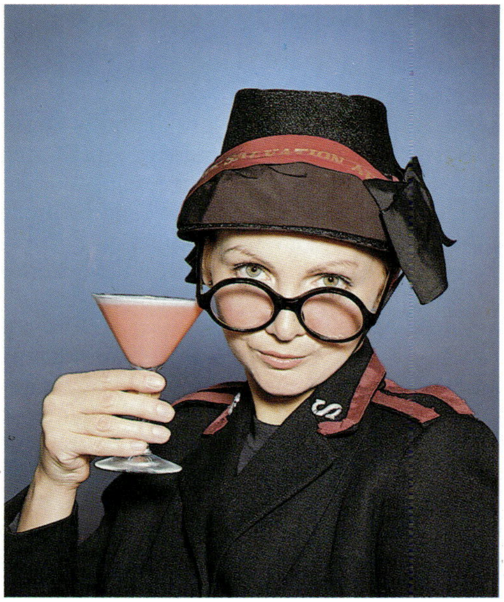
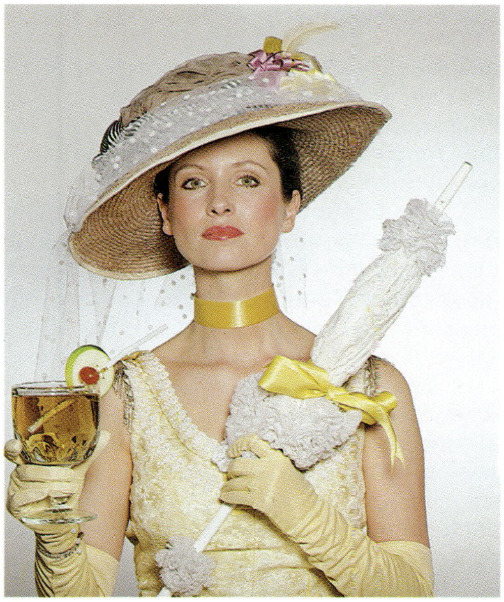

PEOPLE

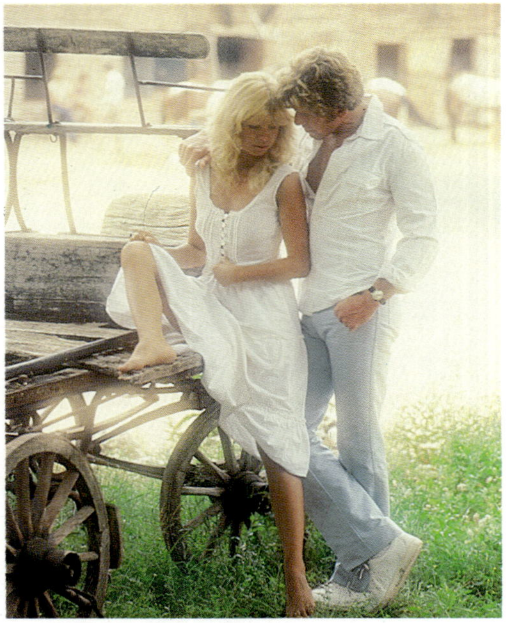

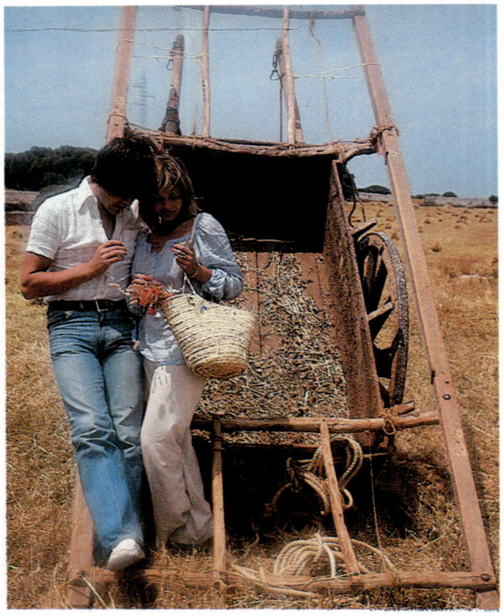

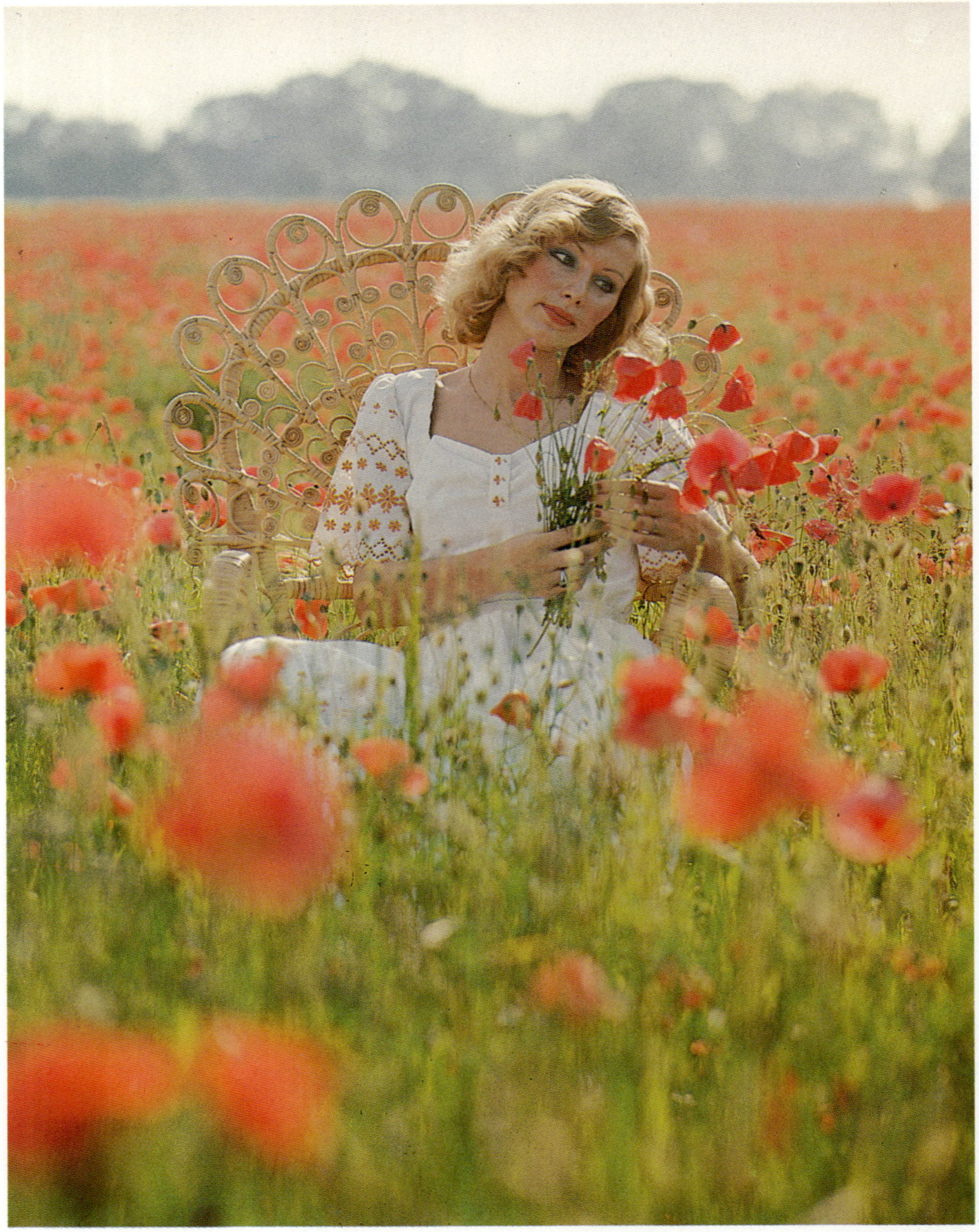

processed as soon as possible after exposure. If you know that the film has a slight colour bias, use a colour correcting gel. Professionals usually buy film in batches, and test the first roll both for effective speed and for colour balance; this is worth considering for the utmost in quality.

Special effects, such as trick filters, split-field filters, and so forth, should be used with great reserve; in this kind of photography in particular, funny colours can often be a substitute for creativity. Novelty is not enough: ask yourself what the picture gains from the use of the special effect. The answer may well be 'everything', but often it will be 'nothing'.

Finally, you will need to be able to handle people, in the style of photography which you have chosen. Taking candid pictures at a beer festival is different from directing a glamour session, which is in turn different from a portrait that is attempting to get under the model's skin. Too many photographers tend to hide behind their cameras: unless you really like people, and are able to get on with them, this may well be a branch of photography to avoid.

CLASSICAL NUDES

These may be either abstracts, as previously discussed, or what might unkindly be called old-fashioned pin-ups. The former requires girls of impeccable form and complexion if it is to be at all successful; abstracts generally have an almost tactile quality, and the sagging breast or wobbly bottom will not project this type of image.

The old fashioned pin-up is generally posed either in the fashion of a Greek statue, or to portray some activity carried to extremes; examples include the girl warming herself in front of the fire, the girl combing her tresses, or sitting on a rock and staring soulfully into the distance. When done well, these photographs can be very beautiful; they have a sort of innocence and purity of line which distinguishes them from lesser nudes. When done badly, though, they resemble Victorian cheesecake or worse. 'Worse' in this case includes those hideous goose-pimpled nudes, lit with three lamps which cast contrasting shadows and in any case are coloured with gels to cast violent smears of colour (usually deep blue, red, and magenta) all over the poor girl's

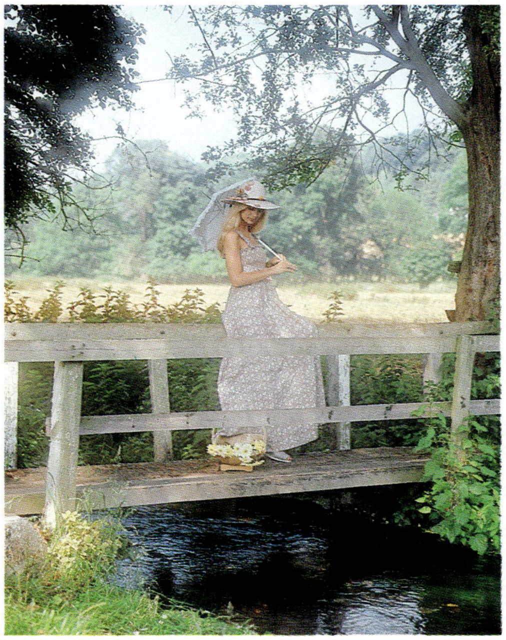

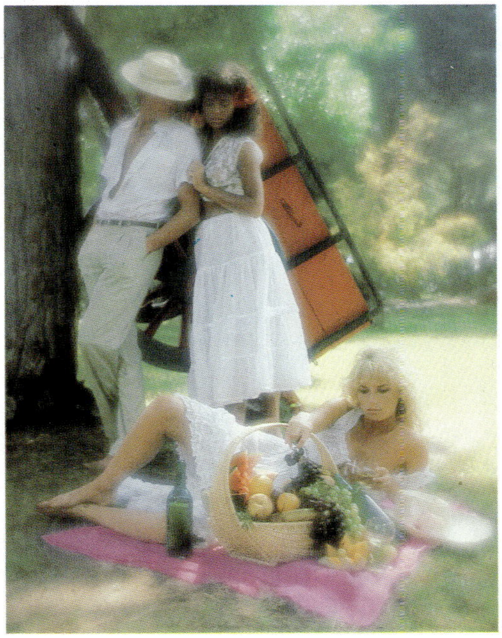

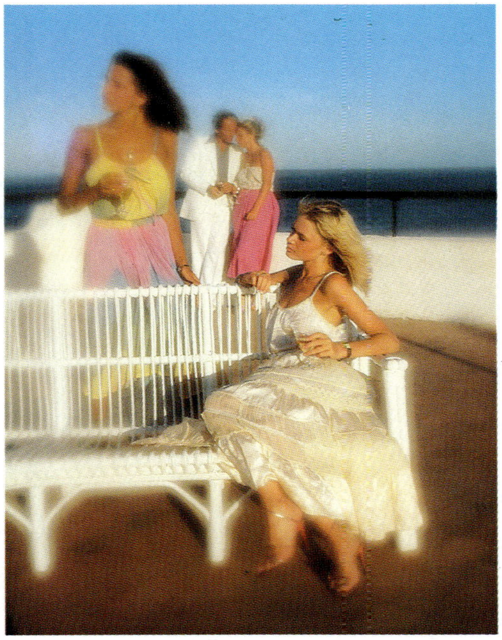

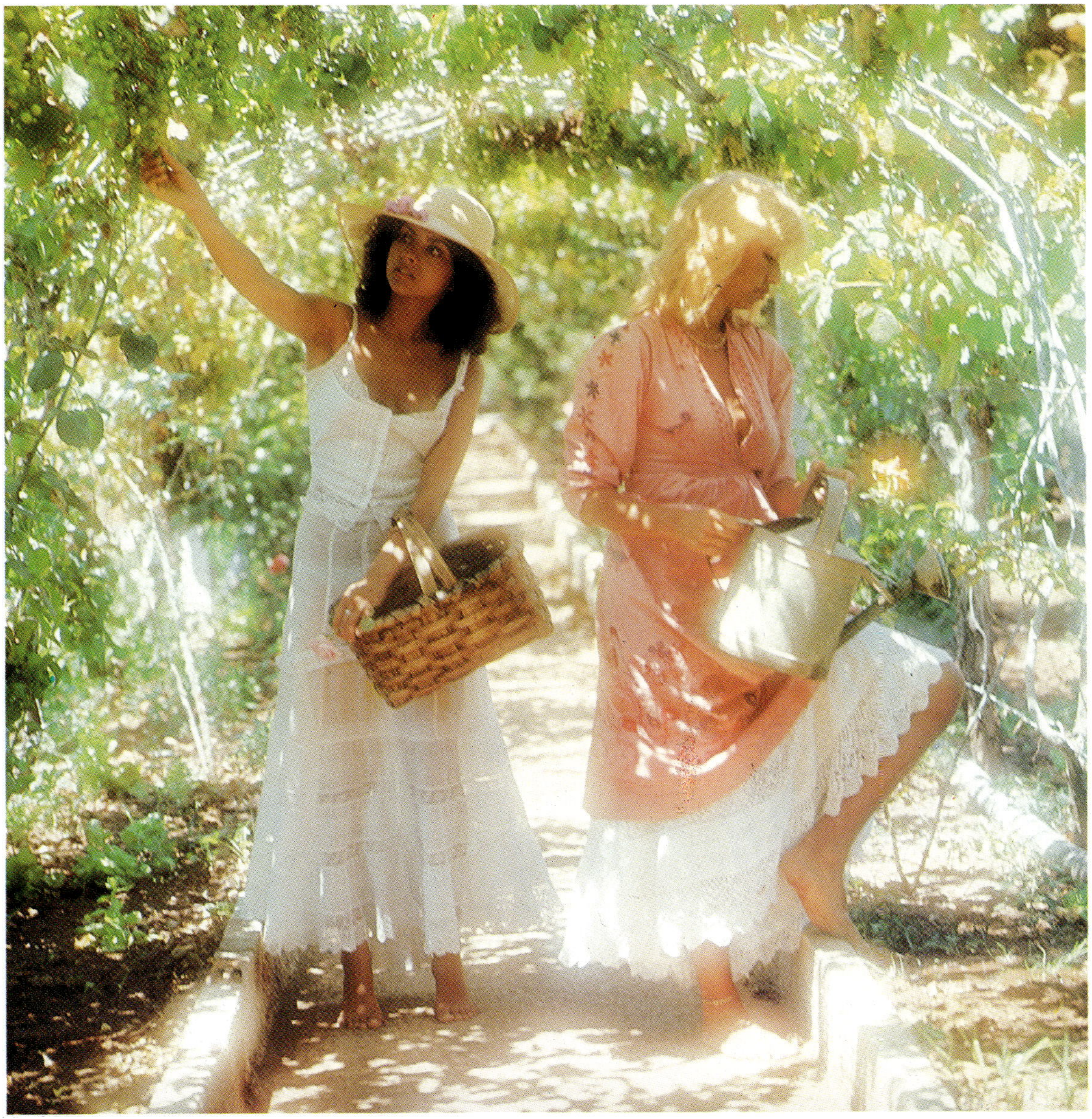

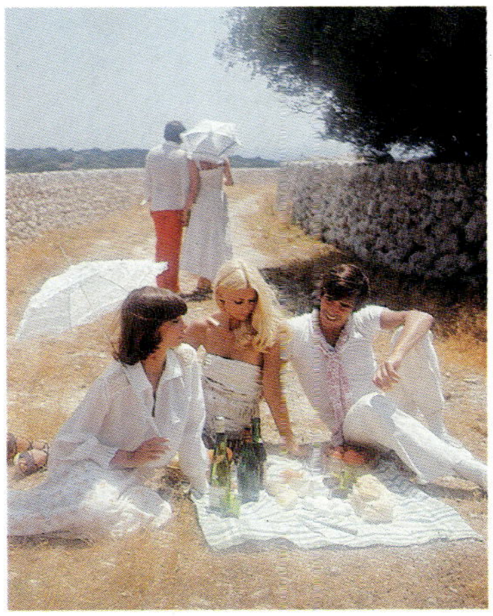

The one 'trick' which is often *appropriate to photographing people is some form of soft-focus or diffusion. It is very much a question of fashion, of course: the undiffused picture on the* ***facing page bottom left,*** *dates from the 1960s. Since the overall effect is deliberately romantic, it is important to choose props, locations, clothes, poses, and lighting which are appropriate. Note the use of soft pastel colours and overexposure to desaturate even the stronger colours, and the generous use of backlighting. As diffusers (such as fog filters) diffuse some skylight into the picture, they often give it a bluish cast. A warming filter, such as an 81A or even something stronger, is appropriate: a scratched 81A combines both effects admirably!*

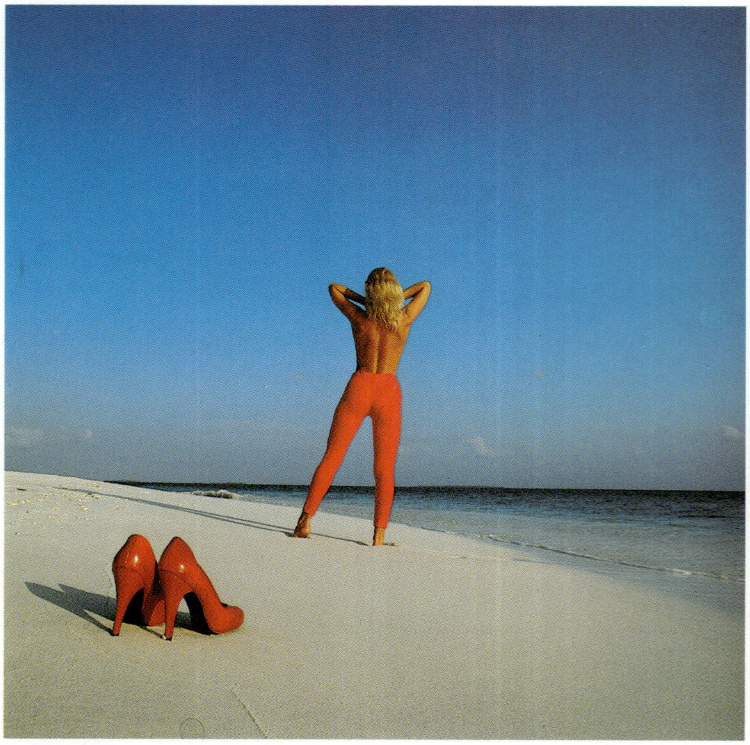

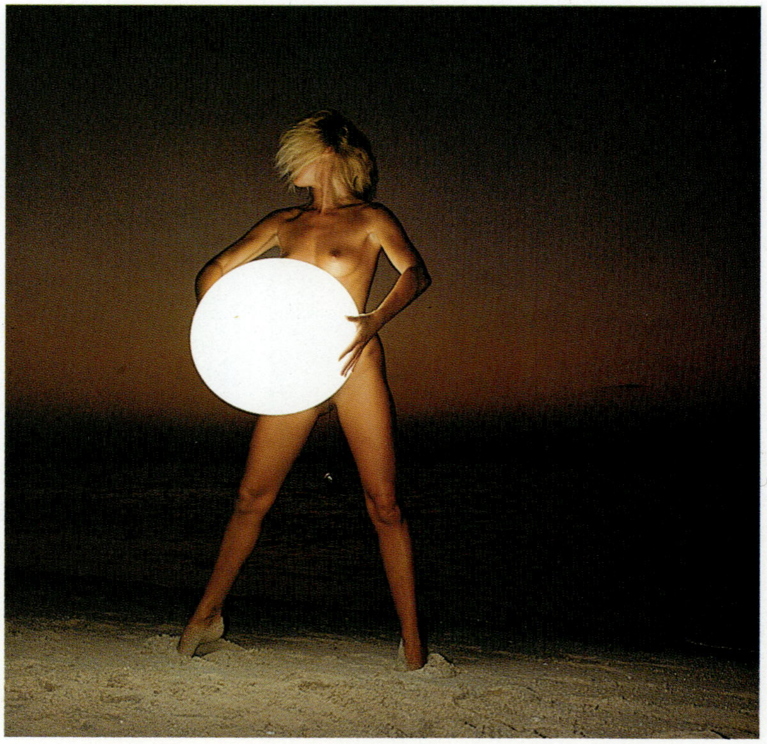

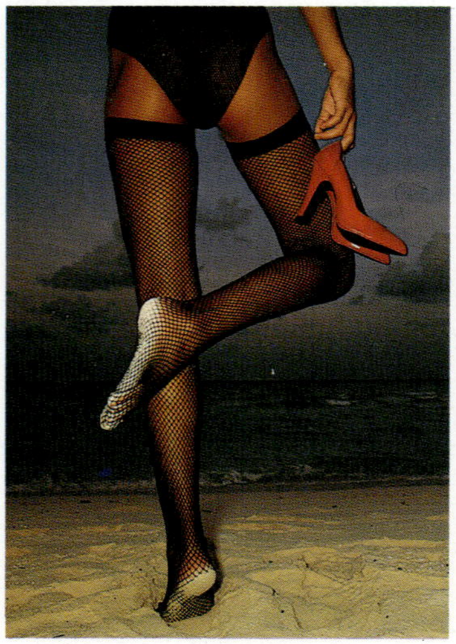

__A conventional flashgun,__ carefully hidden behind rubber balloons was the secret technique used in creating the particularly strong, almost unearthly images shown ***top right and right.*** *Fill-in flash was used to provide the necessary detail as well as to reinforce the feeling of unreality. Most of the other pictures rely on saturated colour and a purity of line which is in itself attractive, quite apart from the attractions of the models; they also illustrate the importance of the background, and of separating the subject from the background visually. The use of medium format (Hasselblad) gives superb gradation.*

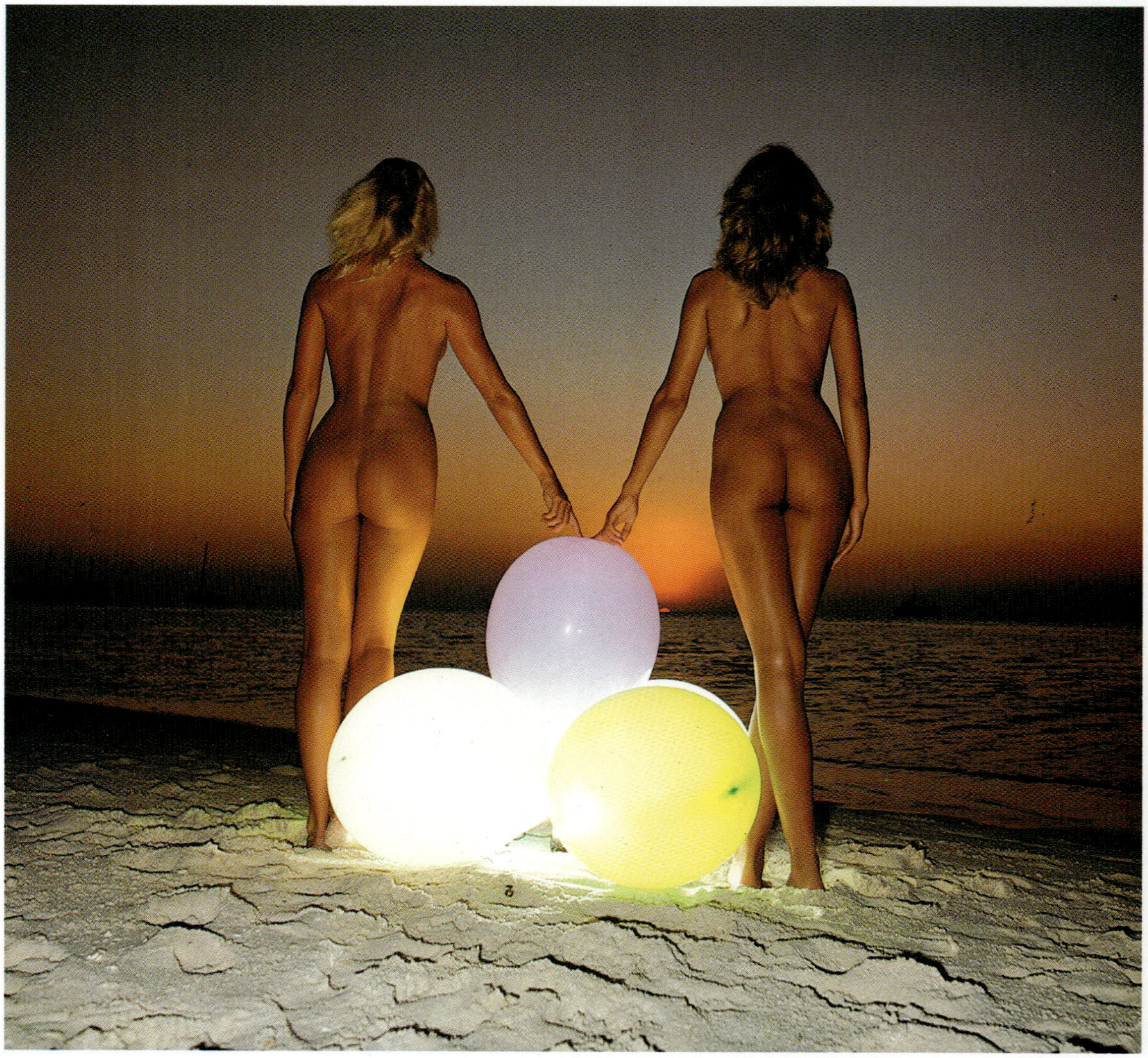

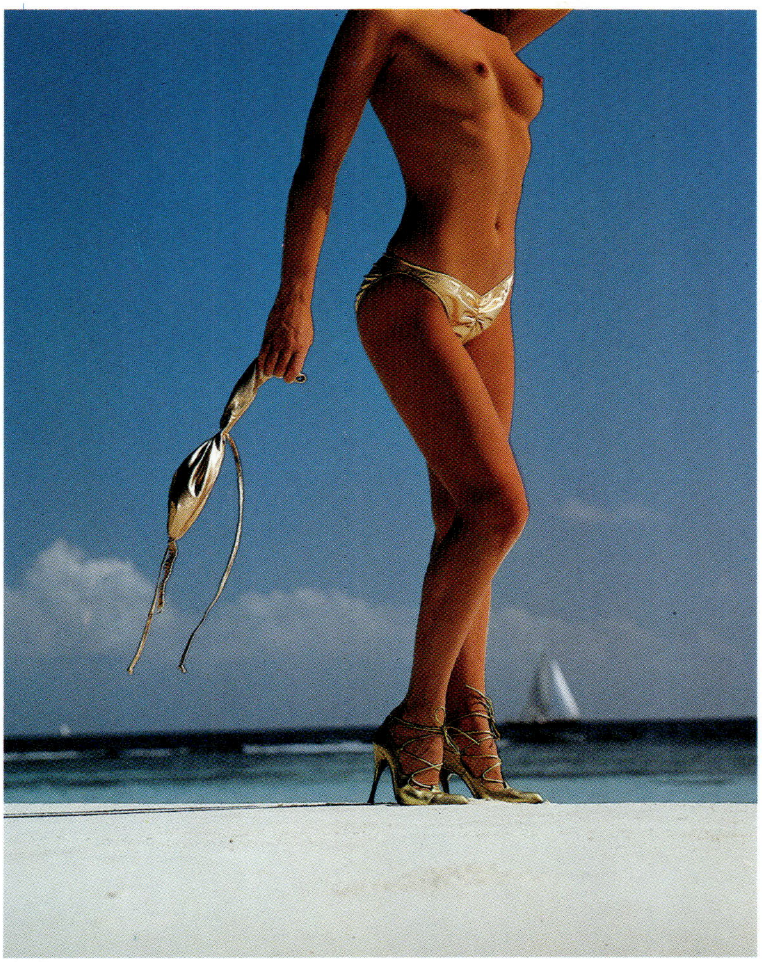
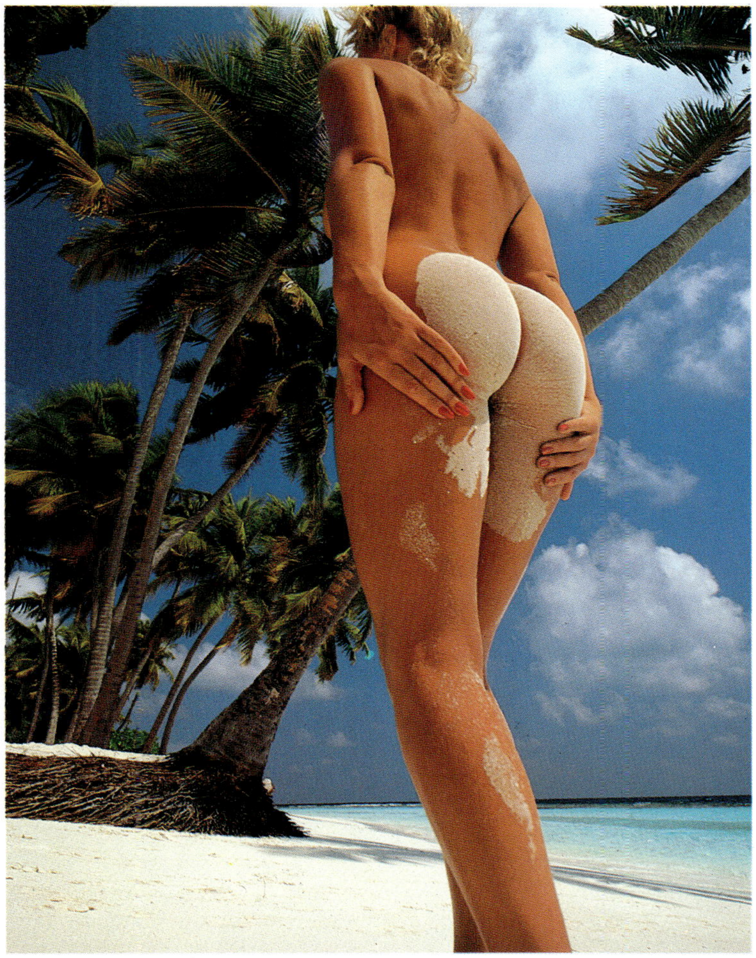
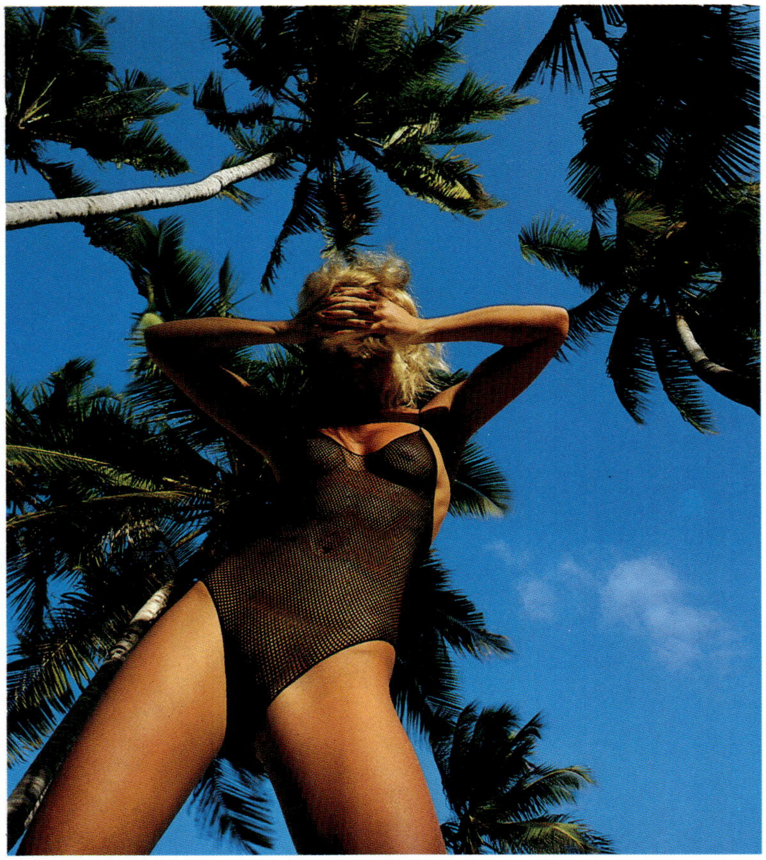
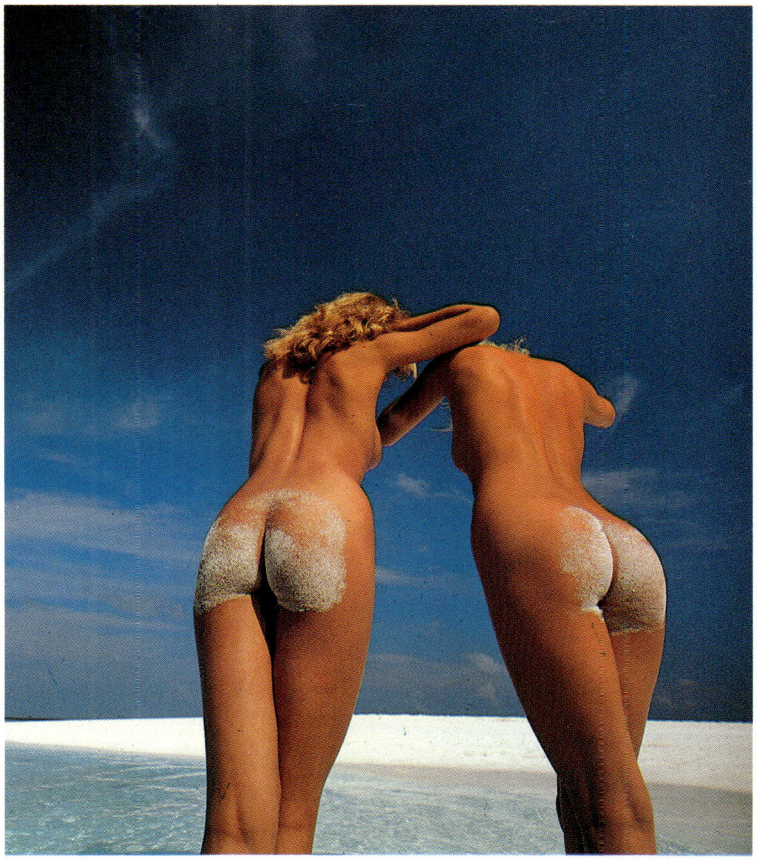

body. This repulsive type of picture has neither the attractive innocence of the old-fashioned nude nor the honest sexiness of the more modern type: instead, it has a certain sleaziness which results from the photographer's refusal to face honestly how he would like to portray the girl, and his inability to do so even if he knew.

This, incidentally, is a fundamental problem when dealing with attractive models. If you fancy the girl, either have the guts to say so (directly or by flirting) or keep it totally professional: innuendo and uncertainty is no fun for either party.

GLAMOUR

The only spark of creativity exhibited in most magazines is in the contriving of story-lines to match the pictures. The girls are usually beautiful, well photographed from a technical point of view, and utterly predictable: the expensive flat, the lacy boudoir, or the well-padded sofa. Devising new surroundings is no mean feat; taking original pictures is nothing short of heroic.

Of course, the average reader does not want 'arty' pictures; he wants good sharp pictures of girls he can fantasise about. Even when a really masterful photographer in this *genre* finds something new to say, the magazines prefer to run something in the same old mould.

Of late, a certain degree of departure from the super-sharp fantasy babies of the 1950s and 1960s has been seen in a return to romanticism, with soft focus, desaturated colours, and a sort of impressionist 'veil of light' over the pictures; this is further explored in the next chapter, 'The Romantic Image'.

DIRECTING MODELS

In this style of photography, you call upon the model to portray some person who is real only in your mind. Some photographers prefer to be totally autocratic, and to order the model to do this and that, but this only works at all well (if at all) if the photographer is very experienced and sure of himself and the model is a professional who can do as she is told. With amateur (or less martinet-like professional) photographers, and amateur models, it is much better to work together towards the kind of picture you want. Much of what is said here also holds true for the previous two categories (nude and glamour).

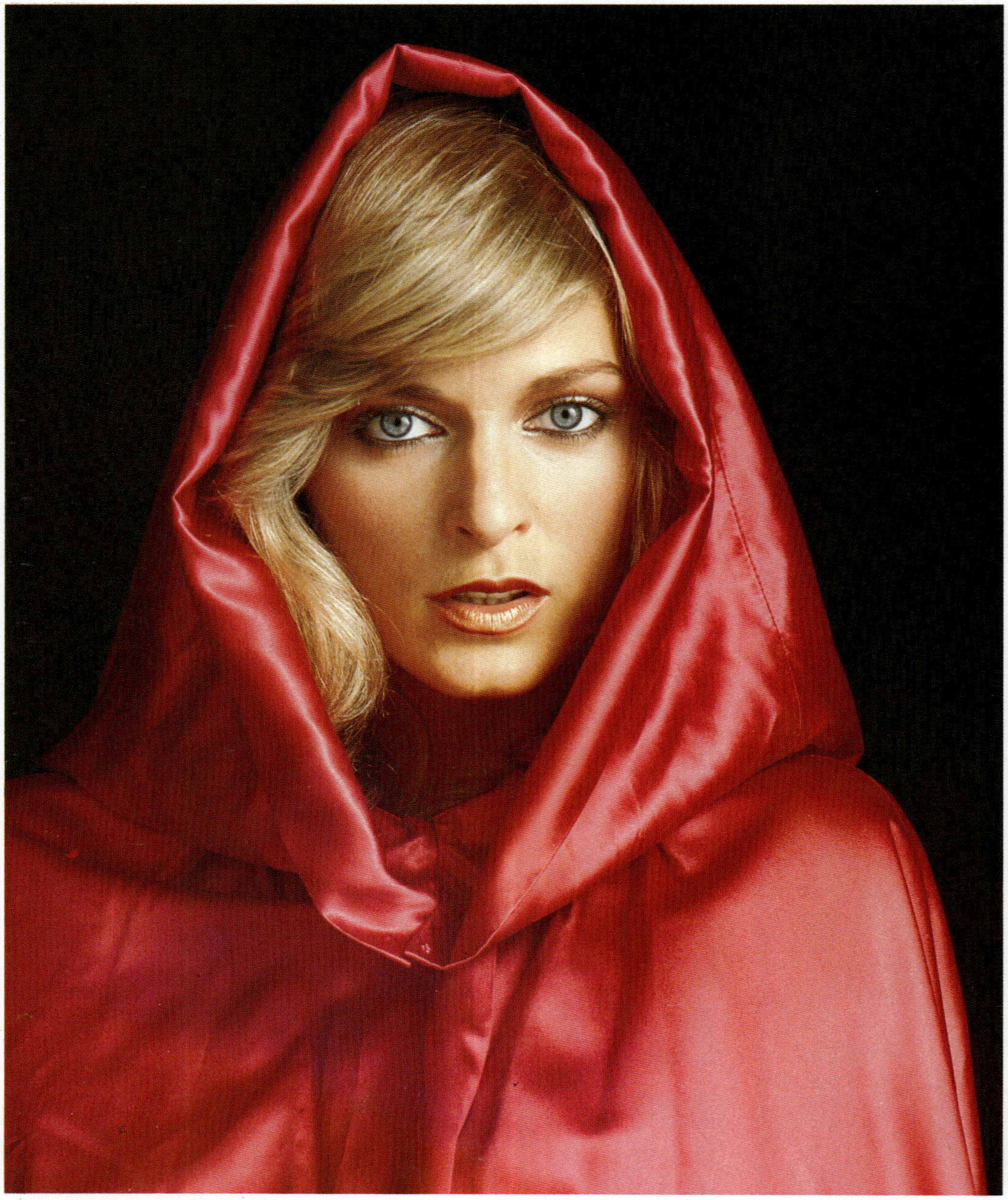

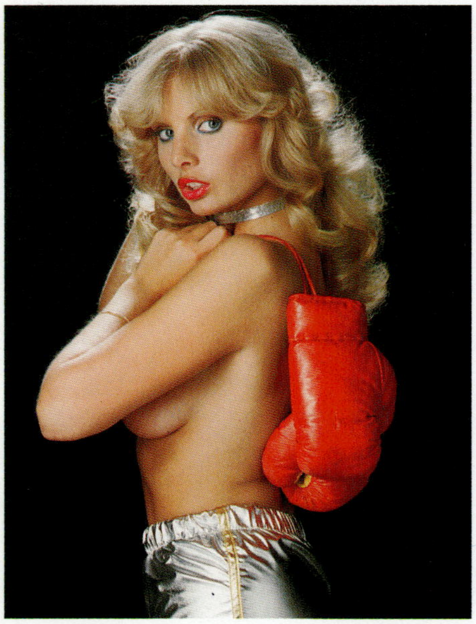

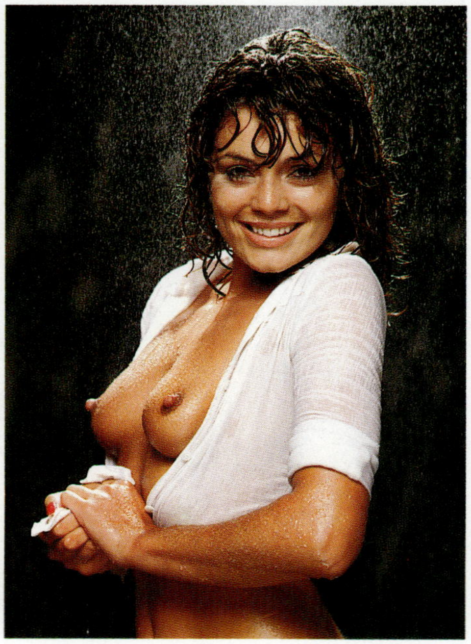

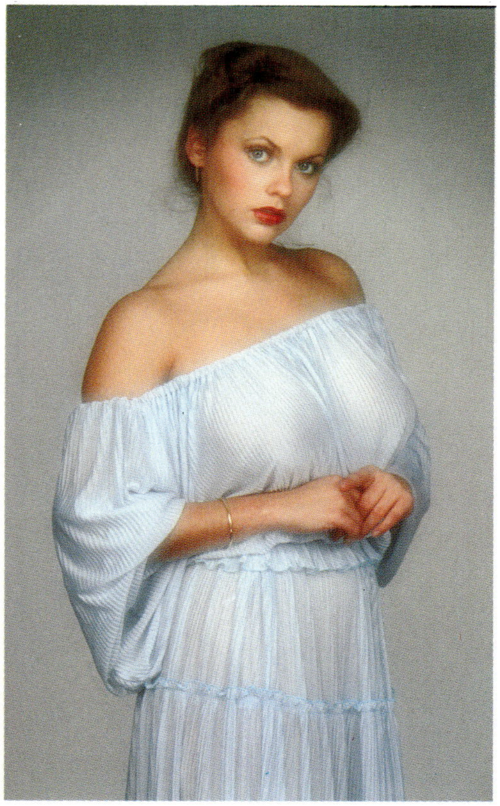

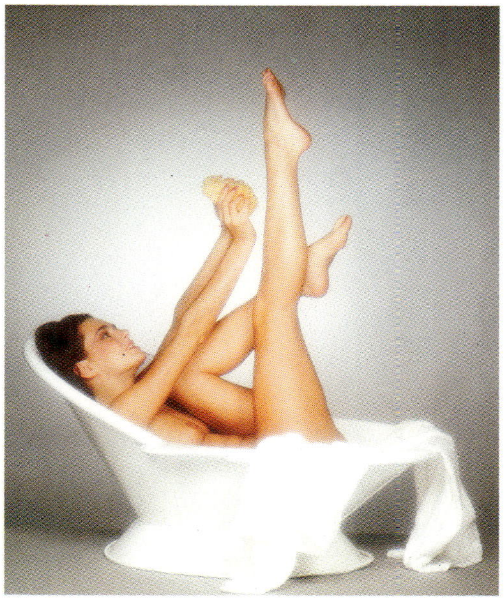

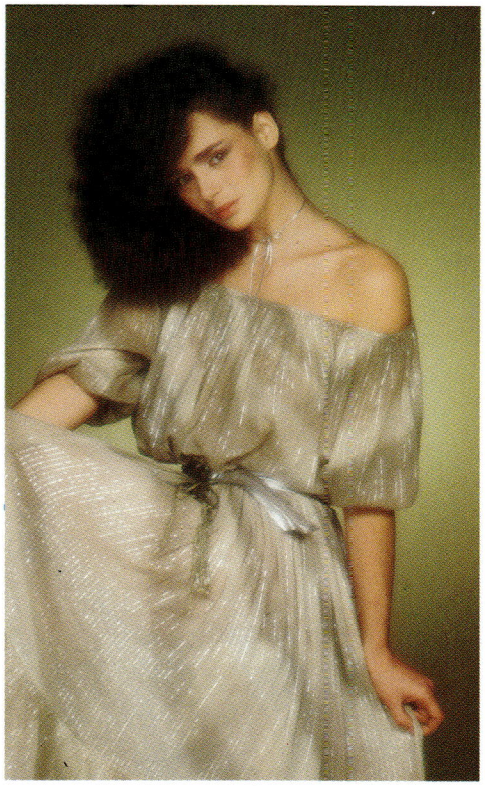

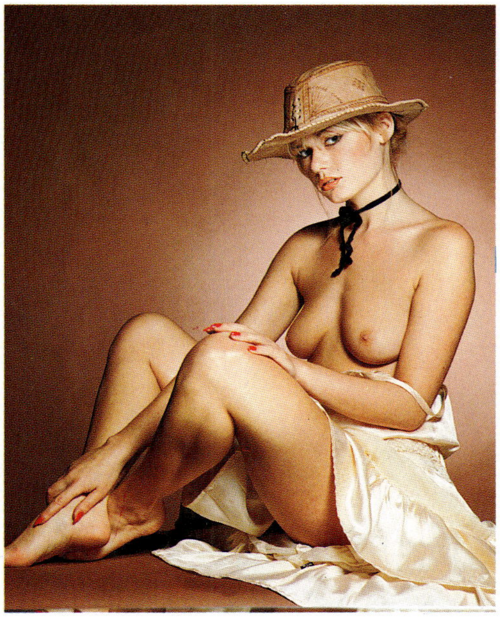

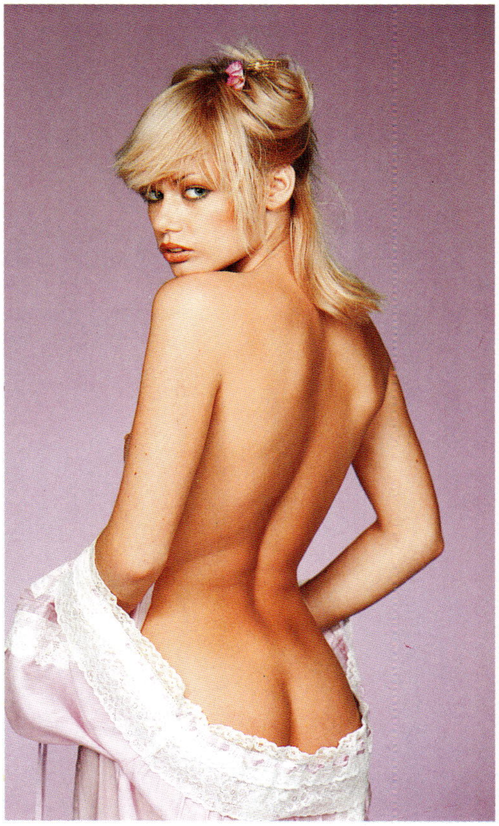

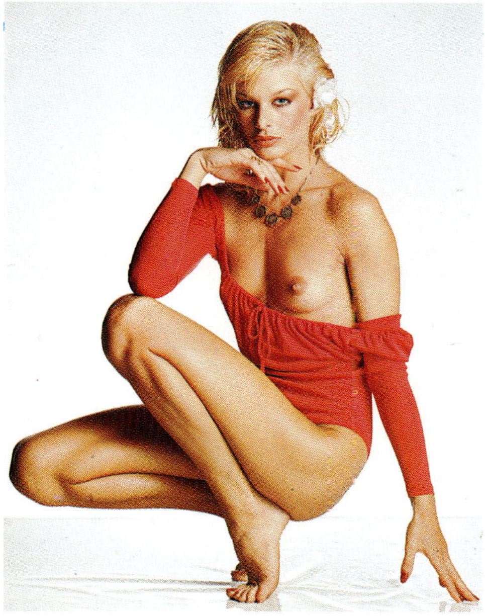

Always have the highest regard for your models' feelings; pretty girls in particular can be extremely insecure and easily offended, so offer a constant stream of praise and encouragement. A musician being tonguelashed by a conductor can set his jaw and play his heart out, 'just to show him'; a model does not really have this option. Few people look good (or respond well to directions, or have many ideas they are prepared to communicate) if they are at all upset.

Be reasonably sure of what you want, and that the model can provide it. If you are after flashing eyes and sultry *machismo* don't use a clean-limbed blue-eyed blond-haired Englishman. Work towards what you want; don't expect to get it first time, unless your model is psychic. In the same vein, make sure that you have any props you need, that the surroundings are right, and so forth.

Truly successful pin-ups need *not be very revealing. In all but one of these pictures the impact comes mainly from eye-contact and the model's expression; the bath shot succeeds by old-fashioned innocence and romantic prurience.*

Finally, don't get too carried away on a tide of *simpatico* for the model; it is all too easy to get some fantastic shots, which suffer only from the slight drawback that they are totally unsuitable for the purpose for which they were taken. To an amateur, this may not matter too much (though it could be a warning for future sessions); the professional makes a shot list.

PEOPLE

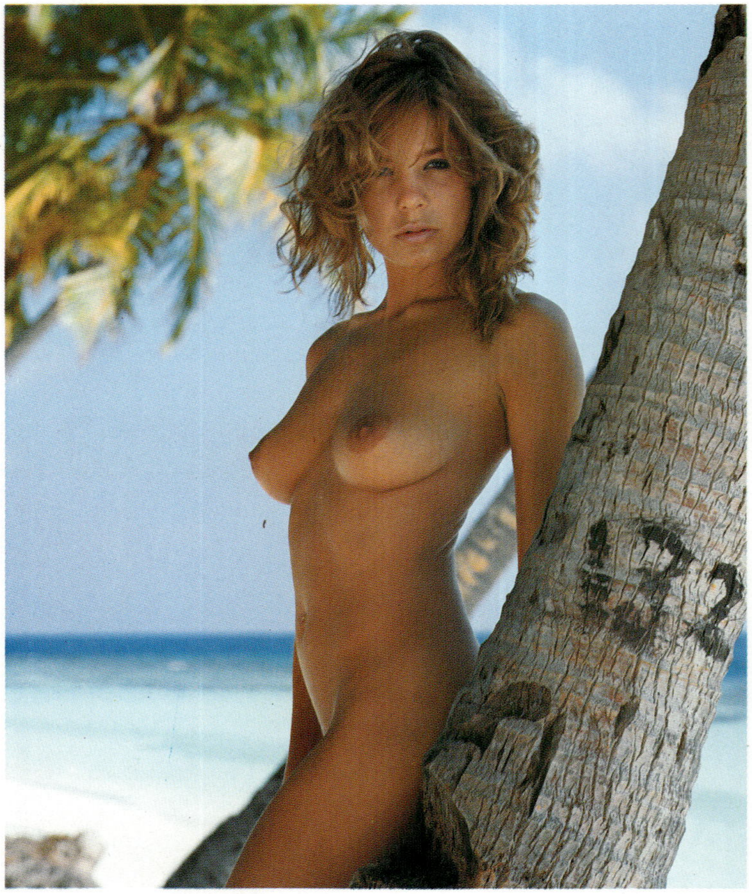

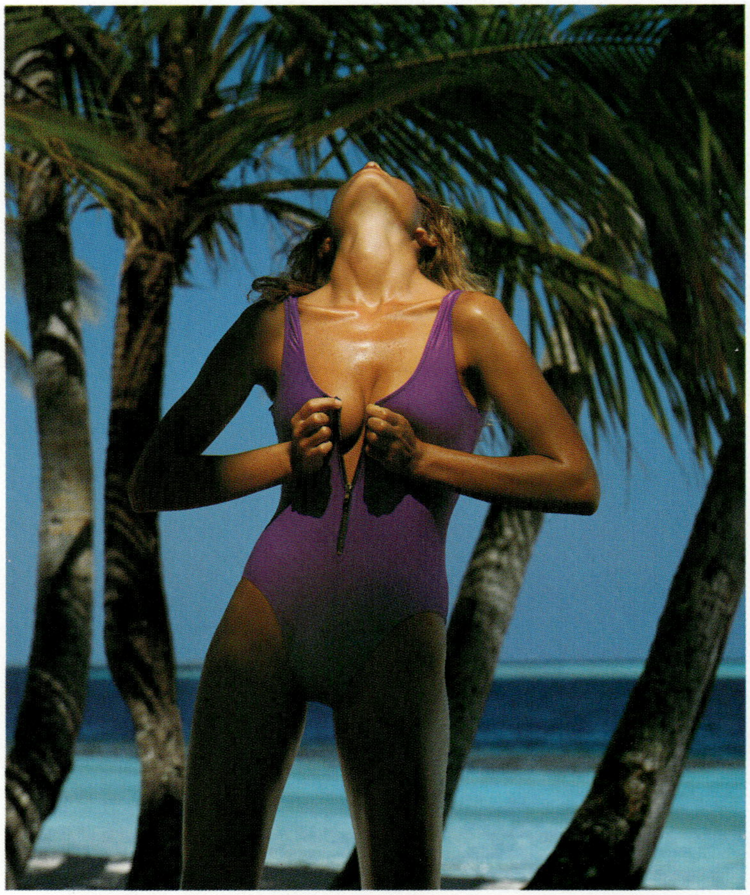

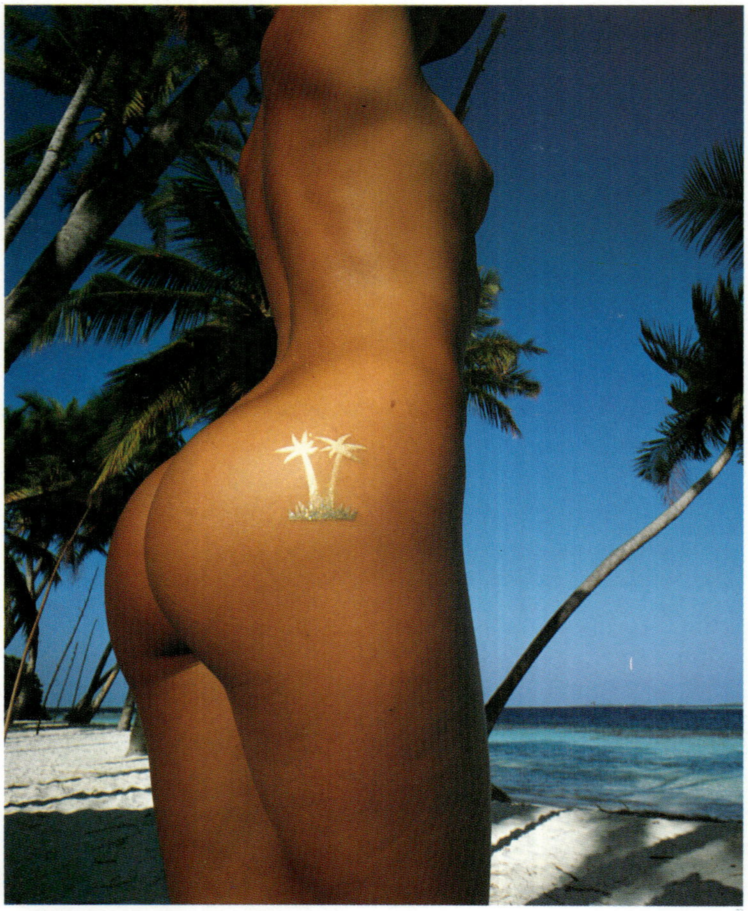

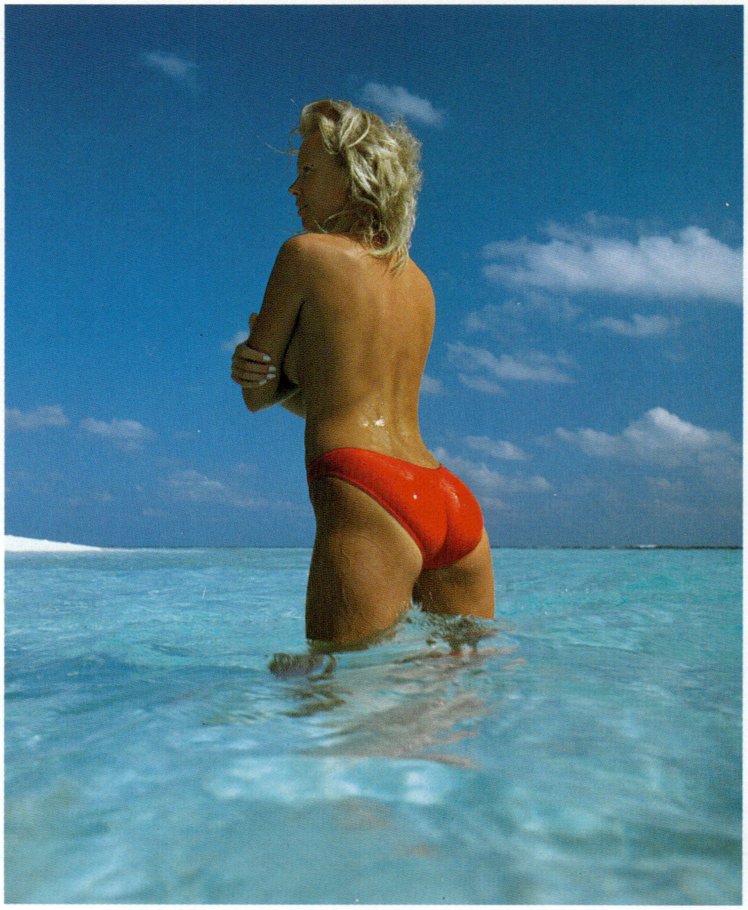

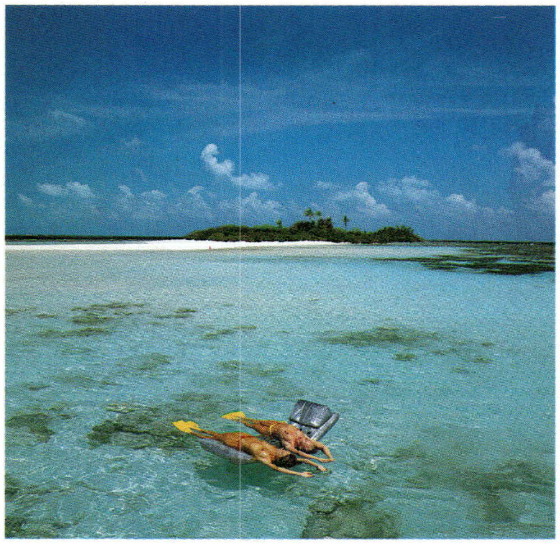

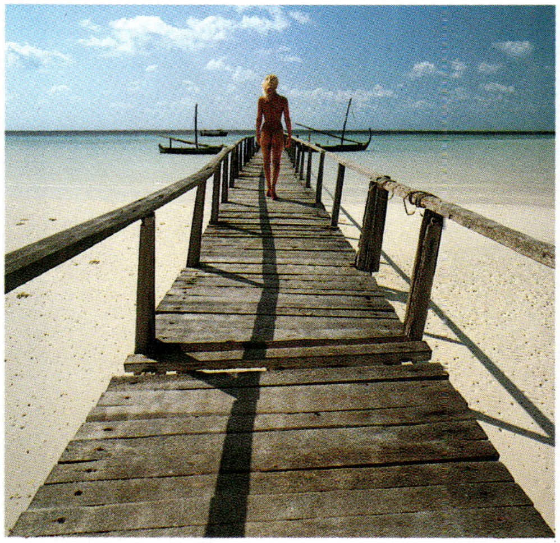

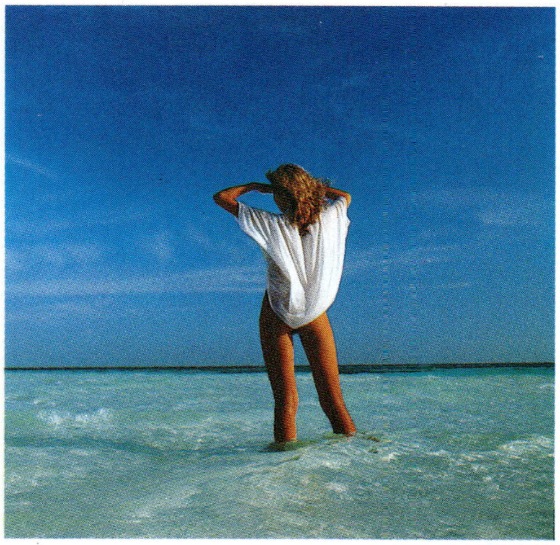

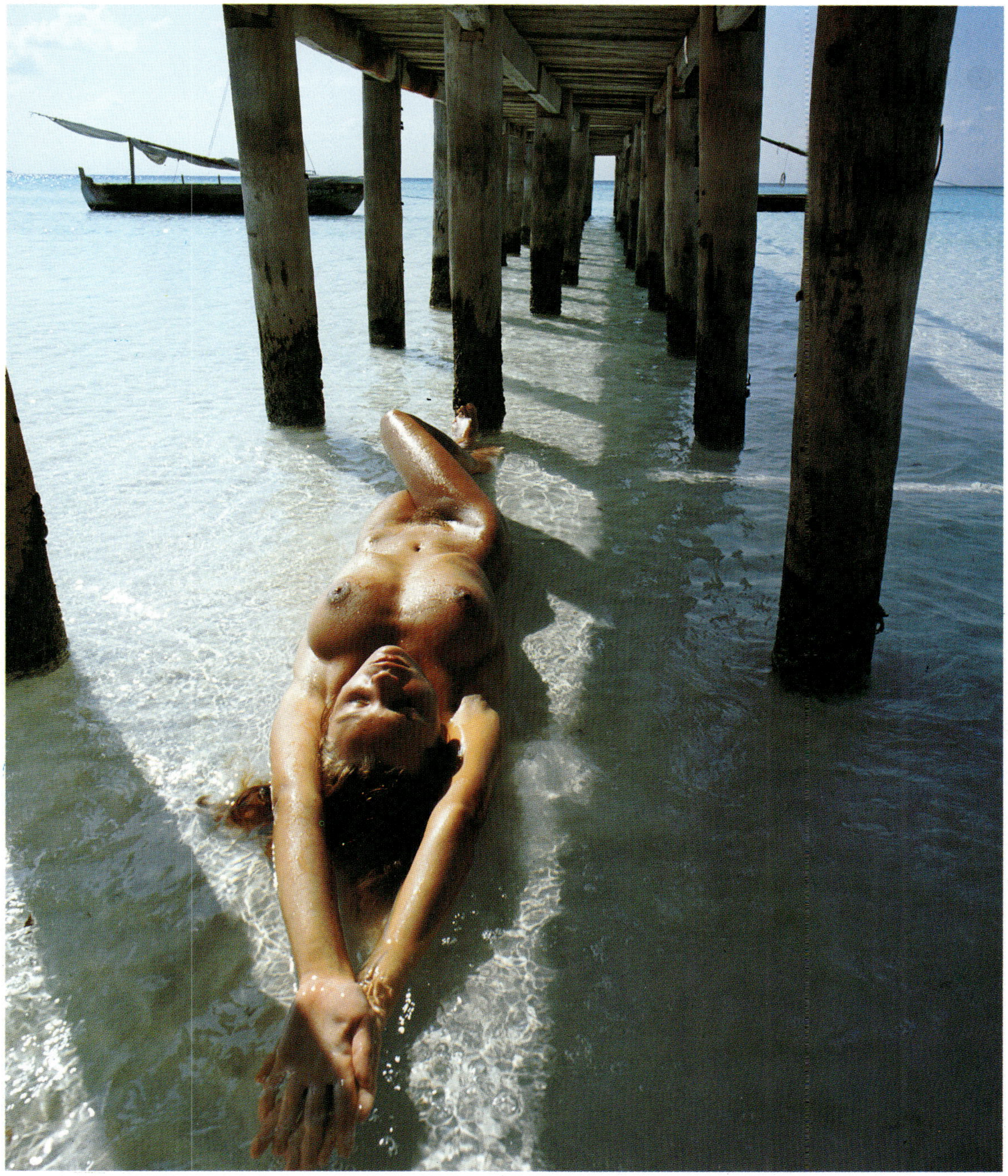

Merely because your subject is *a beautiful girl, there is no need to fill the frame with her. She can be an element in a larger picture – the jetty,* ***above centre and left,*** *or the sea and sky,* ***top left and right.*** *Slight underexposure accentuates a tan and saturates colours.*

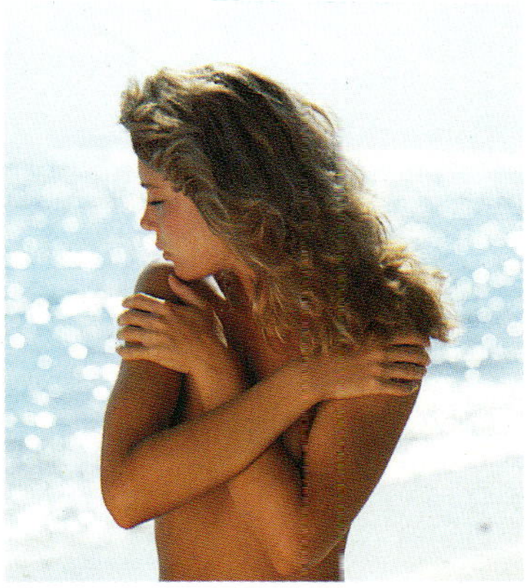

The problems of exposure can *be considerable on the beach. In the small picture* ***above,*** *correct exposure for the model has led to a washed-out background; in the picture* ***facing page bottom right,*** *the underexposure necessary to capture the deep blue of the sky and the lighter blue of the water has meant that the girl's face is very dark. The other three pictures on the opposite page show the use of fill-in flash. On the* ***top left,*** *the aim was a balance: in the pictures on the* ***top right and bottom left,*** *the background is slightly underexposed for extra saturation and impact. All pictures: Hasselblad with underwater housing and tripod.*

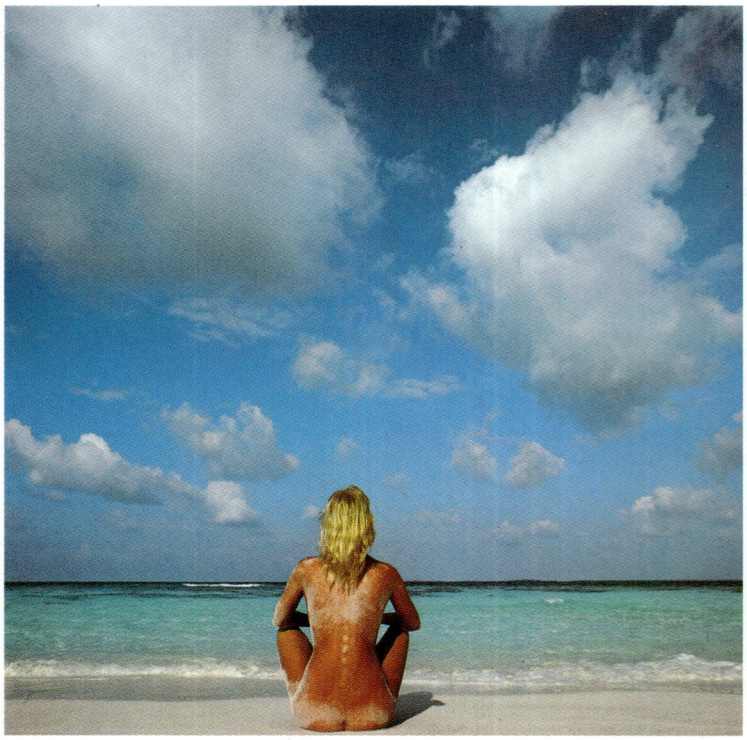

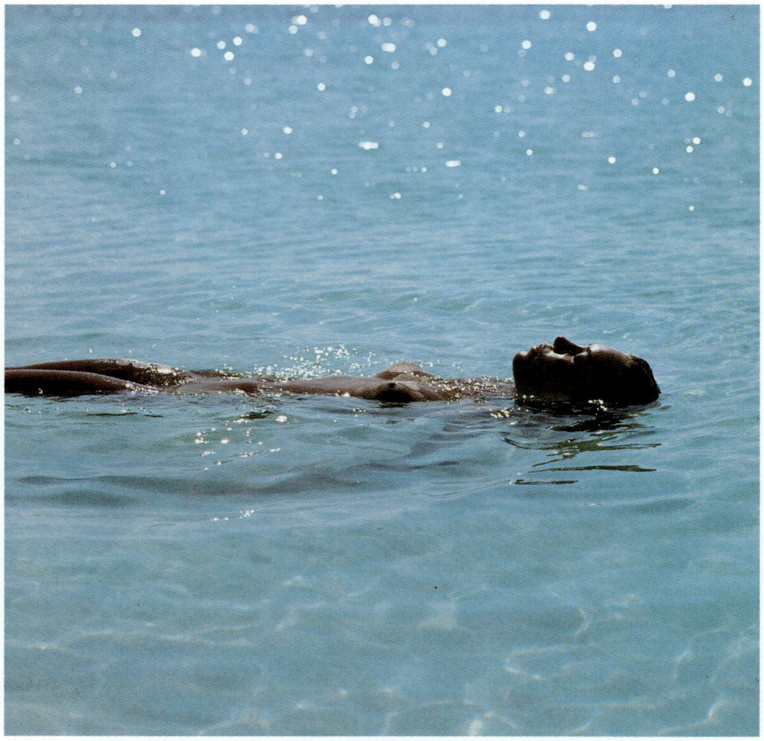

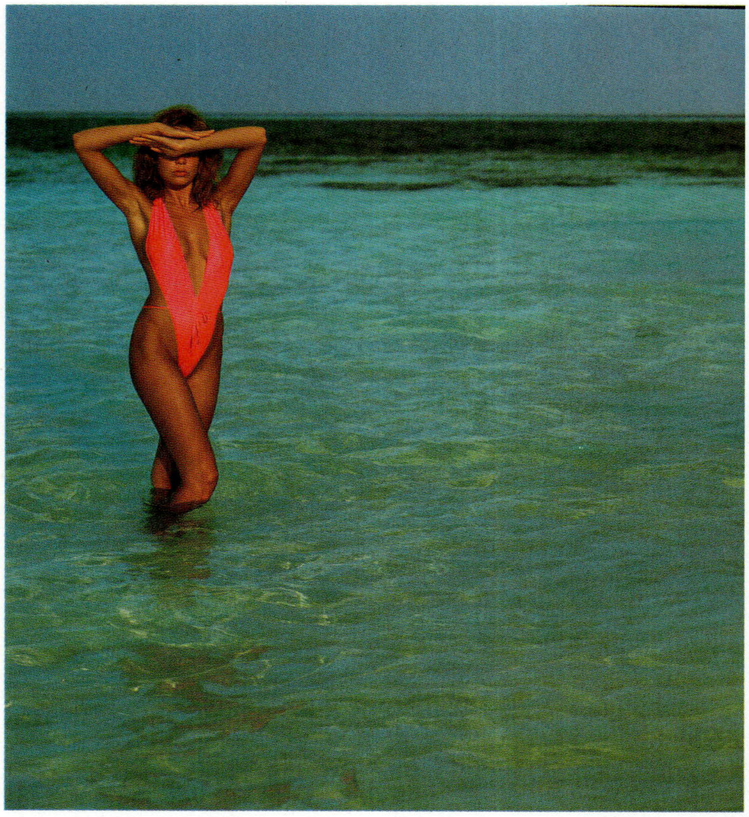

__Girls, sun, sea, and sand may__ sound like paradise – but they are a nightmare for equipment. Ideally, you should use underwater cameras or housings; at least, tape over all cracks and take great care to avoid splashing. Unless you use a sealed-leg tripod such as the Benbo, always rinse the tripod legs in fresh water after immersion; salt water can corrode light alloys beyond repair in a few hours.

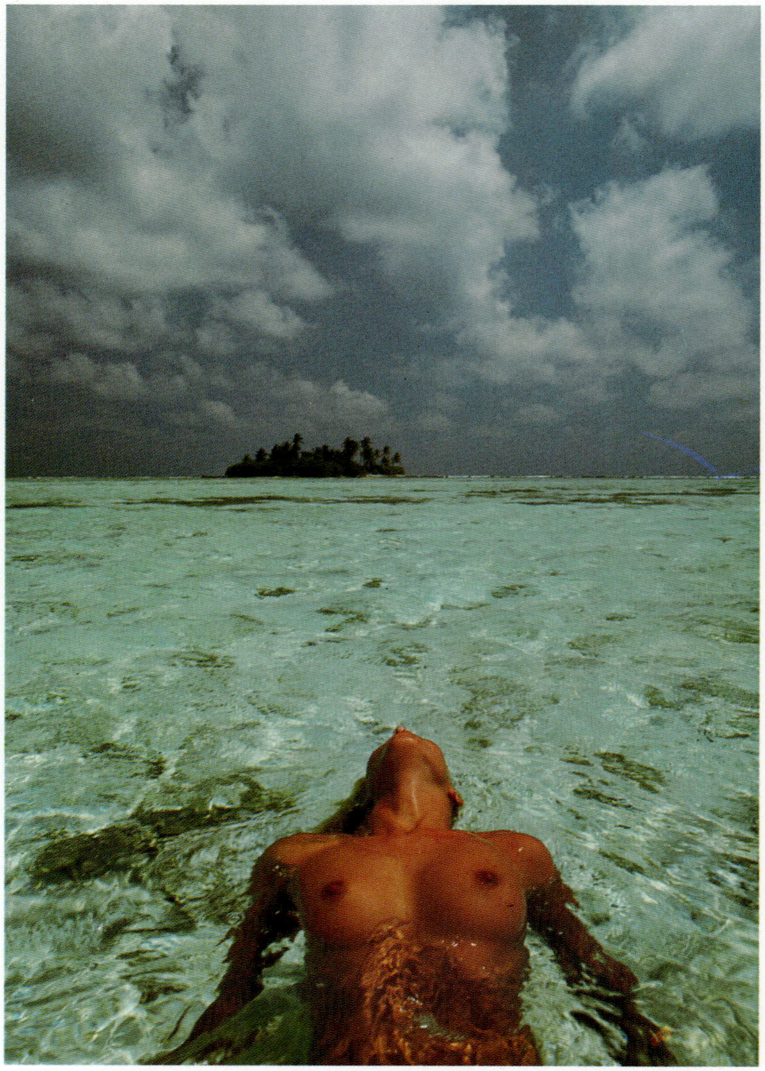

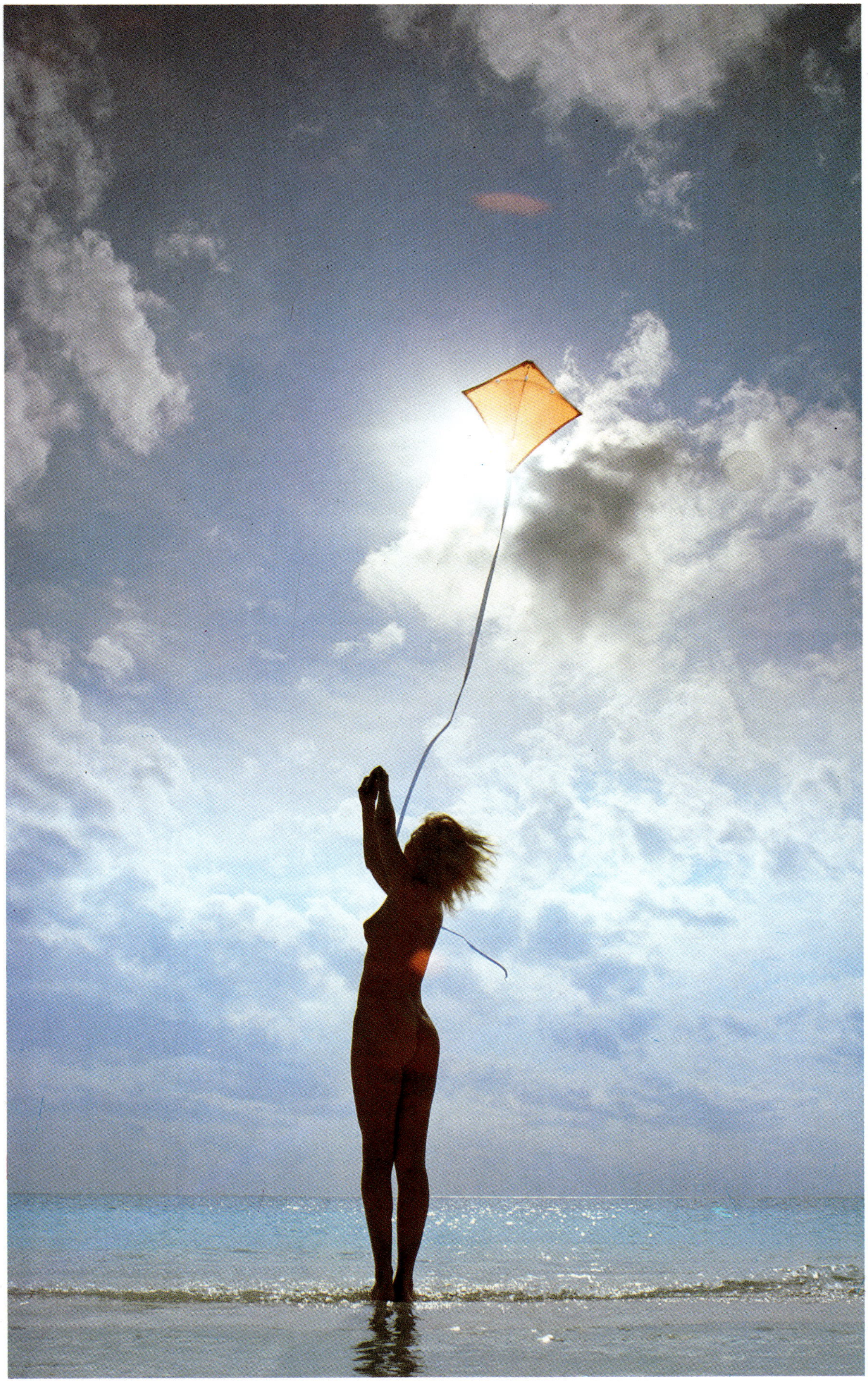

Unusual lighting effects are as *important in glamour photography as anywhere. In the picture* ***below*** *the red light of sunset and the darkening sky produce interesting colour contrasts; in the bottom picture, simple underexposure against the sun's reflection is used.*

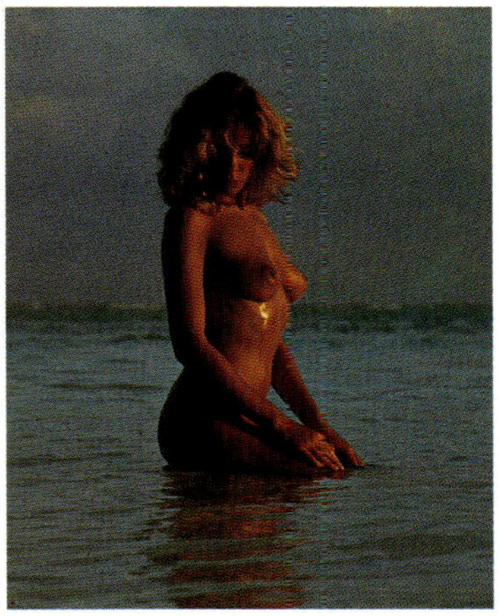

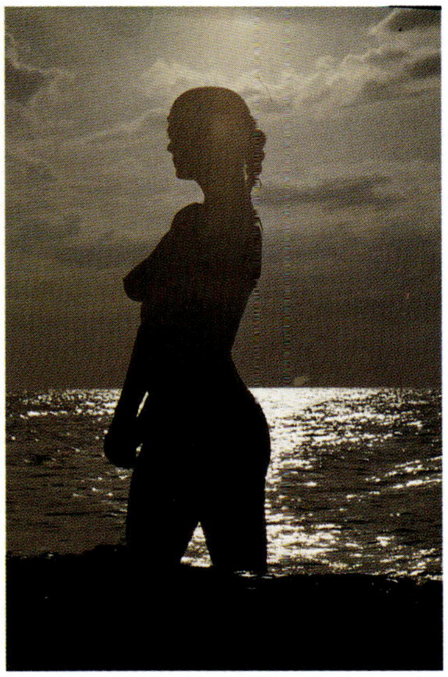

The big picture on the left is *deceptively simple; have you ever* ***tried*** *to get a kite where you wanted it? Exposing for the sky has meant that the girl is reduced to a semi-silhouette, but 'fill' comes from light reflected from the sea and sand; mentally, we supply more detail than there is. Two flare spots, one above the kite and one on the girl's back, are slightly distracting, but that they are not worse is a tribute to the design and multi-coating of modern lenses.*

PEOPLE

THE MASK BEHIND THE MASK

Some maintain that it is arrogant even to pretend that you can say anything which is truly about another person; they say that every statement you make, in word, deed, or picture, reflects only you. Whilst there must be a certain amount of truth in what they say, I distrust so extreme a posture. If you can really get to know someone, you may be able to get close enough to capture something of the way they see themselves, or at least of that underlying something which most people agree is the character or nature of the subject.

Some people can do this very rapidly; they are the great reportage photographers like Bert Hardy. Others take a few hours; the best thing to do is to get your subject to talk about himself (or herself) and just listen. Study the gestures, try to work out what is important in this person's life (you may be able to use an appropriate setting) and generally intrude as little as possible. Of course, you can bend the rules a little and interact with the subject to a greater extent; the picture will then reveal a little of him and a little of you. Some subjects only come to life in this way, and (infuriatingly enough) they tend to be the ones who present the most faces to the most people. I do not mean this unkindly, as I myself have significantly different faces for my drinking friends, my publishers, my Buddhist teacher, and so forth. With luck, the face that you get will be one which is recognisable to other people.

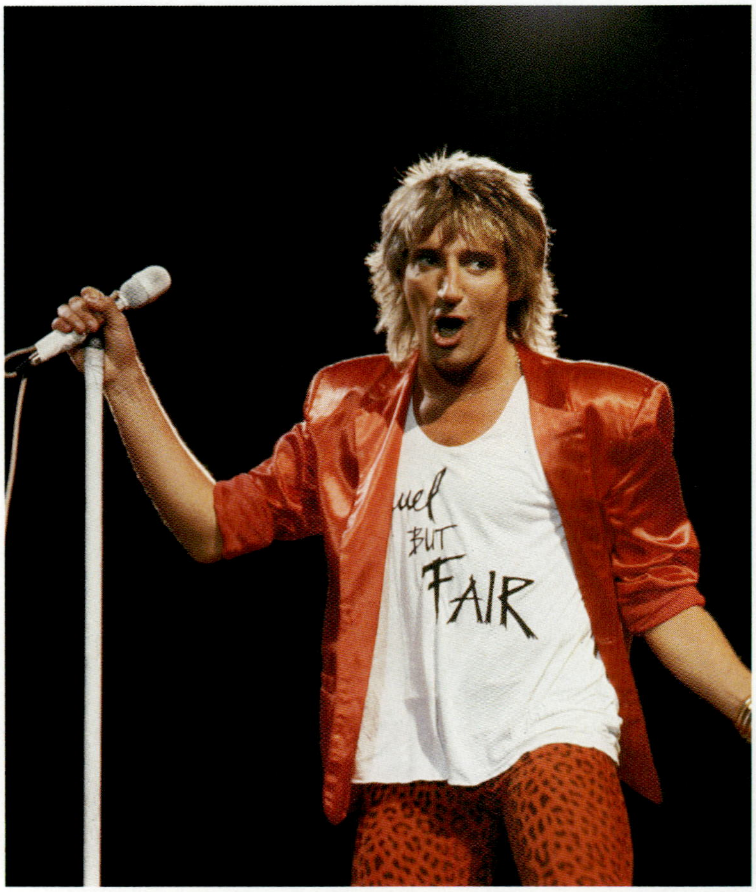

THE MIRROR

The mirror reflects whatever is put in front of it: it does not direct, or interact, or record. For obvious reasons, a photographer cannot be a perfect mirror (if only because he <u>does</u> record). It is possible, though, to get some interesting pictures by telling people that you will photograph whatever pose or aspect of their personality they choose to show to the camera.

The drawback with this approach is that most people are either self-conscious or over-inclined to intellectualise: they put on so carefully considered a face that it is hardly worth seeing. There are half a dozen standard pictures – hand behind the head, body grotesquely bent in a bow, teeth-bared smile, head thrown back, and obscene or aggressive gesture – which recur time after time.

The most successful way to employ it is to direct the photographs at first (no matter how lightly) and then gradually withdraw direction; once the subject gets some idea of what <u>you</u> are after, they may get some ideas of their own. I have always found that the best pictures of this kind are of children: they are unselfconscious and original, and they are so seldom asked how <u>they</u> would like to do something that they react extremely well. The other type of person who responds well is the creative artist or writer, who usually needs a very strong self-image in order to survive, but does not have the repertoire of stock gestures which actors so often fall back upon.

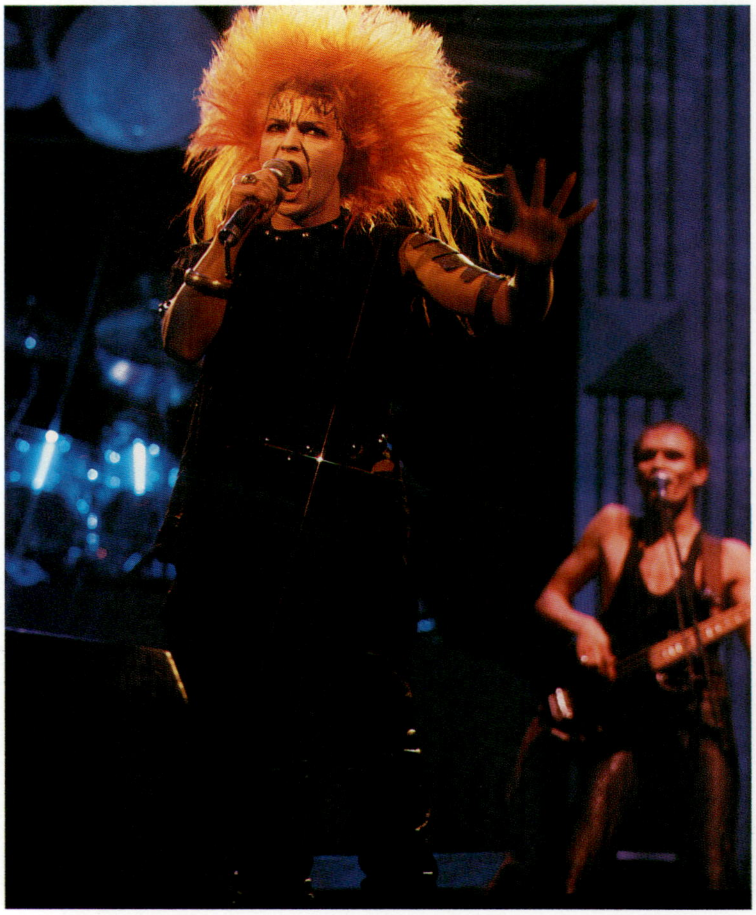

The carefully constructed *public face of a pop-singer is a good place to start trying to capture what is 'typical' in a person; because all actions are carefully considered to support the image, you do not need to hunt very much. The only real difficulties are technical: All these pictures are by available light and make use of the rapidly-changing stage lighting. For this sort of picture, there can be no real substitute for using a lot of film. All of these were shot on 35mm, where the low cost per frame and fast action are essential. Be prepared to reject up to 90% of your pictures, but do not reject blur and odd colours out-of-hand.*

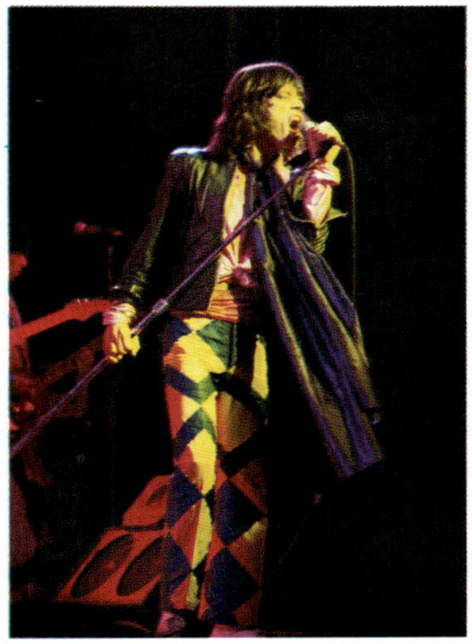

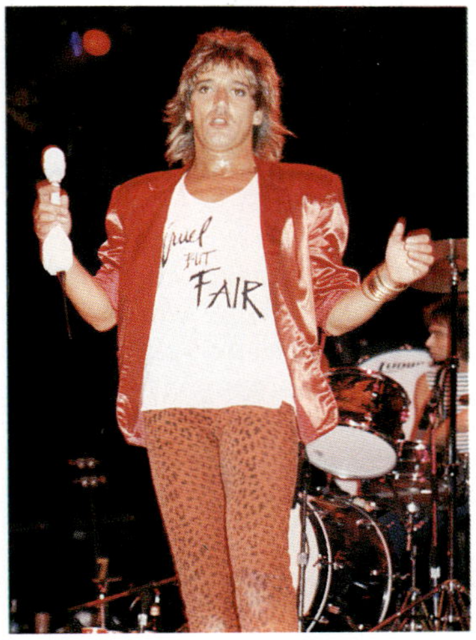

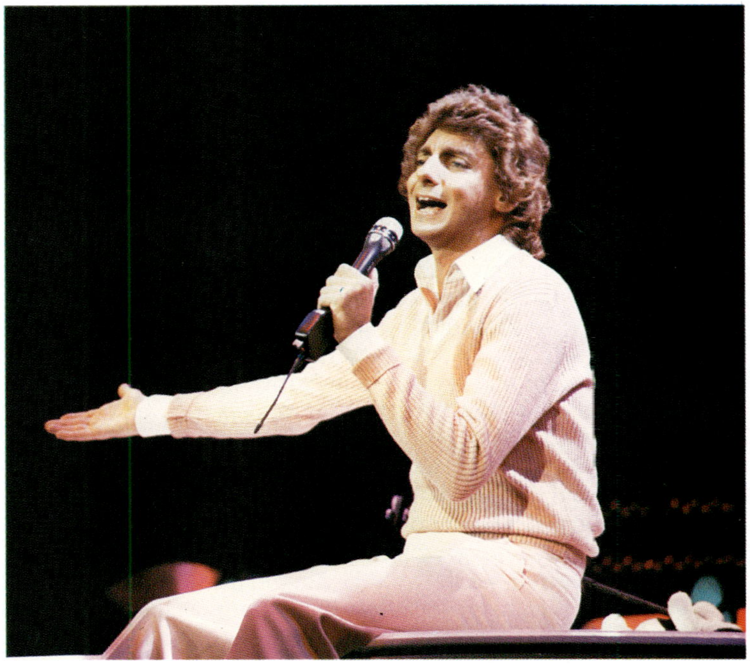

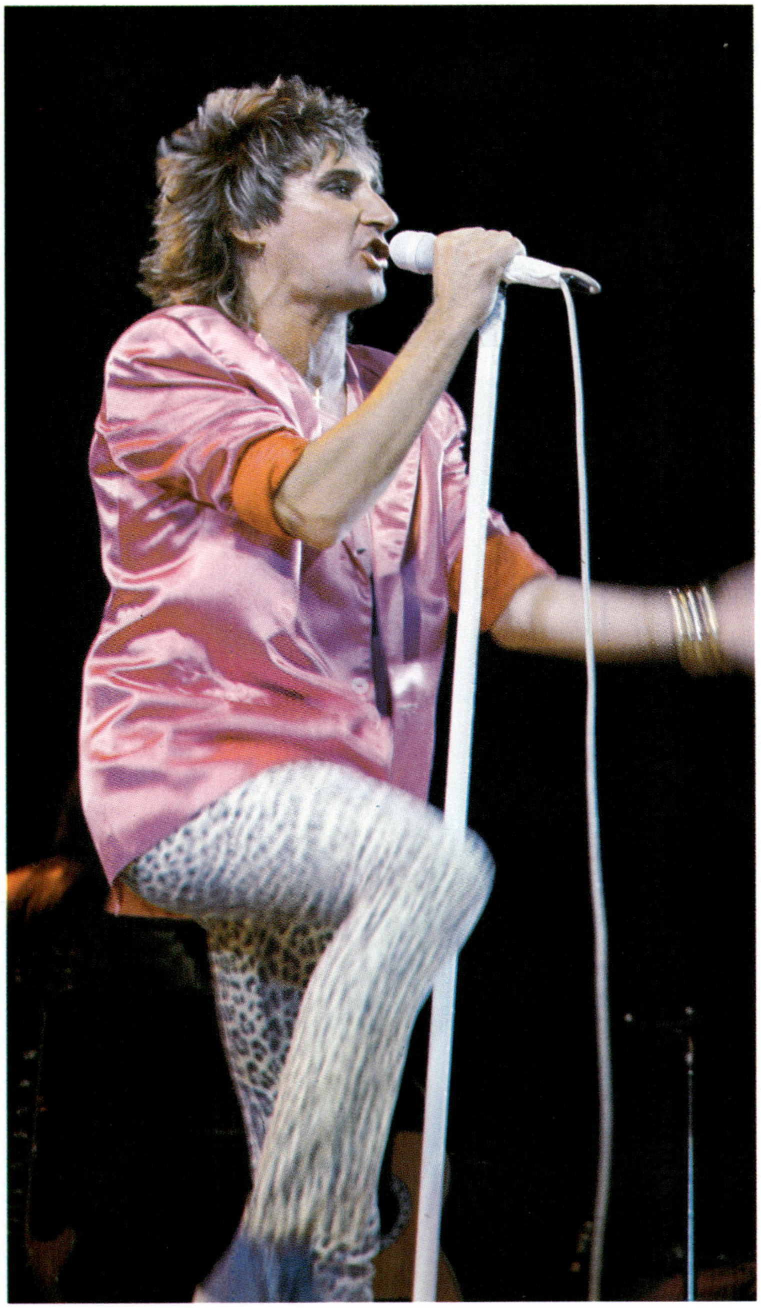

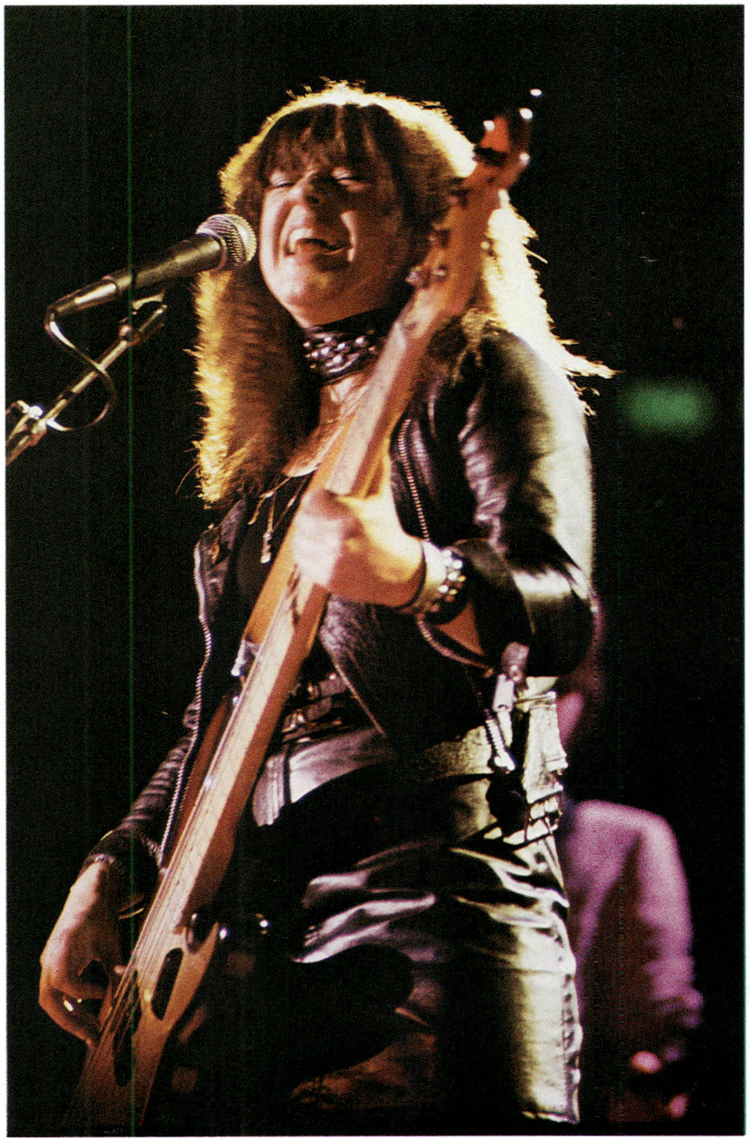

PEOPLE

There is a recognisable style of romantic or nostalgic photography which gained ground in the 1970s. It eschews bright saturated colours and razor-sharp definition, and it is suitable (or has been adapted) for everything from portraits via erotica to recreations of scenes gone by. A number of different techniques are used, singly or in combination, and they are considered below.

Soft focus, the oldest of all the old-fashioned tricks, can be achieved in a number of ways. The best is the use of a special soft-focus lens, which gives a sharp image surrounded by an unsharp penumbra or corona (depending on whether you are using negative or positive film): it thereby differs from an out-of-focus image, which has no sharp central image, but renders a point as a blur of more-or-less equal intensity.

But soft-focus lenses are expensive, and in any case rare in 35mm, and so a variety of diffusion discs is available which give a similar (though not identical) effect. The best are probably the Zeiss Softars, with their little embossed lenticles, but these are extremely expensive and are only available for a limited number of cameras; of all the others, the only way to see if there is one which suits you is to read through the filter manufacturers' catalogues, and then to try the filter out on your own camera, at a variety of apertures. Almost all soft-focus lenses and attachments vary in their effects with aperture, and what is perfect at one aperture (usually wide open, or close thereto) may be a disaster at another.

After soft focus, there are a number of different ways of affecting the colour. A simple one is to overexpose the film, so that there is an atmosphere of lightness and ethereality: this has been done so often with ballet dancers that it has almost become a cliché. Because the overexposure required can be quite considerable – often two stops – fast films are the norm for this sort of treatment: after all, with a 2-stop overexposure, even 400 ASA is effectively only 100 ASA, Kodachrome 25 would be down to 6 ASA!

A rather more ingenious effect, which can only be done in two stages, is to underexpose the film quite severely – again, by anything up to two stops – and then to lighten it by duplication, either by recopying onto slide or by printing: this gives the kind of flat, faded colour which characterises David Hamilton's work, which has proved so successful (and commercial) for his beautiful photographs of young girls.

Another technique uses the granular structure of the film itself. The pioneer of this technique, and certainly one of its greatest exponents, was Sarah Moon, who used (and still uses, if

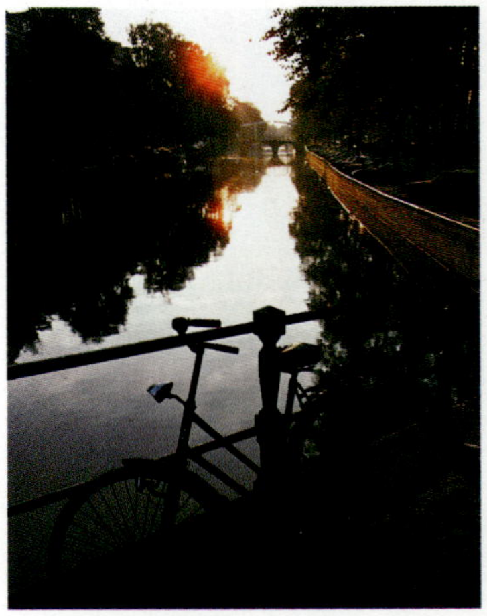

***Bicycles and swans both** have an image which conjures up the past; soft-focus, **below,** increases the effect. There is a vocabulary of 'instant nostalgia' which derives as much from the media as from reality; we have a conditioned response to some things we have never experienced except at second-hand. Whilst it may sound cynical and manipulative, an awareness of such popular imagery may often be used creatively.*

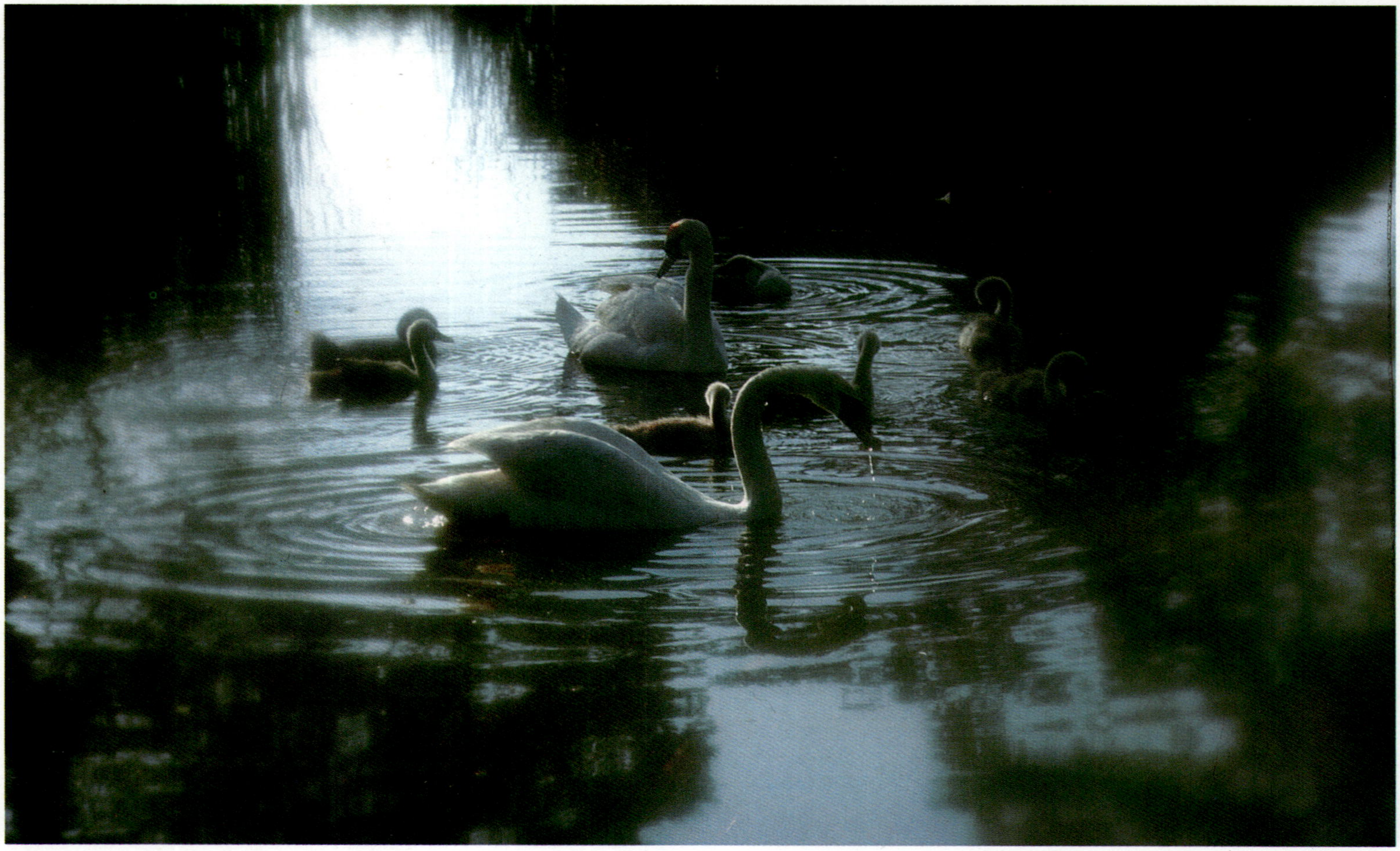

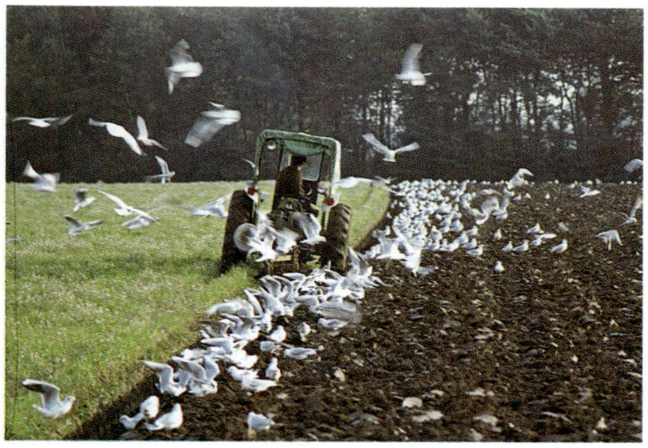

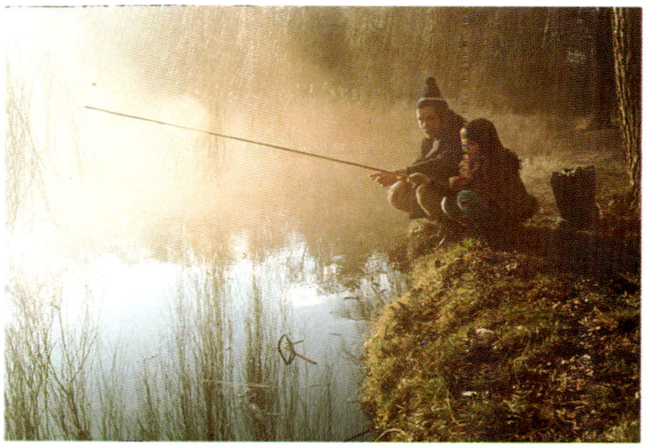

***The man and boy fishing left** and the golden littoral **below** are both beautiful pictures which through their use of colour and light transcend their subjects. The other three are much more calculated and contrived. The monochrome filtration on the two bottom pictures concentrates attention on the subject by removing distracting colour contrasts: the picture **top left** romanticises farming.*

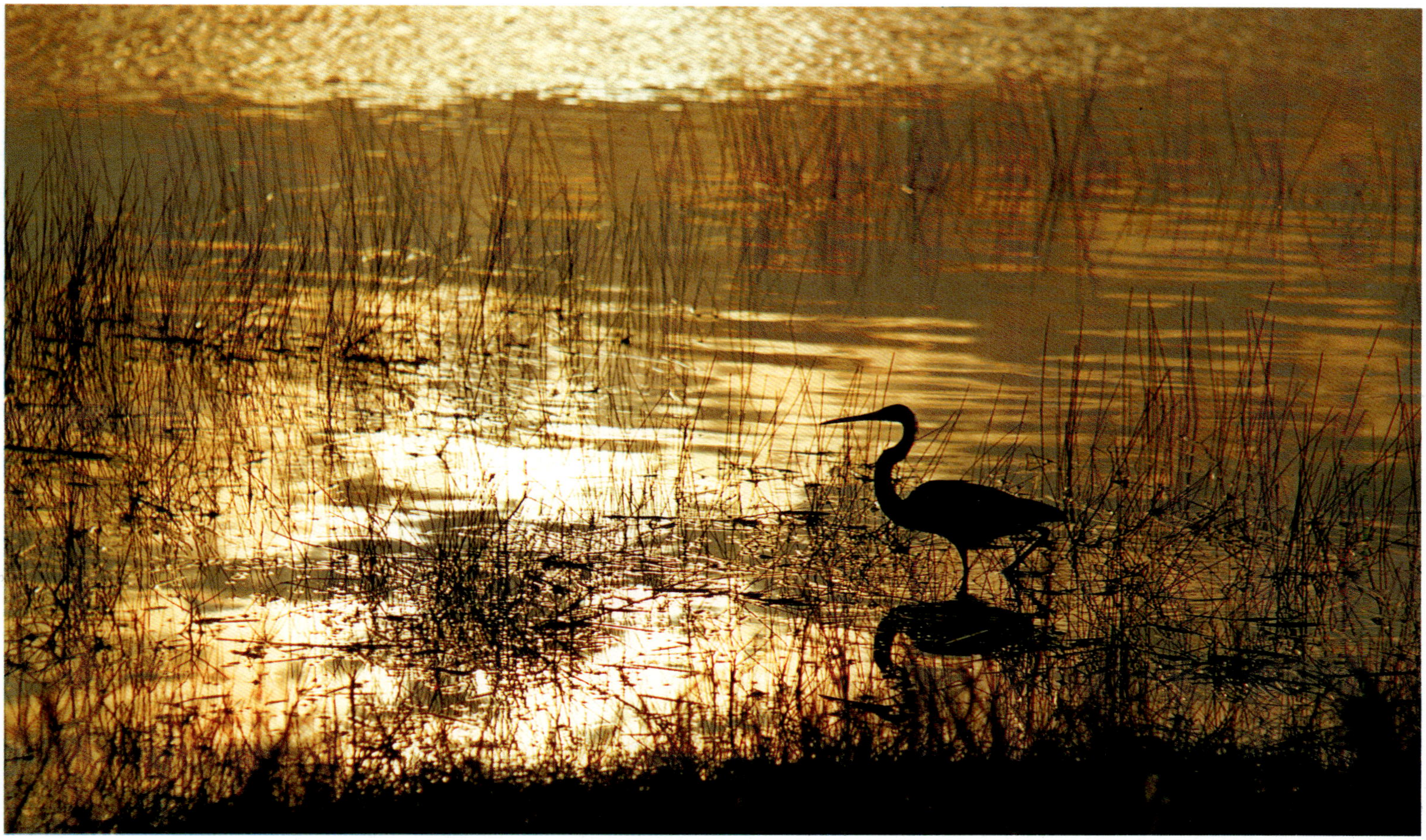

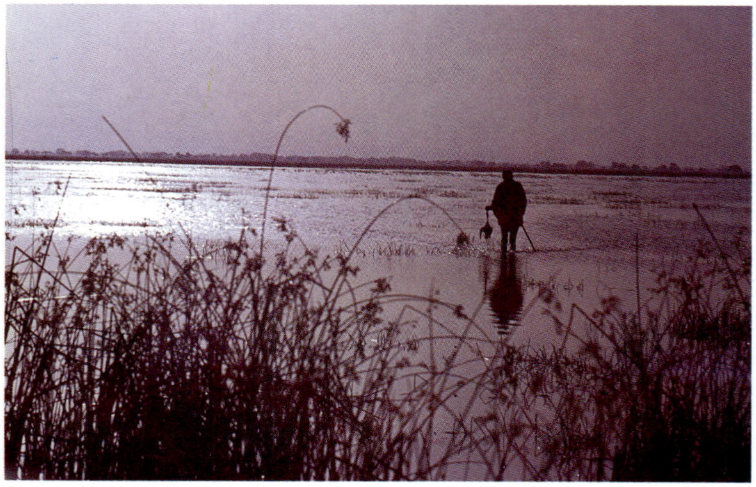

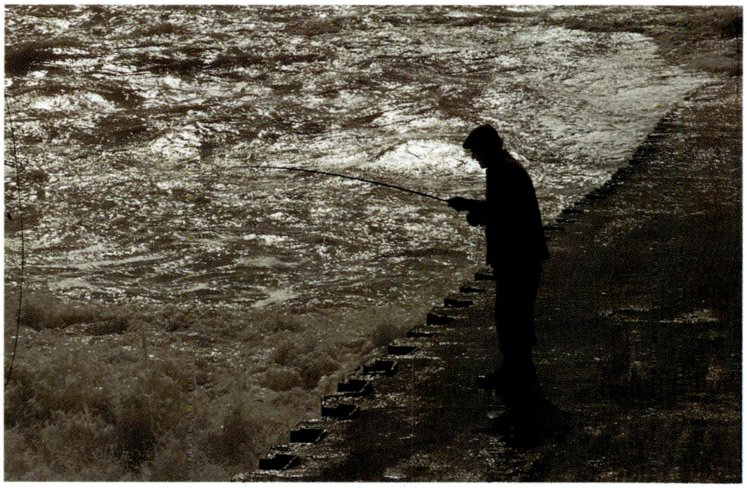

THE ROMANTIC IMAGE

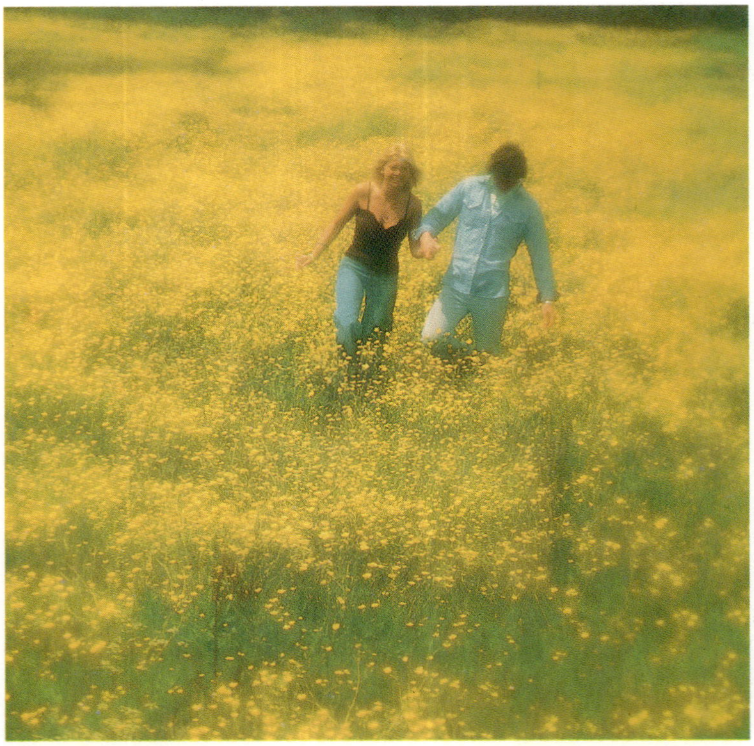

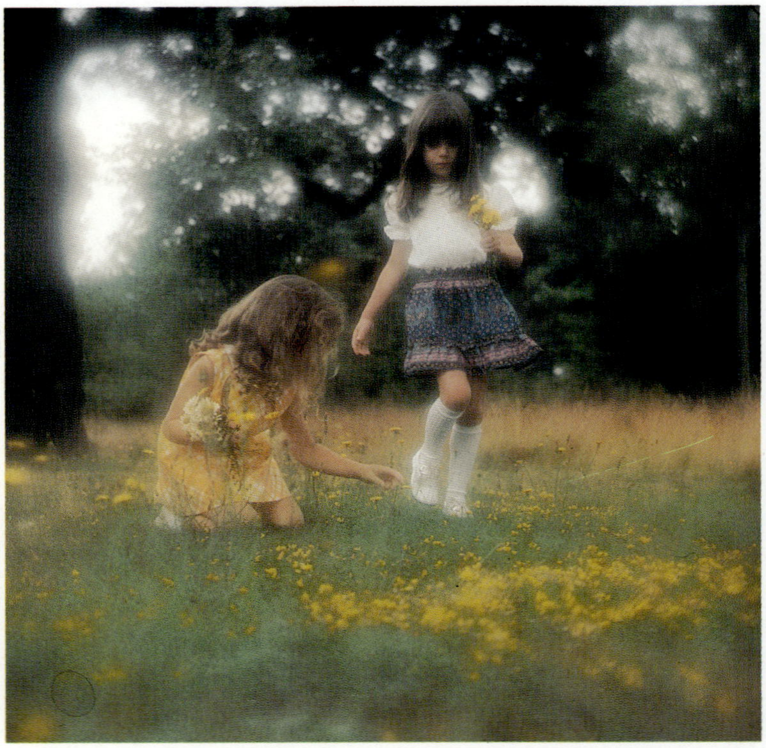

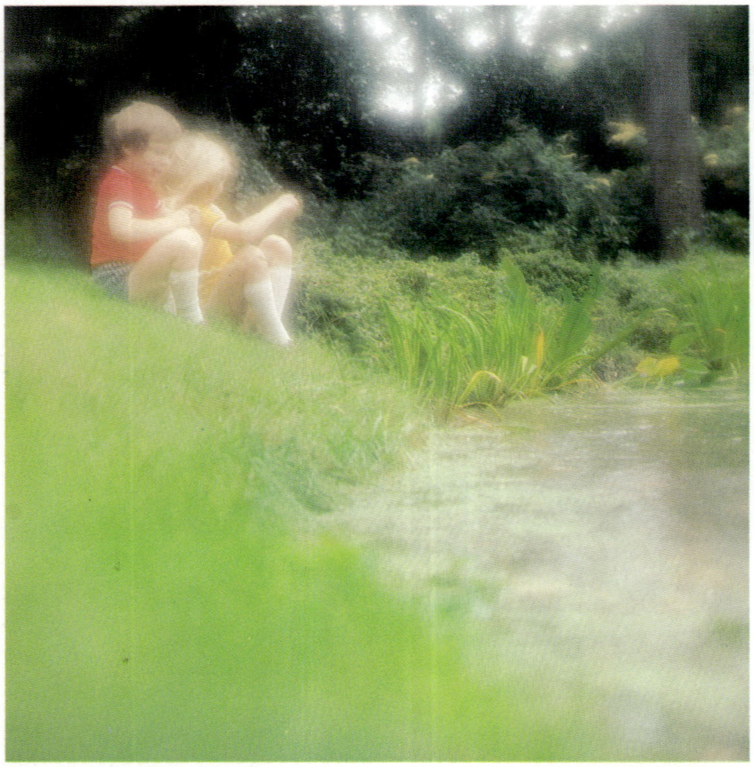

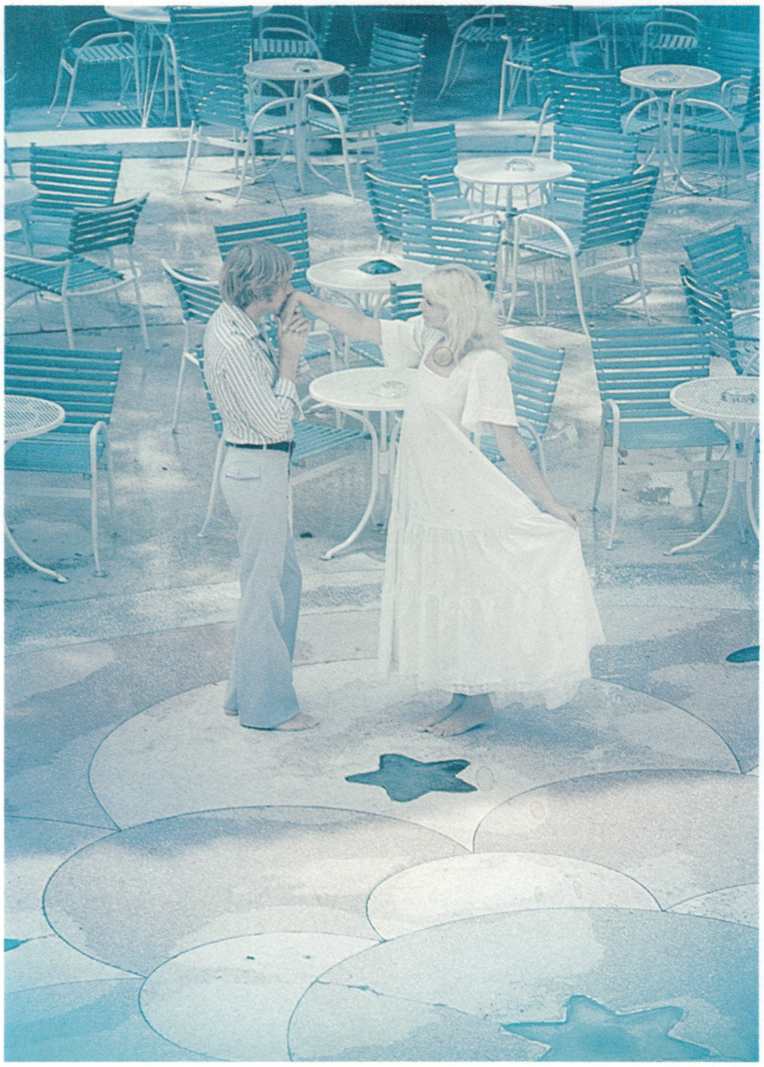

she can get it) GAF's 500 ASA colour film, an outrageously grainy material which nevertheless gave superb effects when correctly used – as it was in her hands. Others have carried it to extremes, composing the picture in the very centre of the film and then duplicating it up to full-frame again so that the dye structure gives a 'pointilliste' effect reminiscent of Seurat.

Almost by definition, the romantic image is a set-piece, not a reportage picture. In general, there are four categories of such pictures, and by applying the techniques described below, these can be extended to whatever ideas the photographer has in mind.

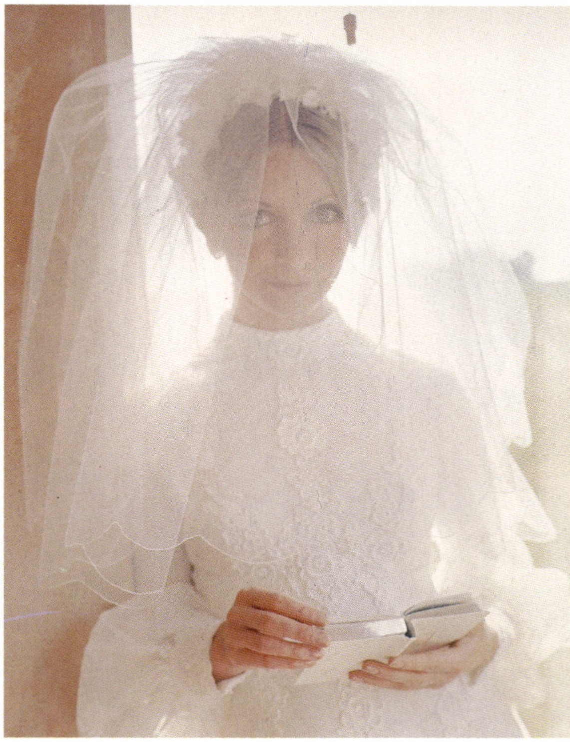

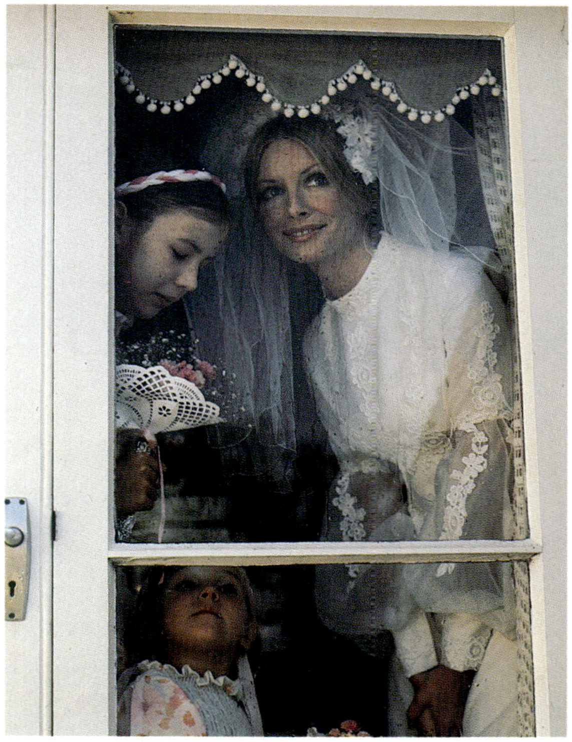

The pictures on these two *pages illustrate the fine line between creativity and cliché; in any case, the distinction must be a personal one, based on whether a picture 'works' for you or not. The shot through the rain-streaked window* ***left*** *is truly creative, as it not only finds a way of surmounting a difficulty (the rain) but even manages to turn it to advantage. At the other extreme, the couple running through the flowers* ***facing page top left*** *is blatantly a 'formula' shot, but nevertheless successful in its appeal to publishers. It is nonsensical, however, to dismiss all fashionable or special-effects shots out of hand: often they will be extremely acceptable to the subjects, and sometimes they can be very attractive.*

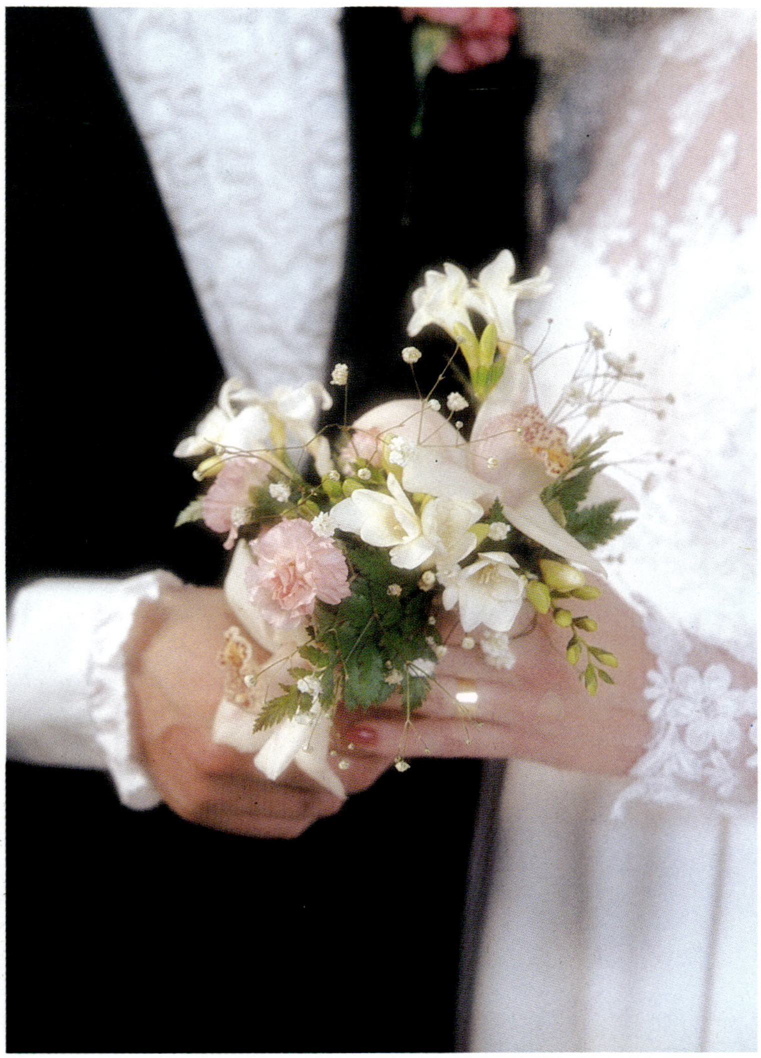

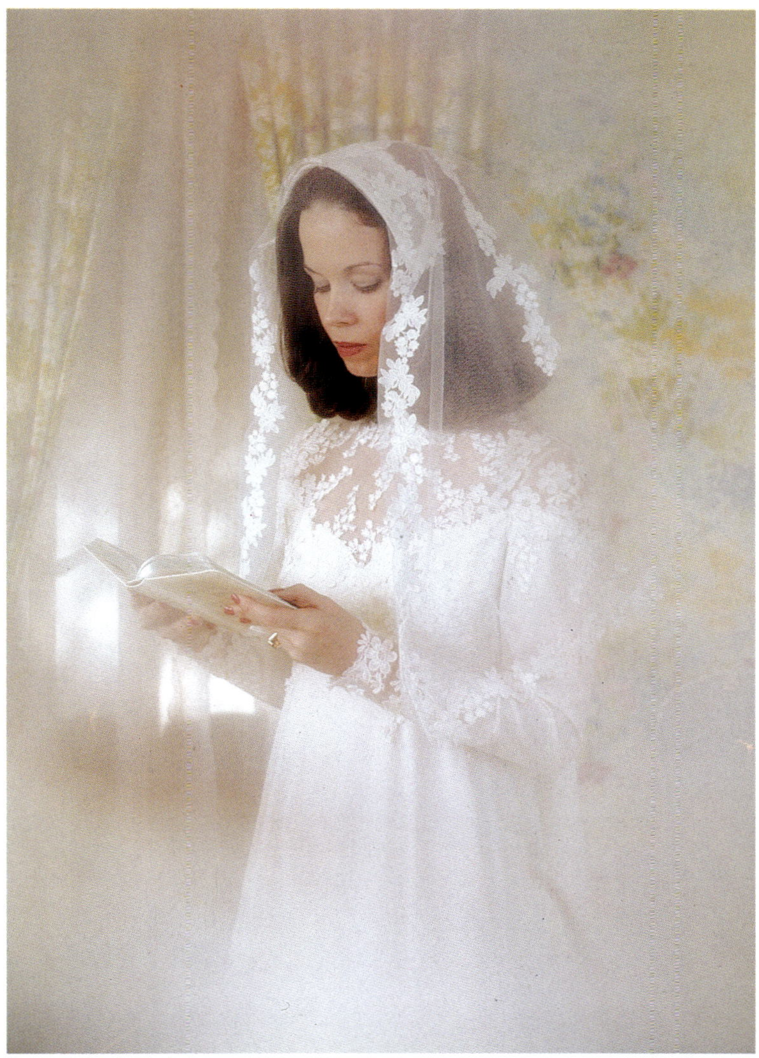

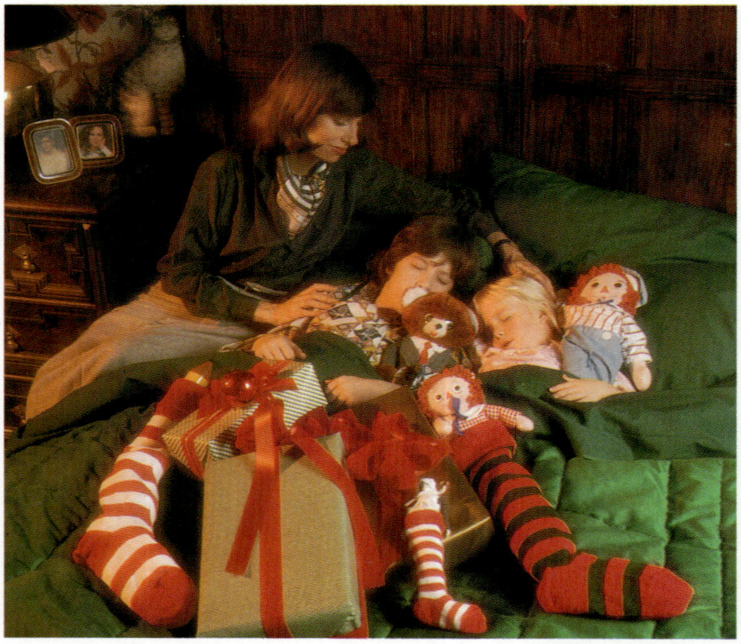

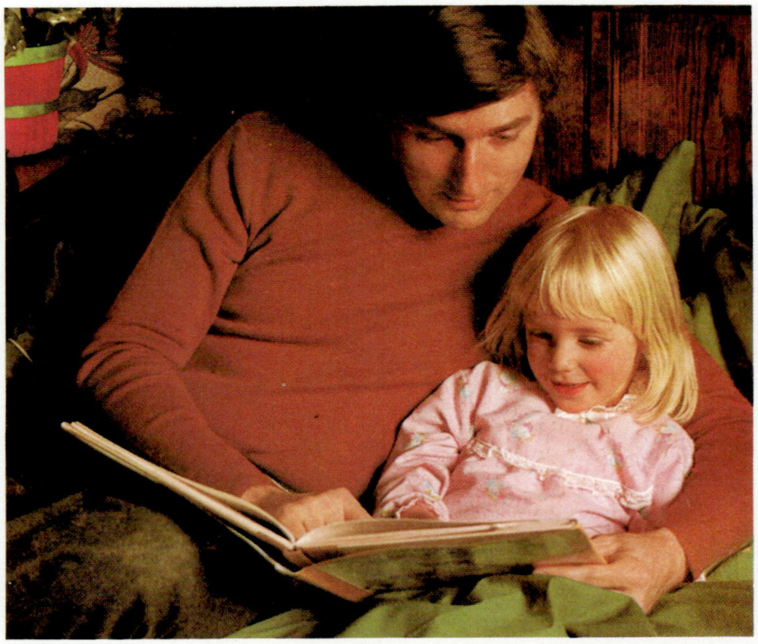

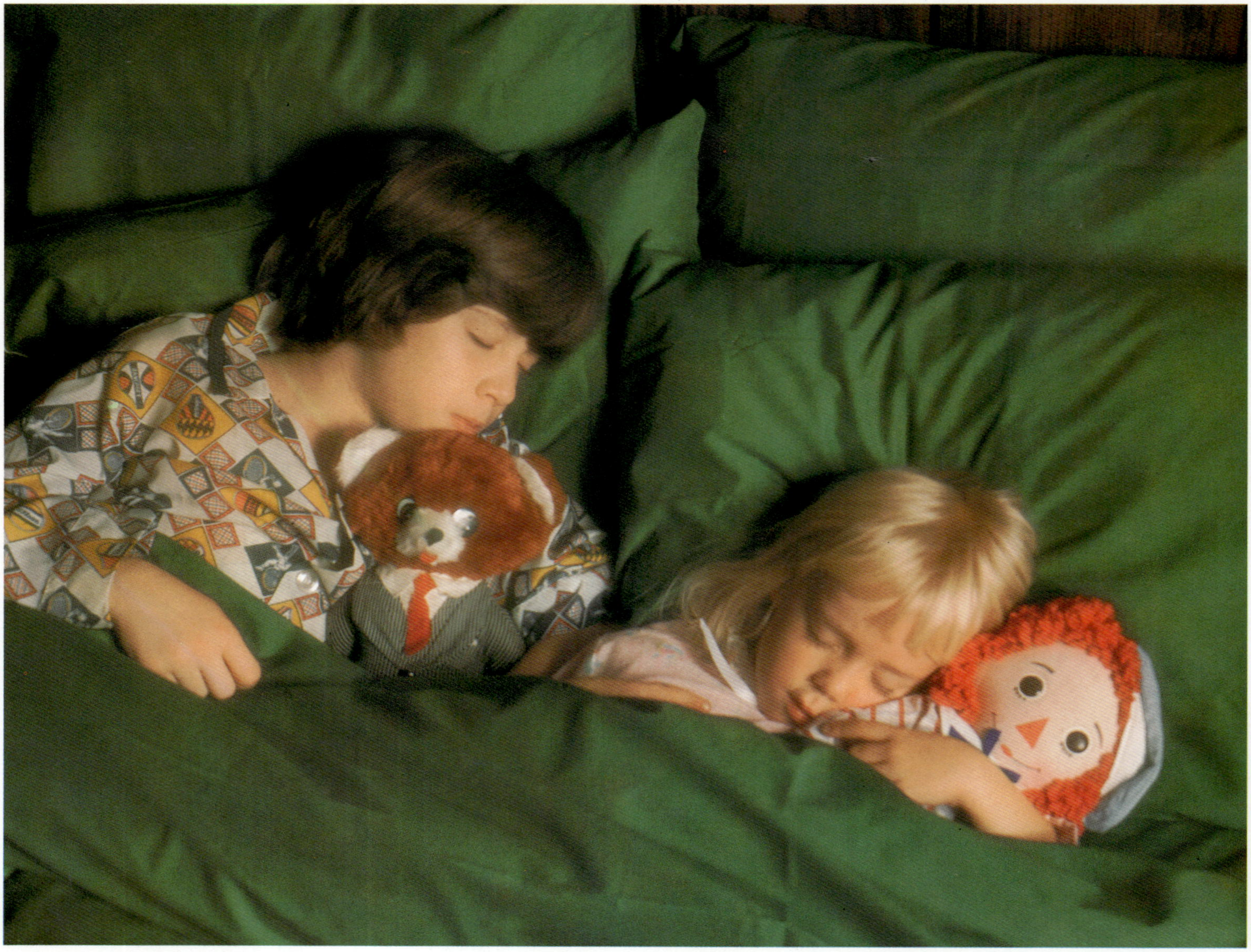

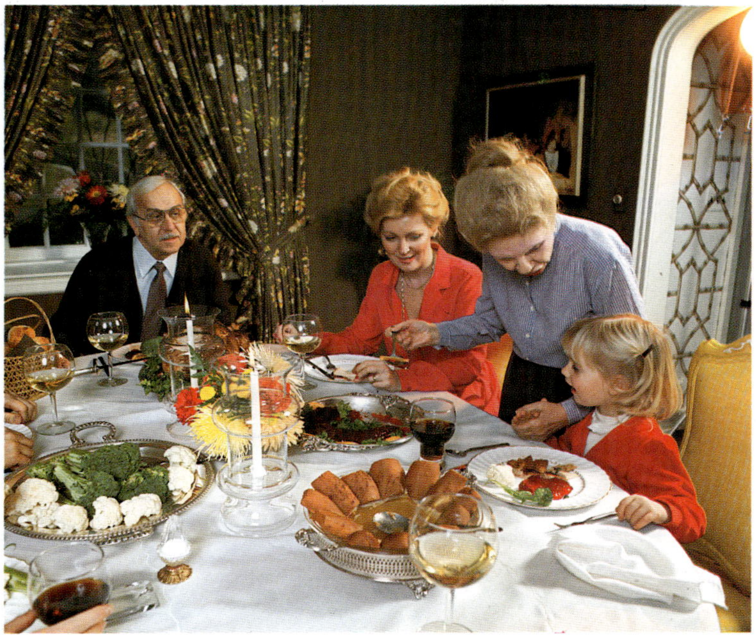

and the mood of the picture may be varied from 'high key' (with few or no dark tones) to 'low key' (in which dark tones predominate).

The third type of lighting is the effect light. Effect lights are used to add highlights to the picture, but great care must be taken that they do not throw shadows which conflict with the key. Typical uses of effects lights include backlighting, or rimlighting, which is particularly effective on hair or fur, and lights used to give sparkle to jewellery.

Finally, there is the background light. This is thrown not upon the subject but upon the background, and may make it uniformly lighter than the subject, uniformly darker than the subject (in extreme cases the background is left unlit, or lit only by the spill from the other lights), or with some sort of shading or modelling to give the background an unobtrusive shape which (usually) concentrates attention on the subject.

Such a lighting set-up may be used with or without soft focus; traditionally, there was always at least a trace of diffusion, but after a long period in which all soft-focus was disdained, quite intense diffusion is returning. The SF-Fujinon lenses for view cameras are probably the best available at the moment, though Rodenstock Imagon users would (with a strong case)

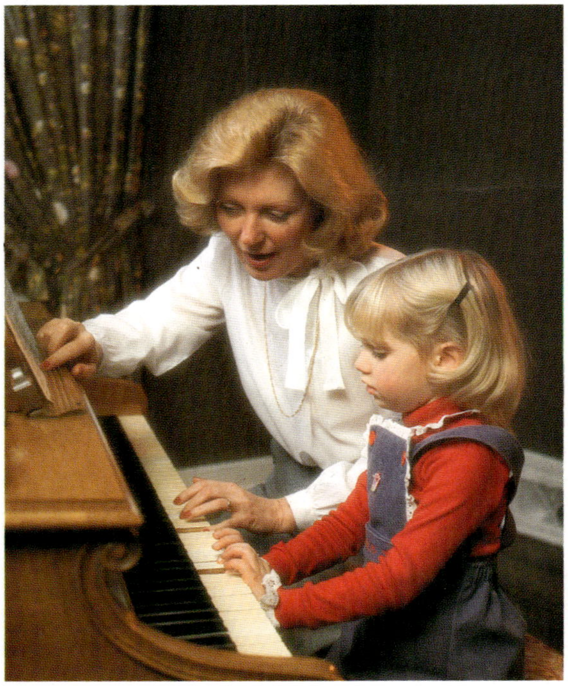

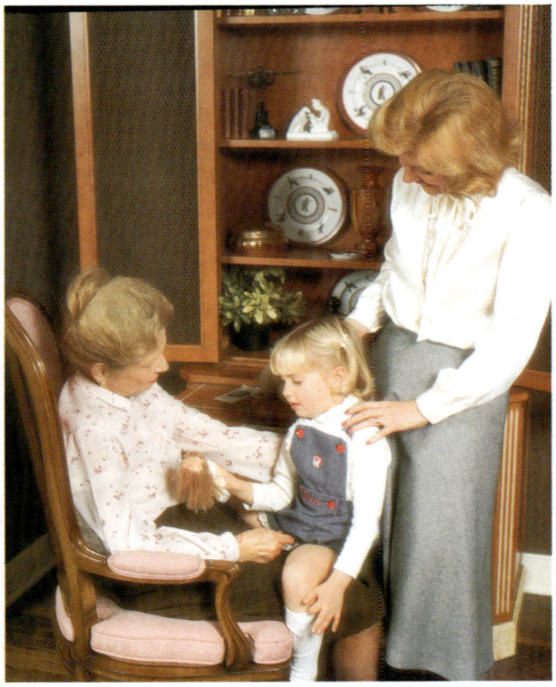

***All of these pictures** are unashamedly posed versions of something which really happened. They were all shot on medium-format cameras, with lenses from 80mm to 150mm; a touch of soft focus has been used in some. Getting a natural effect in such pictures is not as difficult as it might seem, as all you have to do is to get the parties believing in what they are doing. The little girl **facing page, top right** really is listening to her father reading a story, and the piano lesson on this page is genuine. The photographer must be unobtrusive, and fully in control of his equipment: clattering about changing lights, and taking meter readings, and constant false starts are all disastrous.*

PORTRAITURE

Although available light may be used, far more convincing effects are obtainable with fully controlled lighting.

The classic lighting for a portrait makes use of four types of lighting: each may consist of a single lamp, though it is by no means unusual to use more. First, there is the main or key light: this is the one which establishes the shadows, and (except for special effects) comes from above camera level to strike the subject obliquely. It must be the only light which casts shadows on the subject (because split or double shadows are very distracting) but these may be more or less sharp: at one extreme, a spotlight is used, and at the other, a powerful 'trough' or 'northlight'.

The next lamp is the fill, a flat soft light from the direction of the camera, which lightens the shadows cast by the key. By manipulating this light, the dramatic effect of the key is altered,

dispute this; in 35mm there are a couple of proprietary soft-focus lenses which are no more than an achromat in a focusing mount, but are capable of quite excellent results. One slight problem with these lenses is their very cool colour rendition, caused by their simplicity and rather old-fashioned coating: an 81-series filter may be advisable to warm the image up a little. Mamiya also offer soft-focus lenses for their rollfilm reflexes: the days are now long gone when unkind wags could assert that the entire range of Mamiya mid-format lenses were soft-focus, but it is true that for cheap soft-focus effects a Mamiya C3 with the oldest possible lenses, used at full aperture, is superb and gives some substance to the old gibes – and, of course, they can always be stopped down for critical sharpness.

The props used with portraits depend very much on the character of the person you are portraying and on the effect you want to create, but unless you are very confident and very skilled,

THE ROMANTIC IMAGE

simplicity is generally better than complexity. Plain backgrounds, a simple chair, perhaps a desk or table, are all that you need. It is often very rewarding to try for a formal portrait of a child; children can have immense natural dignity, and a portrait which captures this can be very successful.

Whether photographing children or adults, it is always a good idea to have them bring along some prop or possession of their own which they feel happy with. This has two major uses: one is that it acts as a sort of pacifier, and gives the subject something familiar to play with during the essentially unfamiliar activity of having their picture taken, and the other is that it can be a very telling feature of the portrait. Many people have something which is always associated with them – a piece of jewellery, a pair of spectacles, a pipe, or whatever – and if this is included in the portrait it can be a powerful recognition aid, the kind of thing which makes people say, 'Oh, it's just like her.'

PASTORAL

It was the fashion at Versailles to ape the country life: jaded noblemen dressed as honest shepherds pursued their giggling consorts, who were similarly disguised as shepherdesses. There is a similar branch of photography, which dwells upon the pastoral: golden cornfields, sunny days, wild flowers, and so forth.

The first, and most essential, thing is to put the right girl in the right setting: rosy-cheeked blondes are the ideal, surrounded by the kind of landscape described above. Sultry brunettes, or fragile sylphs, are not really on, and nor are overcast days.

Because this is so arrantly a put-up job, the technical approach is usually utterly over-the-top, with lashings of soft focus, and anything up to a stop's over-exposure to give the right airy feel. Given the reflectivity of corn, even two or two and a half stops may not be unrealistic; the single stop applies when using an incident light meter, the higher figures when using reflected-light (especially built-in or TTL) meters.

Props are important, and must again be pastoral. Light-coloured clothes, with or without tiny floral prints, and even white, Alice-in-Wonderland aprons, are the thing; and uncomplicated hairstyles supported by Alice bands will further the illusion.

Grassy banks are ideal, especially if a tree is available for background, but steer clear of hedgerows (which are often visually interesting in their own right, and distract the eye from the subject) and beware of dappled sunlight unless you are using fill-in flash: the differences in light intensity between the shaded bits and the unshaded bits is such that the film cannot satisfactorily record it. The dark parts come out inky, or the light parts burn out – or in severe cases, both. Furthermore, the light is likely to be very green, and a CC10M filter will probably make the model look somewhat choleric.

A filter which is useful, though, is an 81-series warming type: an 81A, or even the stronger ones (81B, 81C, 81EF), will make the sun appear still warmer – unless you are photographing at dawn or in the late afternoon, in which case the effect may be excessive.

One other technical point is that deep focus is usually more effective than the time-honoured approach of throwing the background out of focus, because this type of picture is somewhat painterly, and few painters employ out-of-focus backgrounds.

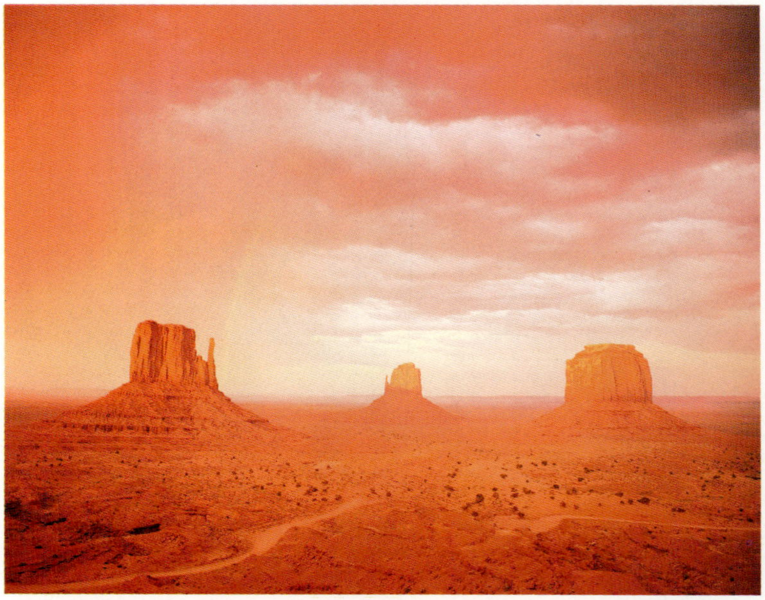

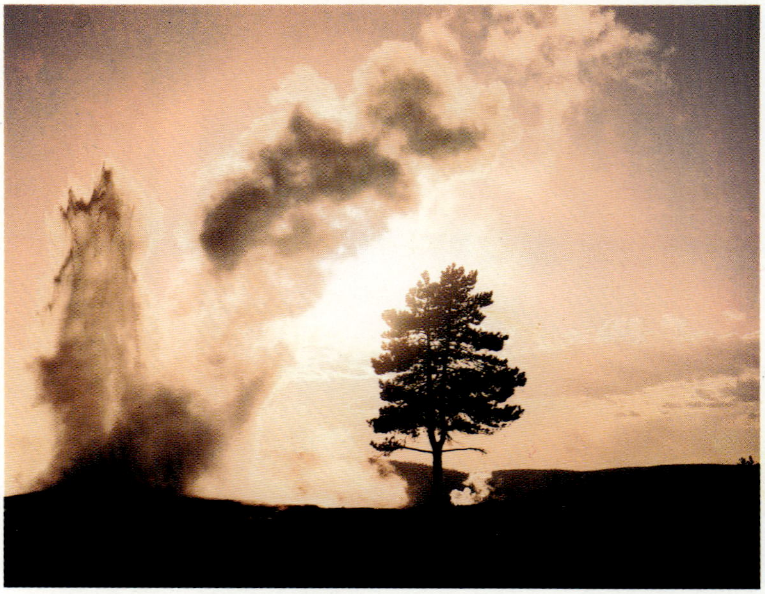

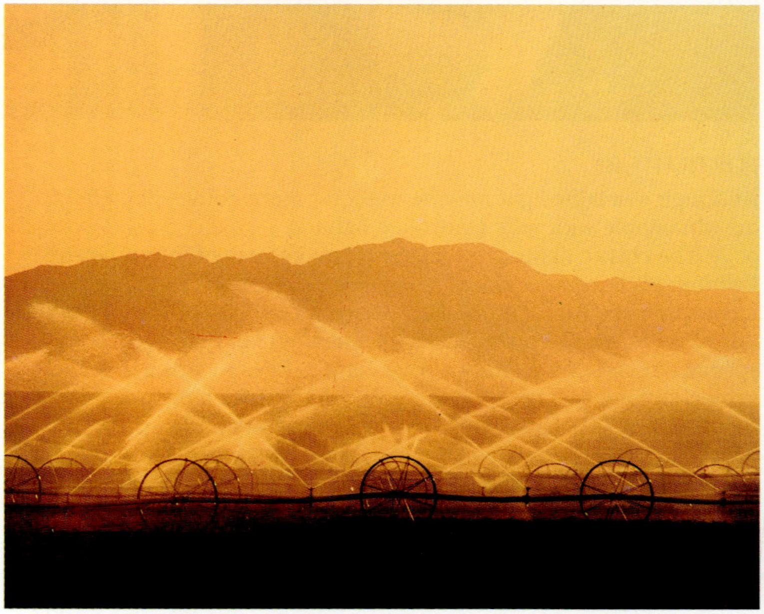

Although the sheer drama of *the landscapes opposite might seem to be the very antithesis of 'romantic,' they could be regarded as the 'macho romanticism' of Jack London and Ernest Hemingway, in which harshness and grandeur replace mere prettiness.*

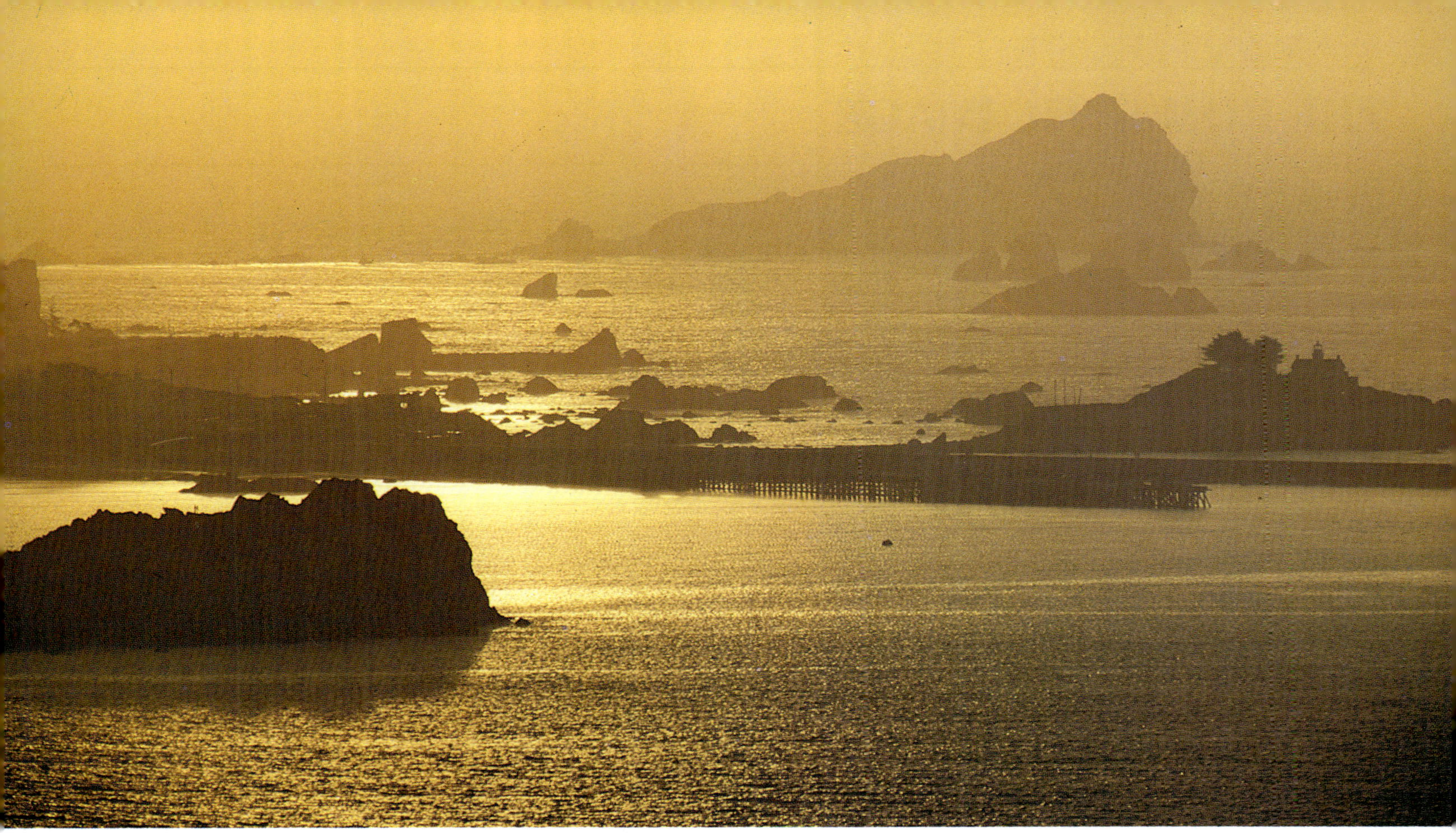

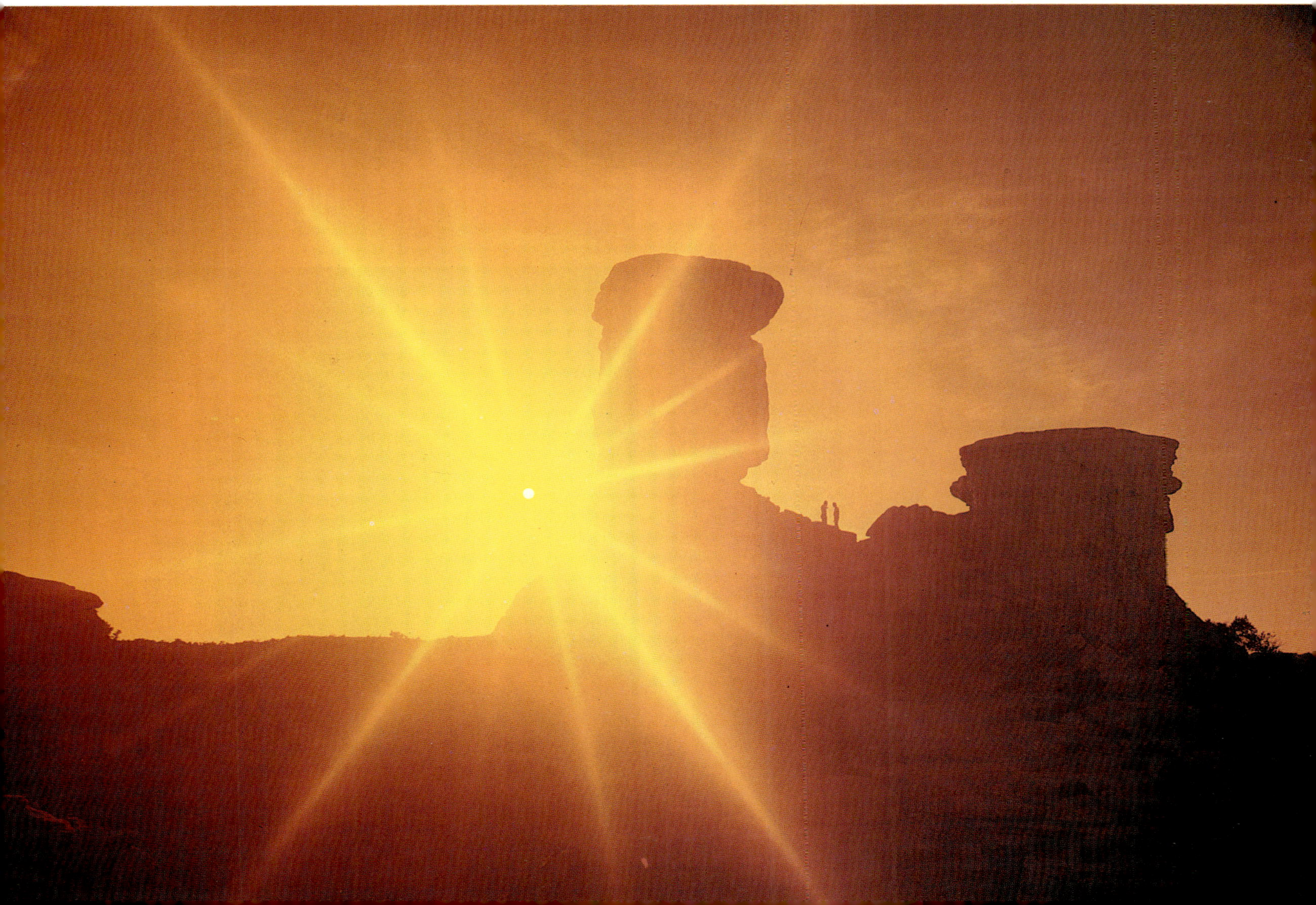

THE ROMANTIC IMAGE

The girl with the cart, facing page bottom left, *is a sort of modern version of the eighteenth century pastoral look in Versailles, and so (arguably) is the picture on the bottom left of this page. The girl in the doorway, the tennis player, and the nymphet in the green stockings are all manifestations of the modern dream-girl: young, hard-seeming, careless. There is an old Tibetan Buddhist teaching: 'If someone I know does something I do not like, may he be my best teacher.' These pictures are an illustration of the need to stay open, and not to place things too rigidly in categories. Romanticism is as closely allied to fantasy as great wits to madness; recognising what it is in a picture which appeals to us is a major step towards being able to recreate that appeal. Some may cavil that any romantic interpretation placed upon a picture of a girl is nothing but a male fantasy, but the depressing logical consequence of that is that we should forswear all romance, and look at pictures of slums and wrecking-yards; better, surely, to stick to romanticism!*

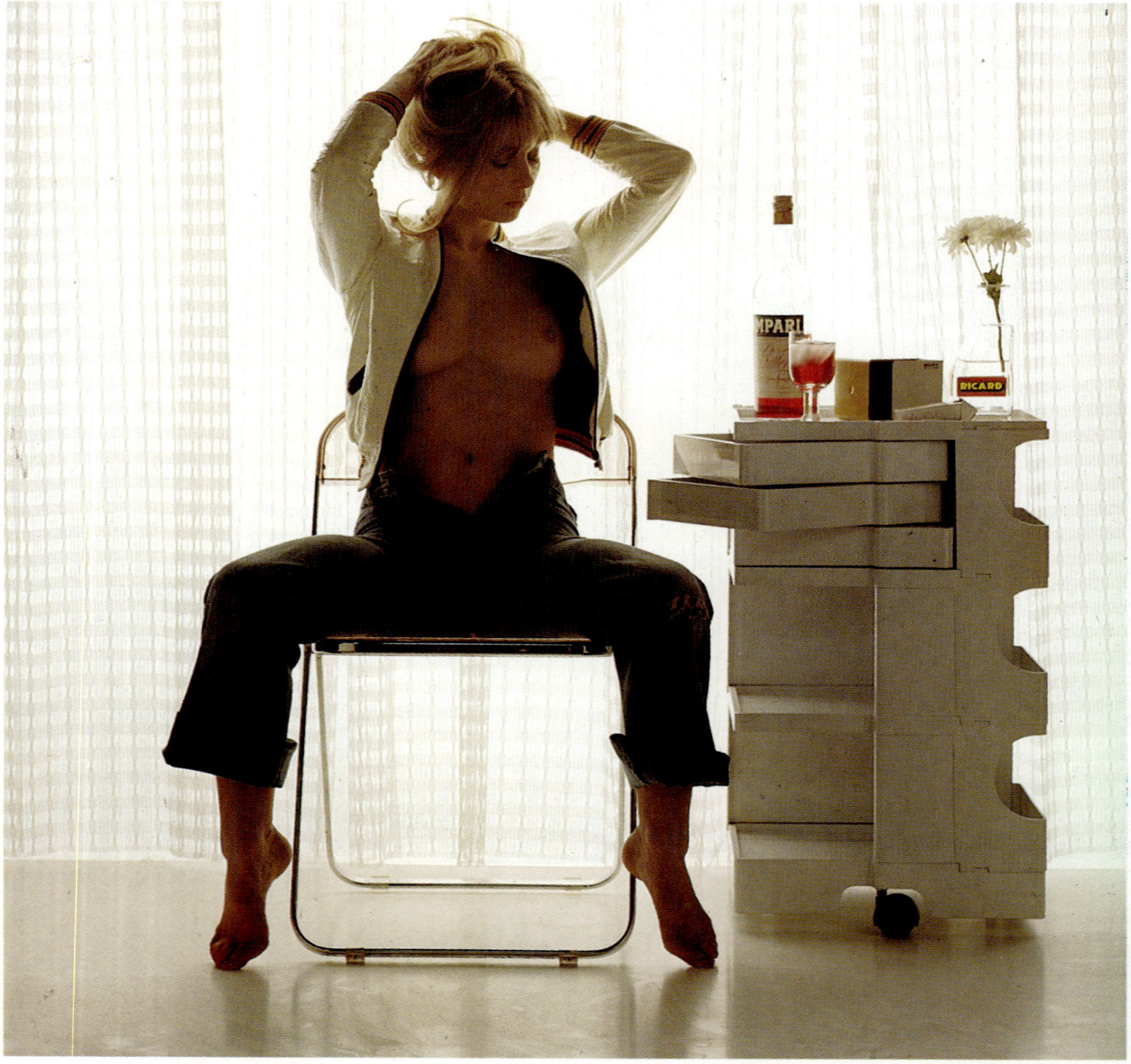

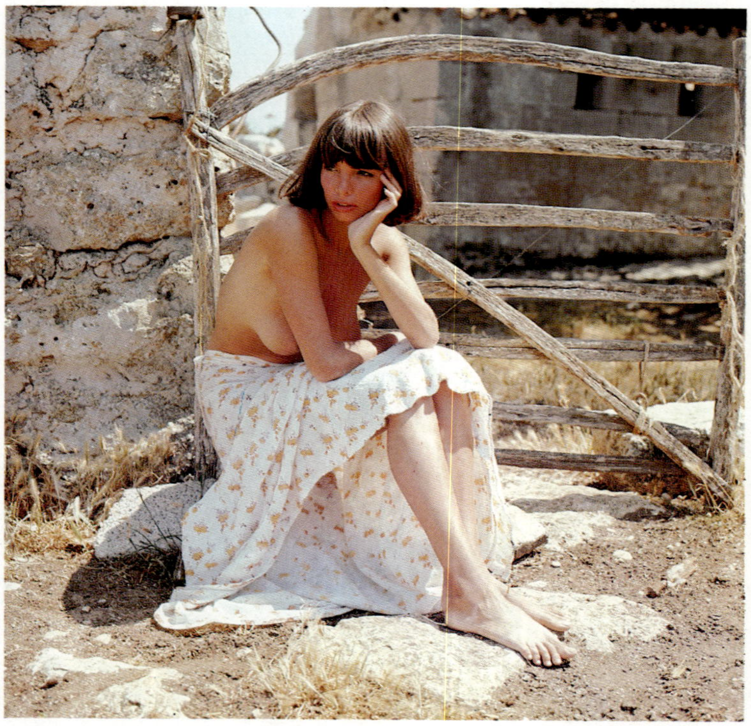

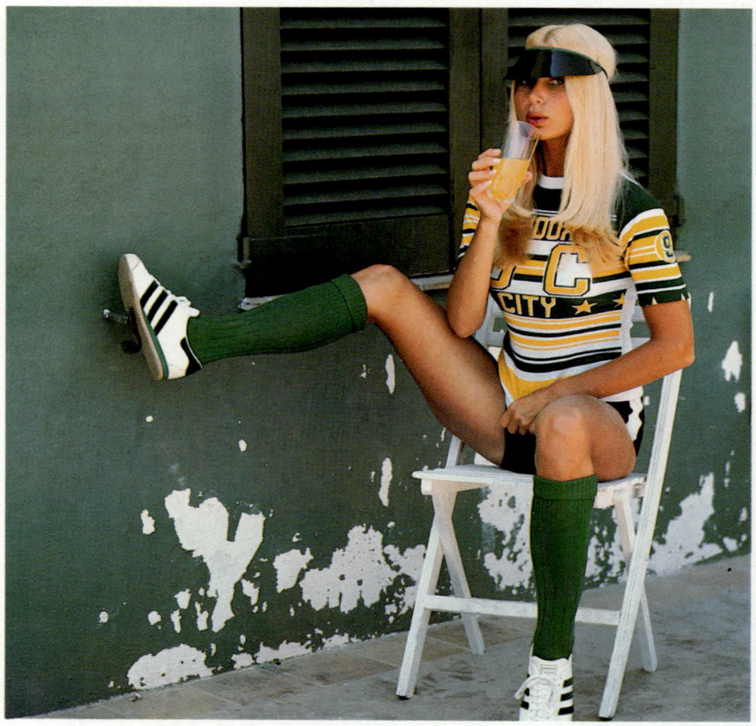

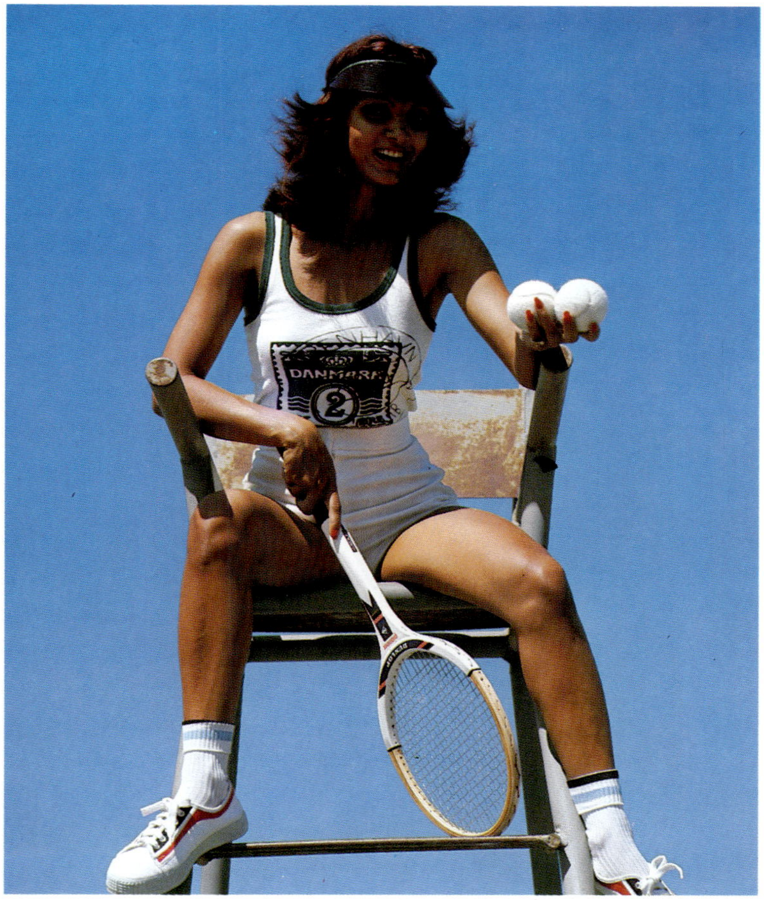
DANMARK
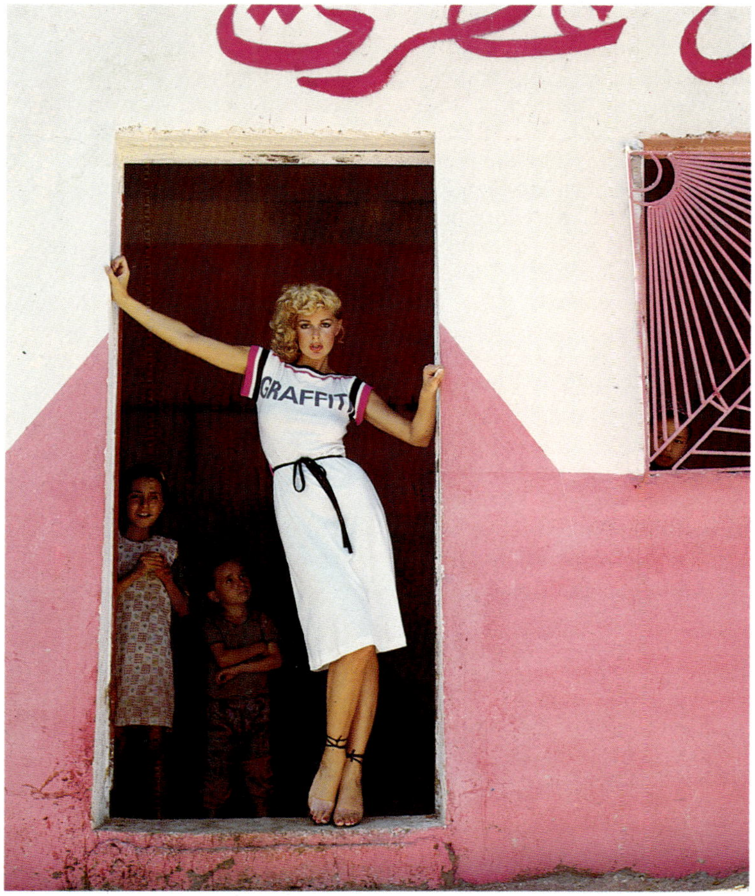
GRAFFIT
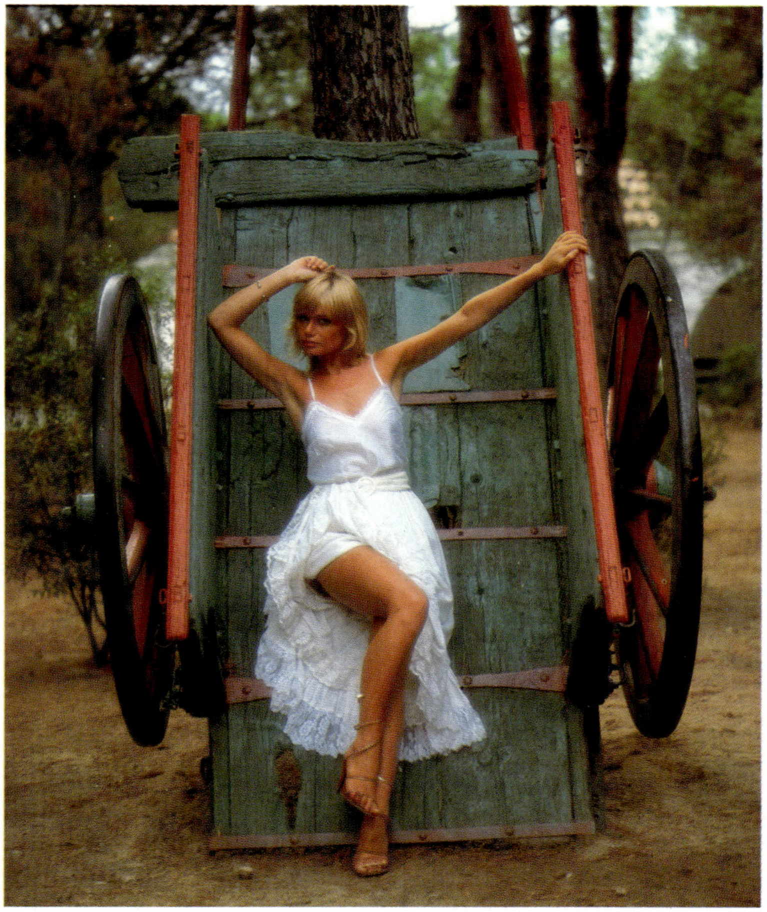
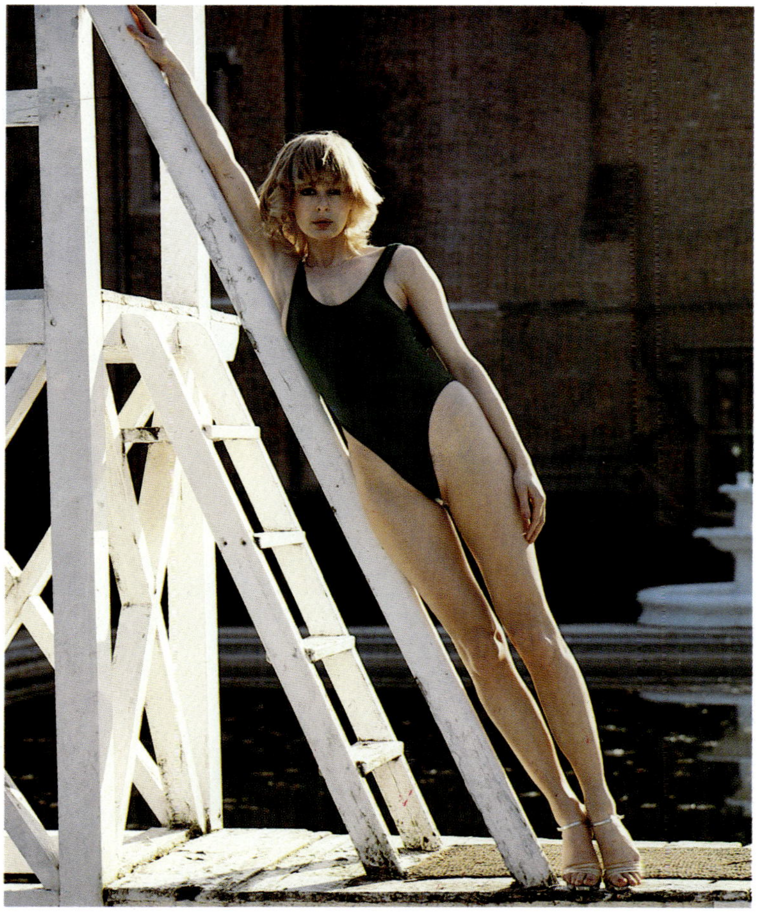

THE ROMANTIC IMAGE

EROTIC

These fall into two camps, the pictures suggesting innocence (or mock-innocence), and the pin-up type. The former is essentially a variation on the pastoral theme, and owes much of its appeal to the fantasy of perfection: if the model showed her awareness of being photographed, the picture would lose its appeal. Instead, they present a unique blend of innocence and availability, and pander to the Cider with Rosie myth of youthful sexual experience in idyllic surroundings – a myth so widely propagated that many people forget the terrors and delights of their own actual experience.

The pin-ups are equally concerned with perfection, but here the settings are much more explicit: luxurious boudoirs, fur rugs, velvet sofas. Here, it is not so much the sexual experience which is fantasised as the beauty of the partner and the luxury of the surroundings.

Either type relies heavily on everything being right, with no dissonant elements. The innocent-looking girl, for example, may be permitted an attractive scratch as if from a thorn – but a spot, a much likelier phenomenon on the average adolescent girl, would be anathema. Again, her clothes must be fitting for a young girl: we do not expect to see her in satin underwear, but in cotton or something similar. Similarly, the adult pin-up must be free from bodily blemish (and the air-brush may be called in to ensure this, as described later) and the surroundings must be free from the paraphernalia which might well be found in real life – empty coffee cups, tissues, etc. Failure to observe these conventions can turn an attractive and more-or-less erotic picture into something little better than pornography.

Hammocks; picnics; rustic *bridges; riverside scenes; pavement cafes; bicycles. In a sense the very subjects are clichés – but they represent something we can all relate to, and if photographed with impeccable attention to detail are almost always attractive.*

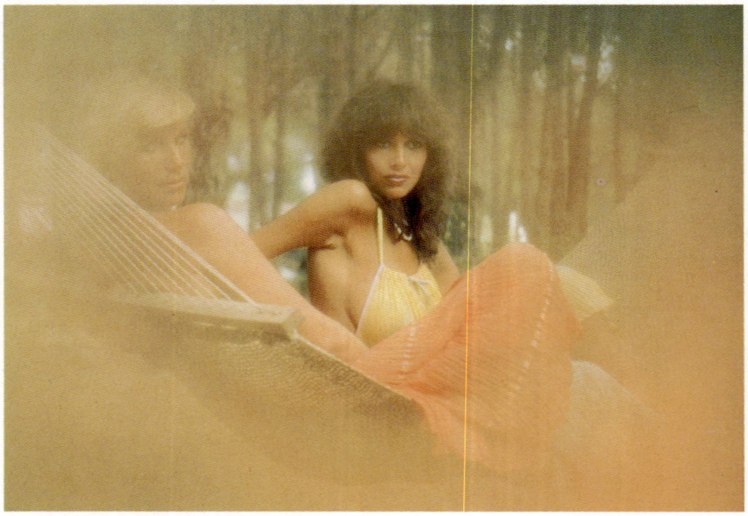

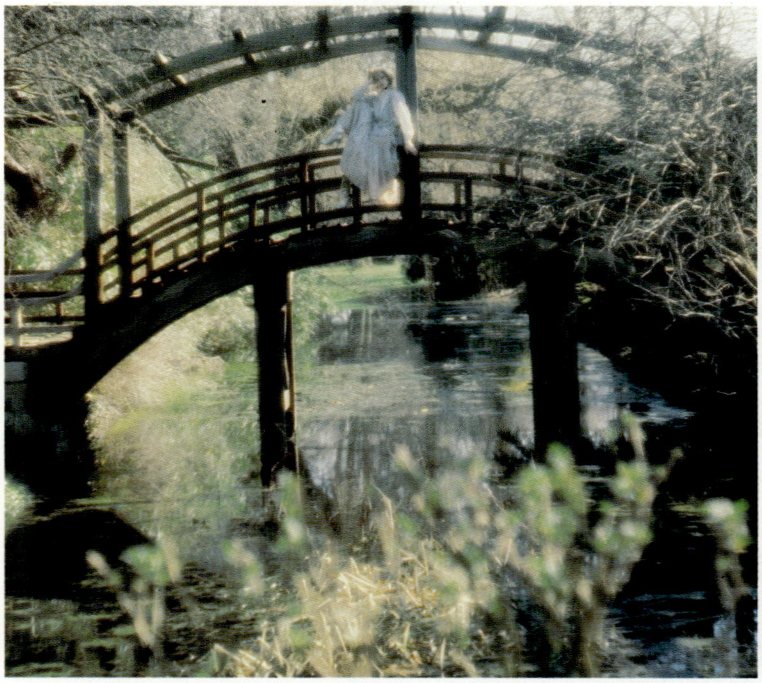

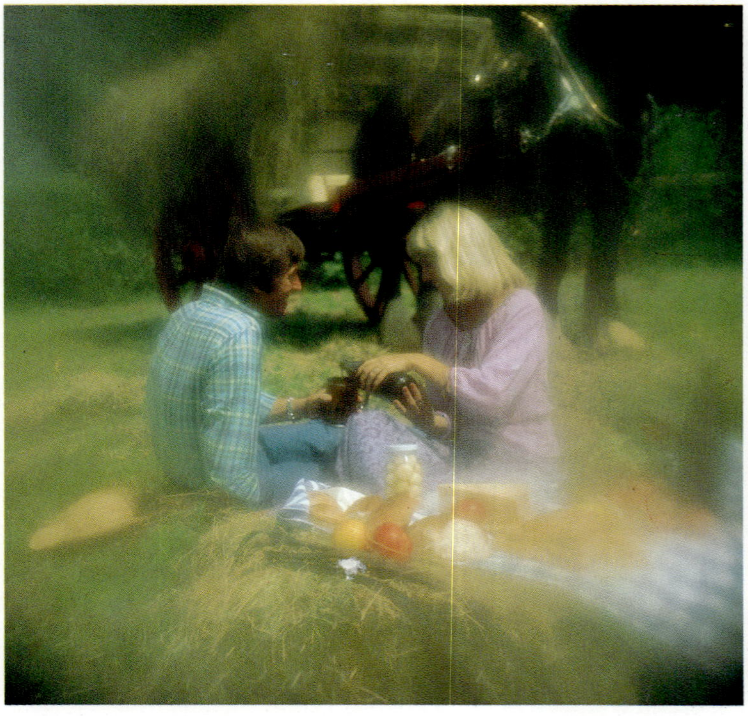

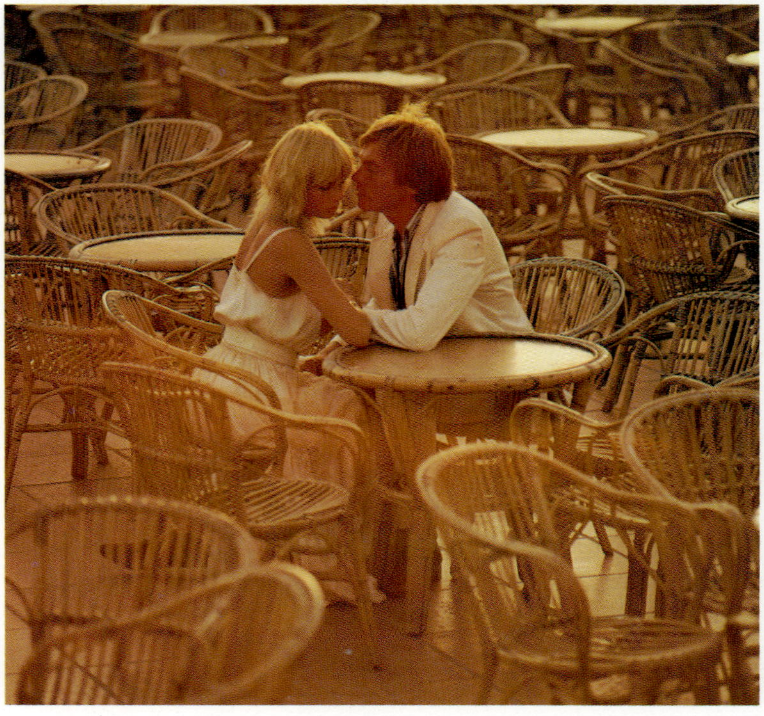

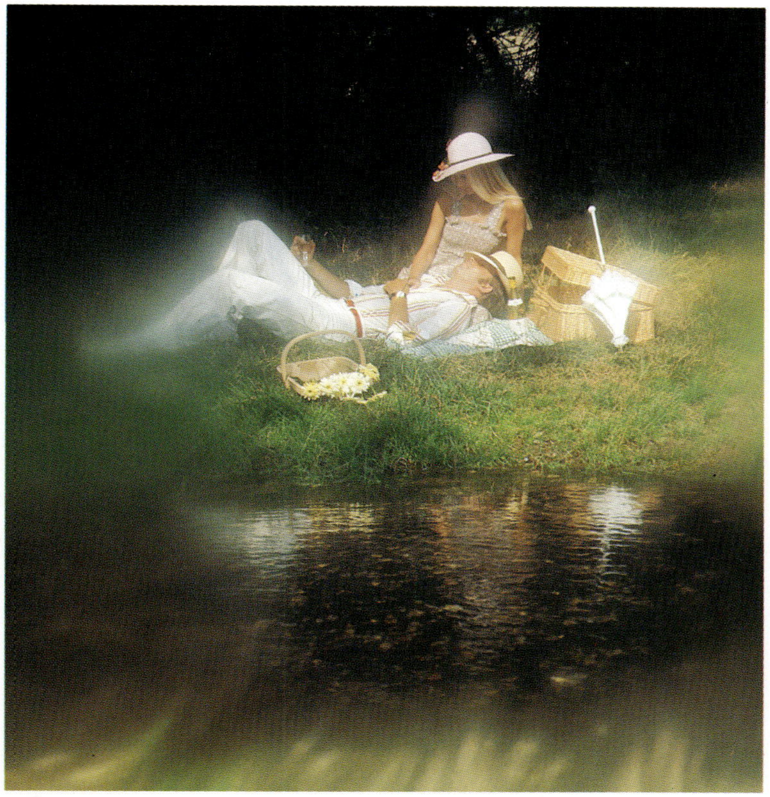

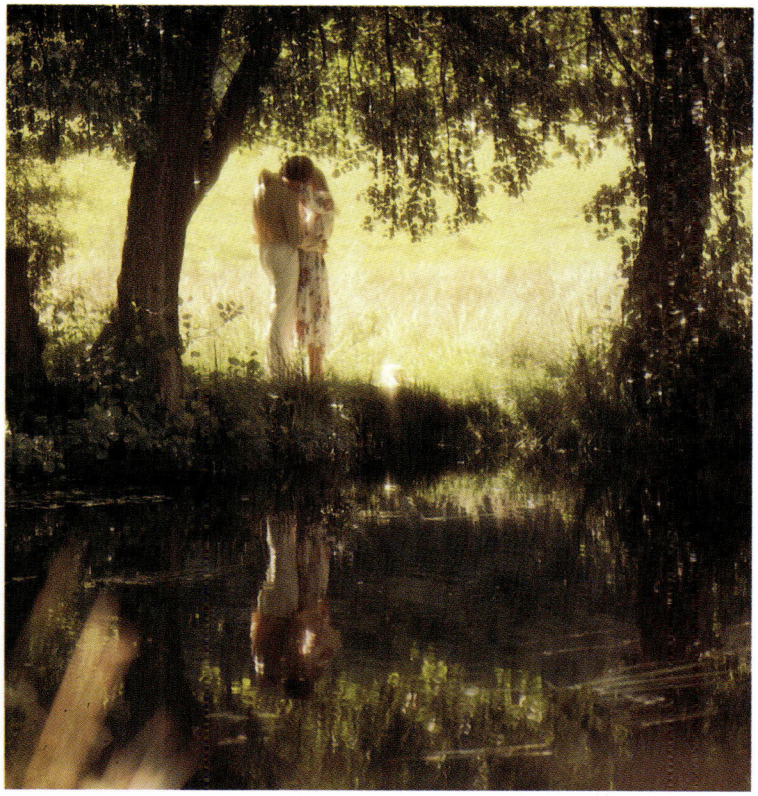

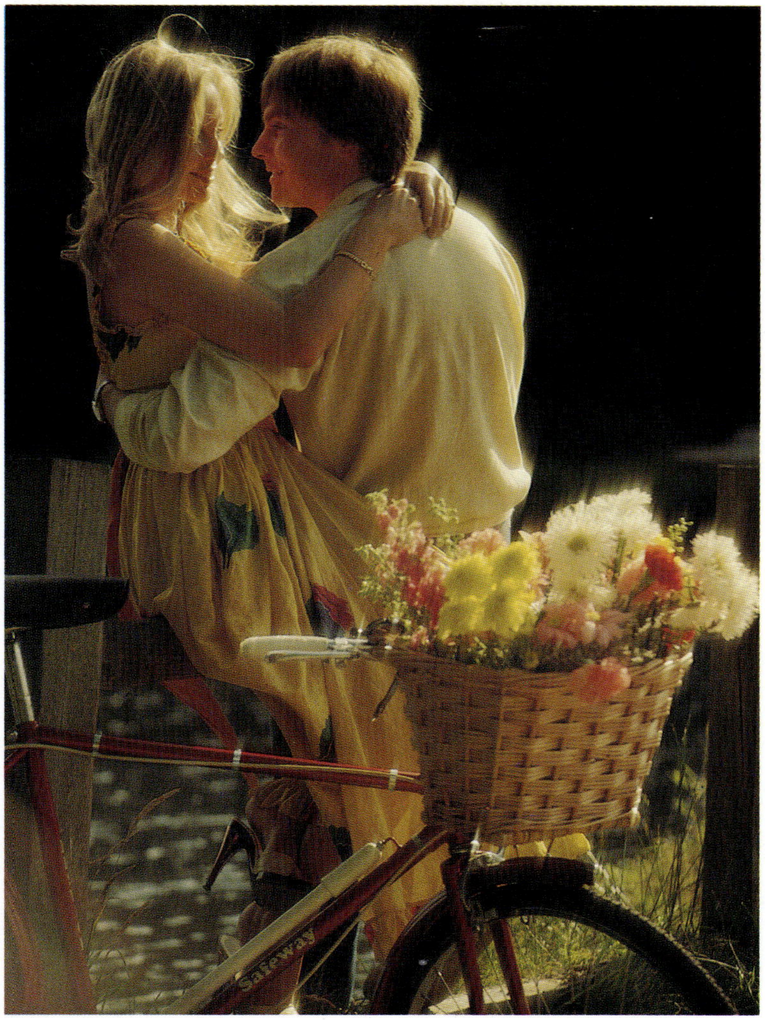

NOSTALGIC

The past which these pictures purport to recreate is more often imaginary than real; it shares this characteristic with both the pastoral and the erotic picture. This has the inevitable implication that the whole effect is carefully considered: once again, no untoward elements are allowed to intrude – and the photographer must also be on his guard for anachronisms, such as a modern wristwatch, or a car or power pylon in the background. When such pictures are produced professionally, it is usual to hire models who look the part; each era has its own standards of beauty, and the girl who is attractive today would not necessarily make an Edwardian beauty or even a 1920s flapper. The same, of course, applies to men – though people are often a lot less careful to be accurate in this case.

Although both technique (usually soft, faded colours) and subject must be right, there is a third matter which must be considered: composition and posing. People nowadays sit in a different way from the past – we are more relaxed, more used to soft furnishings and warm rooms, and less inhibited. Similarly, we are much more open to unusual composition in a photograph, whereas a real Edwardian photographer would have been more accustomed to shooting to a set formula. The only way to get a feeling for pose and composition is to look through old pictures, in books and magazines, as much as possible. Of course, there will be little colour (though Autochromes were available in 1907), but surprisingly enough we can get away with more latitude here, provided we stick to the conventions which seem to have grown up of their own accord – principally, little contrast and rather faded colours, easily achieved by means of slight (half-stop) overexposure and perhaps a fog filter – or in any case, no lens-hood and a flare-prone lens. An old zoom, the worst available, can be very suitable, and a further note of realism can be injected by using very long exposures – at least ⅛ second – with the camera on a tripod. Needless to say, slow films are the most useful here, or you can use an ND (neutral density) filter, or even a polarising filter carefully set not to reduce reflections.

LANDSCAPES

Landscapes are an extremely traditional and extremely personal type of photography. Depending on the location, the scale, and the time of year, the range of colour can be almost monochromatic, or downright riotous. The mood can be massive, looming, and foreboding; sunny, summery, and airy; sun-baked and oppressive; soft, rain-soaked and romantic; or a succession of receding planes, like a Chinese painting.

Landscapes are also extremely difficult. Less than any other subject do they lend themselves to the casual snapshot or the record shot. That vast panorama, which looked so impressive in real life, is nothing but a grey-blue smudge topped with a vast amount of sky when it is reduced to the size of a transparency; and that beautiful shoreline is recorded as a thin, uninteresting line between the grey-blue of the water and the white of the sky.

With the exception of deep blue skies or massively spectacular cloud formations, skies on colour print film are pretty much a disaster unless you print them yourself or have them custom-printed. The averaging system used in machine printing reduces them to nothingness. The serious colour landscape photographer will, therefore, normally use colour slide film.

Furthermore, because landscape photography is something of a contemplative pastime (as fishing is alleged to be by its adherents), it is often as well to use a camera which promotes a contemplative frame of mind; most people find that the ground-glass of a reflex (without a pentaprism) or even a view camera has this effect. To be sure, there are masters like Yoshikazu Shirakawa who work quickly with big Pentaxes and the like, but whilst one is still apprenticed to the craft it is generally true to say

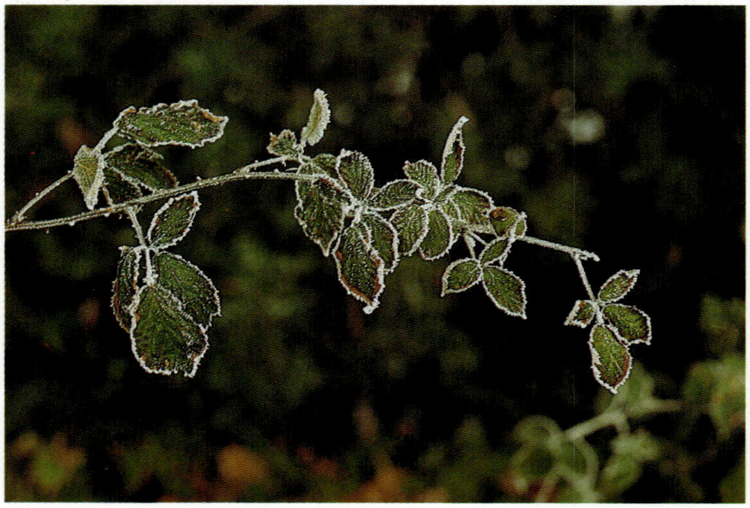

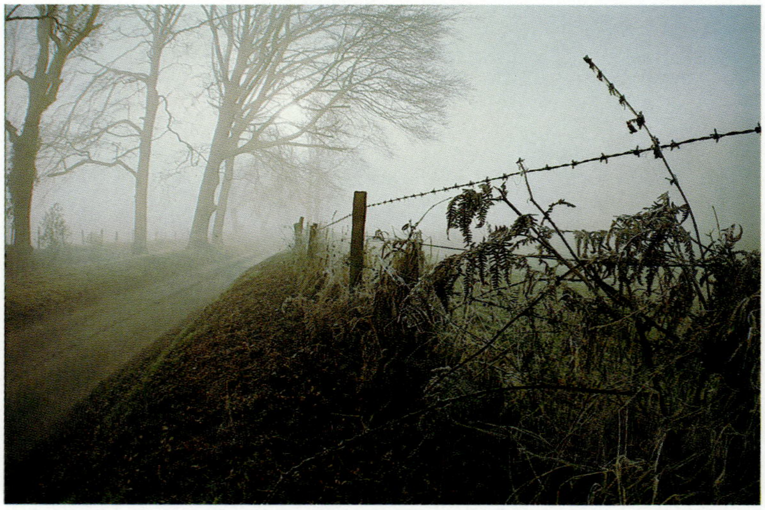

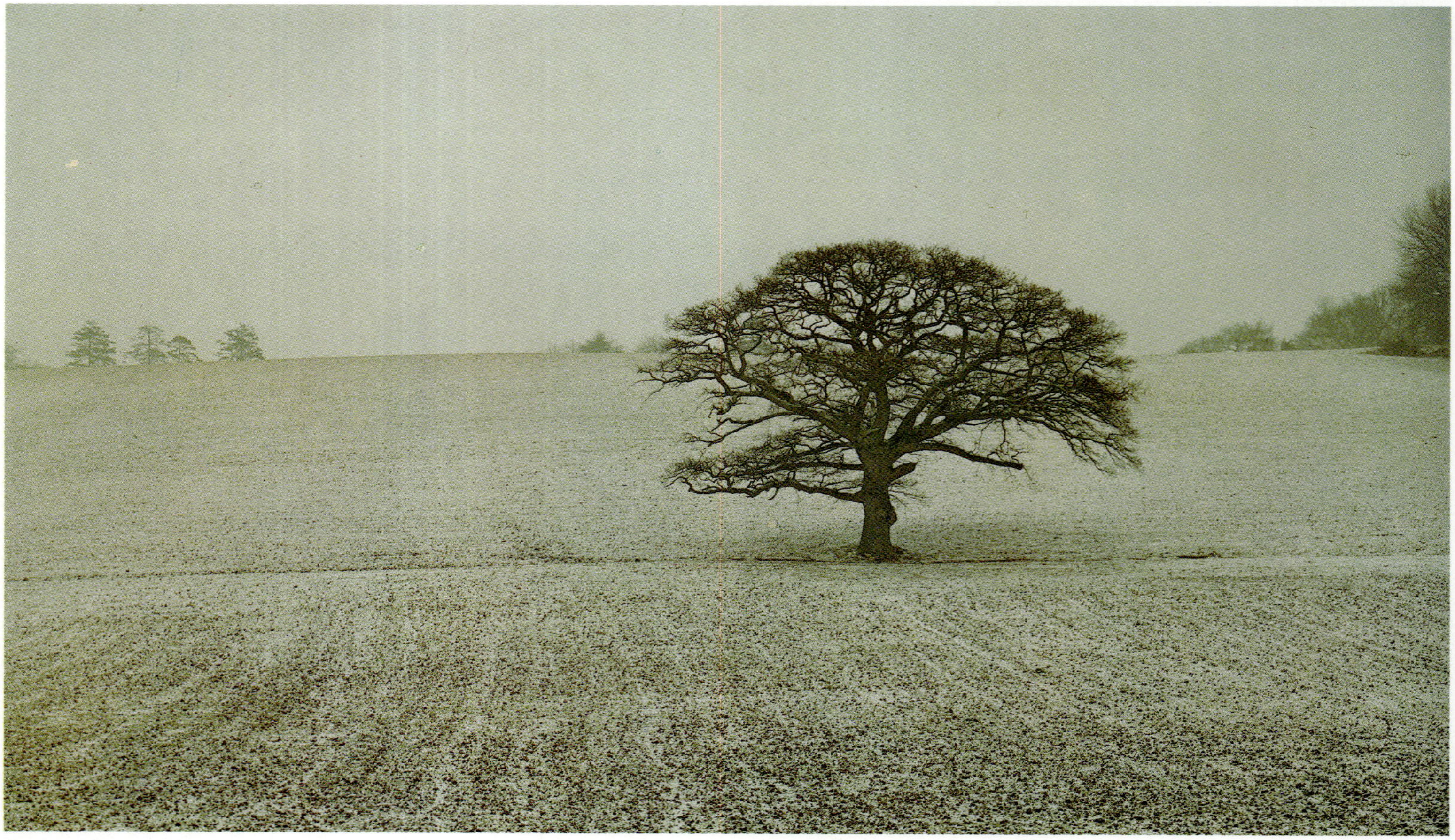

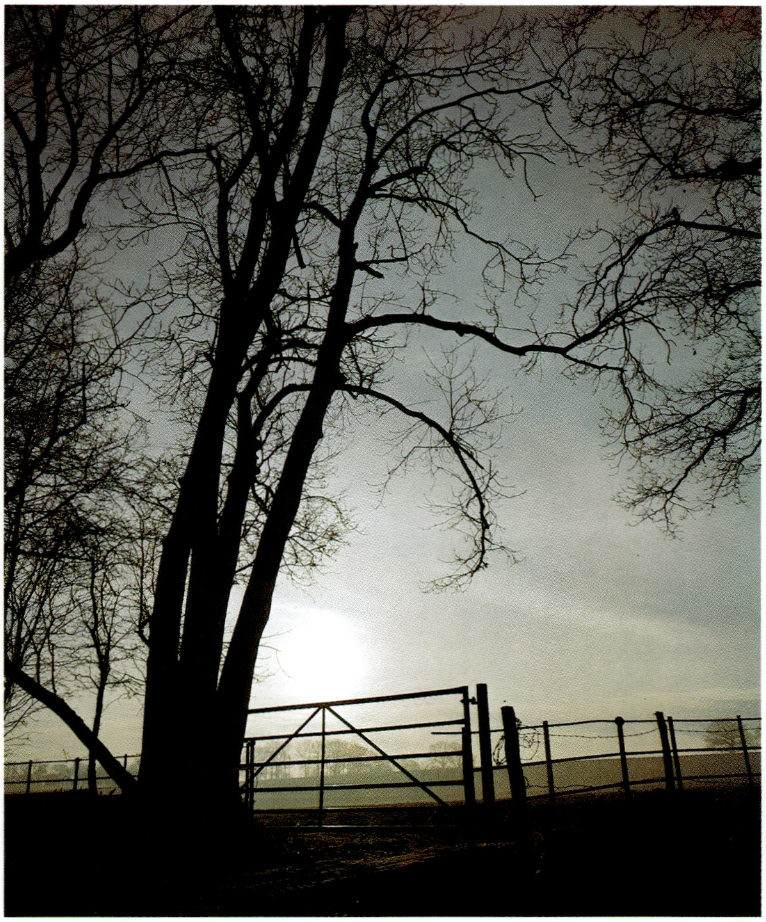

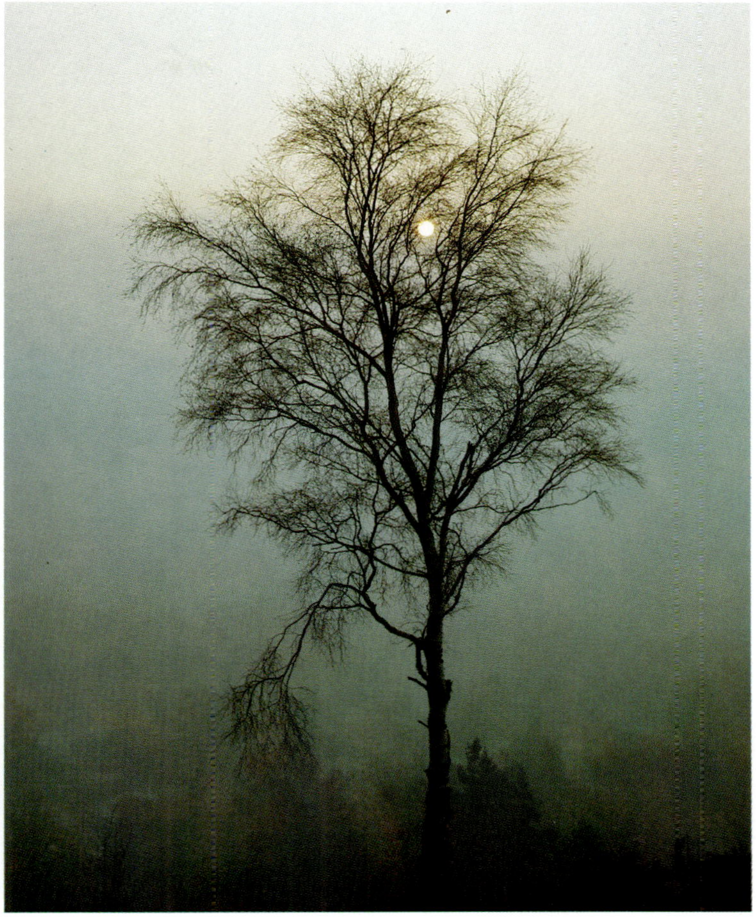

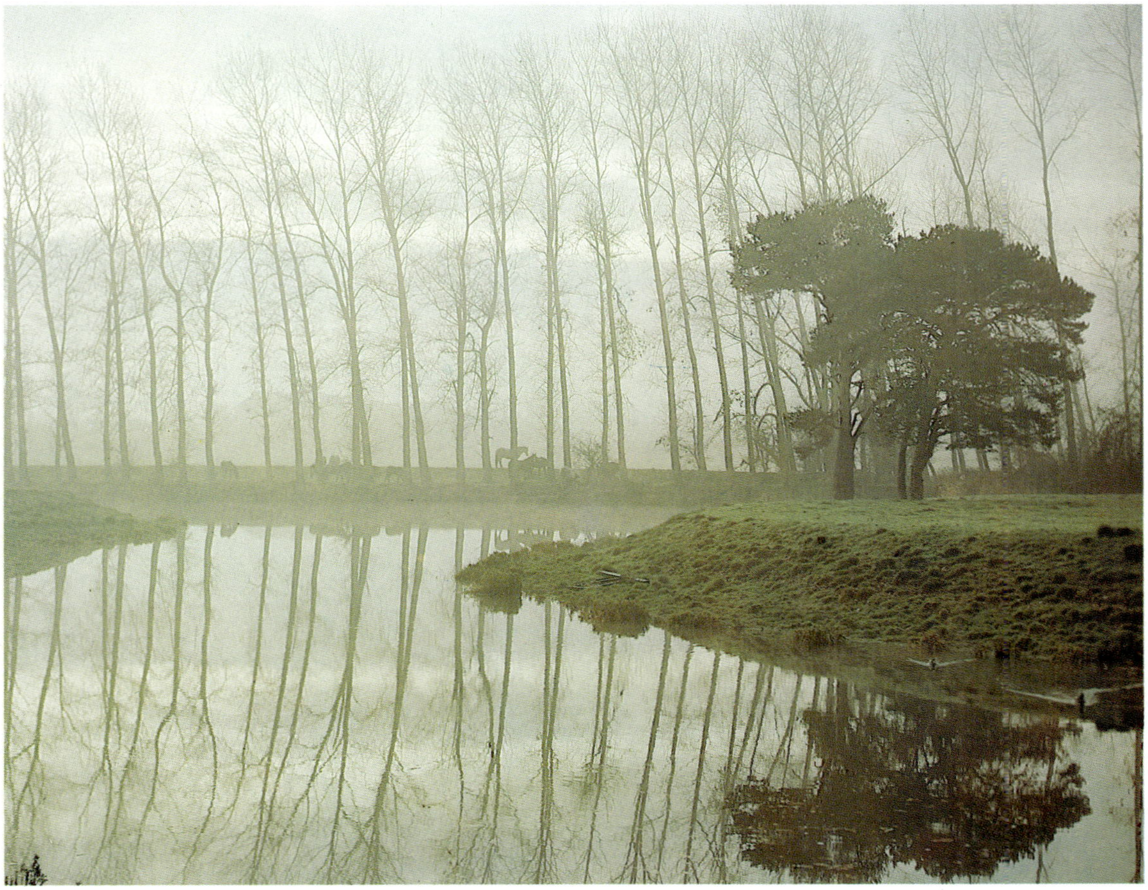

Almost all serious landscape *photographers gravitate sooner or later to medium or large format, with 4 x 5" the acknowledged leader. It is not a question of the equipment making them better photographers; rather, it is that the best landscape photographers, the ones who care the most about landscape, buy the most suitable tools. It is possible, though, to get similar results by using 35mm like a large format camera. First, use fine-grained film: Kodachrome for preference. Secondly, always use a tripod. Thirdly, make each exposure count. Walk around until you have exactly the right viewpoint: select the right lens: meter carefully: compose unhurriedly. 'Machine gunning' very rarely works. As may be seen from these pictures and those which follow, the noonday sun is best left to mad dogs and Englishmen. Here, mist, dawn, and frost have all been used for their own special contribution.*

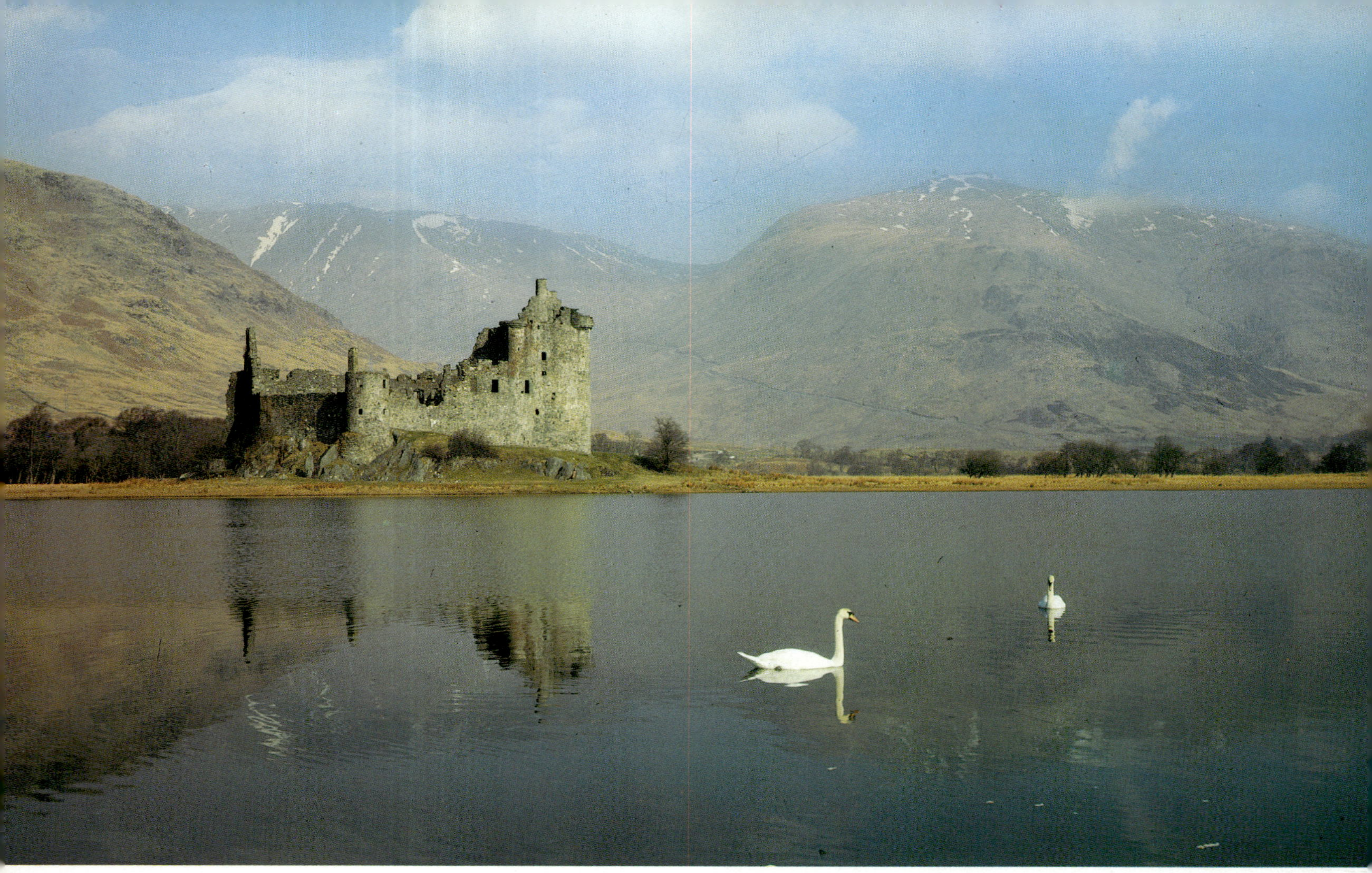

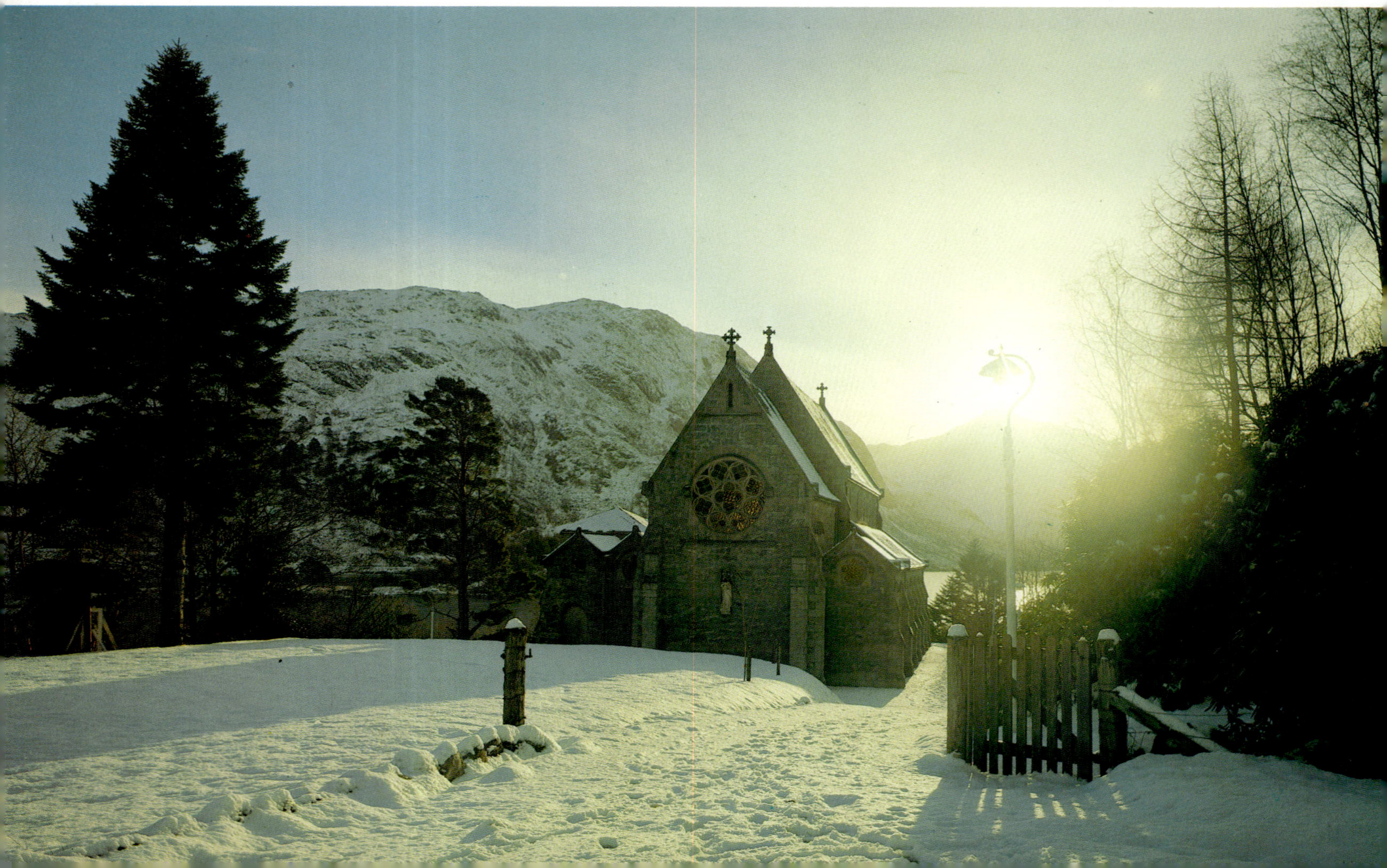

that an ounce of forethought is worth a pound of snapshots.

Big transparencies also have their advantages. It is easier to study the relatively expansive screen of a medium- or large-format camera rather than the tiny jewel-like image of a 35mm camera. Even more important, the bigger picture seems better able to capture the subtle gradations which characterise some landscapes, and the vivid interactions and interfaces of colour which characterise others. Some landscape photographers use old folding cameras, taking eight 2¼ x 3¼" pictures on 120 film: the viewfinders may not amount to much, but the amount of information on the negative is impressive. These are particularly favoured by those who use negative film and do their own printing.

Finally, on the equipment front, a tripod is a useful accessory. Once again, it promotes the contemplative aspect of the process, and it also gives a feeling of occasion. Whilst some photographers would decry this, many agree that the landscape is something you have to measure up to; a mediocre photographer cannot reduce it to his own scale as he could (say) a portrait or a nude. Either he succeeds, or he fails utterly.

After this, it is a matter of the kind of landscape which you want to take.

To begin with, the detail is a good place to start; a single cottage, surrounded by hills, perhaps. Even a patch of flowers, or a ruined shepherd's hut, can be a successful picture. It allows you

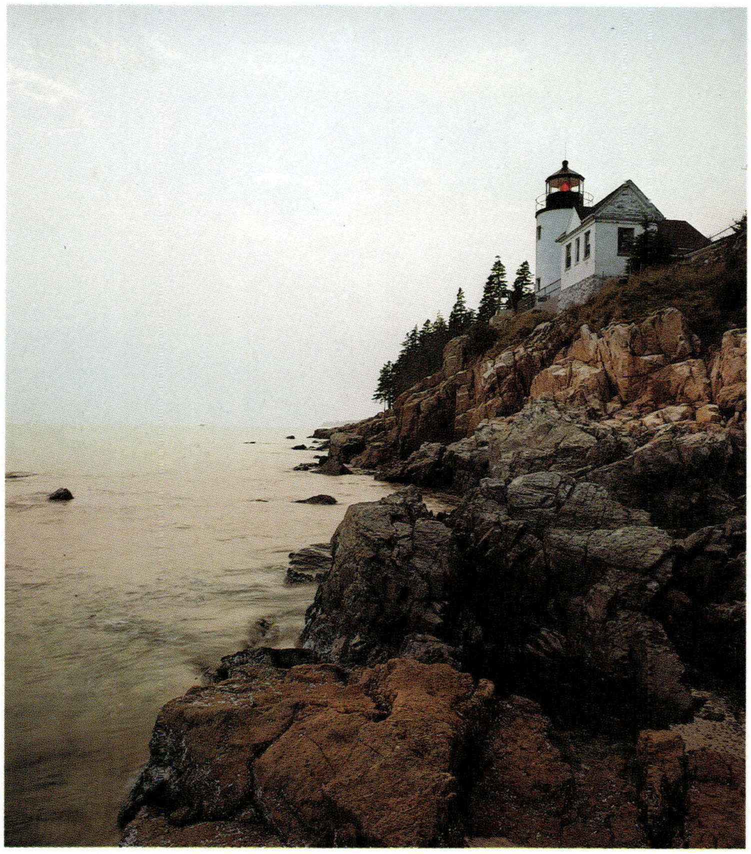

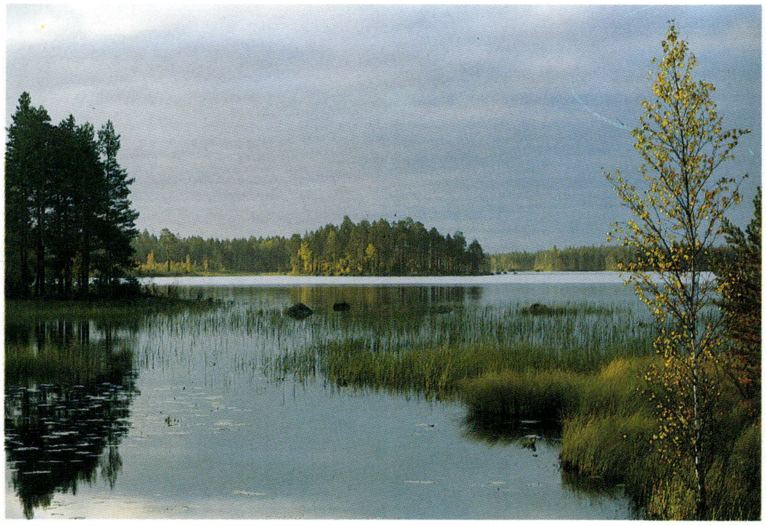

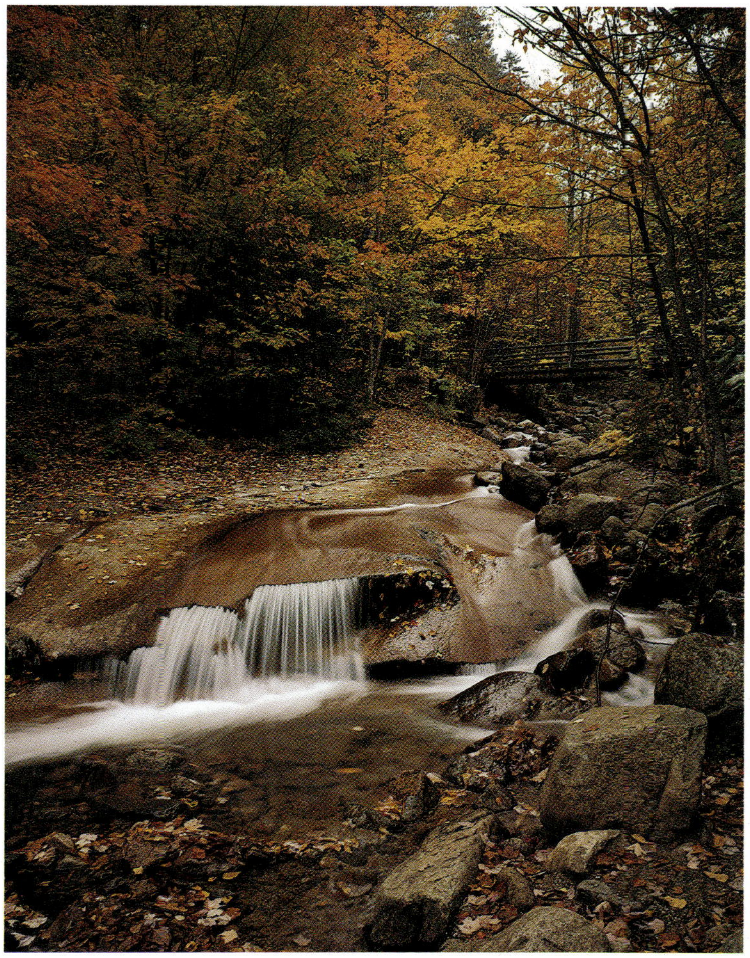

The only way to get the swans *where they were needed,* ***facing page top,*** *was to wait; the only way to photograph the church at dawn was to get up early.*

Attention to detail, and a willingness to work for a picture, are evident in all the pictures on this page.

to concentrate on form, on the overall shape of the picture (remember earlier remarks on composition), and encourages you to watch out for dissonant areas of colour. A good trick here is to examine the out-of-focus image, which subjugates form to colour. Furthermore, with a detail it is harder to fall into the classic trap which awaits the novice landscape photographer: no main subject.

After you have mastered the close-up detail, you can begin to take more and more in. For close-ups, a standard lens is frequently ideal. After that, landscape photographers begin to split into two groups: those who advocate wide-angle lenses (to capture the sweep of the landscape all around) and those who believe that they can better control their image by using a longer-focus lens to select what strikes their eye.

LANDSCAPES

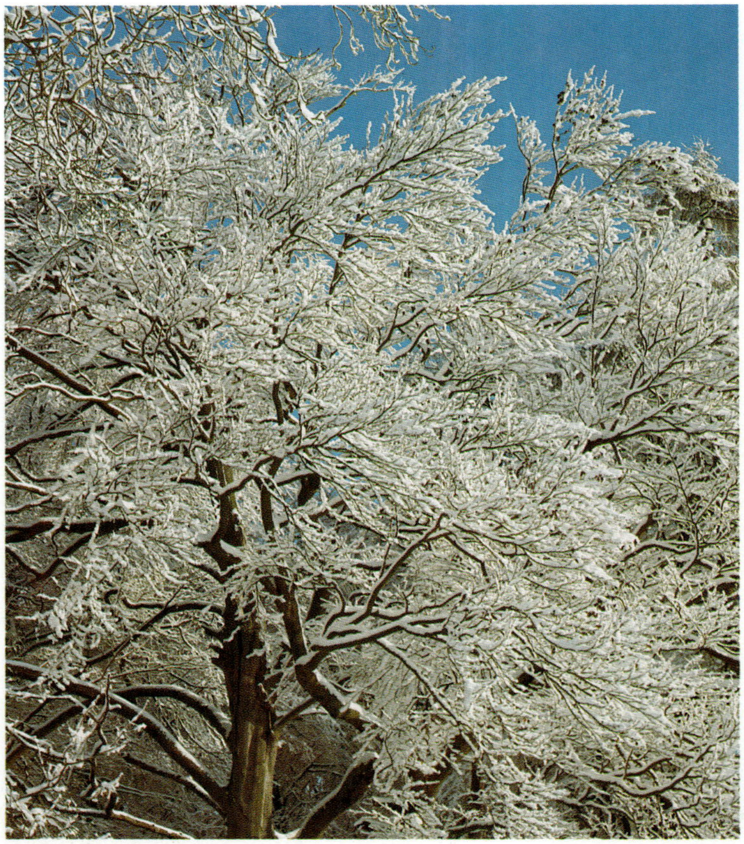

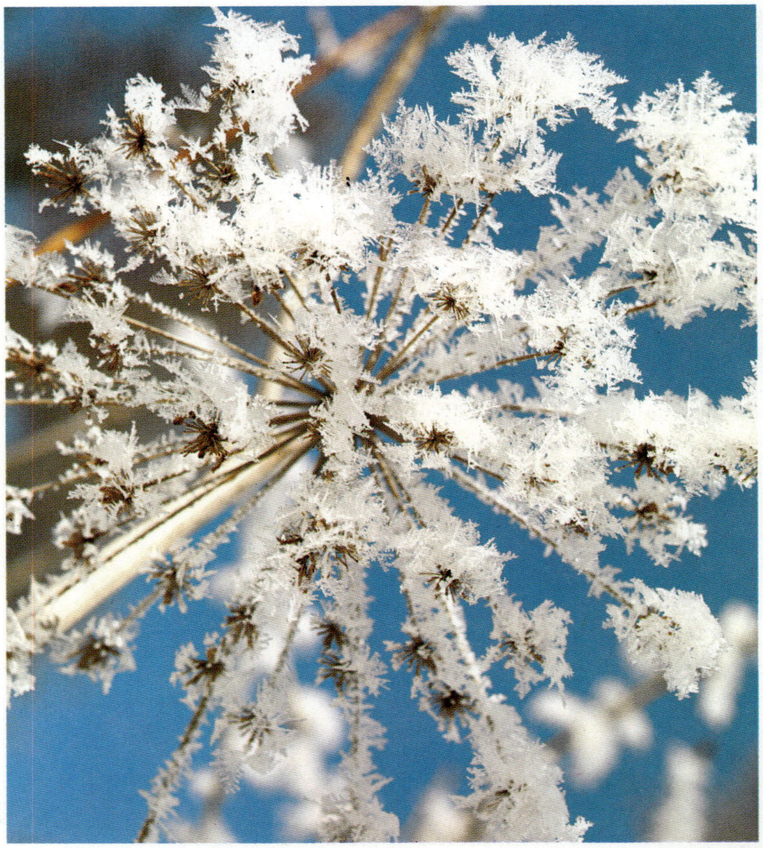

A 5 x 4" camera was essential *to capture all the wealth of detail in the snow scene on the right; carrying camera and tripod on a winter's morning was not easy, but the results justify it.*

Neither view is in itself 'correct'; the most that can be said is that the choice of lens depends about equally on the terrain and the photographer. In the mountains, the long-focus approach is frequently all but essential. Otherwise, a picture taken across a valley may be utterly unimpressive – though, of course, if the mountains are big enough, or the photographer chooses his viewpoint carefully enough, even a wide angle would be perfectly suitable. For views of rolling countryside, or pictures with a strong foreground and an extensive background, then a wide angle may well be more appropriate.

It is when you begin to tackle the larger subjects that you begin to appreciate the importance of knowing your countryside, as well as just loving it. For many years, for example, I have been fascinated by the white china-clay mines and waste dumps in Cornwall, my native land. I always promised myself that I would photograph them; but when I came to try it, I found it vastly more difficult than I had expected. There were too many greys, and browns; the white I had in my head hardly existed. As I explored, though, I came to realise that my memory was not really at fault: there are white roads, and white rivers, and a fresh dump is glistening white, but I had been going to old and disused dumps. I also began to appreciate the other colours: the deep milky blue of the water in a pit, reflecting a summer's sky; the sage-green of the hardy plants colonising the old dumps; the battered, rusty kettles; the lorries in enveloping clouds of blue-white dust.

There have been other places, too. The wild rough scenery of Big Sur is another thing I want to photograph – but I hardly know where to begin. The ominous darkness of Dozmary Pool, where the giant Tregagle roars, and where no sensible Cornishman would go at night; the creeks of northern California, so like the lochs of Scotland; the incredible Renaissance jumble of Valetta, the 'city built by gentlemen for gentlemen' after the Great Siege, or the Moorish dignity of Mdina, the old capital of Malta which it replaced. It takes time.

As with many other aspects of photography, the landscape makes two demands which are not immediately apparent. The first is that you should be interested in – even in love with – your subject for its own sake: the casual photographer will very rarely equal the man of passion. And the second is time, a lot of time. When I first read the works of Ansel Adams I was struck dumb by the pictures, but almost dismissed the text: I wrote in my journal, "You too can take pictures like Ansel Adams if you are prepared to spend three weeks on each exposure." I now realise that I underestimated: three months or even three years might not be unusual (though you can always do something else in the meantime), and the investment is worth it. The fact that we can capture the picture in a fraction of a second, and even that metering the Ansel Adams way takes a minute or two, blinds us to the question of when that fraction of a second should be. It is rather like some of the more demanding Zen Buddhist practices: perfect inaction, then (at the appropriate time) perfect action. You see why I say landscape photography is a contemplative exercise!

This does not mean, of course, that there is no place for the record shot; but this can only be an *aide-memoire,* and not a creative picture in its own right. It can act as a spur to drive you back again and again until you have the picture you want – but you should not exhibit it as a work of art unless that curious inner voice tells you that it is. Unfortunately, the landscape has been easy meat for the talker and theorist, and the most incredibly tedious pictures have been explained away as art. The simple guide is always the same: 'I may not know much about landscape photography – but I know what I like!'

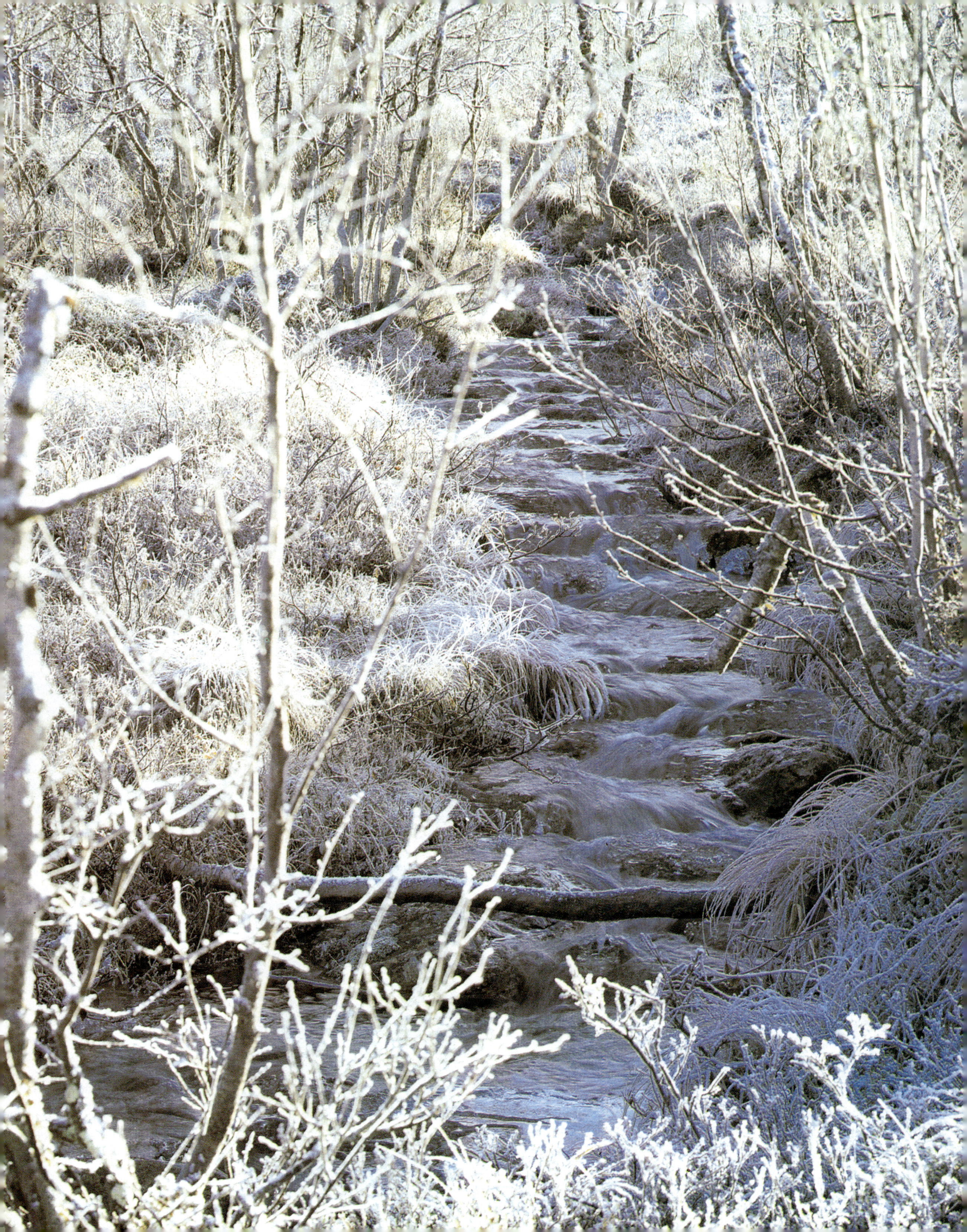

THE COLOUR OF THE CITY

Just as the traditional landscape deals with the colours of nature, so too does the city have its own colours. Because the city is, by definition, man-made, the colours reflect the tastes and fashions prevalent either when the city was built, or at the present.

First of all, there is the cityscape – a general view, in the same way as a landscape is a general view of the countryside. There are of course all the variations in light which are to be found in the country, but in most towns and cities the atmospheric haze which builds up during the day – the pollution, if you like – has also to be taken into account. To show some new office development pristine and sparkling, you would need to get up very early on a summer's morning; but equally, you might choose to use the evening's haze. You could use it, for example, to emphasise the cosiness of a village. I will never forget coming down into Okehampton, on Dartmoor, one winter's night. It was bitterly cold, and I was riding a motorcycle. The town lay in its valley, shrouded in coal-smoke. After the clear air of the moors, it was like breathing tar – but it was also a powerful symbol of the warmth available there, of the sense of being in an outpost in a fundamentally hostile environment.

There are many other ways in which you can match a picture to its lighting and atmosphere. For instance, a grey utilitarian town of the industrial revolution looks very different on a summer's day and on a grey misty winter's day. In the one, the red bricks can be warm and vibrant, projecting an atmosphere of welcome and comfort and the promise of hot tea in back-to-back houses, the hospitality of honest hard-working folk. In the other, the feeling is quite different: of the endless grind, the daily trudge to work, the ever-present threat of the dole queue. Other angles and other lights portray different aspects again: the centre of industry, lively and self-confident; the decaying industrial heartland, discarded as financial wizardry spins more profits than honest toil; the showpiece of modern town-planning; vandalism by architects.

There are also the people to consider in a cityscape. Like the light, they vary through the day. Early in the morning there will be few people; the odd cleaner or early deliveryman. A peak comes at the morning rush-hour, with people and cars packed close together, hurrying, eyes fixed straight ahead, impatient. Then, the normal working day; everyday comings and goings. At lunchtime, a chance to relax; this is when the pretty young secretaries are out buying clothes, the purchasing clerks are eating their sandwiches on the park benches, and harrassed singles are trying to do their shopping. Back to the comings and goings, then the afternoon rush-hour – but more relaxed now, without the deadline of the time-clock. This is the time to stop for a drink, or a bit of window-shopping. Finally, the evening, with night-life of various sorts, teenagers cruising in their cars, cinema queues, strip joints, bars . . . and all this slowly petering out, until the town is quiet again in the small hours of the morning, waiting for the circle to start again.

At night, of course, there are the lights of the city – and the effects vary enormously from twilight through to full darkness, with street lights, traffic lights, store illumination, office lights, advertising signs. These are more fully dealt with later.

Rather than using a wide-angle lens for general cityscapes, which might seem the obvious approach, a long-focus lens and a distant high-up viewpoint is often more effective. The perspective is compressed by the long-focus lens, which often emphasises the character of the city: in Stratford-upon-Avon it could mass together the Elizabethan buildings, or equally it could show the towers of downtown Los Angeles against their background of smog. Inevitably, a long-focus lens emphasises haze, so pictures will be moody rather than needle-sharp. The drawback of wide-angles is that it is very difficult to get a really interesting foreground: all too often, a potentially interesting cityscape is dominated by a large expanse of road or park – though in some cases (as always) this too can be effective.

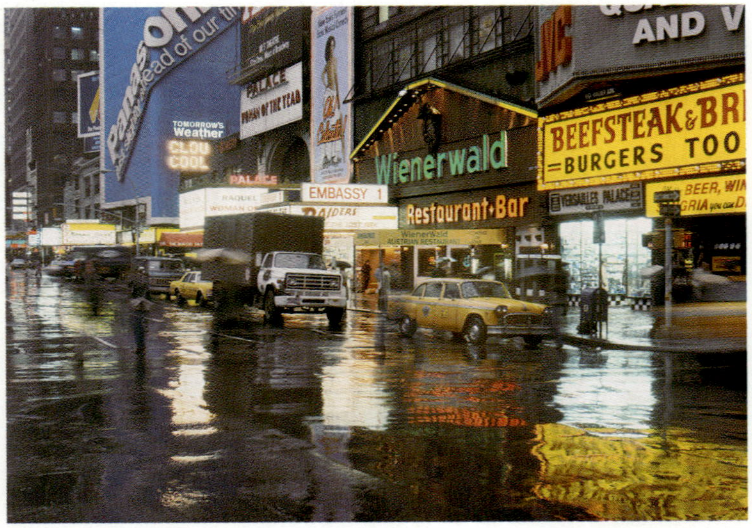

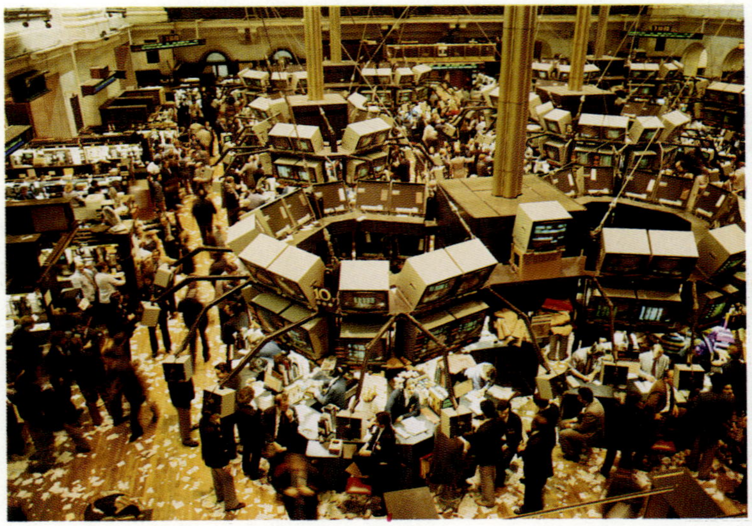

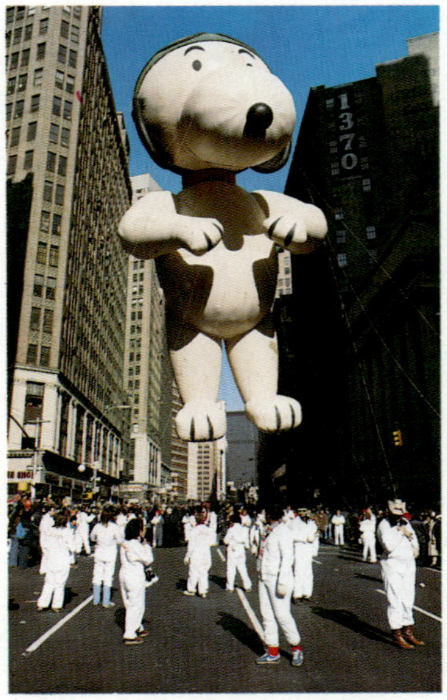

*Often, telling pictures of well-known sights can be made at night. Colours are more interesting, and the lights add an air of fantasy to a scene which might be quite dull in the daytime. Rainy streets can be turned to great advantage, too: the distorted reflections make a far more attractive foreground than an empty pavement. Try, also, to take the pictures which are special to **you**, the scenes where difficulty of access or sheer quirky coincidence mean that not many will see them. The Snoopy balloon always raises a smile, and the interior of the stock market has a bizarre quality to it.*

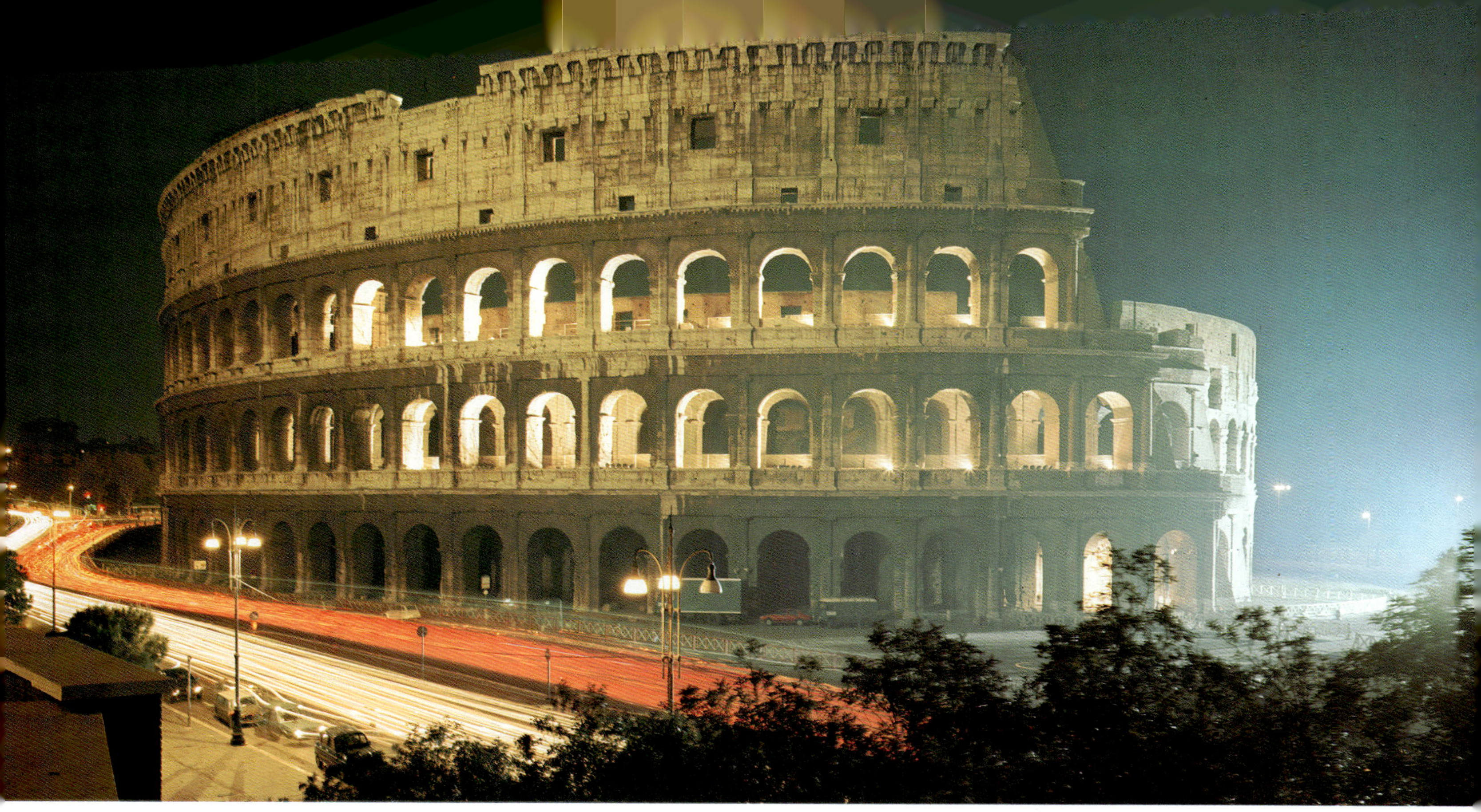

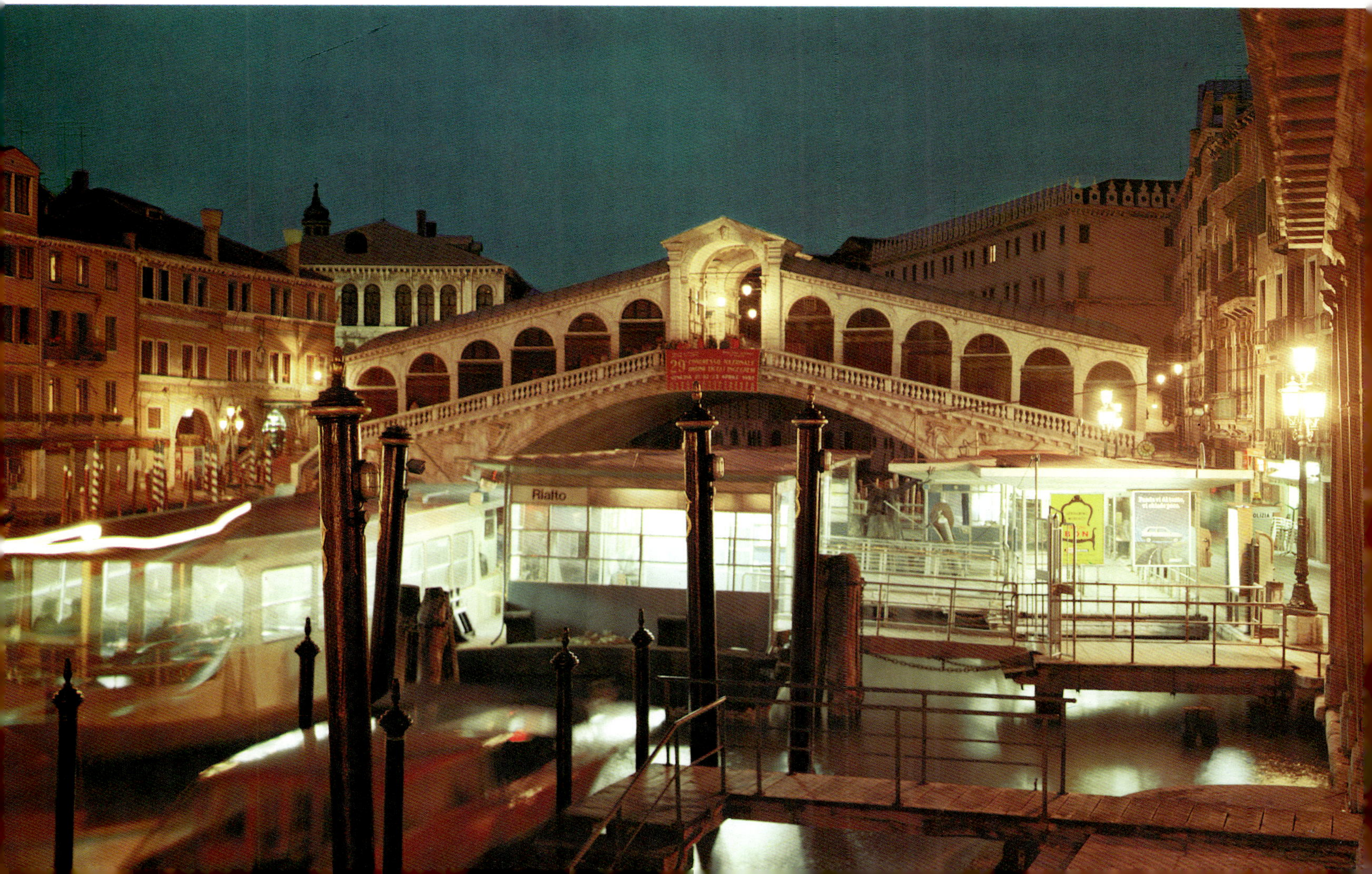
Rialto

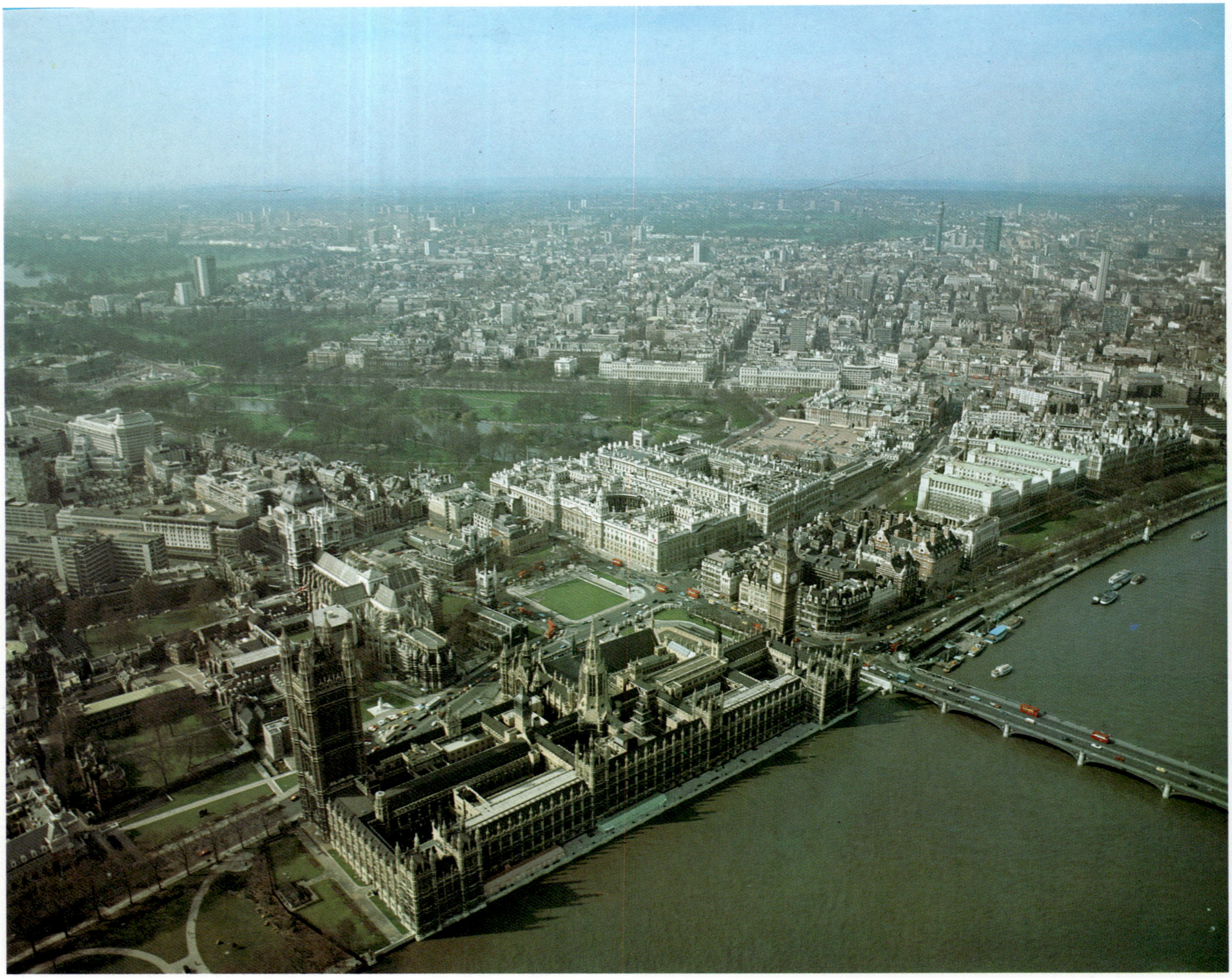

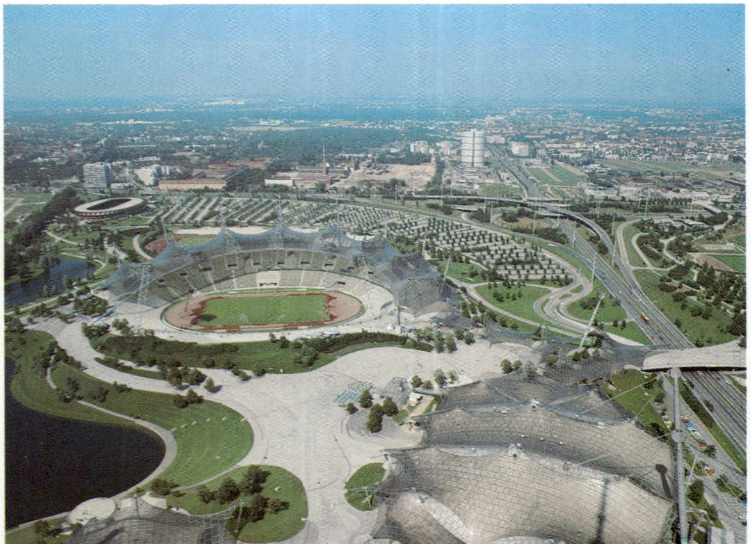

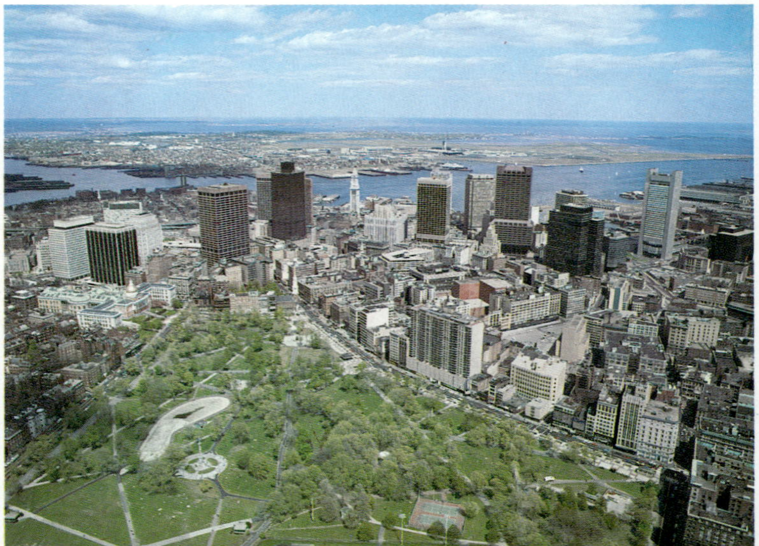

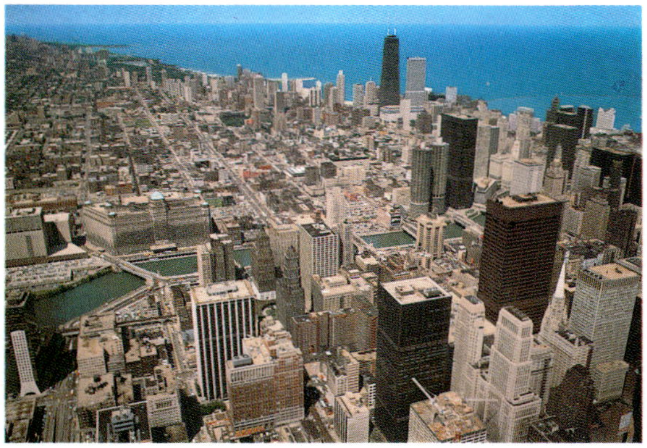

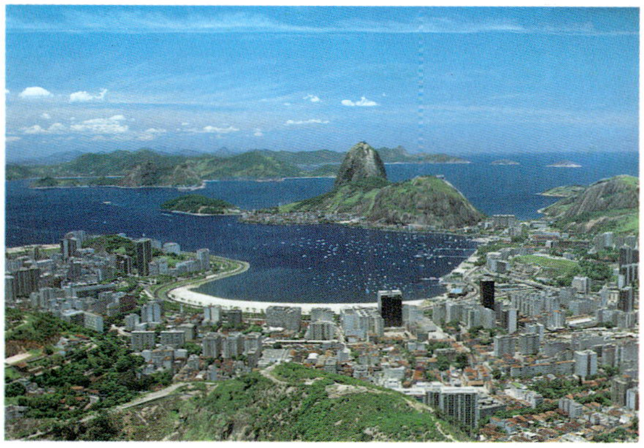

Aerial pictures may be beyond *the reach of most of us, though it is often possible to get surprisingly good pictures by holding the camera close to the window in an airliner as it is coming in to land, and cutting out reflections with a scarf or jacket. Do not hold the camera against the glass, though, as the vibration will cause blurring. Cut blue haze with an 81A filter.*

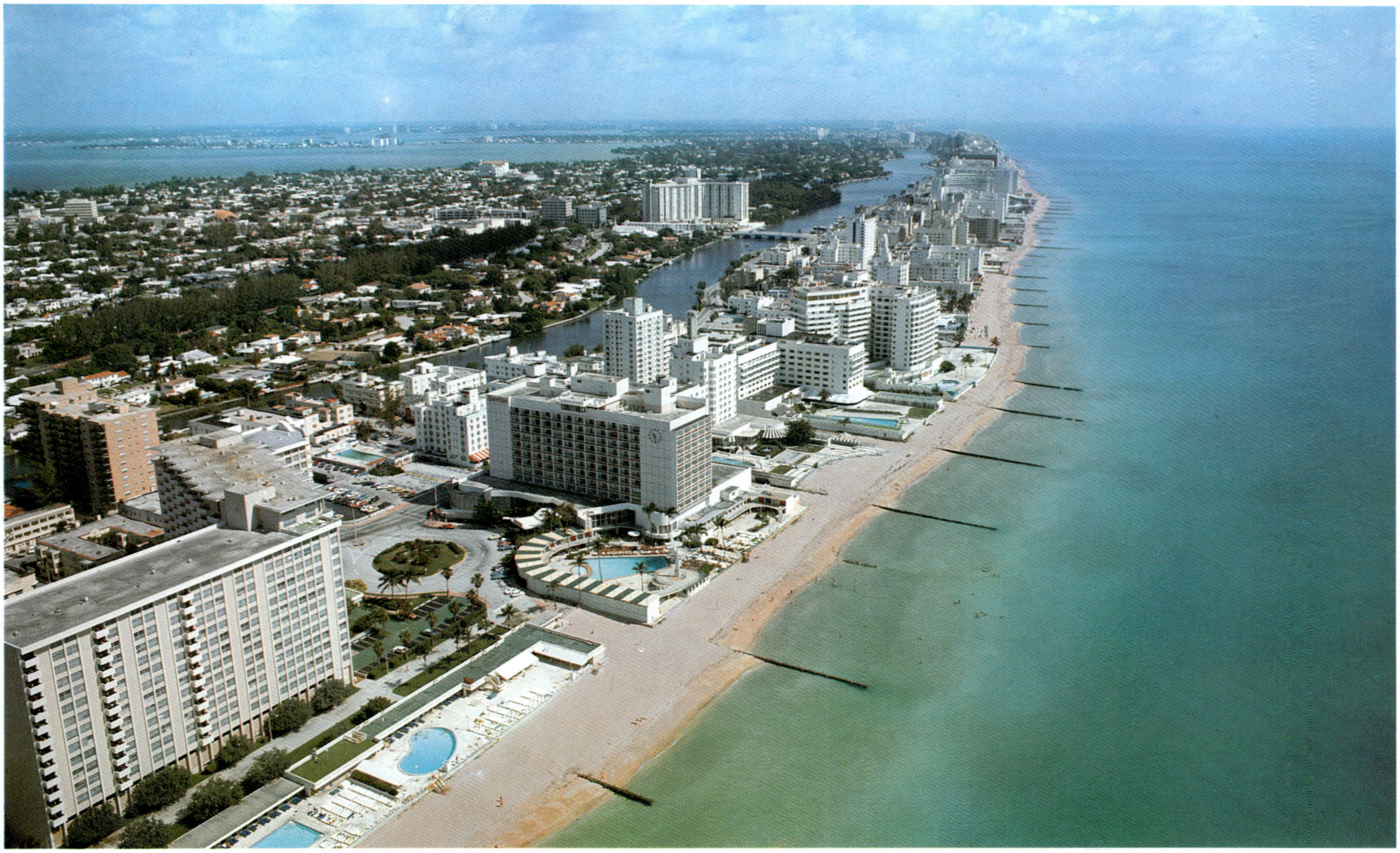

Instead of going for the broad sweep, you may decide to concentrate on details. These may be as large as a building a quarter of a mile high, or as small as a doorknocker.

In order to photograph buildings in the traditional manner – with strictly parallel sides, so as to avoid the 'falling over backwards' look which results from tilting the camera upwards, you need either a perspective control lens or a technical camera (or a higher viewpoint opposite the building!) – and given the price of most perspective control lenses, a second-hand technical camera could be a better bet. The alternatives are to use ultra-wide-angle lenses, and waste half the frame (not very practical with colour slide film) or to use the same wide-angles and tilt the camera very obviously, so that the 'falling over' perspective is quite clearly intentional. You are likely to end up with a lot of sky in such shots, so a polarising filter and a blue sky make for interesting colour.

The day on which you photograph a building can have an enormous effect on the final result. On a bright, sunny day the same building can be made to look cool and airy, or hot, sweaty, and unpleasant, or dank and shadowed. By choosing a misty day it can be made forbidding or familiar; on a rainy day, it might look threatening, or welcoming, or thoroughly wet and uncomfortable. Unless the person who is looking at the photograph knows the building, who is to argue? To accentuate the effect, filters can be invaluable – either subtle, such as the CC05B which gives a wintry tinge or an 81A to warm things up, or downright bold, like a vivid purple or cyan.

There are many details other than buildings, though. For example, you may choose to make bright, bold colour your sole criterion – in which case you are already more than half-way towards abstracts. Bright roadsigns, plastic delivery trays used by bakers, the vivid red-net bags so often used to contain cabbages

THE COLOUR OF THE CITY

Very tall buildings, such as** New York's World Trade Center, allow 'aerial' shots without an aeroplane. Often, though, much more interesting and creative shots can be made by selecting details or small cameos. The graphic simplicity of the bridge, **below,** defies all the 'rules' of composition, but its impact is considerable. A 5 x 4" camera captured the fine detail, but carefully used Kodachrome could give almost as impressive an effect. The fish-eye perspective **facing page bottom left,** has emphasised the closed-in, protected, feeling of the ice-rink, whilst meticulous attention to exposure and colour balance was needed to convey the opulence and elegance of the buffet scene **facing page top.

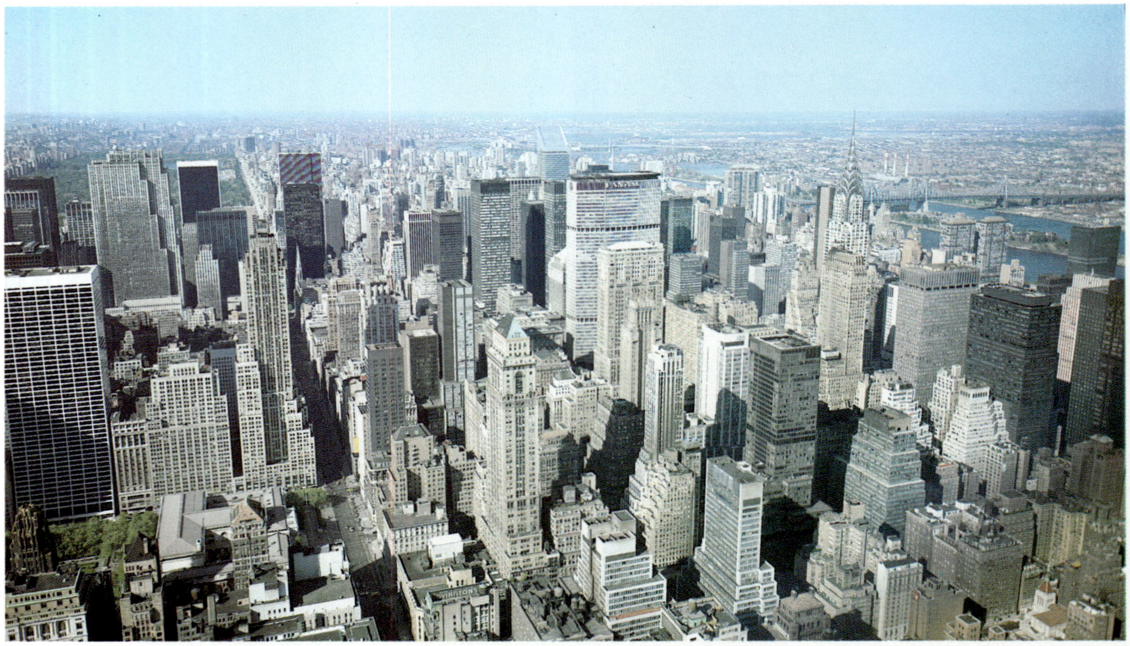

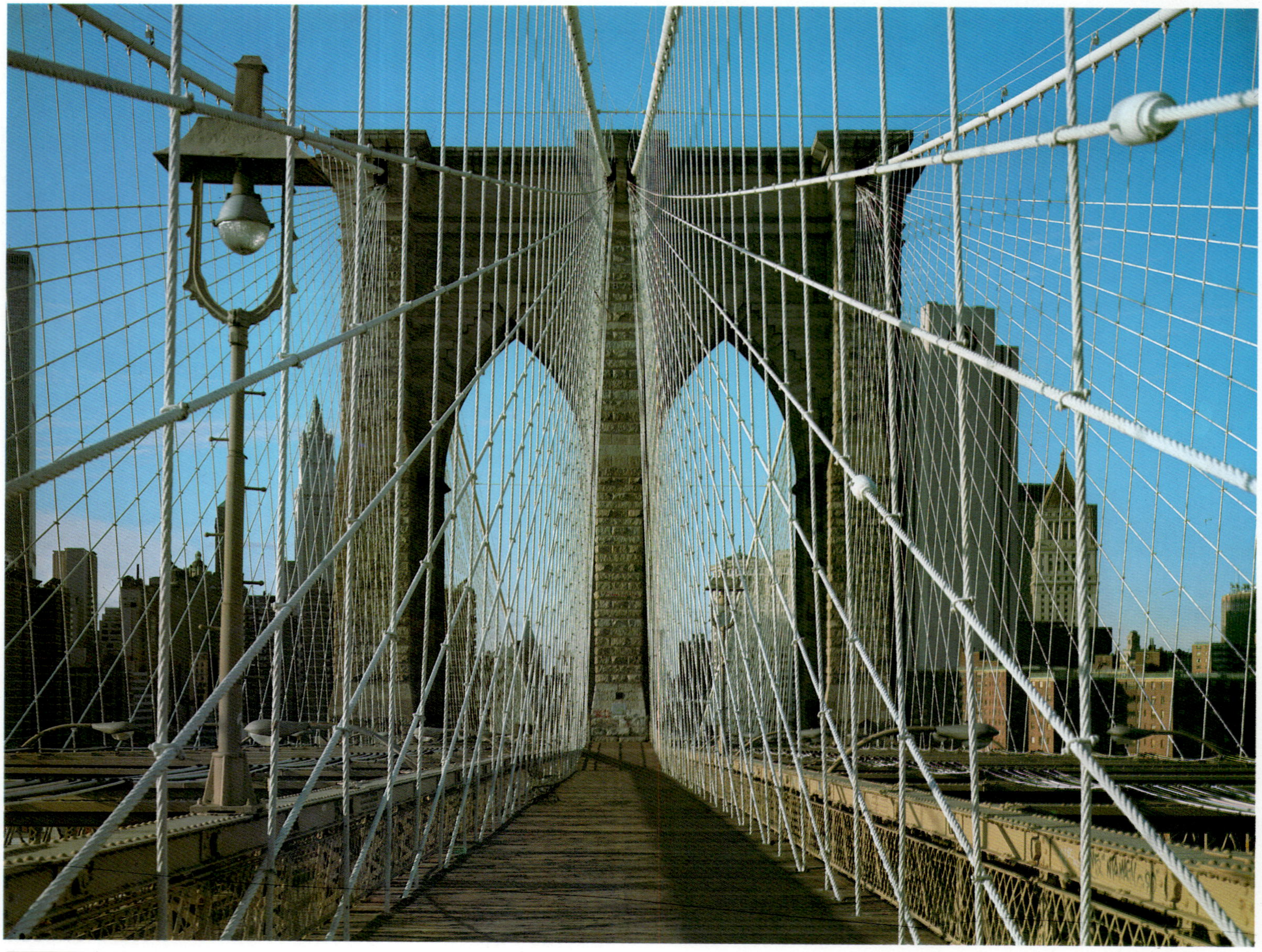

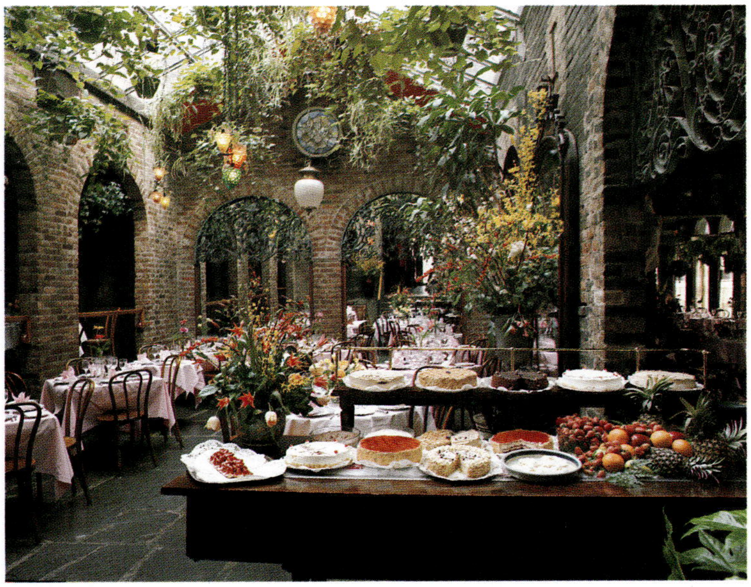

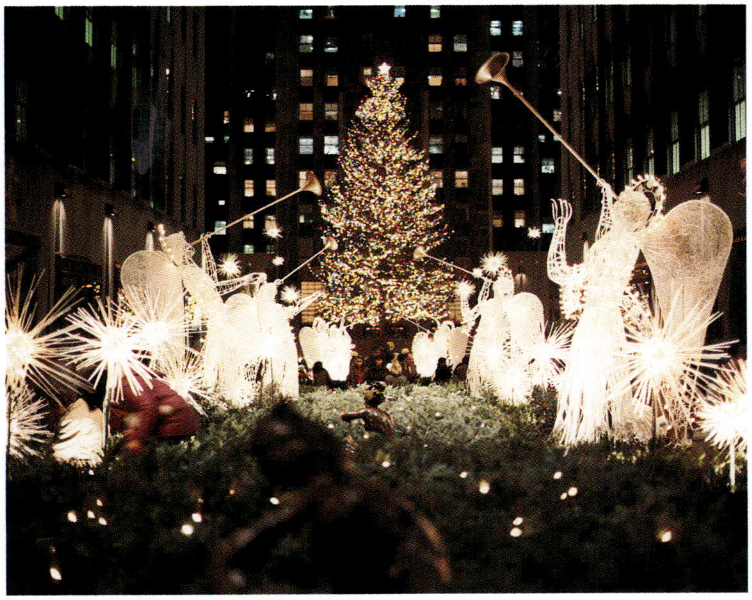

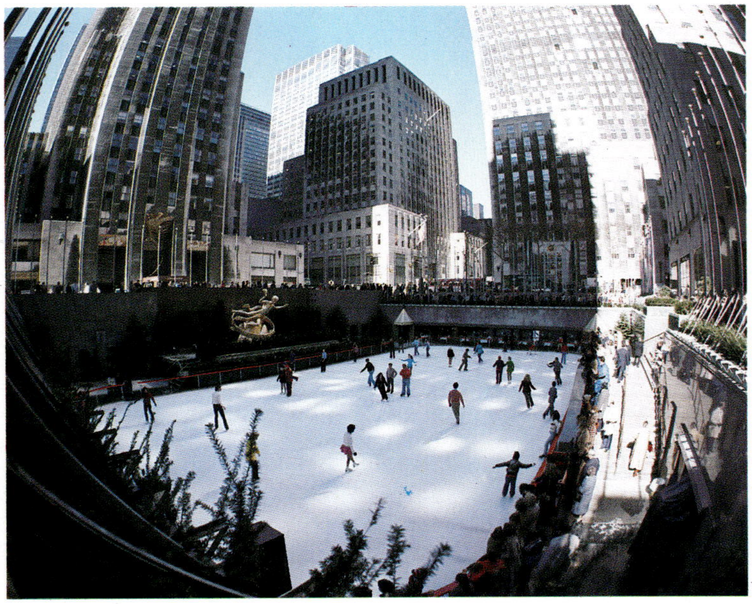

and other green-leafed vegetables at city markets, advertising signs, cars, even rubbish, all can afford brilliant pictures. Underexpose for extra intensity, and to help in spotting the colours, throw your eyes slightly out of focus as described earlier.

Another idea previously suggested, which is particularly relevant here is one of decay. Peeling paint, or partially torn-off posters, or even spray-painted graffiti, can all give sudden and unexpected juxtapositions of colour and shape.

Instead of abstraction, there are also the many tiny details which make a city unique. The roadsigns are an obvious example, though as time progresses these are becoming more and more standardised. Who could forget the British posting-boxes, so bright that they have given their name to a colour, 'pillar box red'. And what Englishman could get over the shock of finding that the Irish paint them green? In London, of course, the big red bus is colourful and distinctive – but here we are getting on to the area of travel photography, which is covered in the next chapter.

Buildings and objects are not the only colourful subjects in the city, either. There are always the people – especially the young people, who usually wear the brightest clothes. The 'punk' fashions must surely be the ultimate in personal colour, with fluorescent green or orange spiky-cut hair, though it must be admitted that the clothes are sometimes rather drab. Surprisingly few people mind being photographed, but if you are of a timid disposition you may find that a 105mm lens, or even a 135mm, is easier to use. Alternatively, use a real wide-angle, such as a 24mm, and get in among them: if you are really close, people tend to assume that you are too close to be photographing them, and consequently ignore you.

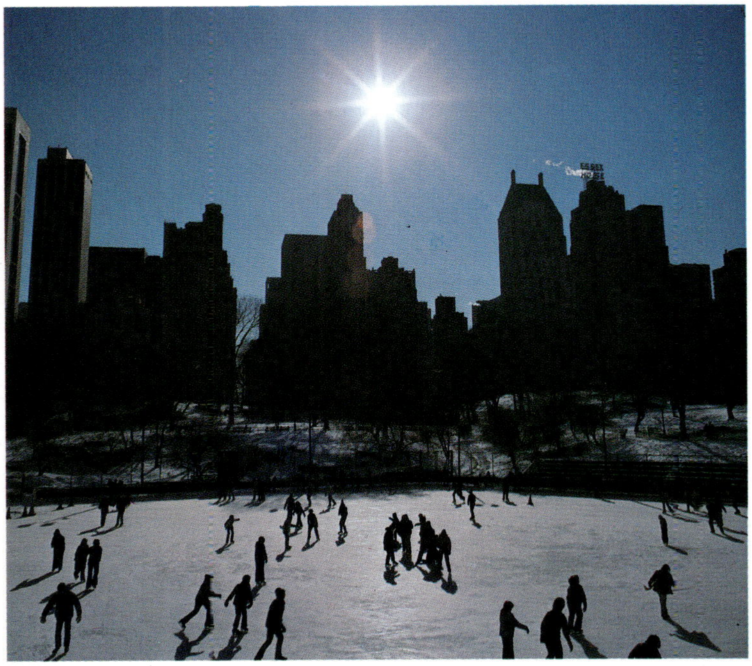

All in all, photographing a city is a question of getting a feeling for the place; of deciding what you want to say with your camera, and saying it. If the city strikes you as huge and terrifying, then try to communicate that. If it seems a haven of civilisation (which, by definition, it is – *'cives,'* from which 'civilisation' comes, is Latin for 'a city'), then portray that. The only way to get good pictures is to have something in mind already, even if it is only something so abstract as 'some typical Venetian colours'. Look and think; and then photograph.

TRAVEL

Travel, especially if it is to somewhere sufficiently remote, can be an excellent way to unleash creativity; but there is always the danger that everything seems so new, so exciting, that we are content merely to record what is around us. Whilst this is a perfectly valid approach, it does not necessarily partake much of creativity.

More than almost any other branch of photography, it behoves the travel photographer to choose his equipment carefully. Buying extra equipment at the destination may be impossible or at best expensive, and there are few things more infuriating than realising whilst on location that what you really need is something which you already have – at home.

One of the greatest difficulties *in travel photography lies in avoiding clichéd views of well-known scenes. A good way to do this is to incorporate something which is not normally shown: the buildings adjacent to the Leaning Tower of Pisa, the ice of a New York winter. The temptation is always to photograph the famous sight and leave it at that, but the incorporation of the ice, of the archway as a frame for the Taj Mahal, and of the gondolas as a foreground to the well-known Venetian architecture, all make for a picture which is very much more attractive than the bare record. The only way to get such pictures is to spend a good bit of time scouting around and planning before actually pressing the shutter release; the Mughal interior* ***facing page bottom right*** *suggests the cool haven which the carved pavilions provide from the glare of the sun, even if the tonal range of the scene is such that shadows are blocked and highlights washed-out.*

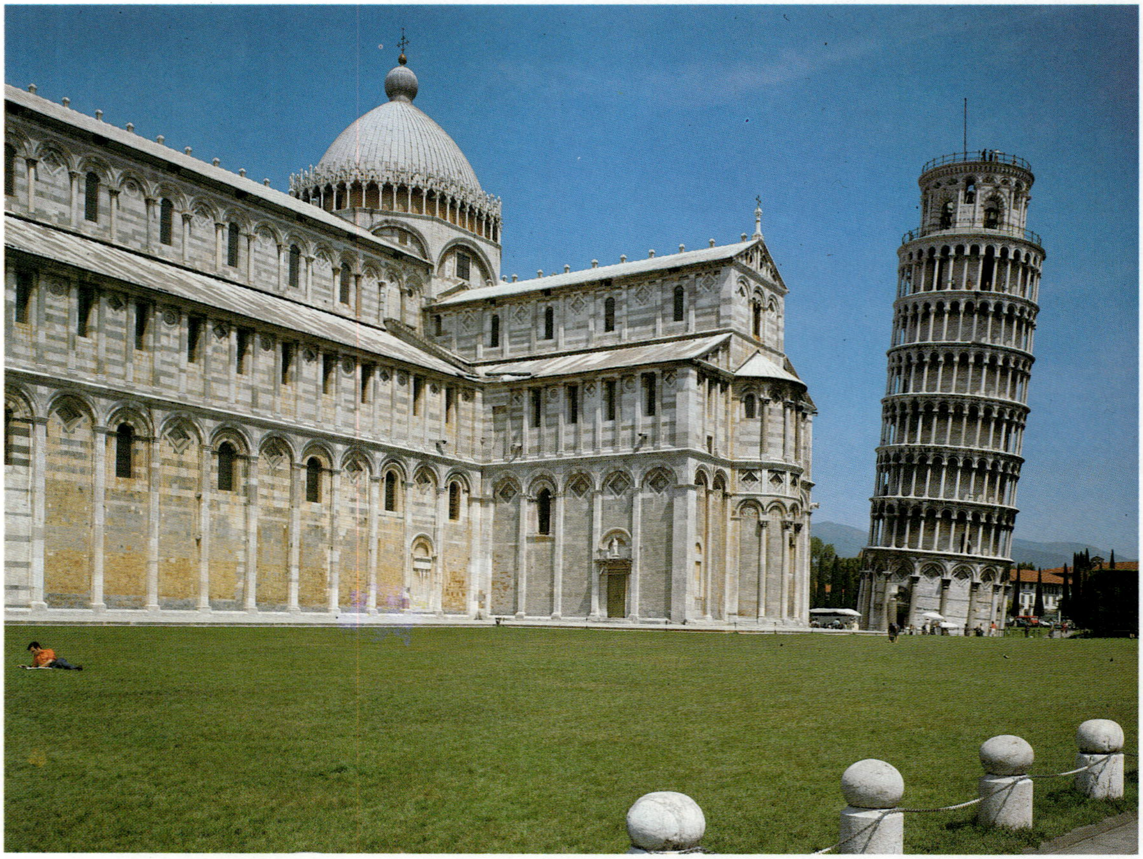

The choice of equipment varies very much according to the kind of things you want to photograph, the intended use of the photographs, the weight you want to carry around, and (of course) the depth of your wallet.

At the one extreme is the minimalist approach; a single camera and a single lens, with perhaps a simple backup. Whilst there is a certain amount to be said for an automatic SLR, there is a great deal more to be said for one with auto and manual options, and a good meter such as a Weston Master or a Luna-Pro. The single lens is open to considerable personal interpretation. I have tried a 55/1.2 (superb for general applications but often too long) and a 24/2.8 (occasionally too wide and sometimes too slow); if I had one, I think I would compromise with a 35/1.4. Others prefer zooms of varying types, but I find that these are so slow as to be useless for many types of pictures – especially if, like me, you favour 25 ASA Kodachrome.

At the other extreme is the everything-but-the-kitchen-sink school, with three bodies, half a dozen lenses, motor drives, etc. This gives you plenty of creative control, but it is an awful lot of stuff to carry about with you. Of course, you can leave most of it at the hotel or wherever you are staying, but then you are effectively back to the minimalist school.

A fair compromise is probably one body, your three (or even two) favourite lenses, and a backup – either a spare body or a complete compact or similar camera (I use a 1936 Leica). It is best not to be too battery dependent, and if you do rely on batteries to make sure that you replace them (and preferably carry spares as well) before the trip.

Of course, if you are considering publication, a larger format camera will be useful; consider a rollfilm SLR or TLR. If the camera is likely to be used in very hazardous conditions, simplicity is important too: a Rollei or similar TLR is about as

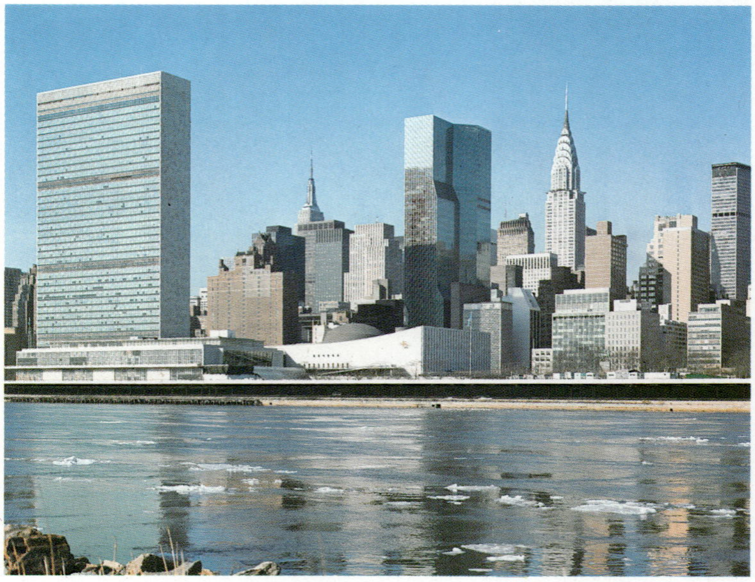

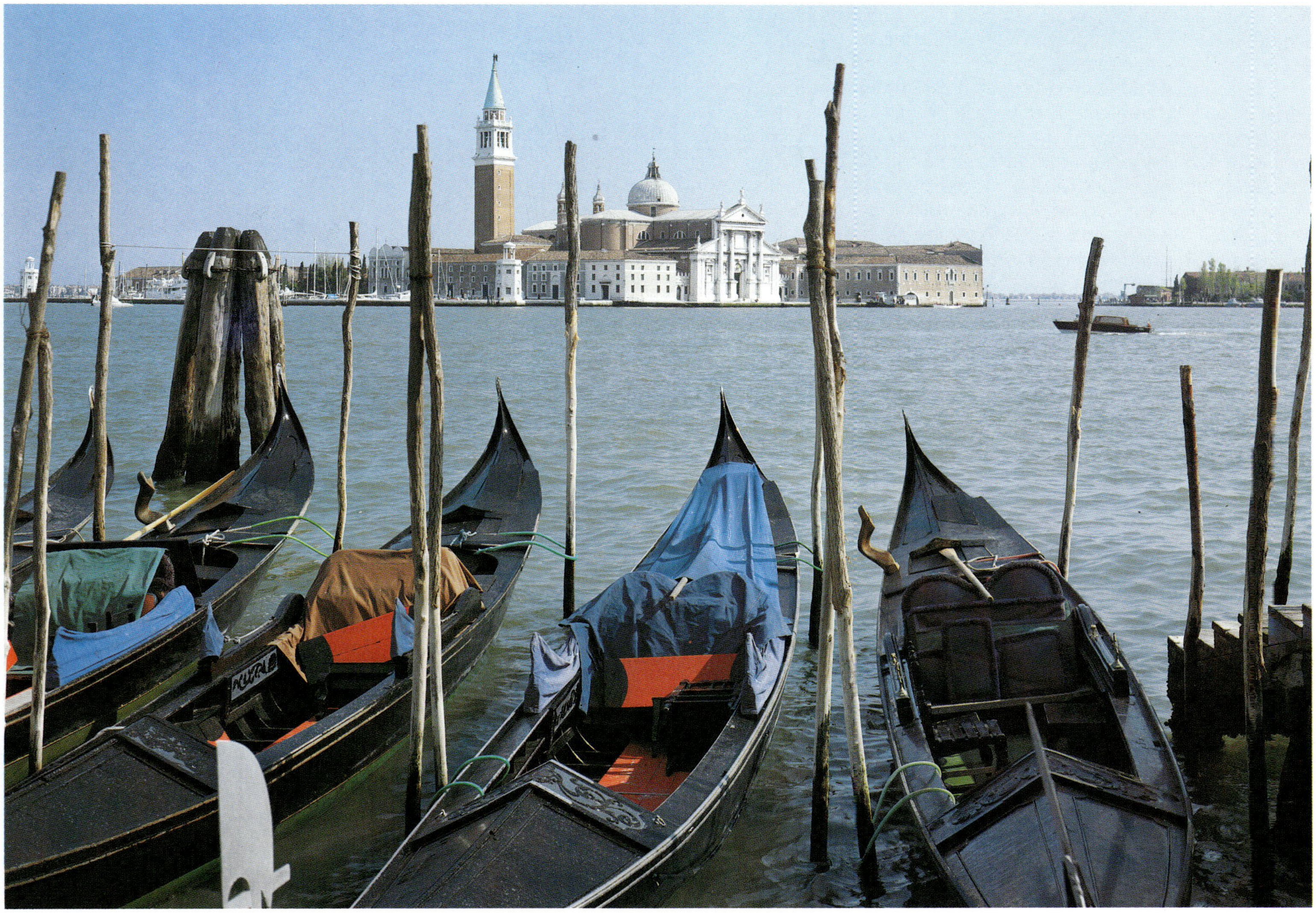

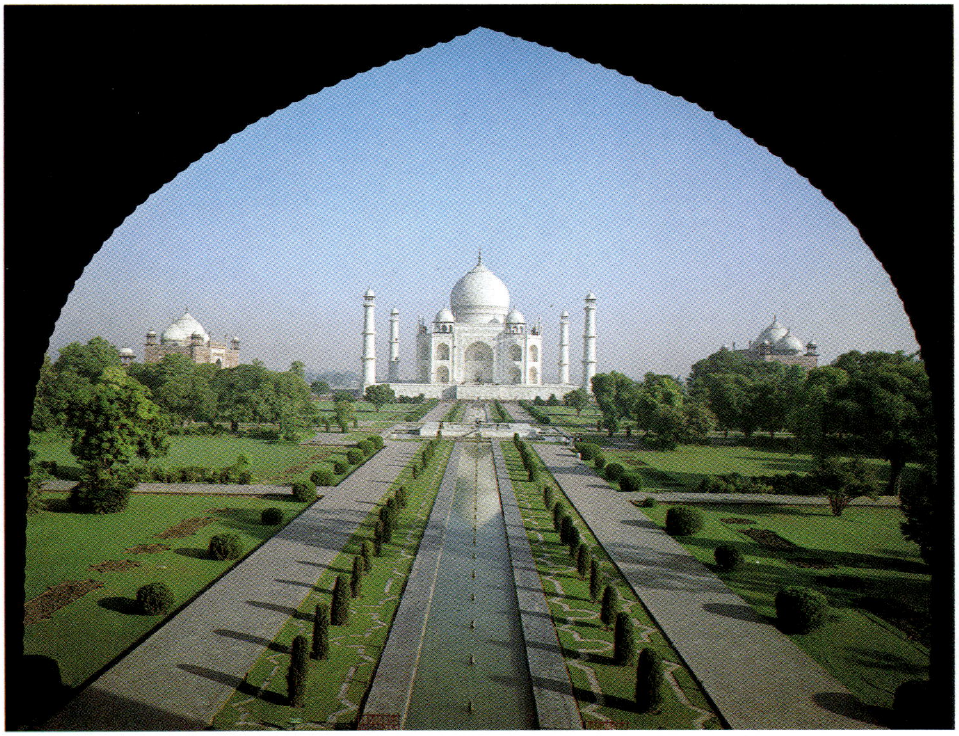

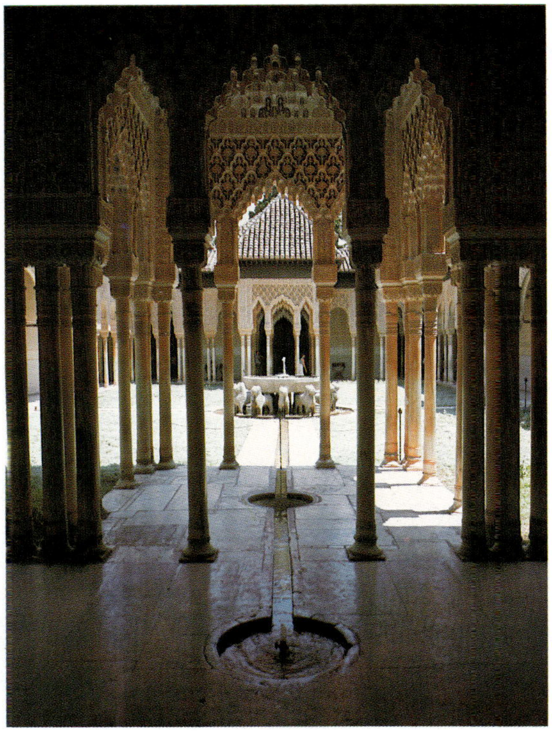

reliable as you can get, though I prefer my (equally simple) Linhof Super Technica 6 x 9cm. Of course, this sort of thing can get pretty heavy and expensive.

It is impossible to be very specific about equipment, though, and it usually takes a couple of trips in order to decide what is best for you. The advice above is pretty general, and based on my own experience; for example, for a recent trip to California's Disneyland I took only an automatic SLR with standard lens, because all that was needed was a snapshot-type approach to illustrate a book on snapshot photography. On the other hand, a trip to India to illustrate a book on Vajrayana Buddhism involved three Nikons, eight lenses, and a Linhof outfit with three lenses and three backs as well as a Hasselblad. And, of course, the trusty 1936 Leica!

Choosing the equipment is not the only thing to do before you go. You should also research the place as much as possible – borrow or buy books on it, see films, go to exhibitions, anything. You can illustrate two types of things. The first is the accepted view of a place – the soft misty green landscape of Ireland, for example, or the bright sun and primary colours of Southern California – and the second is your personal view; in California, you might photograph the astonishing sunsets through the palm trees, the aircraft stacked up over the airport, or the gaudy seediness of the latino down-town area. There is nothing wrong with the 'accepted view' approach, provided it does not become clichéd and obvious, and indeed I find that it is a necessary counterfoil to the more personal type of work. It is also essential, from a commercial point of view, to have 'establishing shots' which show familiar landmarks such as the Golden Gate Bridge in San Francisco or the Parthenon in Athens. The creativity required for such shots may even be greater than that required for ostensibly more original shots; thinking up a new way to photograph the Taj Mahal is a real challenge to creativity.

The research does not stop when you arrive. Buy picture postcards; they show you the local landmarks (useful for establishing shots) and in some cases serve as Ghastly Warnings about how not to photograph somewhere – though more often they are the work of local photographers who have probably tried many angles and had a more-or-less valid reason for choosing the one they did.

A counsel of perfection advises you not to take pictures as soon as you arrive, but to walk about getting the feel of the place. In Bermuda, for example, one of the most striking things is that the greenery really is as lush as it is shown on the picture postcards – perhaps more so. In Los Angeles, the peeling paint and faded colours in some parts of town (especially the *barrios*, where the photographer with an expensive camera ventures at his peril) are quite Mediterranean. This initial walkabout is designed to stoke up your creative fires; the argument is that if you are deprived of your camera, you benefit both by becoming hungry to use it and by being denied the opportunity to take the 'obvious' pictures.

I do not support this view. The walkabout is an excellent idea, but it carries with it a certain freshness of vision. If you are not carrying your camera, you will see things that you want to photograph – and you will later return, with your camera, to try to take them.

The chances are that they will be gone, or at least that your originality of vision will be gone; and worse, because you are trying to recreate the past, you are not open to the present. Certainly, there will be pictures which you will want to take again, and there may well be pictures which you will later discard as rather obvious, but there are also likely to be some really original and spontaneous pictures.

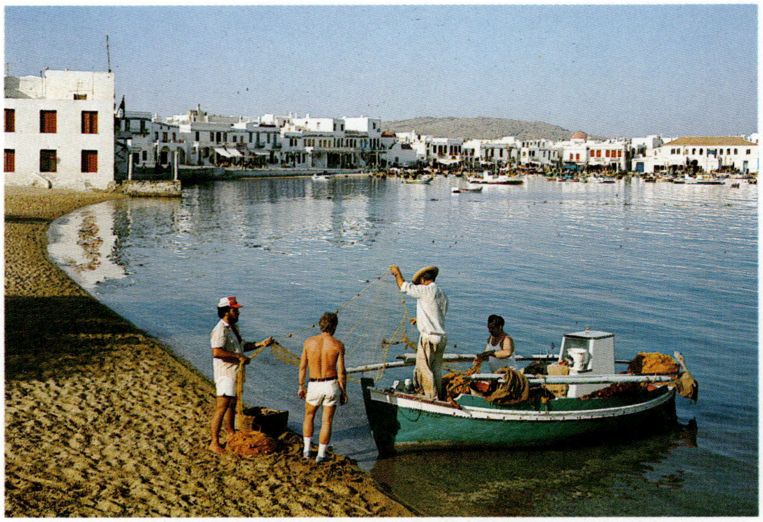

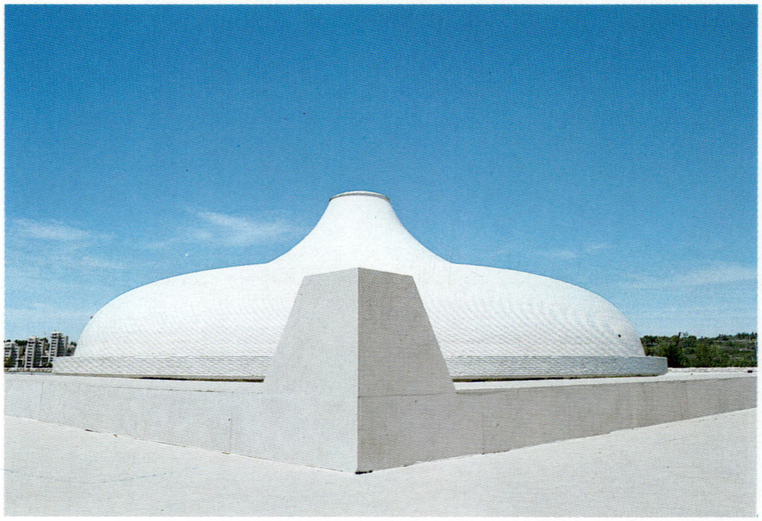

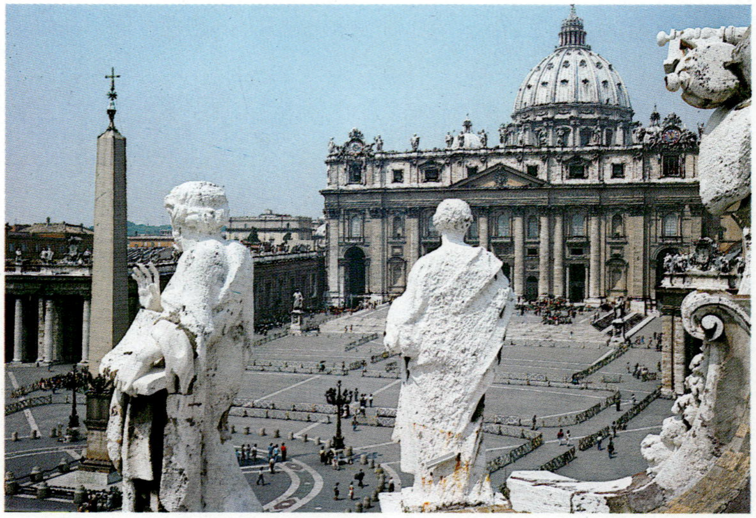

One of the best things about *travel is the way it refreshes our vision. The top picture is essentially narrative: it tells a story about a way of life. The middle one is almost an abstract, and the one above is slightly surreal and threatening. The frozen figures were never meant to be seen from the back, and the contrast between their looming scale and the tiny tourists is rather disquieting.*

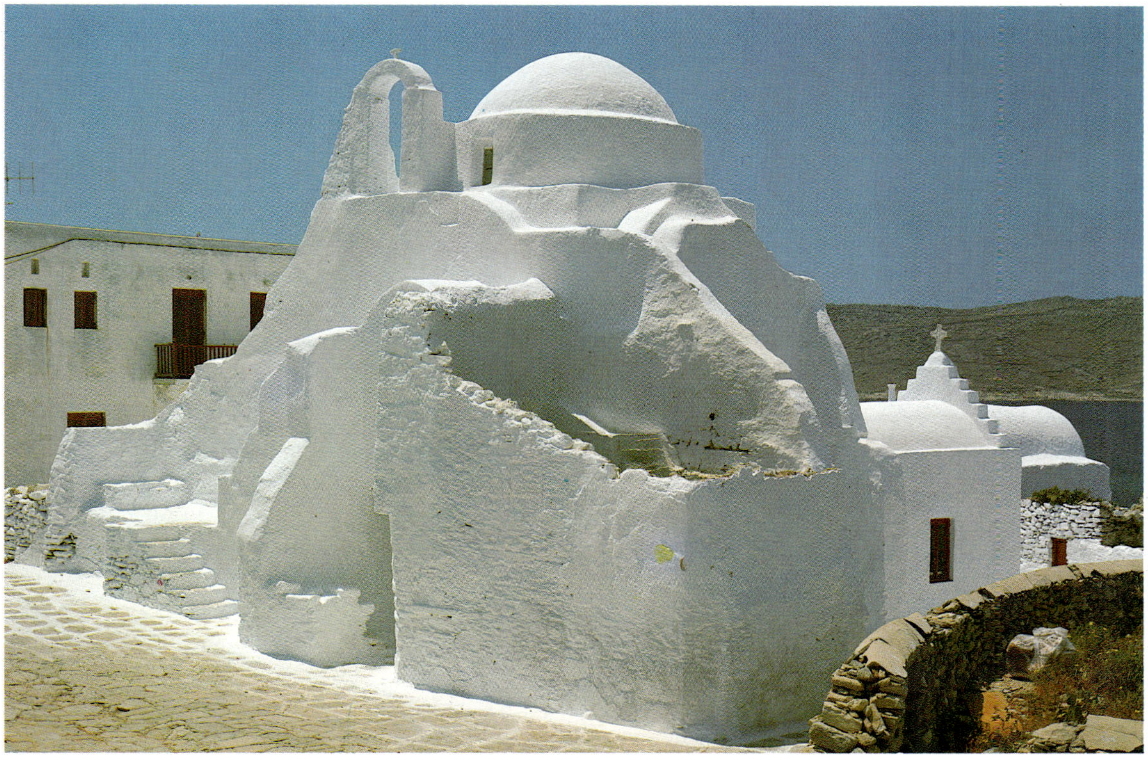

Determining exposure can be** extremely difficult when one is faced with the light colours common in hot countries; when this is combined with the bright clear light of the Mediterranean, there is sometimes a temptation to disbelieve your exposure meter. The best solution is to take an incident light reading and then to underexpose by anything from half a stop to a stop and a half; that way, you will get detail in the whites and magnificent colour saturation elsewhere. If you are using an in-camera meter, aim it at the lightest surface which you want to contain any detail, and give three whole stops* ***more *exposure. Alternatively, take a reading off the palm of your hand, and give half a stop less. These rules-of-thumb are, of course, only a guide: you will need to make adjustments for your particular technique, your film and equipment.*

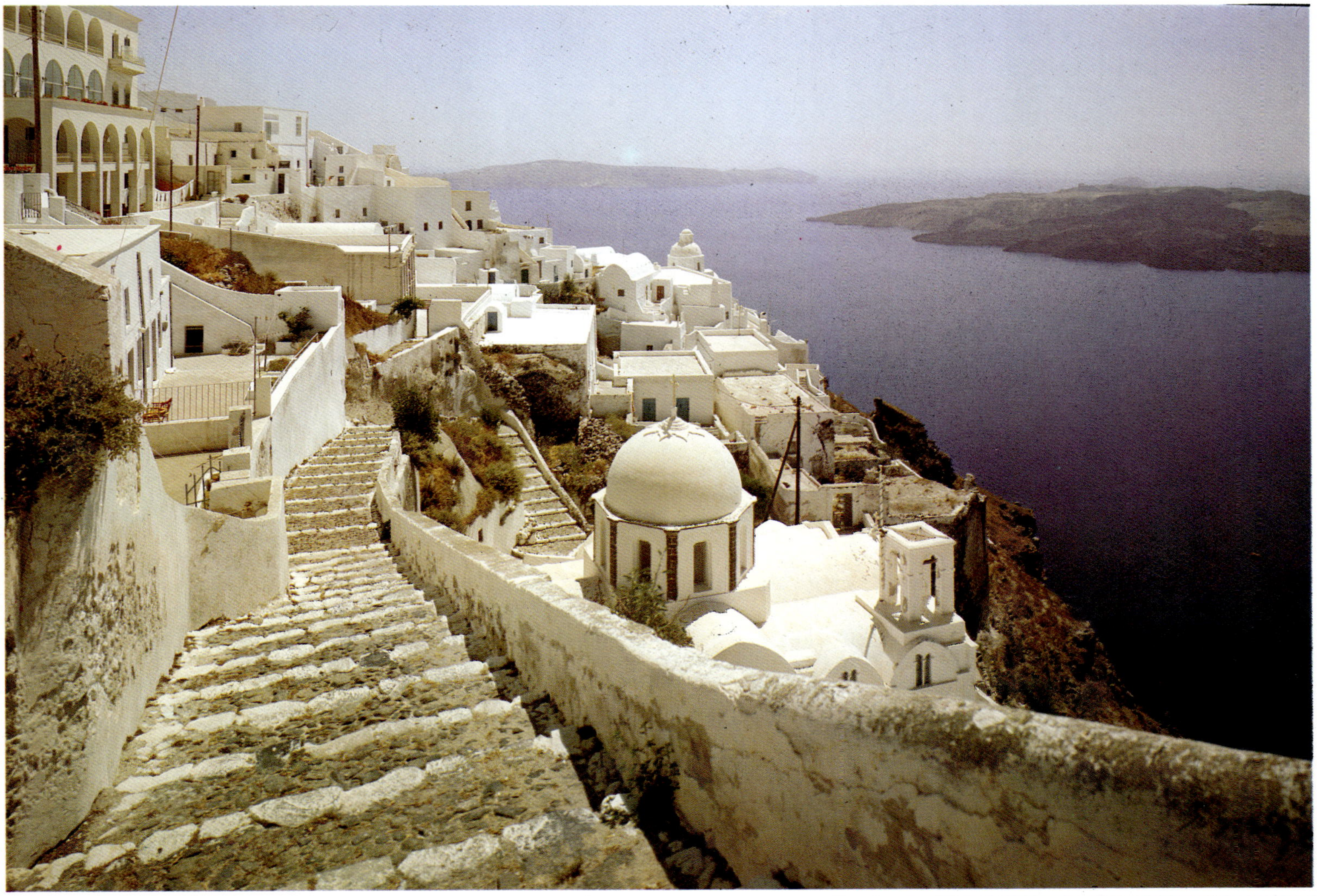

TRAVEL

Successful travel photography is a pretty schizophrenic process. On the one hand, you are trying to show the familiar; things of which people can say, "Ah, yes, I remember that; it was absolutely typical of the place." On the other you are trying to show things which will make them say, "Hey, I never realised that." Furthermore, as nothing short of actually being there can portray the whole *gestalt* of the experience, you are constantly trying to evoke much with little. Perhaps the nearest analogy is with poetry: in the few lines of 'An Irish Airman foresees his death' Yeats manages to summon up the exultation and terror of flying; the silence of the air and the noise of the aeroplane; a deep feeling for the country, and a sense of separation from it; and the essentially similar nature of fatalism and free will. Similarly, Shirakawa's photographs of the Alps, or the Himalayas, or the Grand Canyon, all conjure up a sense of vastness and wonder; of bizarre beauty on a titanic scale; of colours so vivid and yet so unexpected that they remind us of Lovecraft's 'the colour out of space', a wholly new colour never before seen by man.

The important thing is obviously to select from the endless barrage of impressions which you are receiving all the time.

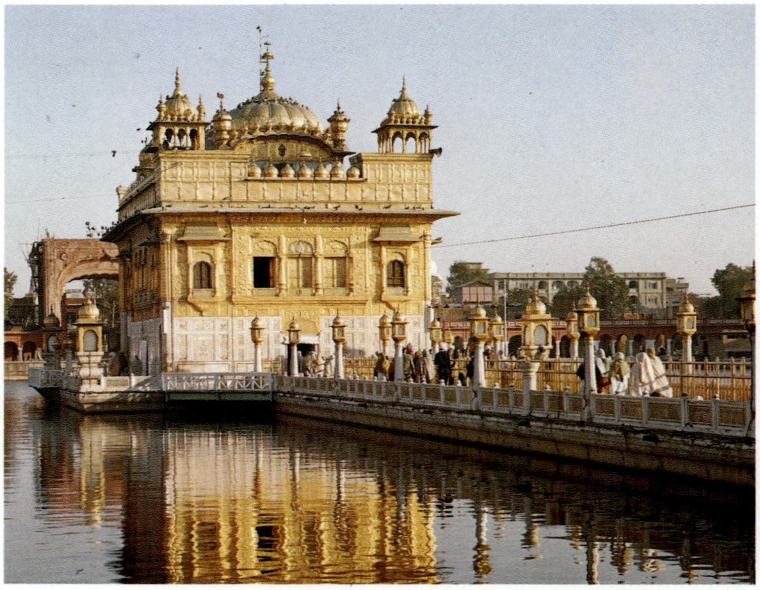

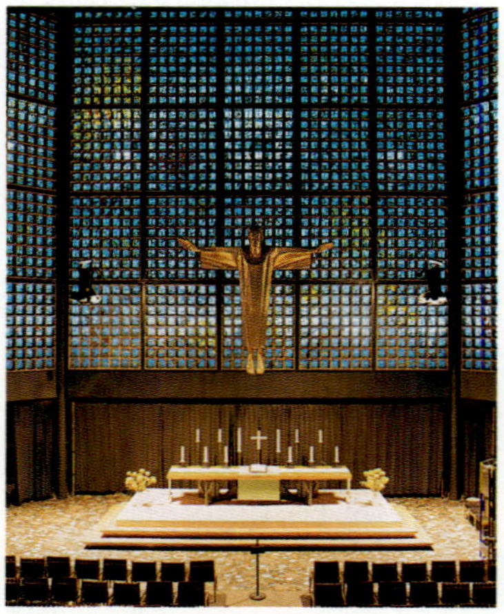

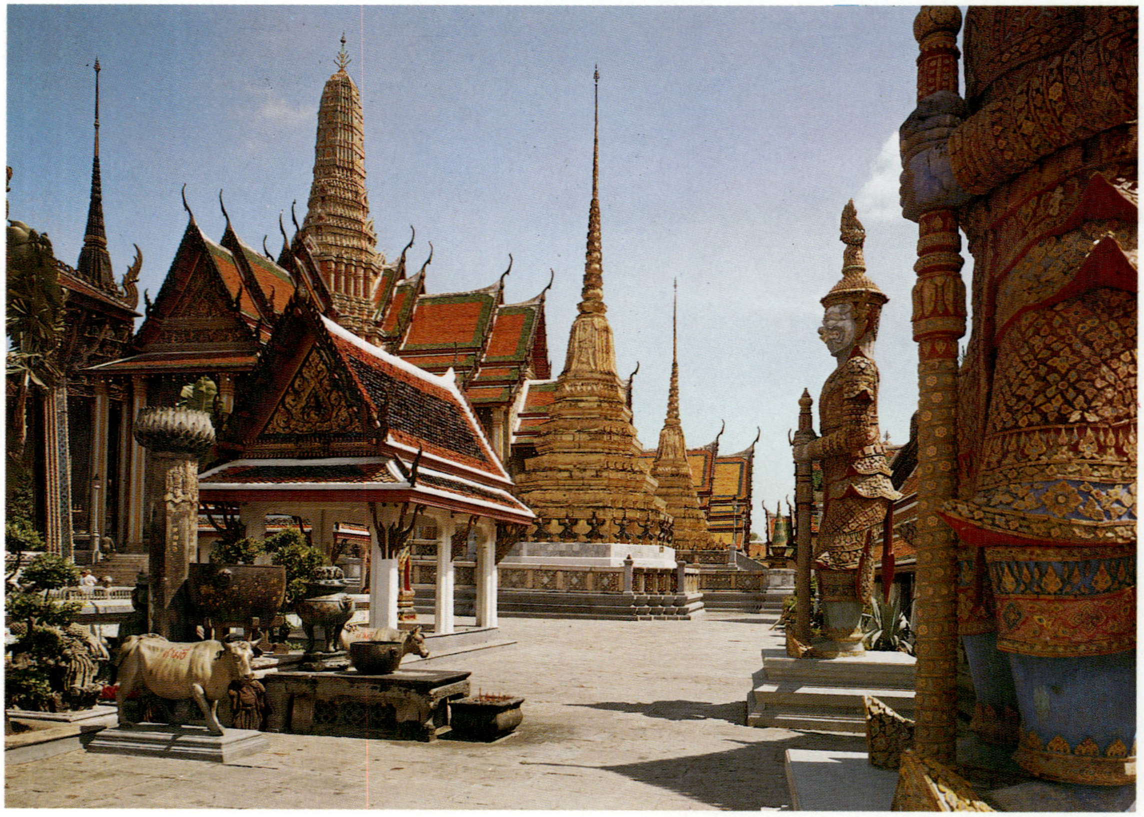

Opinions are divided about *whether to use figures to show scale. My own view is that they should only be included where they are a necessary compositional element, or an integral part of the scene. Thus, the church scene* ***above*** *has no need of a figure, but in the temple* ***right*** *the eye searches in vain for a fulcrum; a figure in the courtyard would help.*

Although the experience itself is continuous and amorphous, there are certain approaches which you can consciously adopt.

The first is the choice of the general picture versus the detail. The traditional landscape, for example, is a general and narrative picture; it shows how quite a large area looked at a particular instant in time, and tells you what was going on during that instant in time. This does not mean that it is devoid of composition; some of the most beautiful landscapes of all time, such as those taken by Ansel Adams and Minor White, are essentially narrative in nature. A different approach, though, isolates a smaller part of that landscape; instead of being very recognisably 'A view from . . . looking over . . .', it becomes, perhaps, 'a typical corner of . . .' (I am not suggesting you use such corny old titles – but they do illustrate what I mean). Elliot Porter's supremely beautiful pictures are often of this type. A yet closer view isolates perhaps a single plant, a part of a building, a sign, or a vehicle or a figure. Coming in closer still we begin to enter the worlds of close-up and macrophotography, dealt with elsewhere. Once again, no one approach is inherently better than any other; it merely depends on which you find the most interesting.

The second is what one might term the 'political' aspect, which deals with how you approach a subject. This is covered in greater detail later, but it is relevant to travel photography, too. Is Los Angeles the long-legged teenagers on the beach? The bronzed surfers? The teeming consumers in the shopping malls?

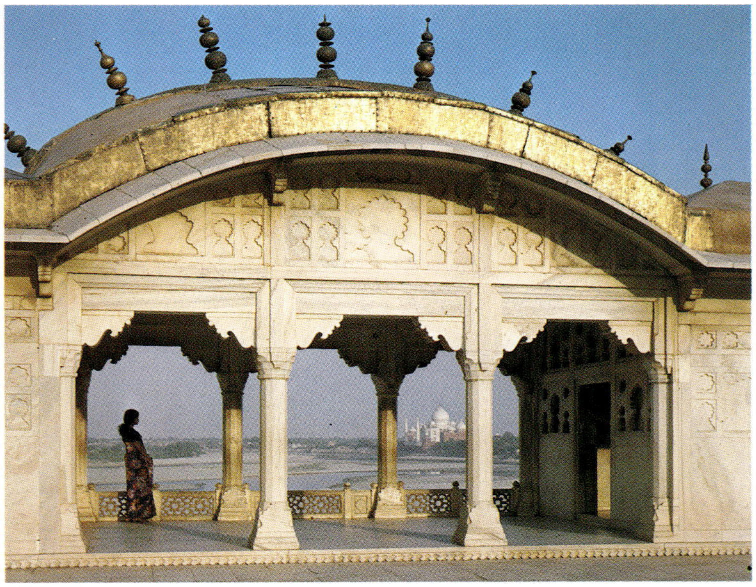

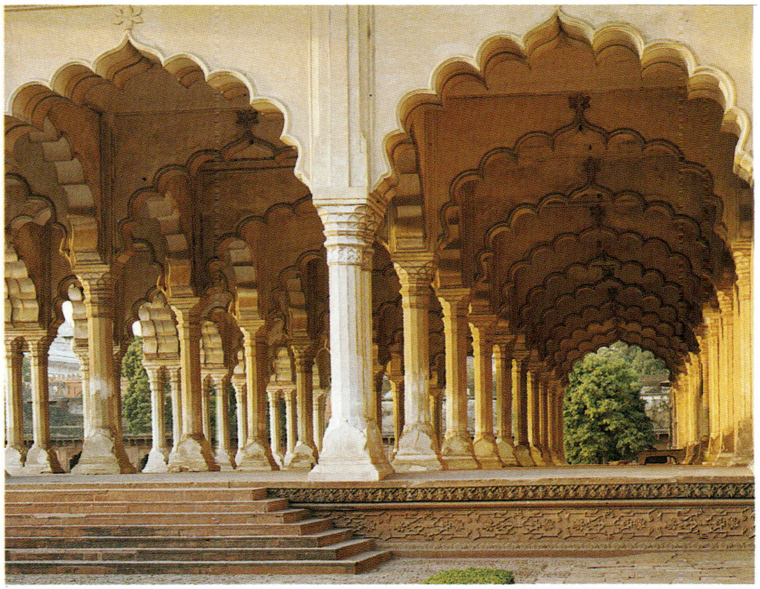

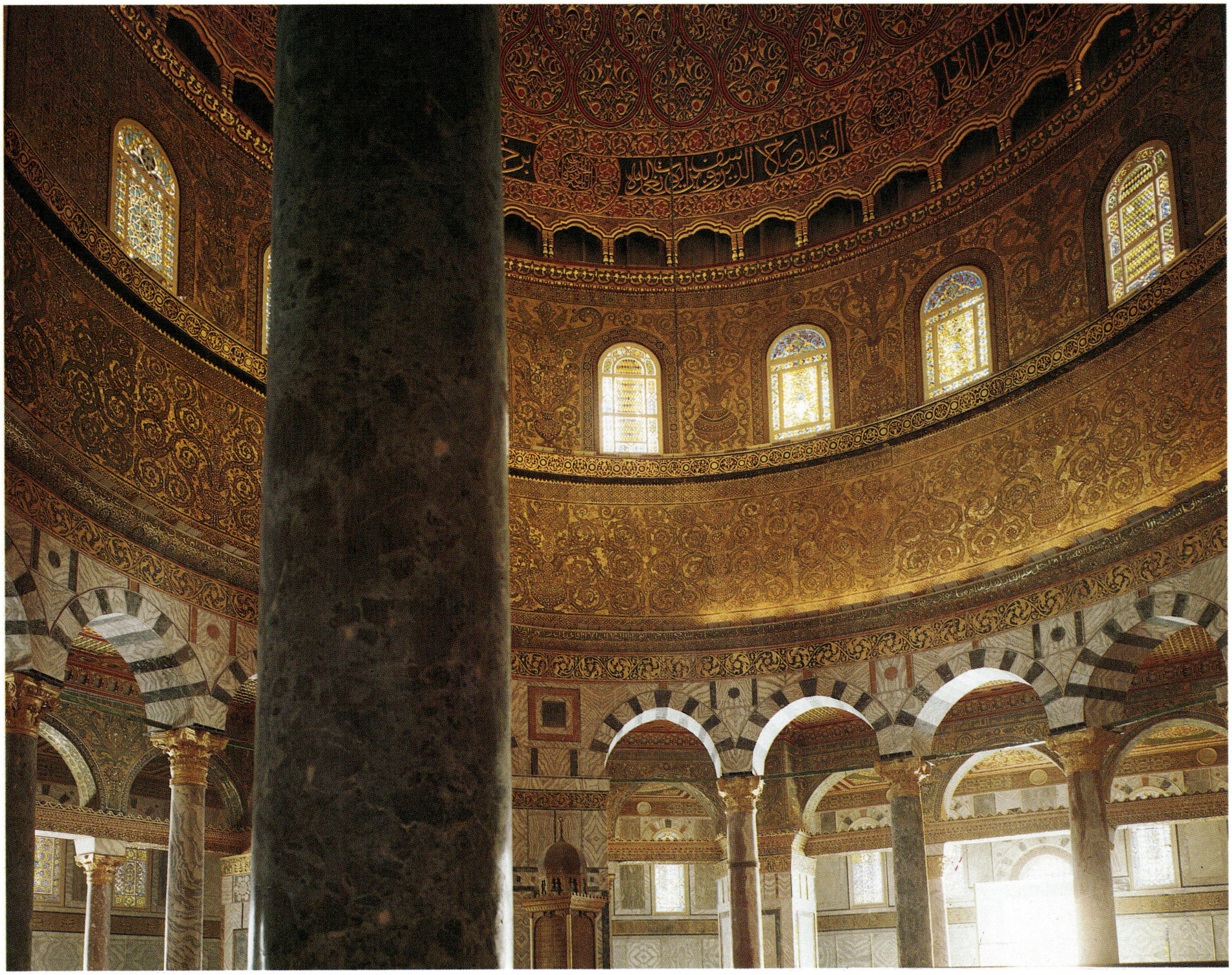

TRAVEL

The crowded freeways? The *barrios?* The mansions in Beverly Hills? The smog? The beautiful rolling hills? The endless suburbs? The tourist traps? The sex shops on the Strip? The star-studded sidewalk on Hollywood? The pumps dotted all over the landscape, pulling the oil out of the ground? The skyscrapers in the financial area downtown? The railroads through the streets? The question is not only one of selection of subject: Beverly Hills can either be a symbol of affluence and success, or of conspicuous consumption and feckless waste – or (and this is the way I see it) a middle-class suburb built by *arrivistes* with too much money for their own good.

The utterly stunning fairy-tale *beauty of the snow scene* ***facing page top*** *demanded great patience and preparation. The potential picture had been observed some long time before the right combination of sunny dawn and recent snowfall presented itself. It meant getting up frighteningly early on several mornings in succession, and carrying a heavy 5 x 4" camera and tripod. The others are also large-format pictures, which entailed a great deal of waiting. Truly successful travel photography is impossible to combine with casual holidaymaking: you have to be prepared to work long hours, walk long distances, and wait until everything is just right. The simplest single tip is always to rise at or before dawn!*

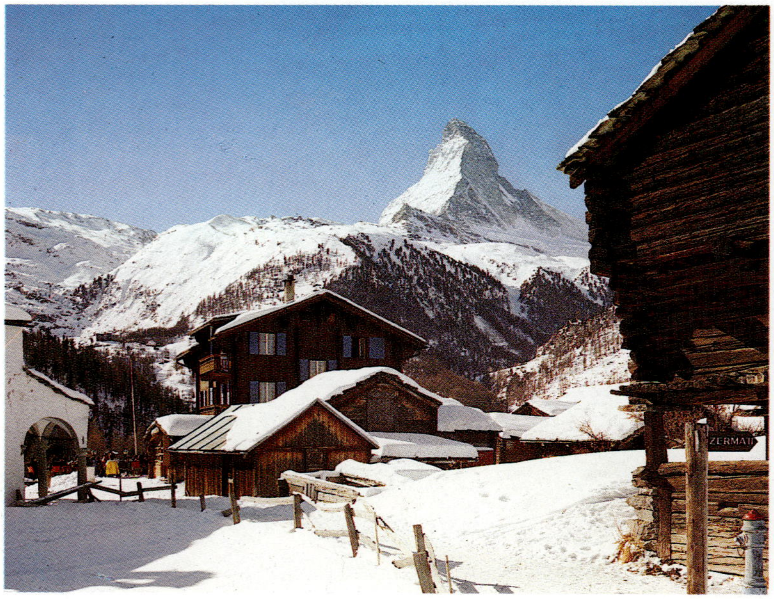

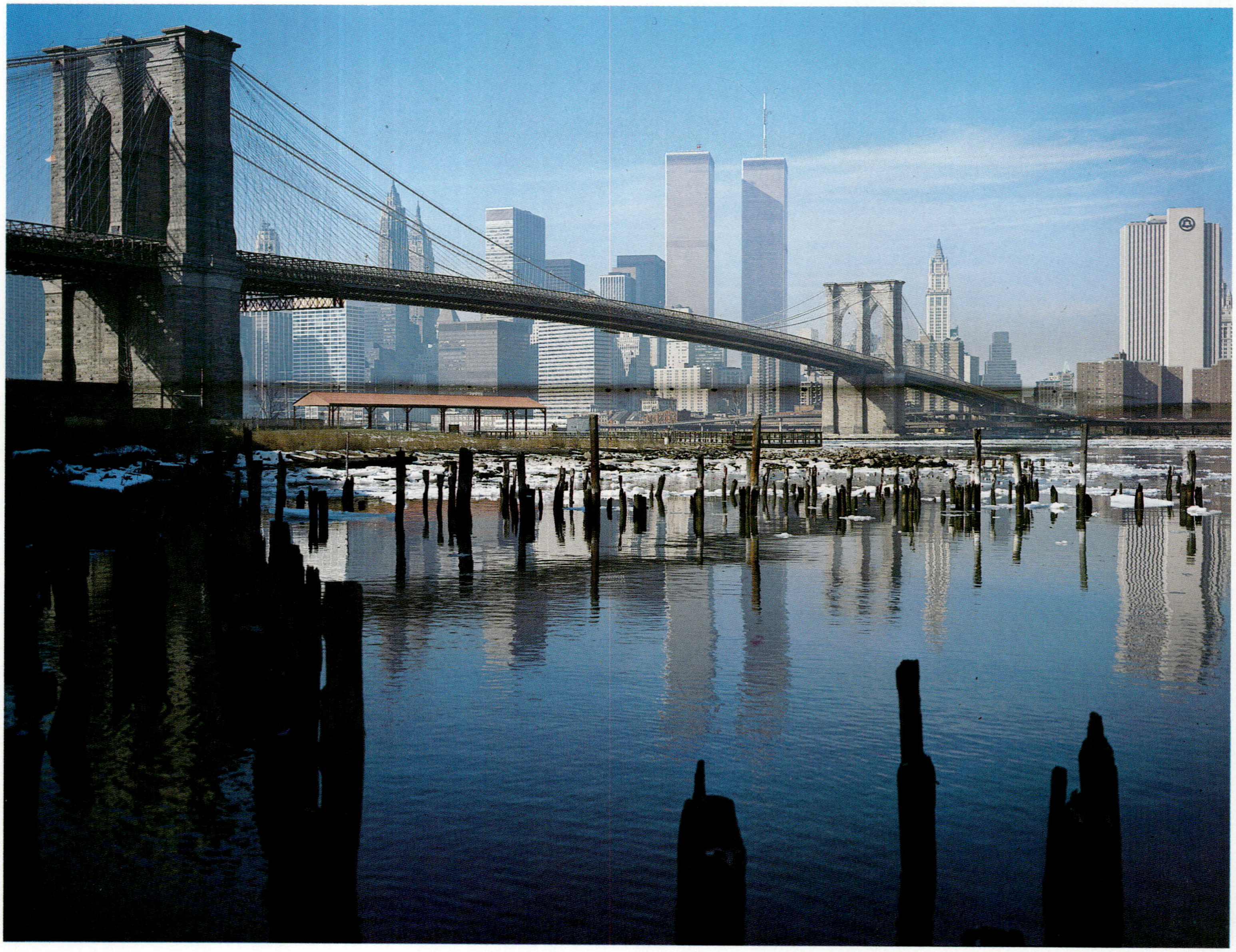

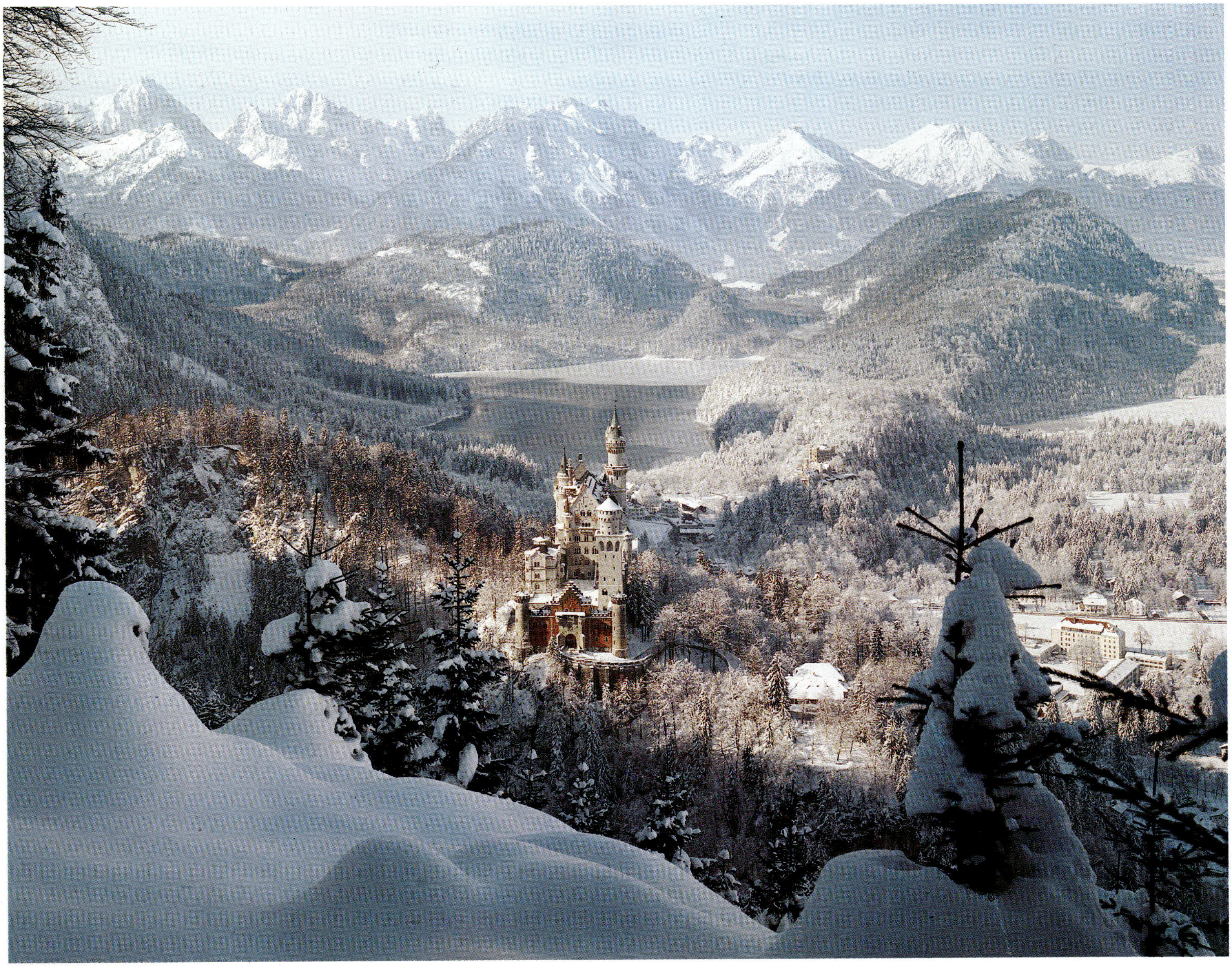

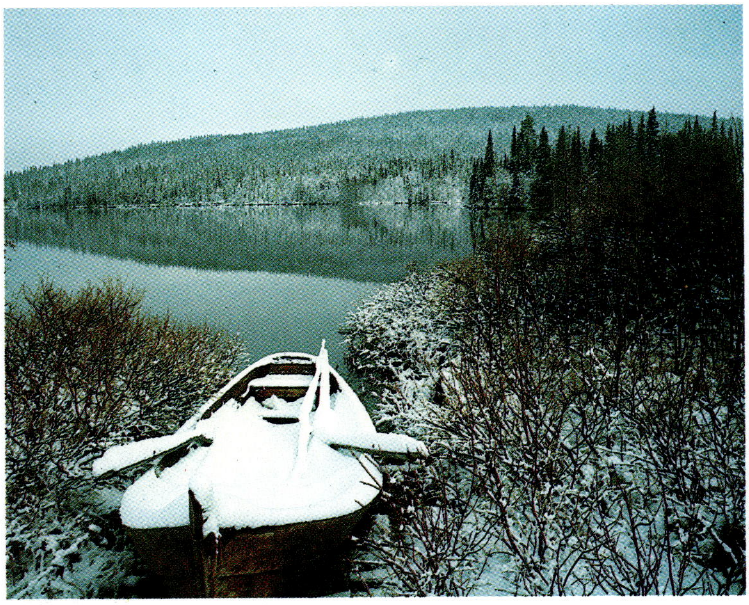

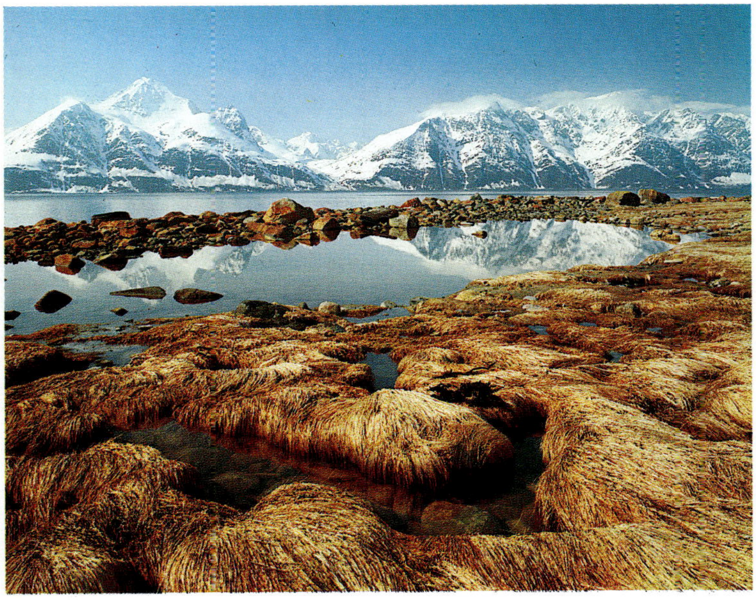

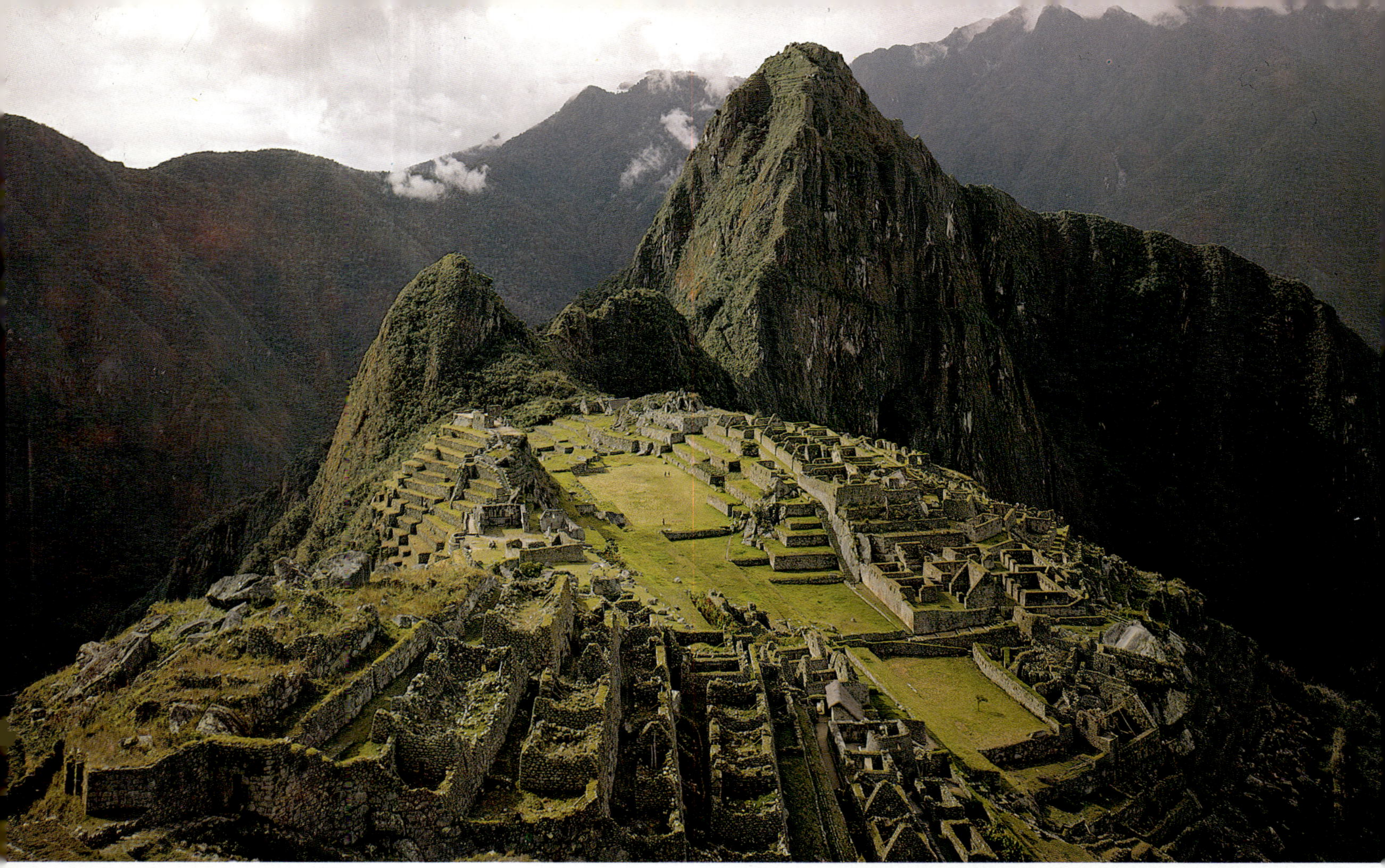

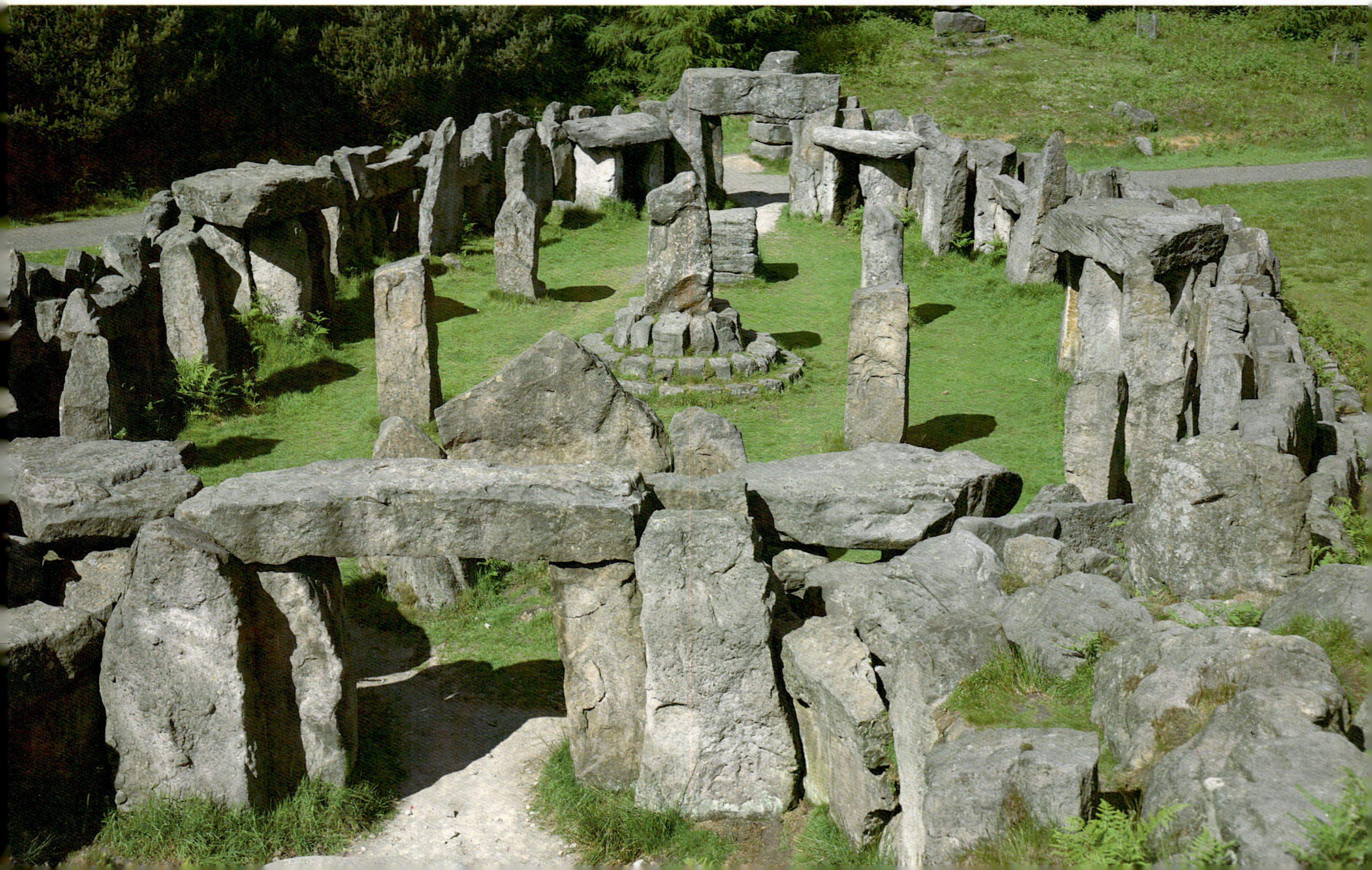

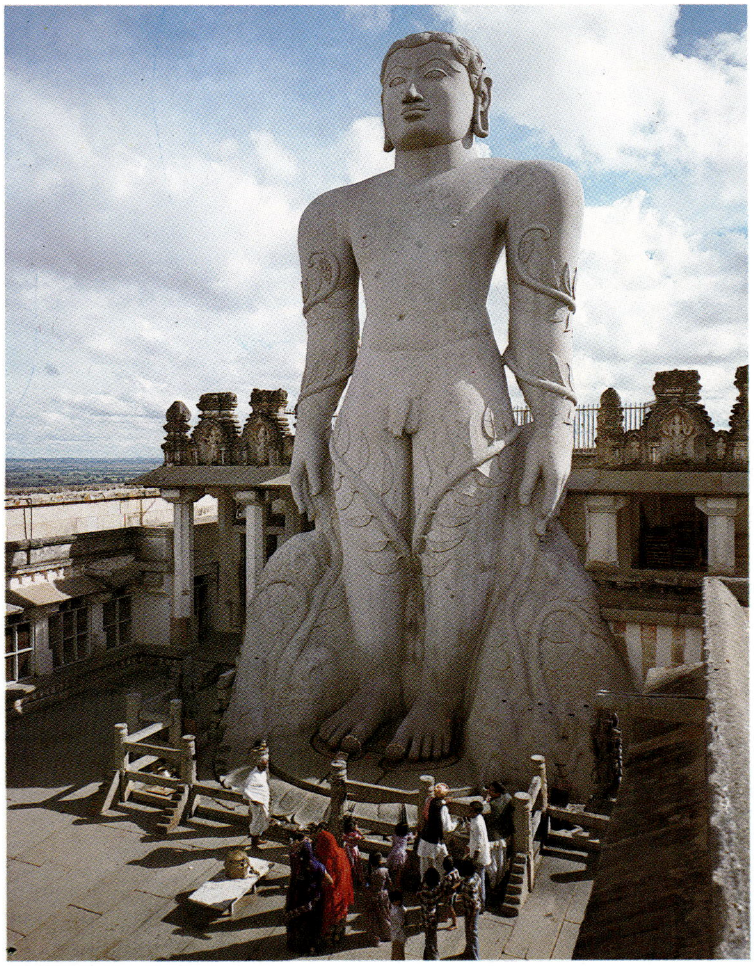

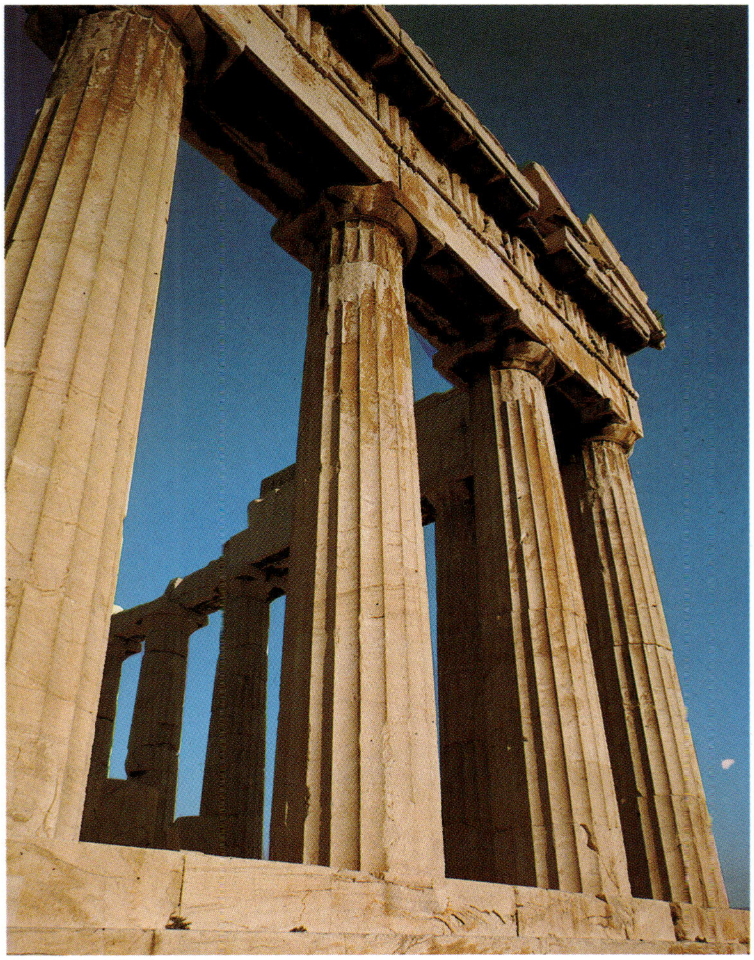

Above and facing page: Ancient monuments and prehistoric sites can serve as sources of inspiration to those lucky enough to visit them.

The small figures of the people in the picture shown ***top left,*** *emphasise the massive scale of the Buddha statue.*

A third approach might be the 'universality' of a picture. There are pictures which could be taken in Death Valley or in Dublin – except that the quality of the light is different. A typical example is sun-and-sand pictures; you might be able to take pictures in Aberdeen which were indistinguishable from those taken in Ipanema, but the weather is likely to be better in Ipanema and there will be a greater chance of finding scantily-clad and beautiful girls. If you like a particular style of photography, but your home town affords little scope for it, you may be able to practise it elsewhere. Pity the photographer of seascapes who lives in Kansas, or the Dutch lover of mountains!

A fourth spectrum to consider is <u>when</u> you take your pictures. The slanting light of dawn is very different from the overhead light of noon, but both can be used to good effect. Although noon is often said to be the worst possible time for photography, there are certain pictures which are enhanced by it. Imagine, for example, that you want to portray the dazzling burning heat of a high summer in Mexico. The almost vertical light, the inky black shadows, possibly the shimmering distortion of heat haze, are all going to be illustrated far better at noon than in the reddish light of dawn.

Weather conditions, too, are important. Dartmoor, in Devon, is a part of the world I like very much; but there are some pictures which cry out to be taken in sunlight, others in mist, yet others in rain or under a blanket of snow. Photographers who admire Ansel Adams are known to wait months for the light to be just right, returning to the same spot year after year until they get what they want. I believe that this is due to an over-strict interpretation of the concept of 'previsualisation'; but I do not deny that (sometimes) it produces the most excellent pictures.

You may wish to consider how important people are to your photography; photographers as disparate as Ansel Adams and David Hockney seem to do very well without them, but Cartier-Bresson and Eugene Smith concentrate on them. Margaret Bourke-White seemed able to produce superb pictures with or without people, and the pictures of Walter Nurnberg seem to use people as archetypes and touchstones rather than as individuals.

Again, there is the question of <u>how much</u> colour you use in your photography. In the hands of a master such as Shirakawa, there may seem to be little difference between even black-and-white photography and colour (though his colour tends to be monochromatic anyway), but Hockney uses picture-postcard colours to excellent effect, as does Harry Callahan. One of my own favourite pictures – a moonrise over a hill in Wales – is composed of a featureless black hill, a featureless deep-blue sky, and a white blob of moon.

All this intellectualising may seem foreign to the direct experience which I have extolled above, but it is in many ways a preconditioning of receptiveness. The biggest barrier to creativity is a tendency to stick to what you know. By questioning your own attitudes you can make those sudden little leaps which are characterised as 'Hey, I could do it that way instead'; and even if the <u>conscious</u> thought does not cross your mind when you take the picture, it is a pretty safe bet that it will be in there unconsciously, and rooting for you.

COLOUR AT NIGHT

Our Victorian forbears distinguished between instantaneous exposures (or 'snapshots') and timed exposures, which might be short enough to be measured by the time-honoured 'one hippopotamus two hippopotamus' method or long enough to determine with a pocket watch; those with a penchant for photographing the interiors of churches frequently ran into half-hour exposures, and on a dim day the enterprising solar artist might well repair to the nearest inn for a leisurely lunch during the exposure.

Even the slowest modern colour films are around a hundred times as fast as a Victorian 'rapid' dry plate, so during the day we no longer even consider 'timed' exposures, at least out of doors. At night, though, we are forced back upon the old distinction.

Contrary to popular belief, hand-held colour photography at night is perfectly possible; and given that this is likely to interest more people than 'timed' exposures, we can consider this first.

HAND-HELD PHOTOGRAPHY AT NIGHT

There are three weapons in the night photographer's armoury. The first is fast lenses. An extreme speed lens is ideal; for the real fanatic, the f/1 Noctilux for the rangefinder Leica or the f/0.95 Canon Dream for the rangefinder Canon 7 and 7s are available at a price. Next come the f/1.2 lenses from a number of leading manufacturers.

Whilst these are very nice to have, they are still considerably more expensive than the f/1.4s and the gain in speed is only half a stop. Furthermore, unless they are from very reputable makers, their optical quality may not be too exciting.

The f/1.4 is probably a good compromise, but it is by no means essential; an f/2 lens can cover a surprising amount of work, and even an f/2.8 is far from useless. Certainly, you would be ill advised to use anything much slower than f/2, but if you look at some of the work done in the 1930s with lenses as slow as f/3.5, it becomes clear that high speed lenses are by no means essential.

Twilight and dawn often *provide magical and at times unusual lighting effects that can be interpreted in various ways.*

Underexposure intensifies the evanescent colours and captures the feeling of half-light.

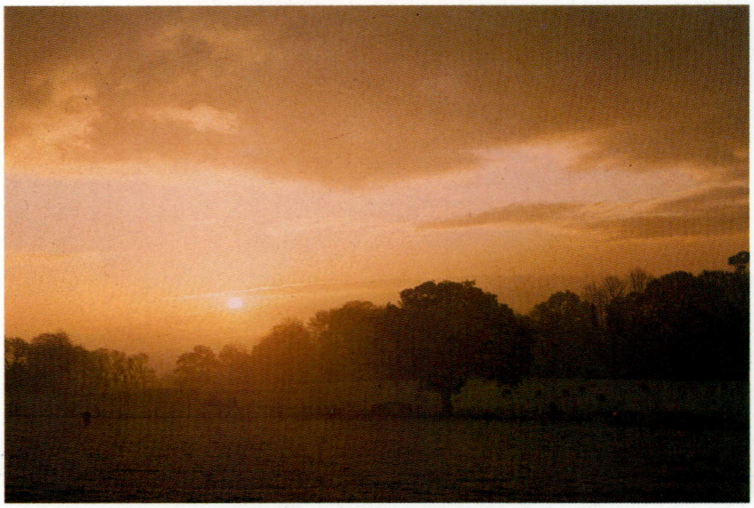

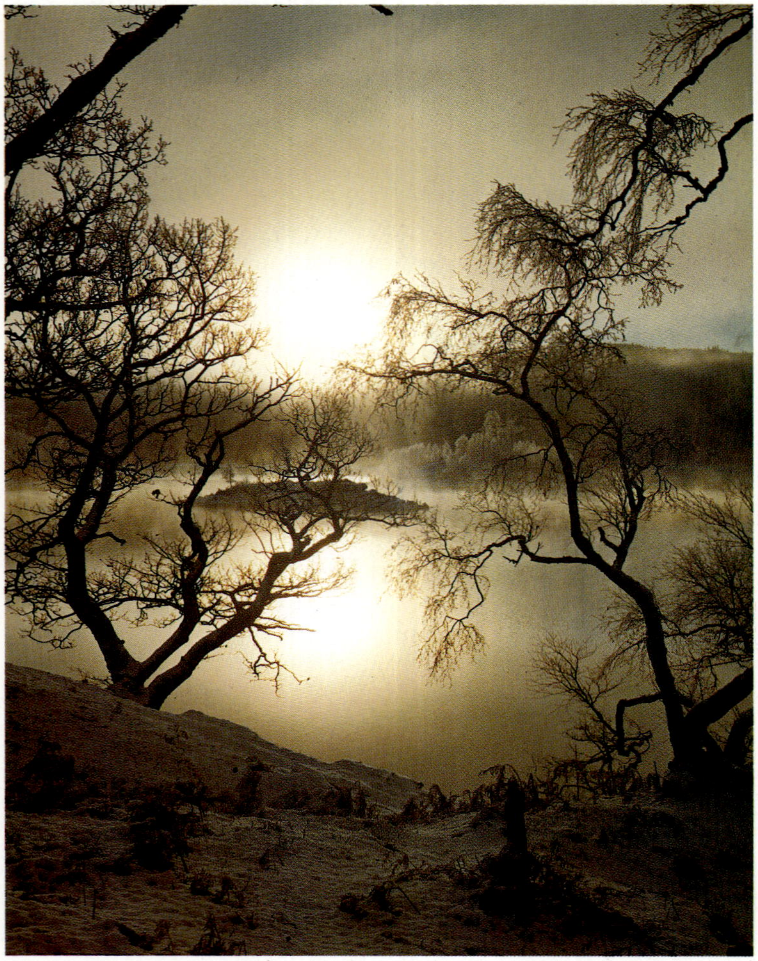

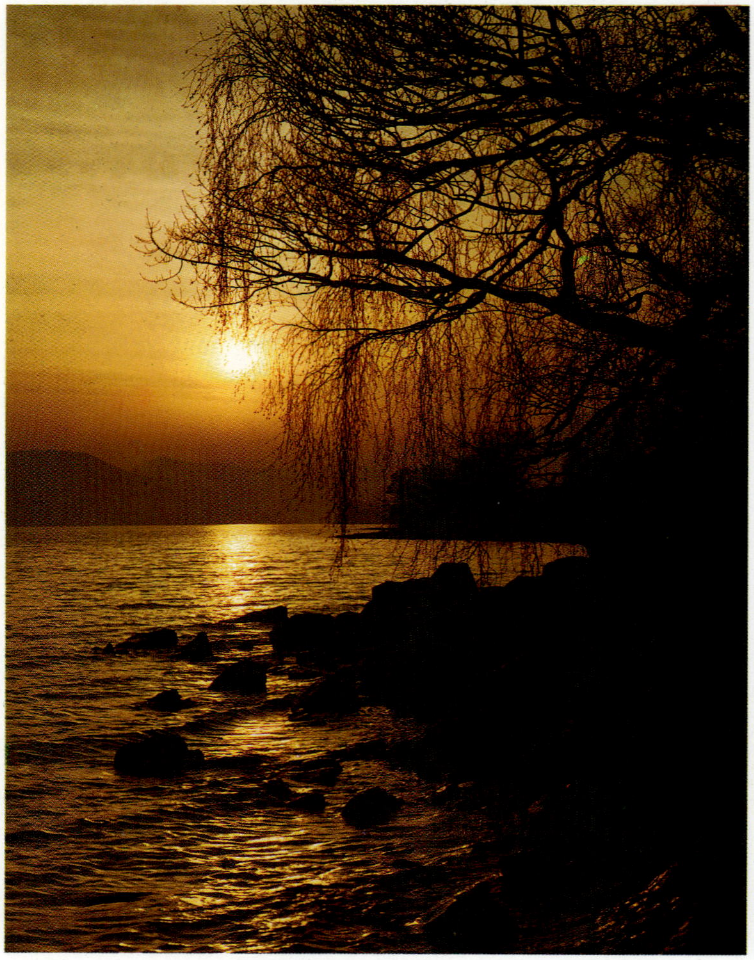

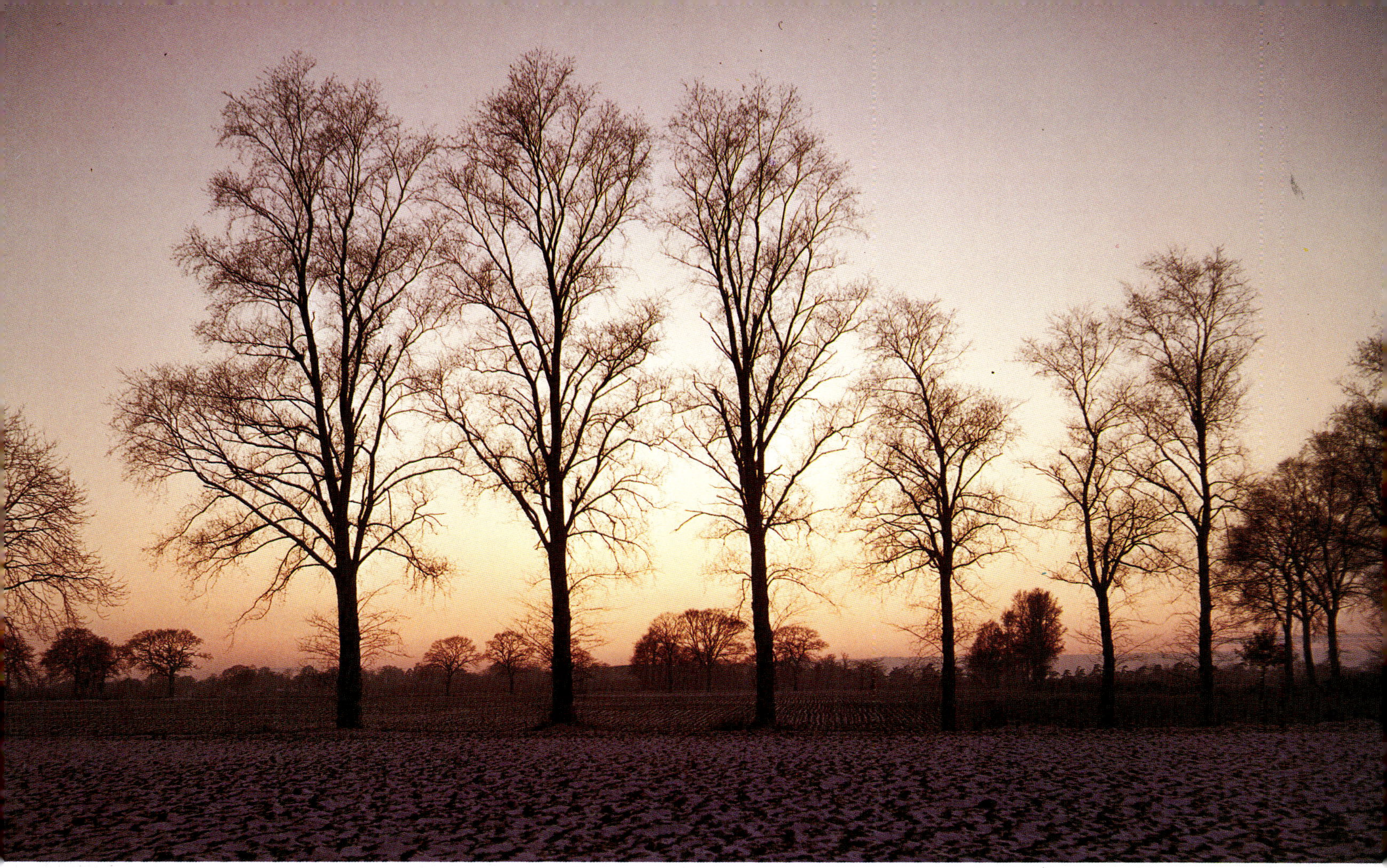

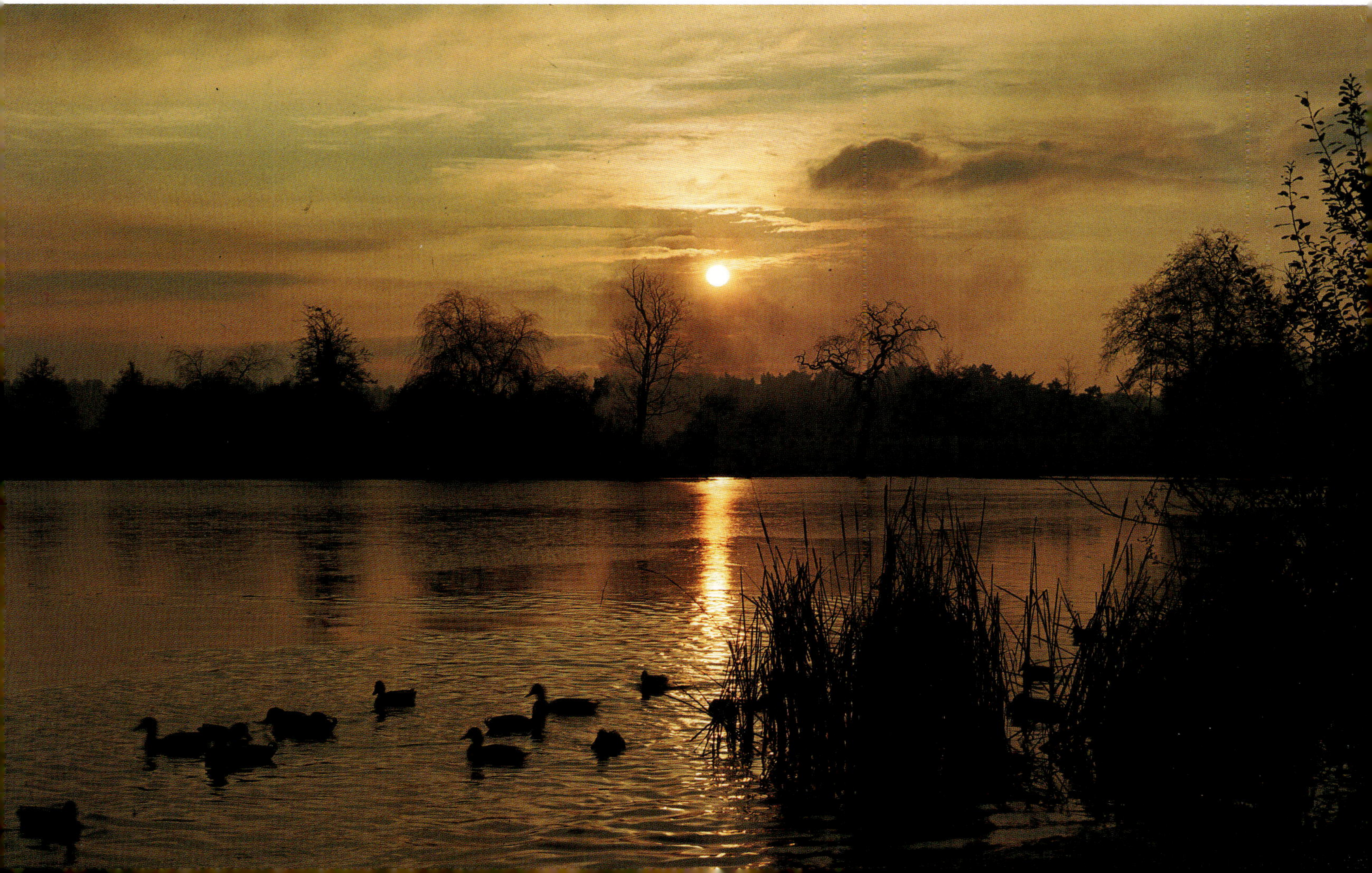

COLOUR AT NIGHT

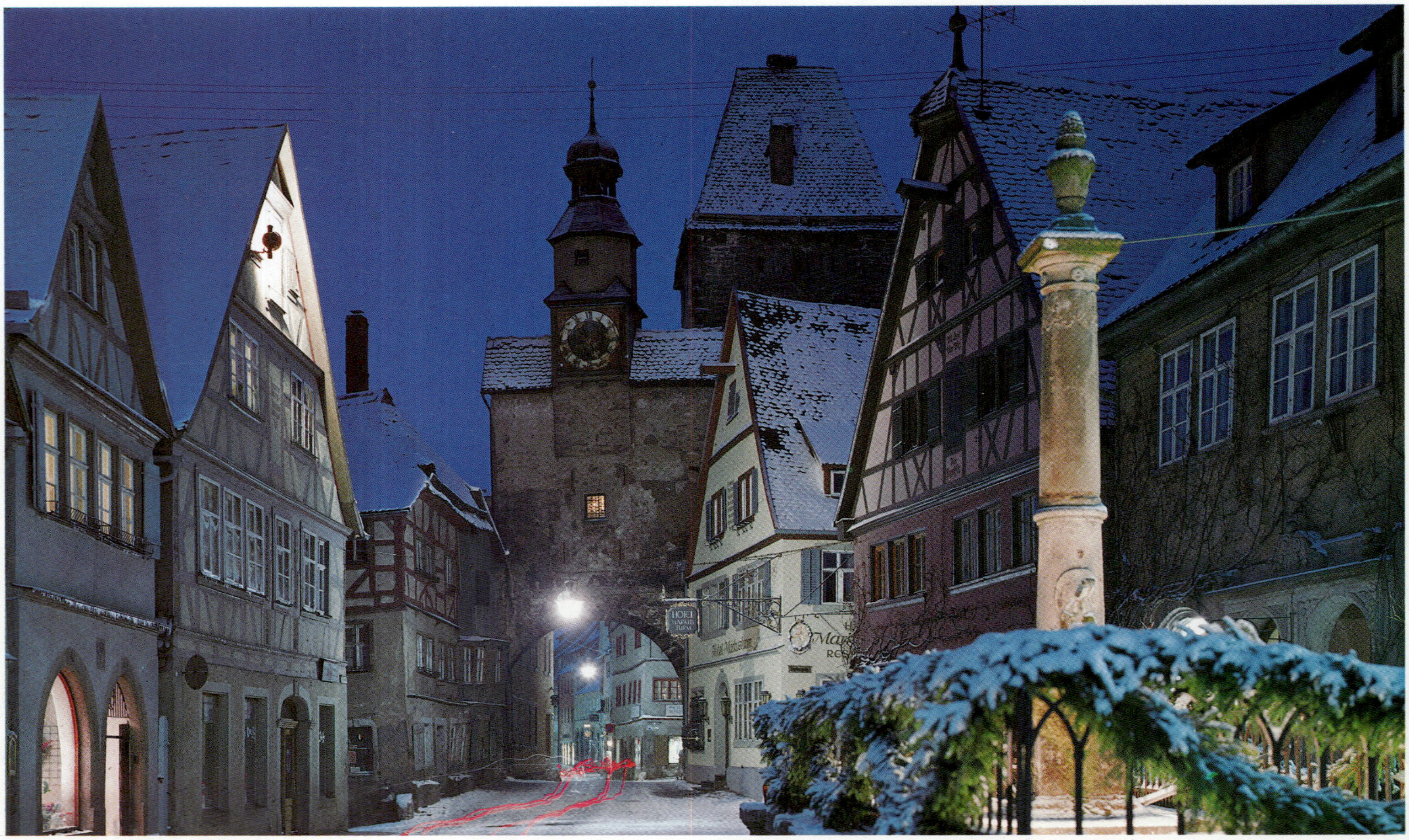

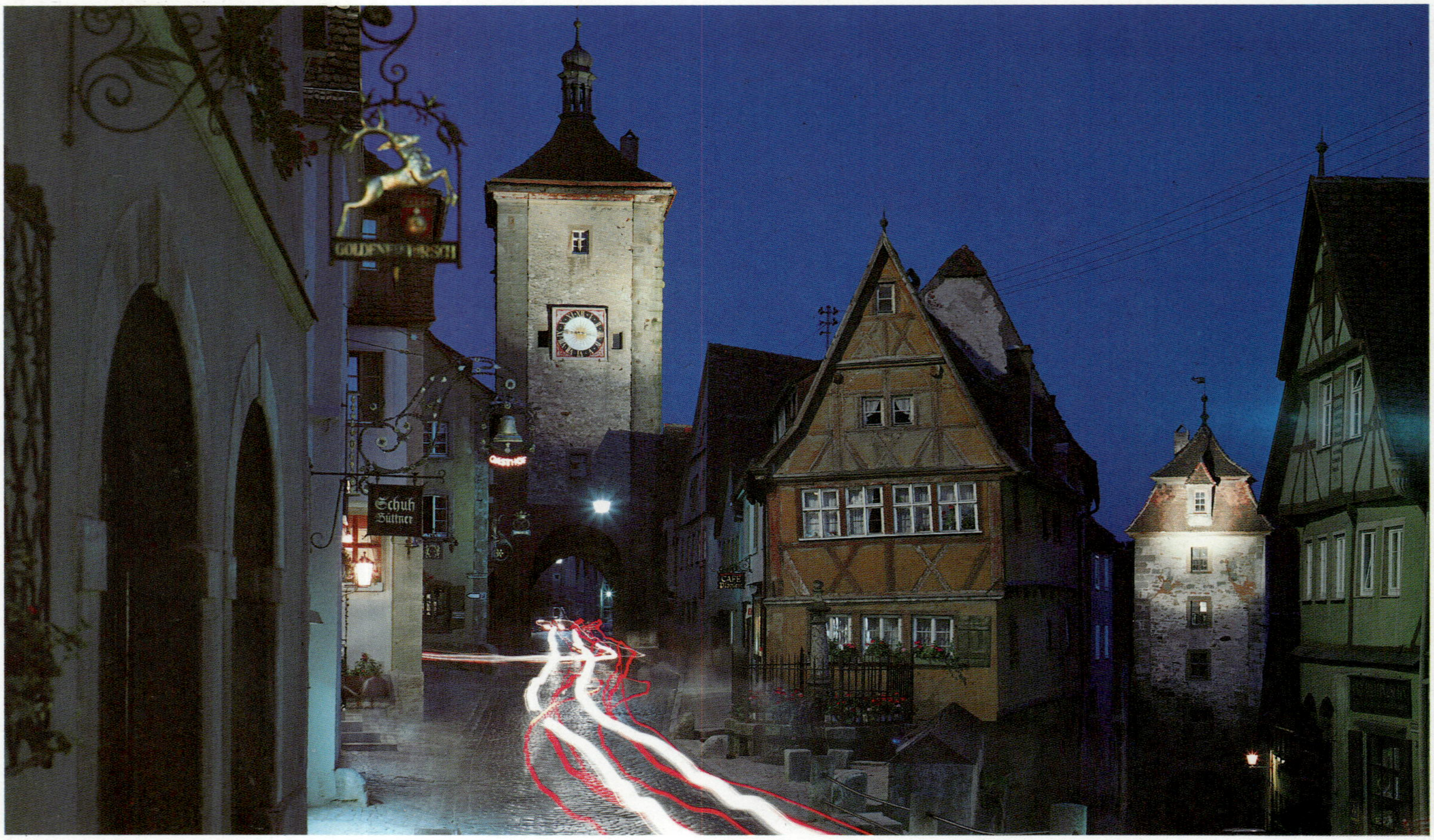

The next weapon is fast film. Here, the modern photographer is incredibly lucky in comparison with his pre-war counterpart. The absolute limit for (black-and-white) pre-war films was about 400 ASA, and now this is available as a standard speed (i.e. without pushing) in both colour print and colour slide. By using faster films such as 3M's 650 ASA or a little 'pushing' in processing (or both) speeds of 800-1000 ASA and more are possible without disastrous loss of quality.

There are, however, two things to watch out for when using these films. The first is that there is a very definite limit to how far they can be uprated; anything more than 100% or *(in extremis)* 150% will lead to colour shifts, thin shadows, colour casts, and all manner of untoward effects. The second is the very mixed colour typically found in night lighting – mixtures of mercury vapour, sodium vapour, fluorescent, and tungsten lighting are by no means unusual, and to expect 'white light' colour rendition is unrealistic.

Fortunately, a very wide range of colour effects is acceptable in a night shot; even more fortunately, the fastest films exhibit the best tolerance for mixed lighting, and for the majority of night shots either the daylight-balanced 400 ASA film or the tungsten-balanced 650 ASA film will give excellent results. To be sure, these films are more expensive than their slower brethren – but the difference is scarcely disastrous (certainly a lot less than buying a faster lens) and the processing costs the same regardless of speed. Admittedly some labs charge a little extra for uprating, but this is far from universally the case and anyway, uprating is often unnecessary.

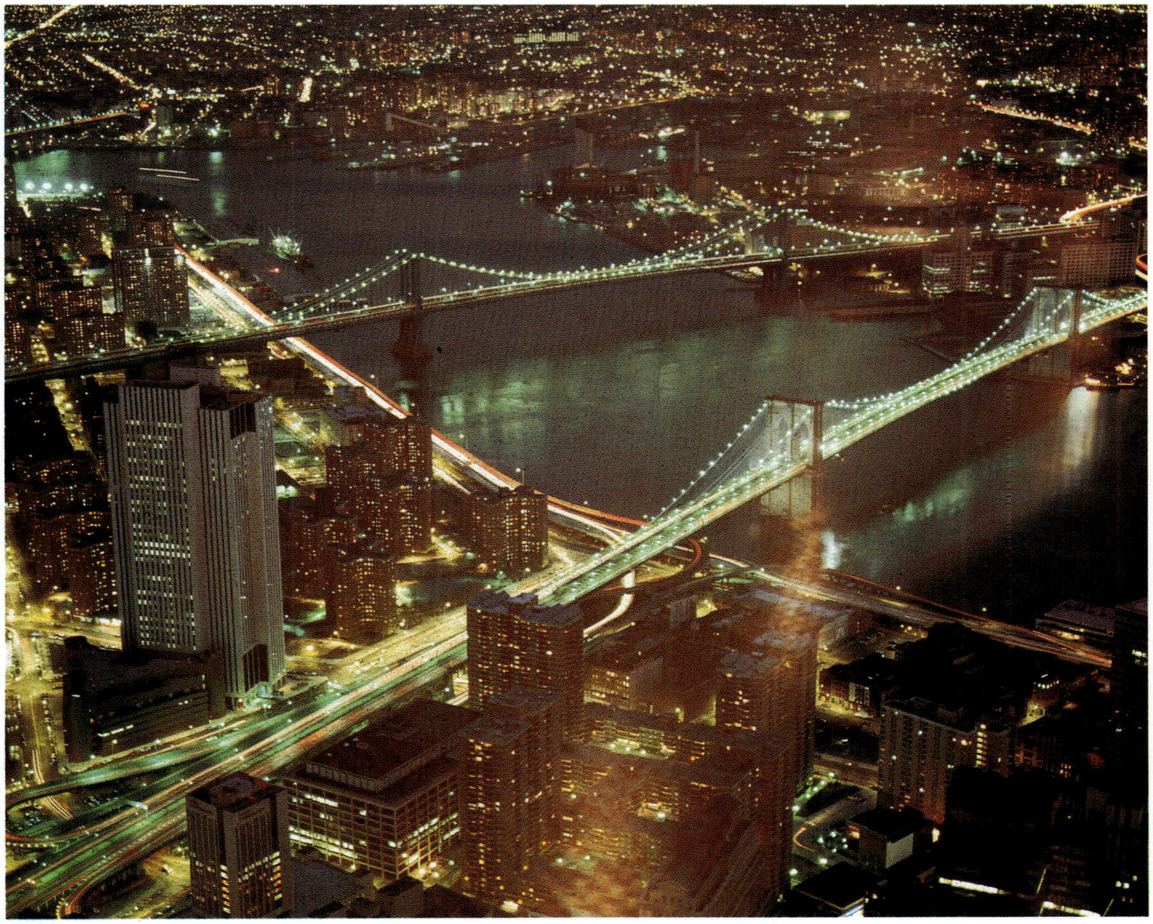

__The squiggly trails of head__ and tail-lights of the traffic in a night shot may be something of a cliché, yet the effect can often be pleasing as shown in the aerial photograph __above.__ In the pictures on the __facing page,__ they add a mystical quality to the sleeping town.

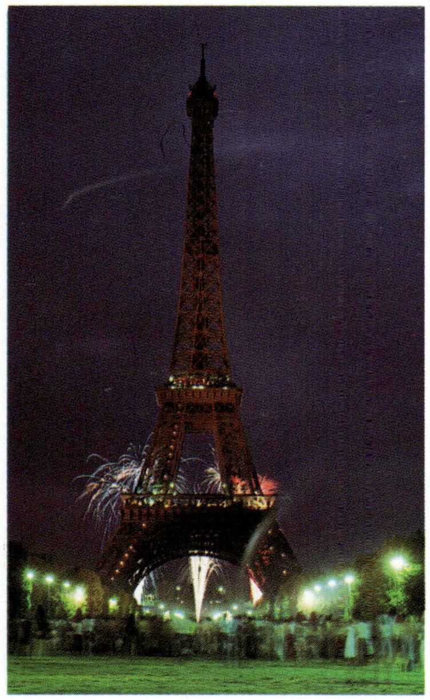

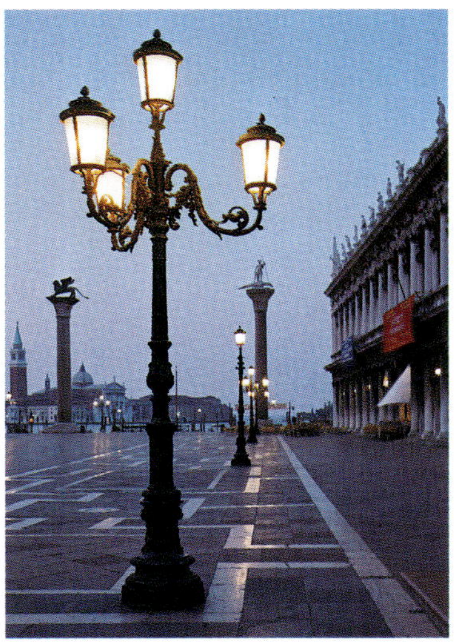

__Many of the most effective__ night-time shots in cities and villages are taken at dusk, when there is still enough light to give an impression of the surroundings but the lamps are lit. This technique is used __above and right.__ A more sophisticated version of the same approach involves making a double exposure a few minutes (or even hours) apart, one for the general scene and one for the lights. Very great care is needed to make sure that the camera is not moved between the two exposures – a solid tripod is essential.

The last arrow in the quiver is a steady hand. Although the received standard wisdom is that you should never hand-hold a picture at less than 1/60 sec. (or 1/30, depending on which authority you believe), you can often get away with slower speeds than this, especially if you can brace yourself or the camera against something during the exposure. It varies widely from person to person, but you may find that by resting the camera on a fence-post or automobile you can achieve a 90% success rate at 1/15, a 50% success rate at 1/8, and some degree of success at even lower speeds.

Remember, though, that even with a slight degree of blur, you may prefer to have the picture rather than pass up the opportunity completely. When I was a student, I used to carry my old Leica, fitted with an f/3.5 lens and loaded with 50 ASA film

COLOUR AT NIGHT

(it was the cheapest available). I have a number of rather wobbly shots taken without support at speeds as long as one full second. They are not artistic masterpieces, but I am still glad that I have them.

As for metering, there is good news and there is bad news. The bad news is that metering in poor light is extremely difficult: the meter may run out of sensitivity, and refuse even to flicker, and in any case the contrast and lighting of a night scene may well differ considerably from the 'typical' scene for which the meter was designed. Spot metering is one answer; zone system metering with a very sensitive meter such as the Luna-Pro is another; a healthy dollop of experience in how to interpret meter readings at night does no harm; but the easiest is to use an exposure table of the type published at the end of this chapter, modifying it in the light of experience as you grow more practised. This fortunately leads us to the good news, which is that metering at night is not very critical anyway.

This is because of the very high contrast which is typical of night lighting, and to a lesser extent because of the different colours of light which are likely to be encountered. With a

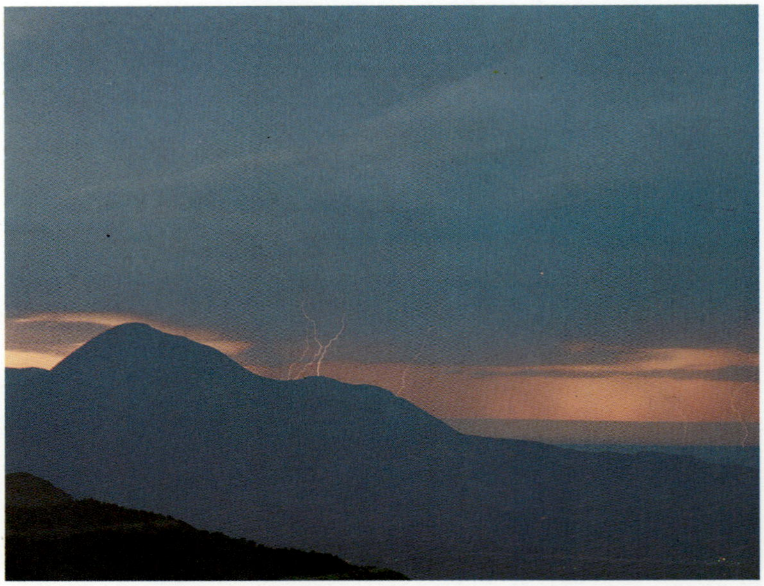

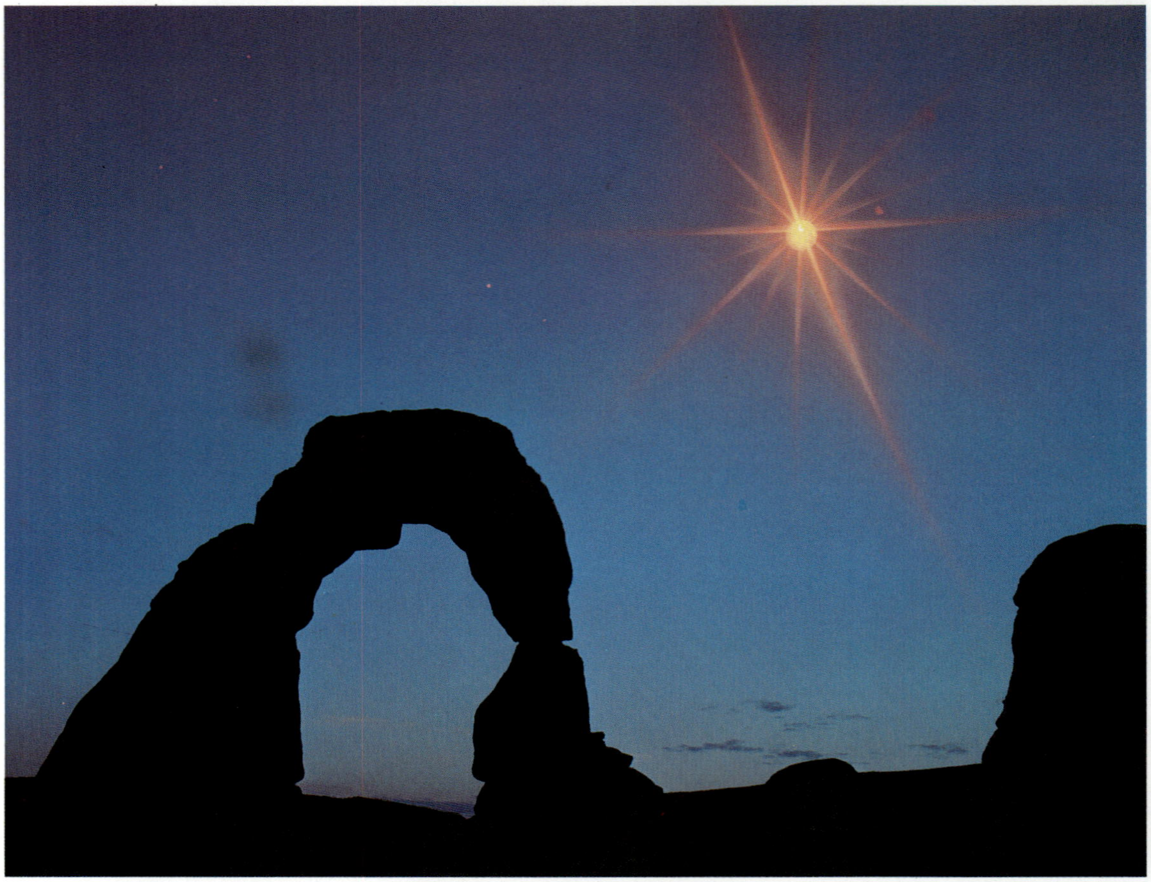

On the immediate right we *have 'nuite Américaine,' or day-for-night; severe underexposure gives the effect of night. The reduction of the subject to silhouette, and the inclusion of a double exposed sun, gives this picture an eerie science-fictional quality. The picture* ***top*** *is a twilight shot of a thunderstorm, and shows the lightning strikes during a long (45-second) exposure; such shots are usually most effective at night. On the* ***opposite page,*** *the moon has been made an important element in the picture. The best way to do this is to use a really long-focus lens – at least 200mm, and preferably 500mm or even longer – or the moon will appear as a minute blob. Exposures must also be brief; at that sort of magnification, the moon fairly races across the frame. A common way to get such pictures is by combining two separate pictures, one a 'stock shot' of the moon and the other of the rest of the subject, with plenty of clear sky.*

conventionally lit daylight scene, we have a pretty clear idea of what we expect to see, but at night we tend to be rather more free of our preconceptions. We are more inclined to accept that the photograph is a photograph, rather than an accurate representation of reality. If the faces are correctly exposed, the clothes may be too dark and the background will certainly be so; but we can look at the faces and accept the picture as correctly exposed. At the other extreme, if the background is lit up like day, the figures may be burnt-out blobs or they may be impressionistic blurs because they have moved during the exposure. If the exposure is long enough, they may even vanish altogether, which is why there are no figures in very early landscape pictures.

Here, though, we are talking about what our great grandfathers would have called 'timed' exposures, and our techniques are rather different.

PHOTOGRAPHY WITH A TRIPOD

Before going on to anything else, it is important to make one point: if colour films are exposed for appreciably longer (or shorter) periods than their designer intended, they cease to respond in their usual manner. They will lose sensitivity, so that

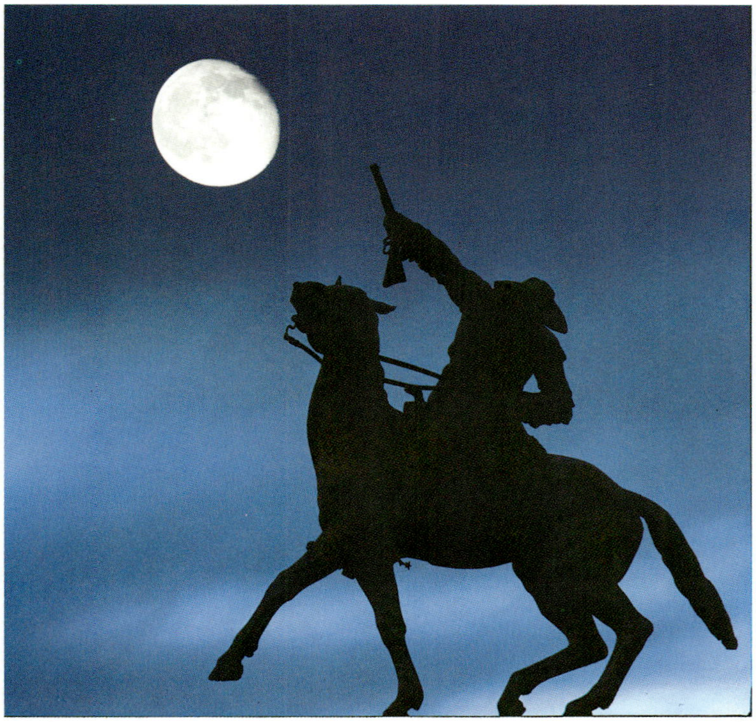

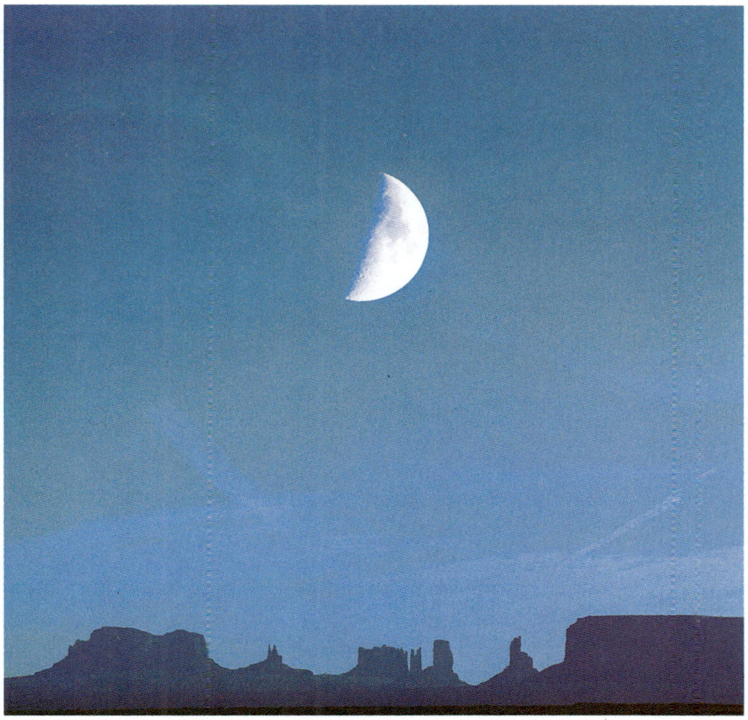

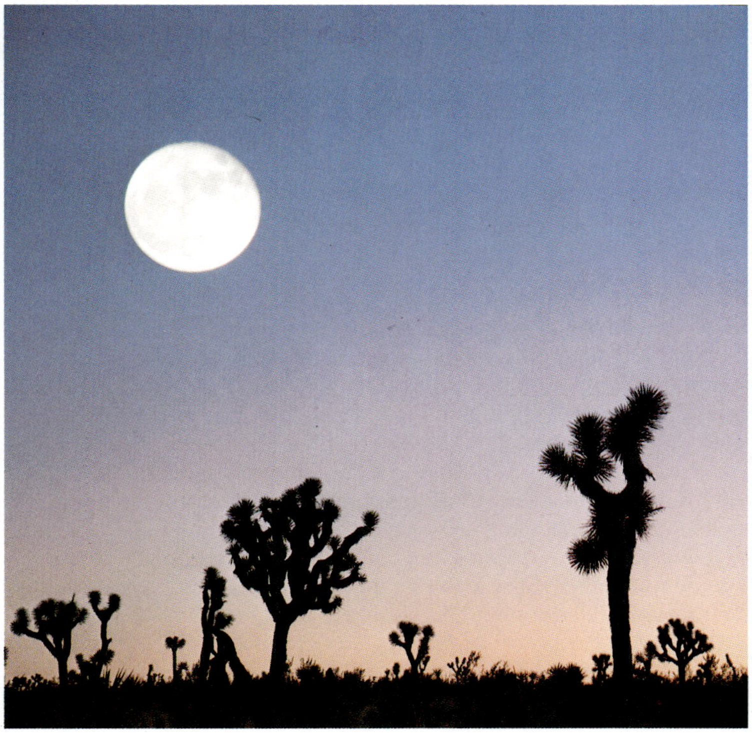

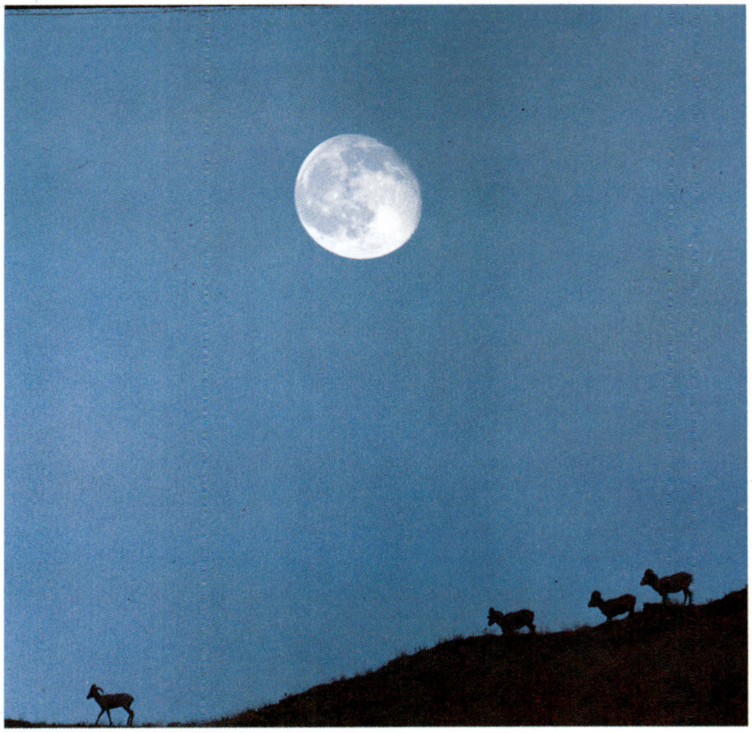

an exposure which the meter would tell us should be thirty seconds might require fifty seconds, and they will change in colour balance so that filters are required to give us a 'normal' looking image. For example, some films tend to go blue if they are exposed for longer than about 1/10 second. The longer the exposure, the more blue they look and the stronger the brownish filter that is required to compensate. Of course, the brown filter introduces a further extension in exposure . . . in practice, this does not give rise to the infinite series of adjustments it might imply, but it can be quite a headache.

These reciprocity defects, as they are called, are not usually significant until you are considering exposures of a second or more. They vary widely from film to film – some films are designed for quite long exposures, and will respond well at five or ten seconds, and the colour shifts and losses of sensitivity are also very different from film to film.

The information you need may be packed with the film, but more likely you will have to write or call the manufacturer; they are all quite willing to help.

With this major reservation, together with the remarks already made concerning the colour of light at night, there is no reason why you should not embark upon night photography with

COLOUR AT NIGHT

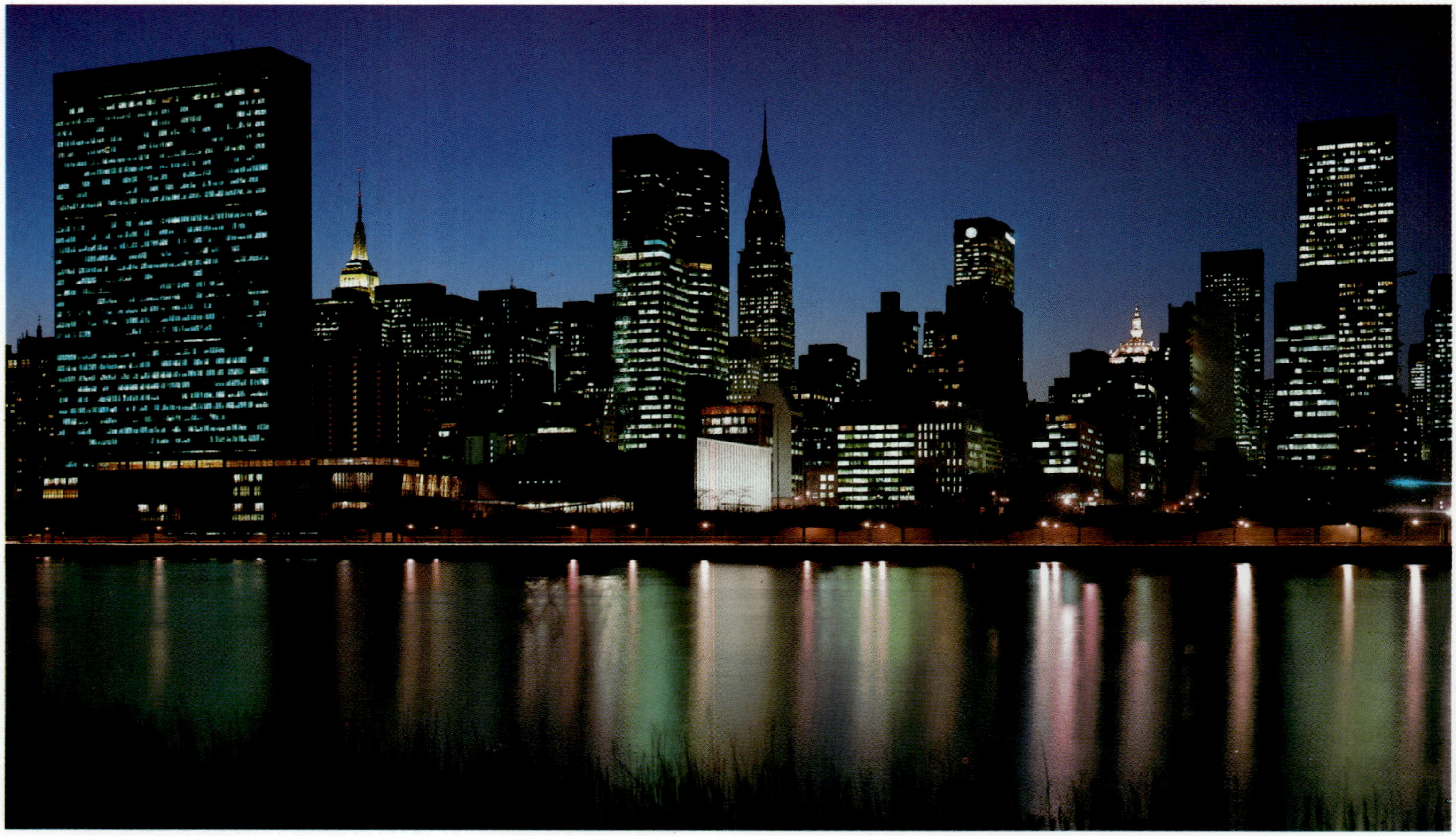

***Even shots like these can be** hand-held if you can find something to rest the camera against – a window-sill, or a wall, or a bollard. A crisp, contrasty lens is essential, or everything will disappear behind a veil of light which masks detail and destroys atmosphere. The pictures **above and facing page top** were taken at twilight; the lower one is rather later on a winter's evening.*

a tripod. A good general guide to tripod selection is to use one as heavy as you can bear to carry and as expensive as you can bear to pay. Light flimsy tripods are all but useless, as they allow a camera to wobble not only in the breeze but also as a result of its own mirror vibration: an old professional trick is to increase the effective mass of the tripod by hanging a full gadget bag from it. If a tripod is too insubstantial to allow this, then it is too insubstantial to be of any use anyway.

There are, however, alternatives to full-sized tripods. One is the table-top tripod, preferably a substantial one: most professionals favour the Leitz model, which is surprisingly inexpensive and doubles as a chest pod, together with either the Leitz ball-and-socket head (frighteningly expensive) or a good proprietary model such as that from Kaiser. Another useful professional standby is the beanbag, which can be as simple as an old sock or small bag filled with sand or even beans: used as a cushion between the camera and any support, it allows exposures of a second or so to be tackled with confidence. With these, a 'hands-on' camera release technique may be permissible, but for the utmost stability you should always use a cable release. If you forget the cable release (and everyone does, sooner or later), try using the camera's built-in self-timer for a vibration-free release.

FLASH OUT OF DOORS AT NIGHT

When using flash out of doors, remember that there will be far less light reflected back from the surroundings than would be the case indoors, so that the flashgun will appear to be giving less light. Furthermore, automation is not much use out of doors; most of the time the gun will be working at full power anyway, and in any case there is the same sort of problem as described with meters, in that the gun is designed to respond to an 'average' scene – into which category a night shot does not fall.

For simple on-camera flash, set the gun to 'manual' and use a guide number 25-50% lower (experiment) than the manufacturer's published number. This should give acceptable results up to the limit of the power of the gun. For instance, one of my guns is rated 100 (feet) at 100 ASA. Out of doors at night I use a guide number of 60 with 100 ASA film, so with an f/2 lens I can use it up to 30′ – though obviously anything nearer the gun than 30′ at that aperture would be overexposed.

A more interesting technique is to use a combination of open-flash and multiple-flash. With the camera on B, each time you double the number of flashes you double the amount of light falling on the film. If you work out, therefore, that you would need to use f/1.4 to get the picture with a single flash, but you are restricted to an f/2.8 lens, you will need 4 flashes (2 x 2). If you wanted to use f/8, in order to get greater depth of field, you would need to use no fewer than 32 flashes (2 x 2 x 2 x 2 x 2).

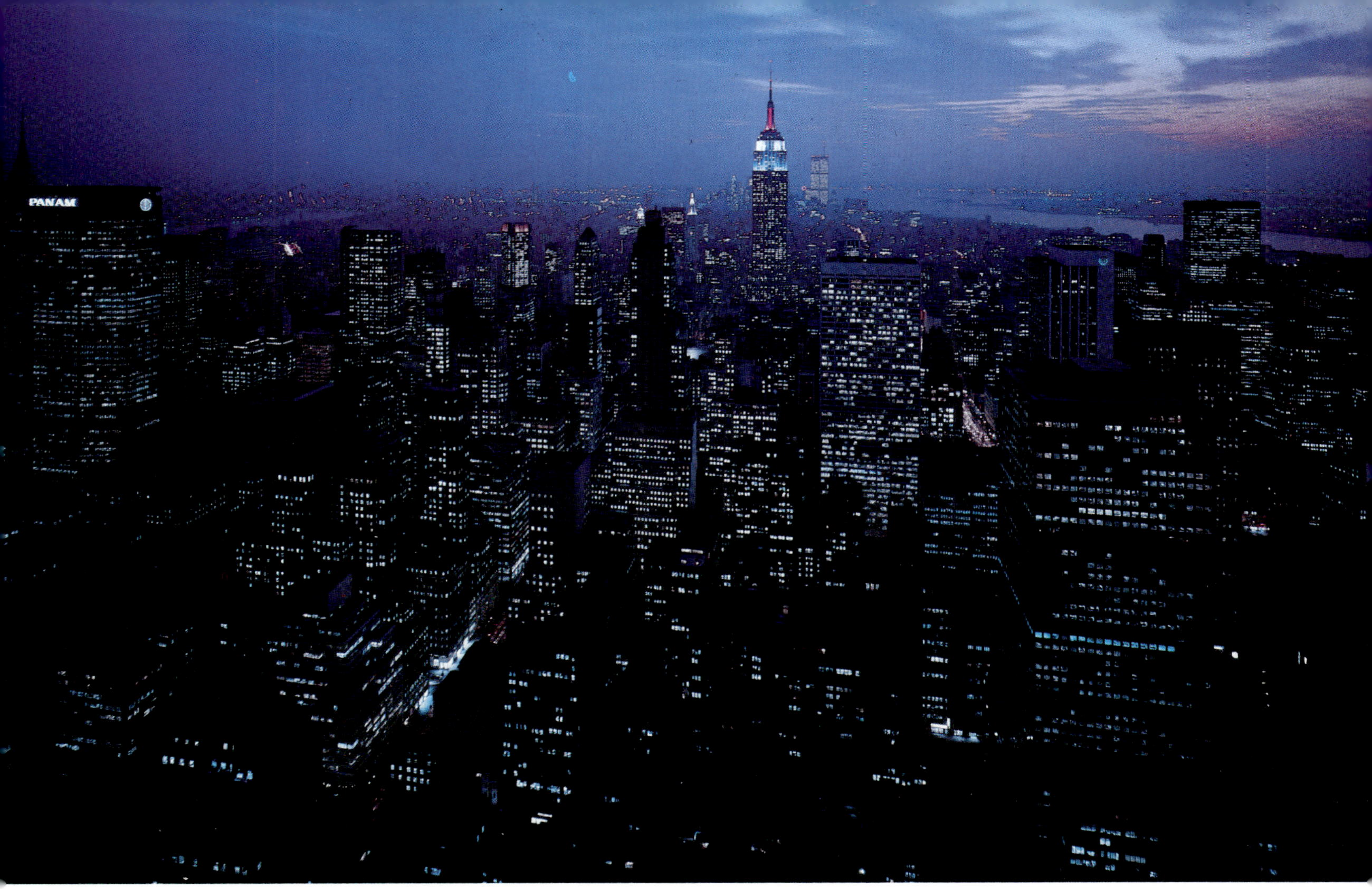
PANAM

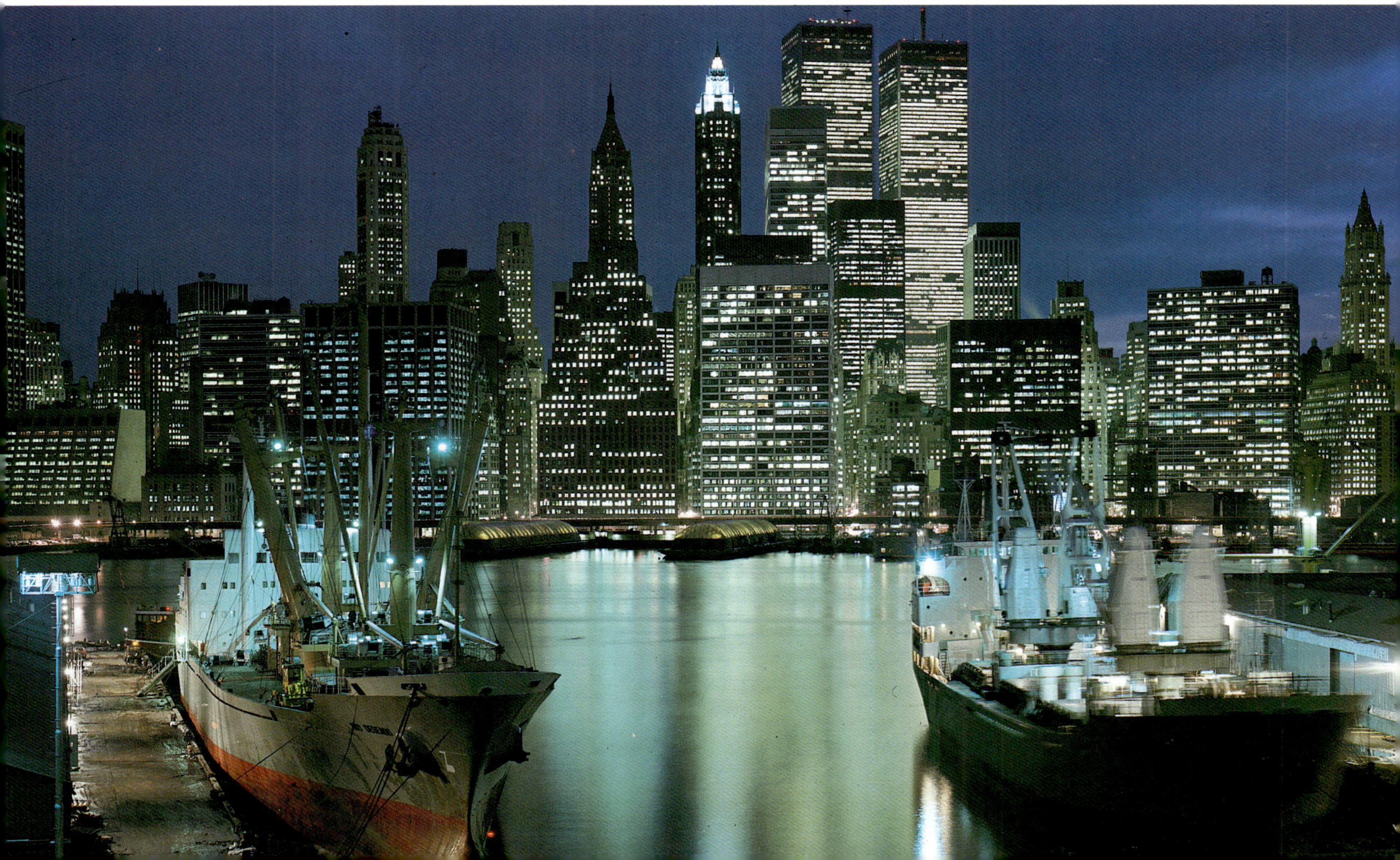

COLOUR AND ACTION

The most obvious thing about action photography is that it freezes a section of time; the dancer, the skier, the racing driver are all fixed in a single pose. The camera can fix things as we see them – or as we think we see them, which is effectively the same thing – or it can show us things we cannot normally see: the snow kicked up by the skier hanging in mid air, or a twirl of colour as the dancer pirouettes.

There is, however, more to it than this. For example, action may be emphasised by the use of bright or dissonant colours: to return to the skier, the picture seems much more action-packed if it shows white snow, blue sky, and brilliant red ski-clothing. The drably-clad skier against a backdrop of pines looks a lot less exciting, even though he may be travelling as fast as his brightly-clad counterpart, or faster. Also, the choice of lens, camera angle, and composition can make a vast difference – though we will return to this later.

Finally, you really have to be familiar with your equipment. The ability to make rapid adjustments to speed, aperture, and focus is essential, and practice at reloading fast, perhaps on the run, is often very useful. There is no real need for a motor drive unless you want to trigger the camera remotely; in fact, the indiscriminate use of a motor drive not only uses up film at an alarming rate, but also diminishes your chances of getting the picture you want. Anticipation, and serious thought about when is the best time to press the shutter release, can give much better results than simply keeping your finger down on the motor drive button. With a 5fps drive your chances are not too bad; with a 10fps drive they are excellent – but you will be reloading the camera once for every 3-7 seconds shooting.

Aside from the technical considerations, there is also the matter of knowing what you are photographing. This is even more essential in natural history photography, where the old

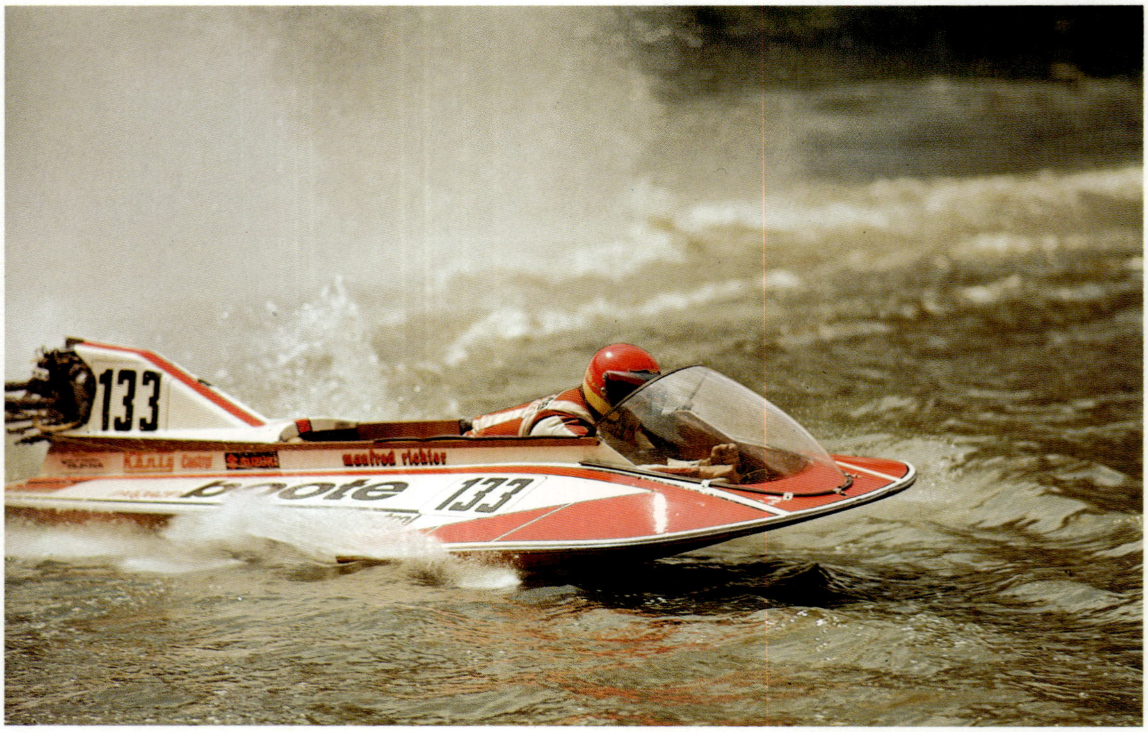

Every one of these pictures has *some blur in it somewhere; the creative aspect of this lies in balancing blur and sharpness to give the impression you want. Experiment and experience, and your own preference, are the only teachers.*

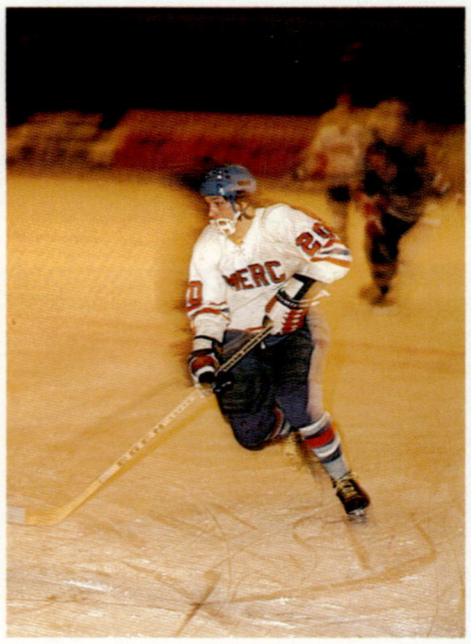

With regard to equipment, the usual rule applies: use what you have. There are, however, two or three technical points which can make life a good deal easier.

First, interchangeable lenses are a boon. It is in the nature of action photography that you cannot always be as close as you would like; the standard 50mm lens fitted to most 35mm cameras is often too short, and the 35-40mm wide-angles fitted to many compacts are extremely limiting.

Instead, a short telephoto in the 85-105mm range is very useful, or (for those sports where you really do have to keep your distance) a lens of 180mm or even more. The 135mm focal length is often an unhappy compromise, and really owes its existence to the fact that it is the longest focal length which could accurately be coupled to the rangefinder cameras of yore.

Secondly, fast lenses and fast film are often called for. Unless you are photographing an event where there really is an enormous amount of light about (such as a skiing competition), you may find that the fast shutter speeds required mean that you need correspondingly fast lenses; and if you want to stop down as well, for maximum depth of field, then fast films will be essential.

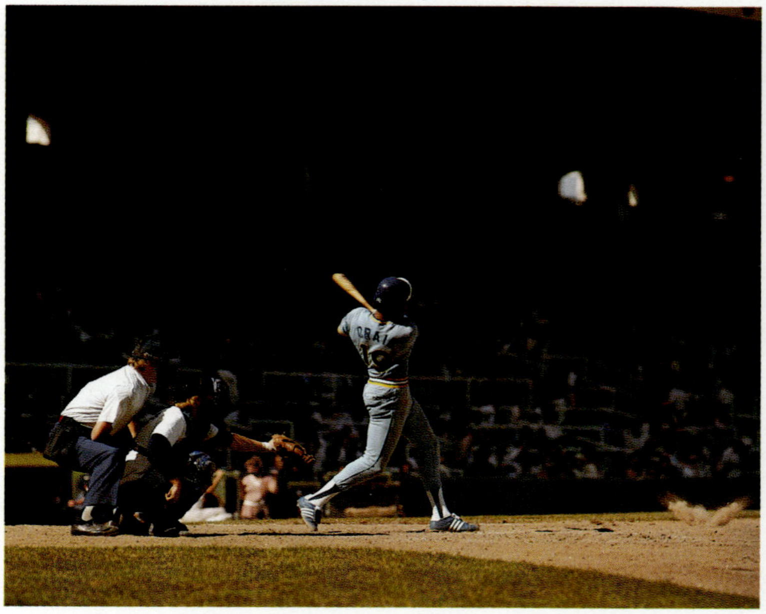

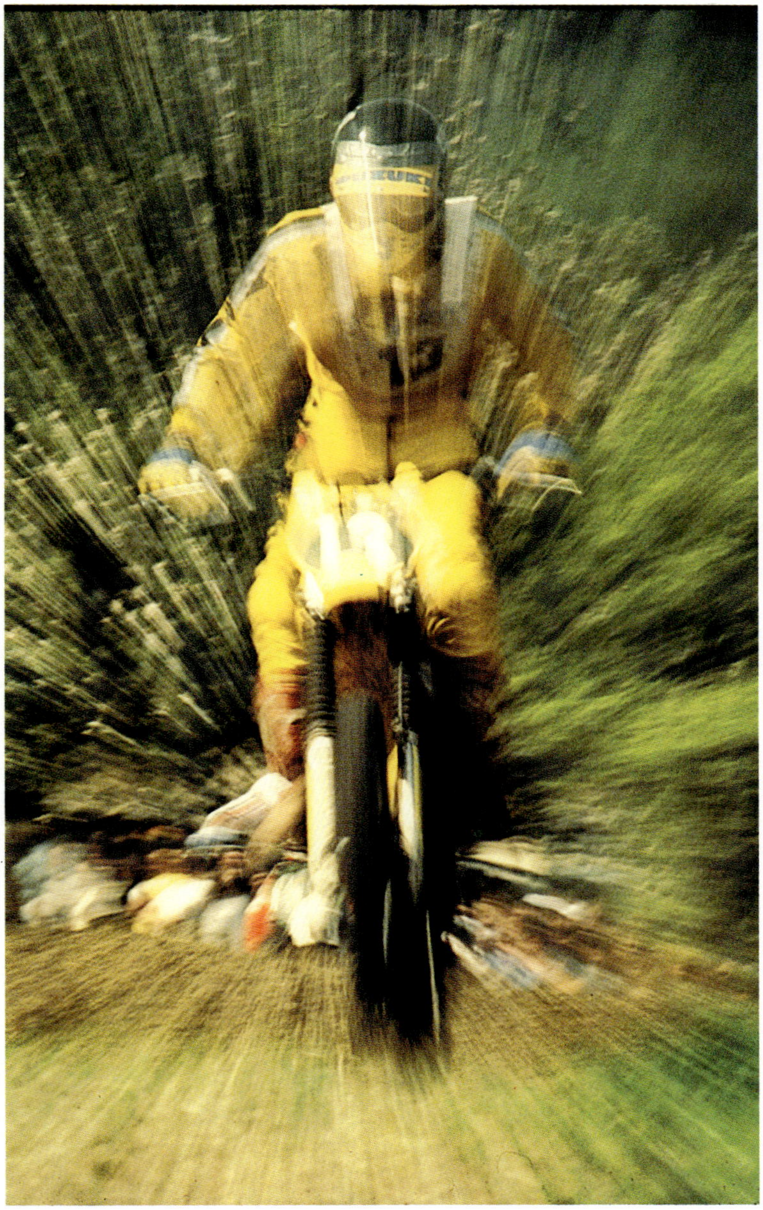

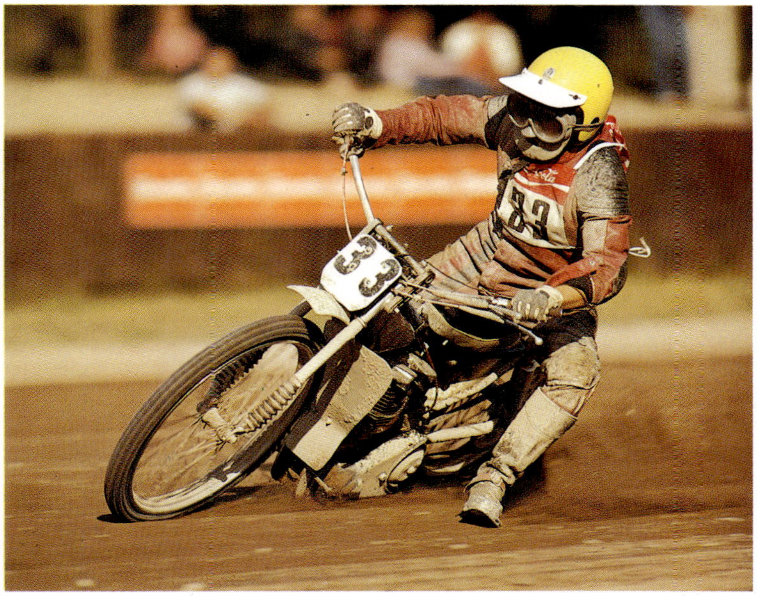

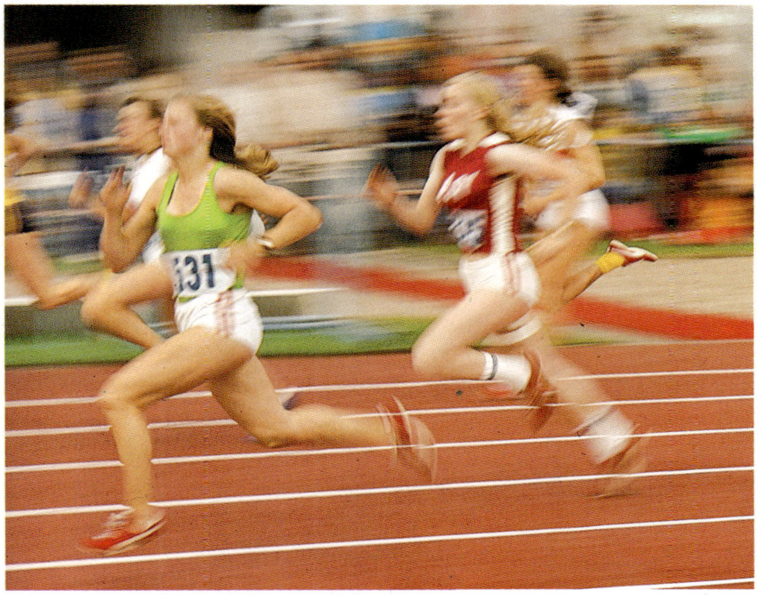

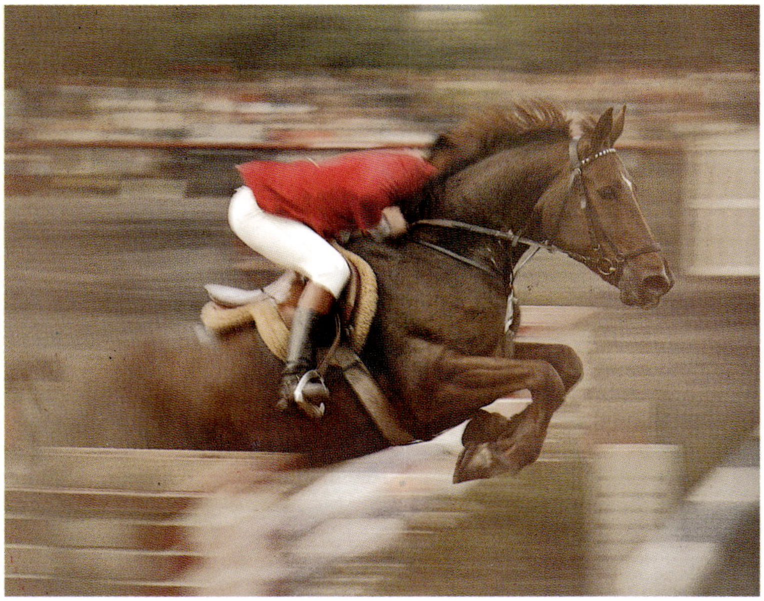

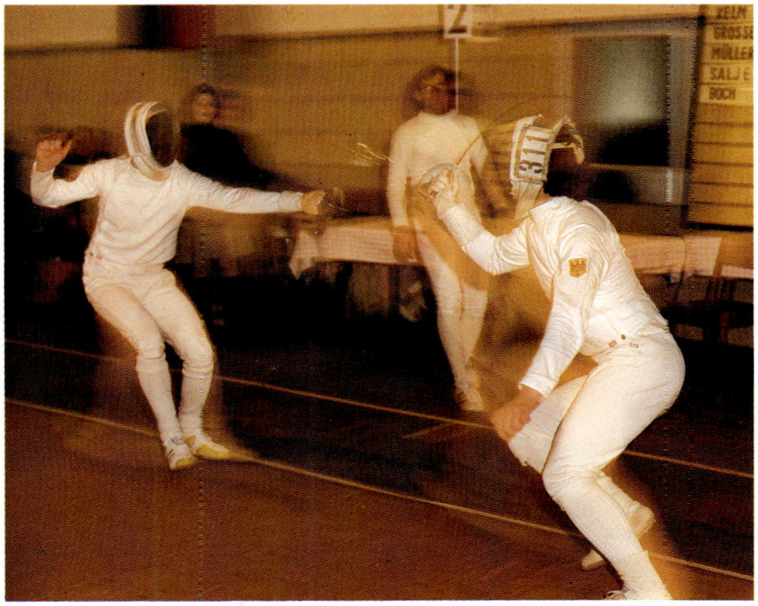

COLOUR AND ACTION

Experience and anticipation *are a very important part of any sort of action photography: the better you understand what you are photographing, the more you are able both to spot a good picture and to see it coming. Few people would go so far as to become bullfighters, but in less demanding activities it is always a good idea to get some personal experience if you can. With this sort of fast-moving and often unpredictable action, you are caught in a trap. You need long lenses, to pull the action close; small apertures, to cover errors in focusing; and fast speeds, to reduce camera shake. Your only saviour is fast film – and then you have grain problems.*

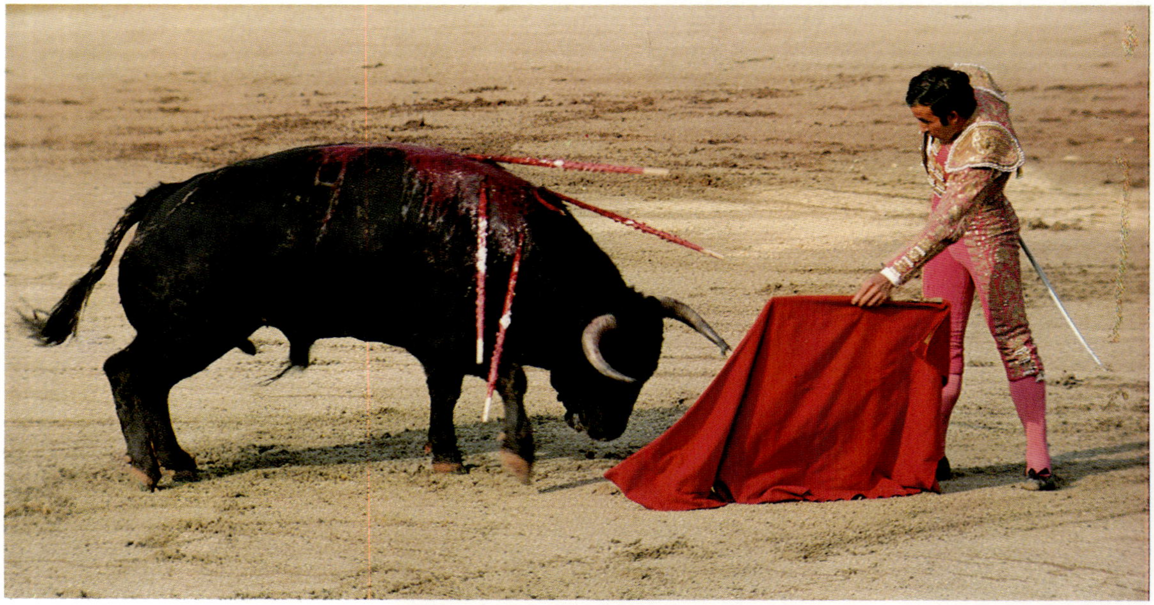

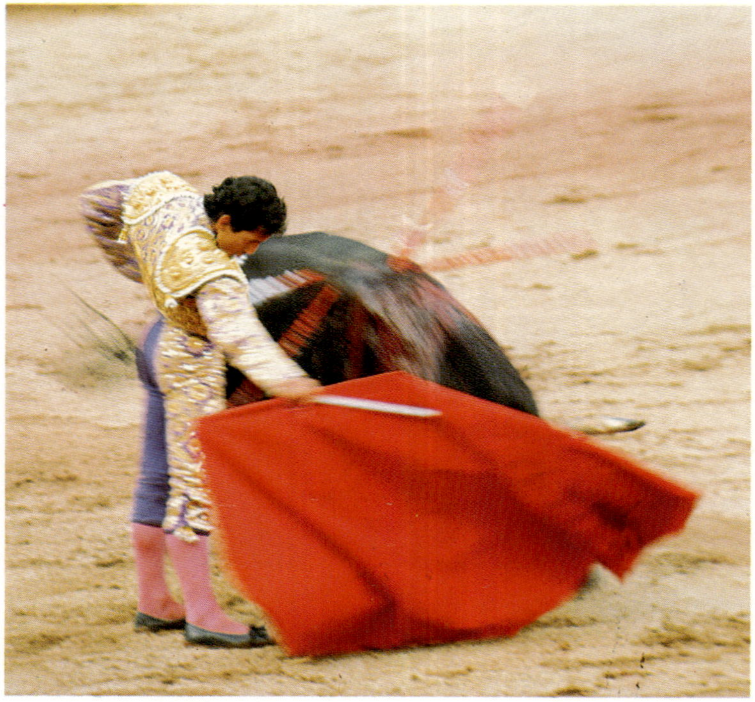

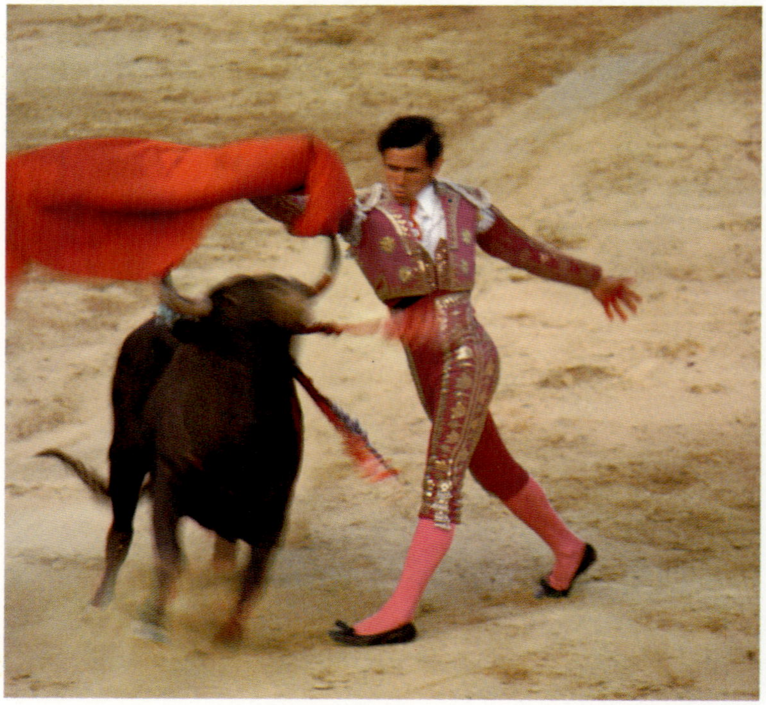

injunction is, 'Biologist first, photographer second' but you will always get better pictures if you have some knowledge of the subject you are photographing and some previous experience, so that you know what focal length lenses to use and where the best angles are. For example, at the first four-wheel-drive meet I went to, I took quite long lenses; I did not realise just how close you can get to the action. Now, the longest I take is 105mm, and I find that I use lenses as wide as 35mm quite regularly. It is best of all if you practice what you photograph, be it ballet or all-in wrestling; but even if you do not, then at least spend some time learning about it.

FREEZING AND BLURRING

It is quite tempting to divide action pictures into two types, the 'frozen' and the blurred. The former uses the highest shutter speeds possible to make sure that nothing in the picture is blurred; in the extreme example, drops of water hang in mid-air as if weightless, and divers are transfixed in time, their bodies just breaking water as unyielding as glass. This used to be considered the standard; it was normal in pre-war photography books (and even for quite some time afterwards) to quote long and complex tables of shutter speeds required to stop various kinds of action at various distances. Apart from such implicitly unnerving ideas as standing within ten feet of an express train moving at sixty miles an hour, there were multiplication and division factors to be considered according to whether the movement was at right angles to the line of sight, oblique to it, or (another alarming thought) coming straight towards you.

The blurred approach, on the other hand, can go to the extreme of showing a few impressionistic whirls and labelling them 'Andalusian dancers'; at an exposure of a second they might be Andalusian, Gipsy, or Republican. Periodically this becomes an overwhelming fashion, but used with discretion it can be very effective indeed.

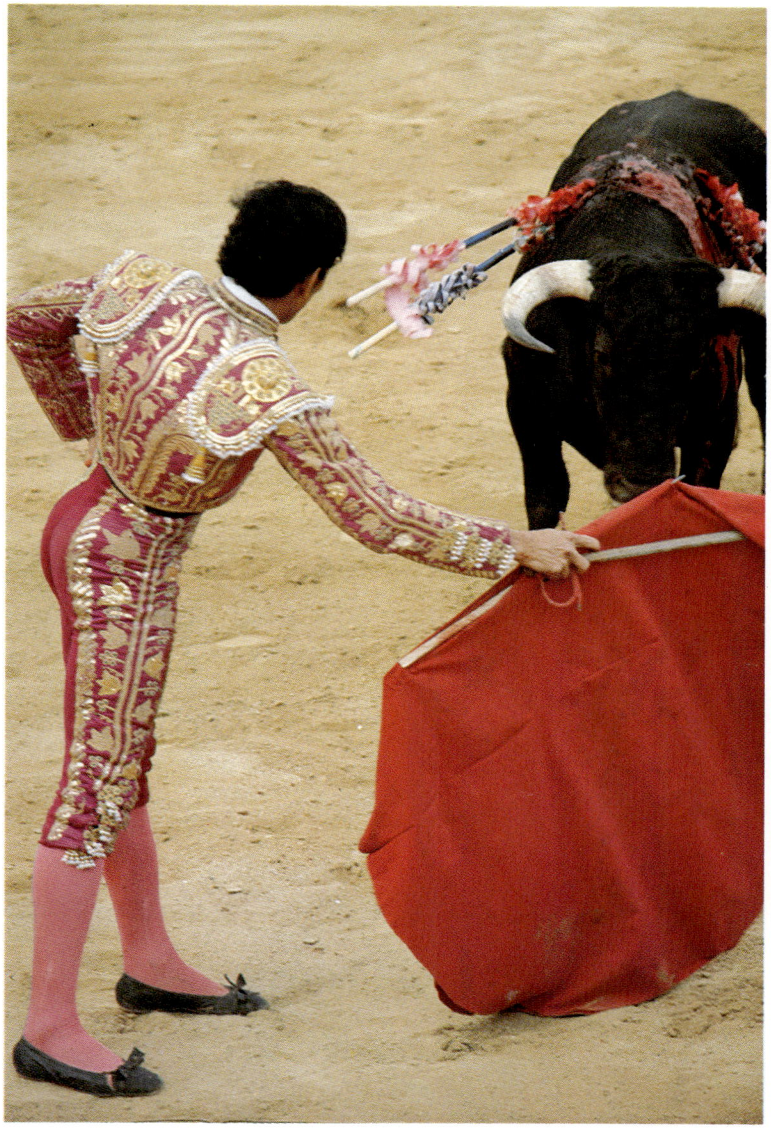

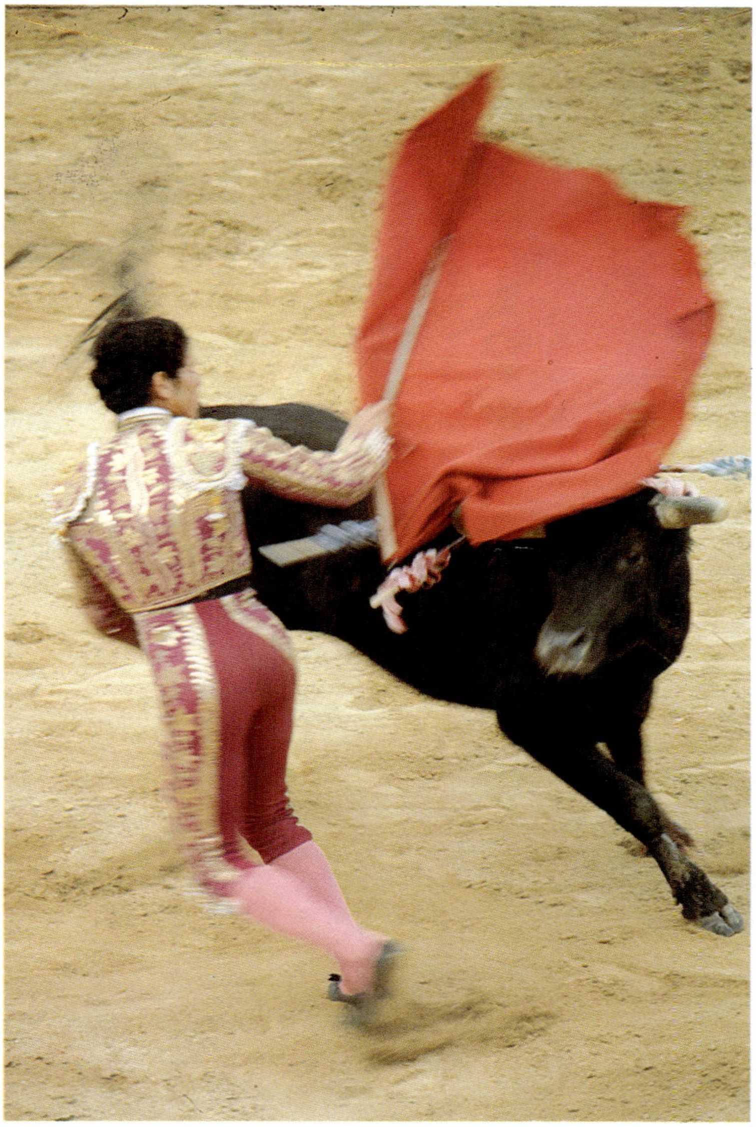

The temptation to make the clear distinction should be resisted, though, because it encourages the use of the two extremes of the shutter-speed dial without considering whether a better effect might not be attained at a more conventional speed. For example, a speed of 1/15 might be enough to show the body and face of a runner with considerable clarity, whilst blurring arms and legs into an impression of effort and speed. This idea of 'compound motion', some of which may be frozen and some not, is extremely important. For example, you might want to show a racing car razor sharp, but leave the wheels a blur. With a swimmer, you could run the whole gamut from a 'fully frozen' 1/2000 sec., through a picture which held the figure sharp but showed some blurring of the water or one which kept the face reasonably sharp but blurred the arms, to a sinuous blur of action which recalled the shape and motion of a fish.

You can also mix a number of sharp images to give the impression of blur and movement, or mix a sharp image (or images) with a blurred one. The former is normally achieved with stroboscopic (multiple) flash, but with some cameras it is possible to use the motor drive to give multiple exposures on a single frame; even if the camera does not specifically provide this feature, pressing (and holding) the rewind button may have the same effect. Alternatively, a straightforward multiple exposure may be possible.

The usual way to get a blurred image plus a sharp one is to use a long exposure and fire a flash during that exposure. If you want to use synchronised flash, you will need to plan the exposure so that the sharp part is at the beginning; it is generally more convenient to use 'open flash' and fire the gun manually. This has the added advantage that you can make more than one flash exposure. For obvious reasons, exposure determination is difficult and a fair amount of experiment and bracketing will be necessary. Another possibility is again a straightforward multiple exposure.

In fact, when you start considering the possibilities of this sort of photography, the options are almost endless. For example, if you use a tripod you can hold the image still at one (or more) points, and pan or tilt to create blur; you can use the various 'motion' attachments marketed by filter manufacturers, which are essentially curved prisms, to 'smear' part of the image; or you can zoom during exposure.

Although the zoom has become almost a cliché, there are still many occasions when it can be used. It requires quite a lot of practice if you are to avoid jiggling the camera or shifting focus, but if you combine it with a flash exposure even this is not a problem. Usually, the most convincing results are obtained by using synchronised flash and zooming from the longest focal length to the shortest; that way, you get the subject sharp, but

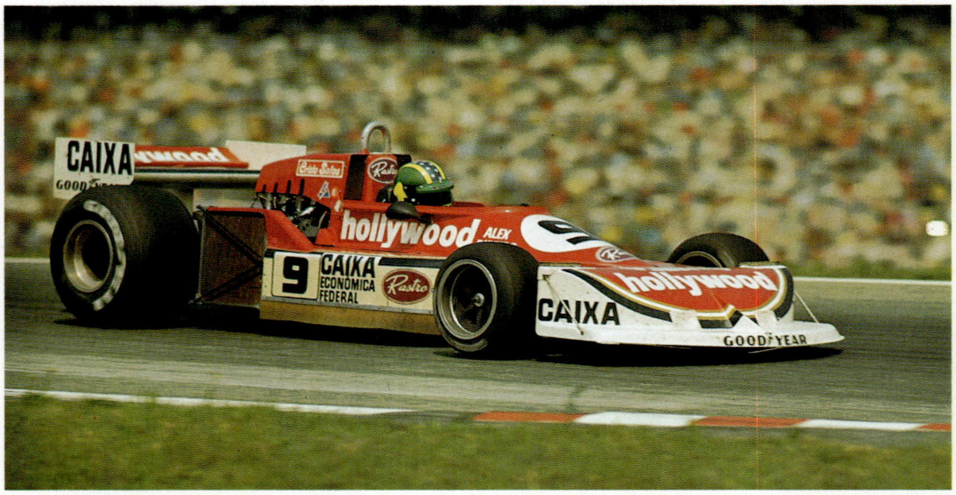
CAIXA
hollywood
9
CAIXA
ECONOMICA
FEDERAL
hollywood
CAIXA
GOODYEAR

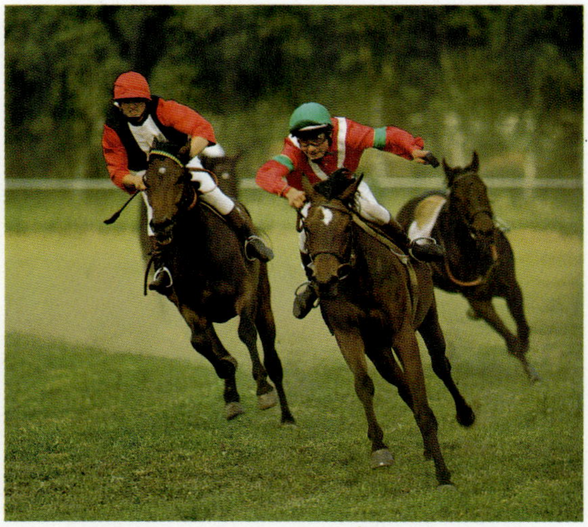

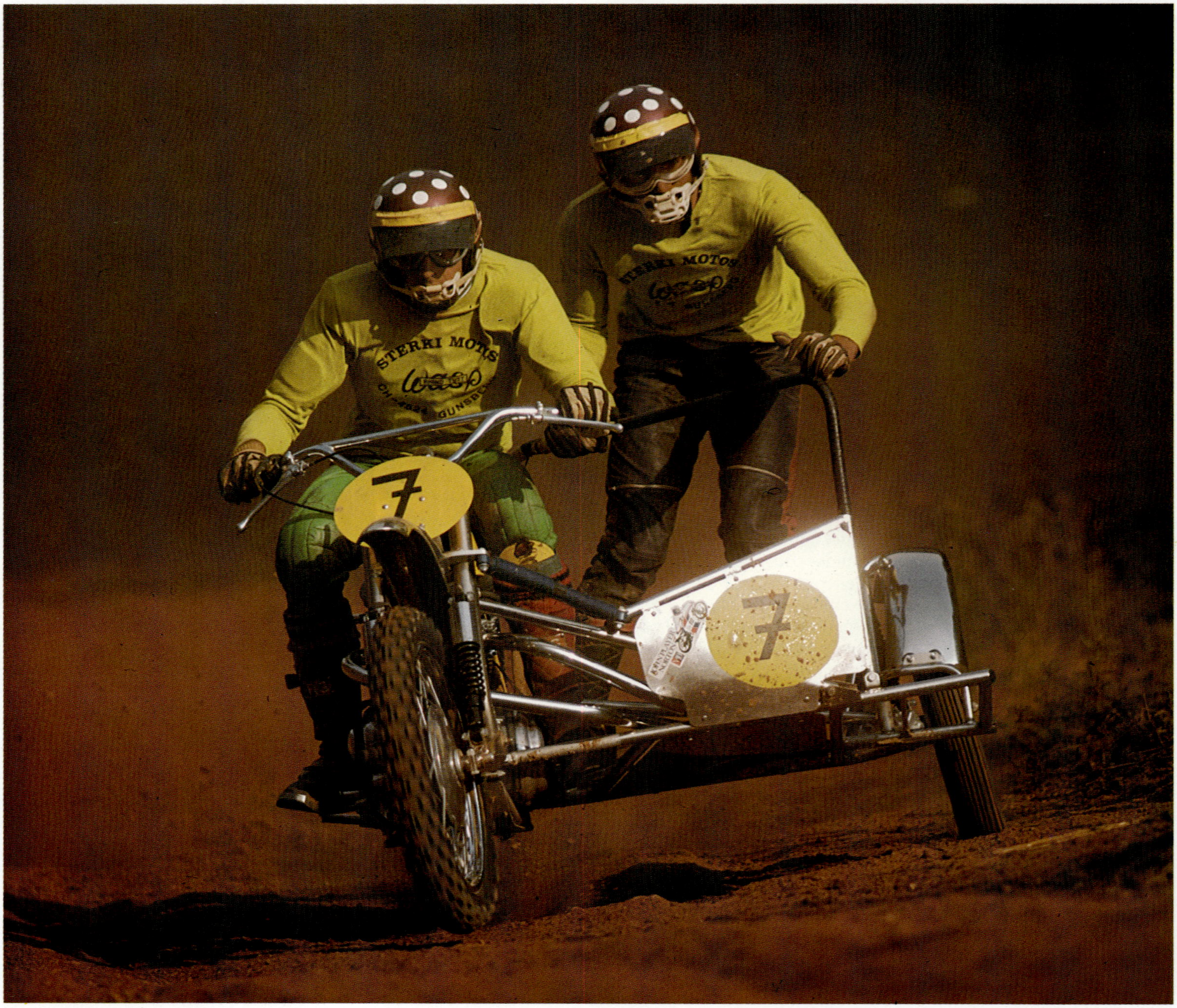
STERKI MOTOS
7
7

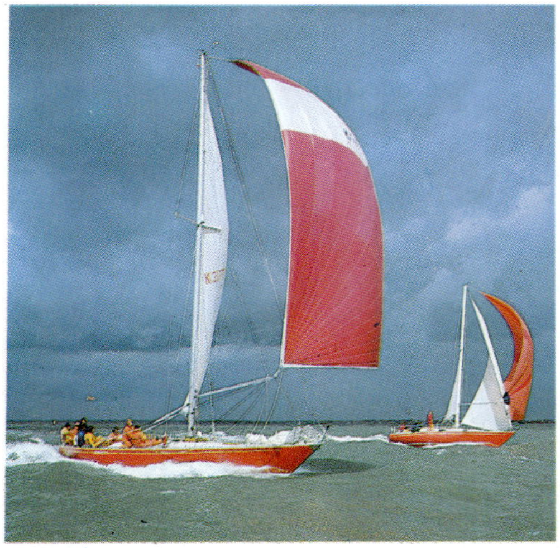

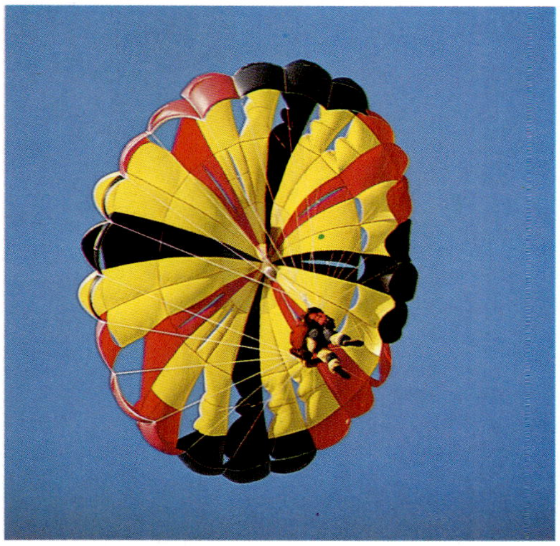

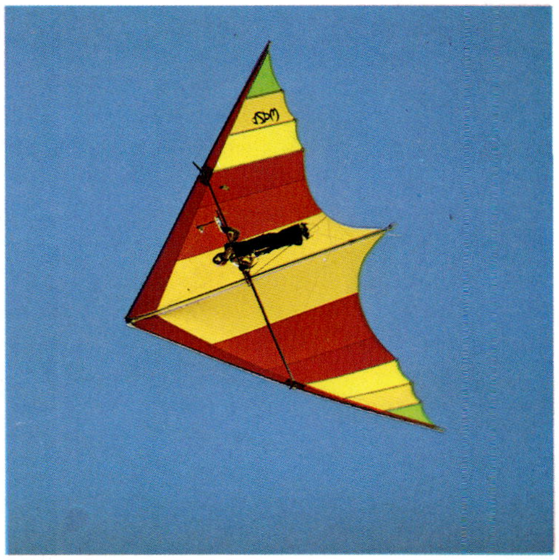

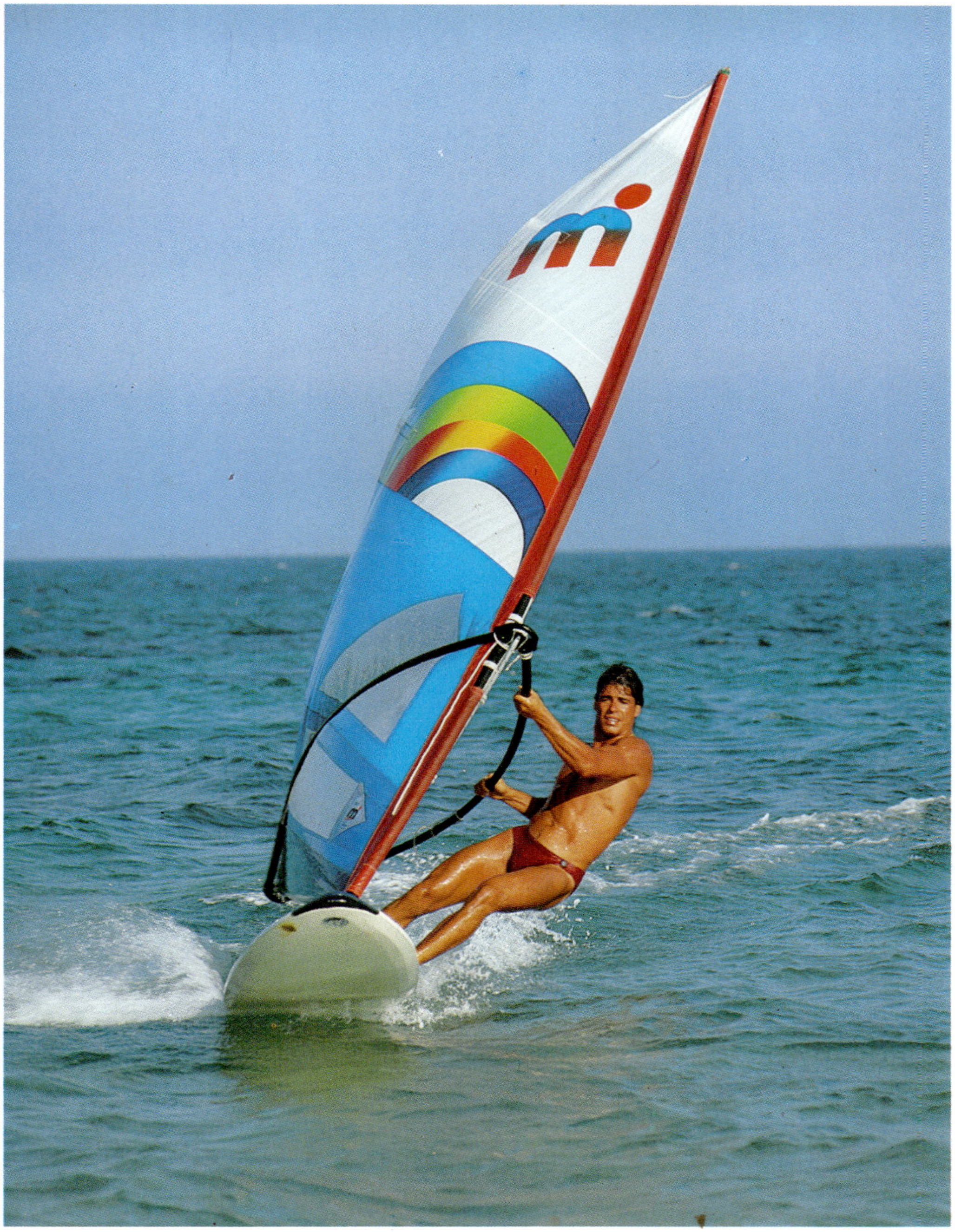

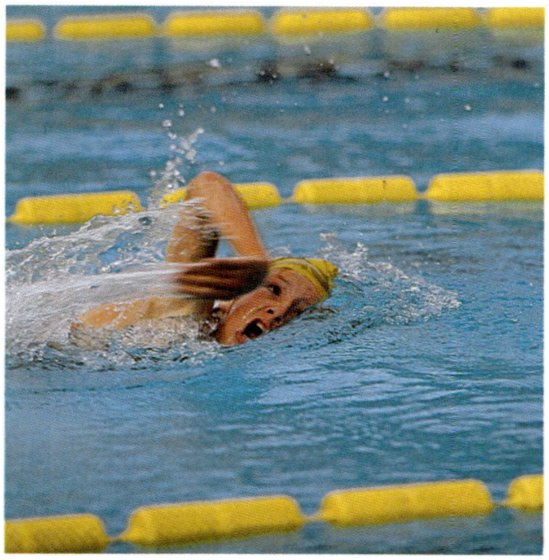

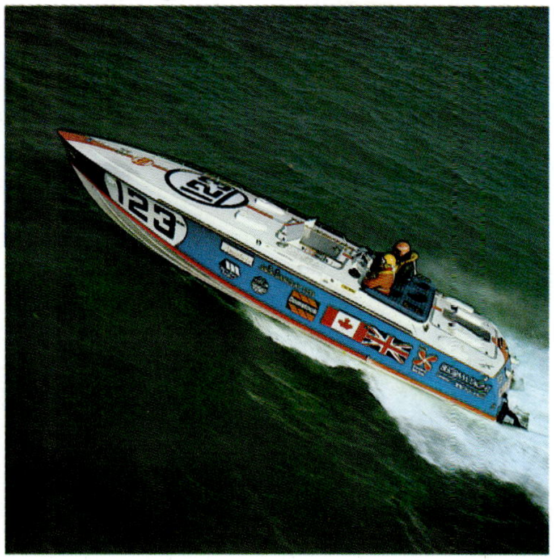

Mentally, we always tend to *associate colour and action; any picture which panders to this preconception stands a good chance of success. It is usually very important to fill the frame with the action: most action sports require a great deal of featureless track, water, etc., which if allowed to fill the picture can be very boring.*

surrounded by 'action streaks' as though it is exploding out towards you. Incidentally, it is not necessary to use a zoom lens to achieve this effect; the change in angle of view of any lens as it is focused will give a similar effect. All that you have to do is 'pull focus' during the exposure – the angle of view narrows as you focus closer.

A technique which makes use of blur and motion is panning. If you follow a moving subject, keeping it in the centre of the viewfinder, then you can use a much slower shutter speed than if the camera were fixed. In extreme cases, this allows you to render sharp a subject which you could not otherwise photograph: a racing car might require a 1/3000 sec. exposure to 'freeze' it without panning, and only 1/500 if you panned. Even with slow-moving subjects, though, panning can be very useful. First, it allows the use of shutter speeds which accentuate the kind of compound motion already referred to; secondly, it allows you to use smaller apertures (either because they are all that you have or for increased depth of field); and thirdly, it blurs the background in a way which suggests great speed. This last effect can be particularly effective, whether used to convey an accurate impression (of, say, a racing car) or something more subjective. A runner, for example, can be made to look as if he is literally 'travelling like the wind'.

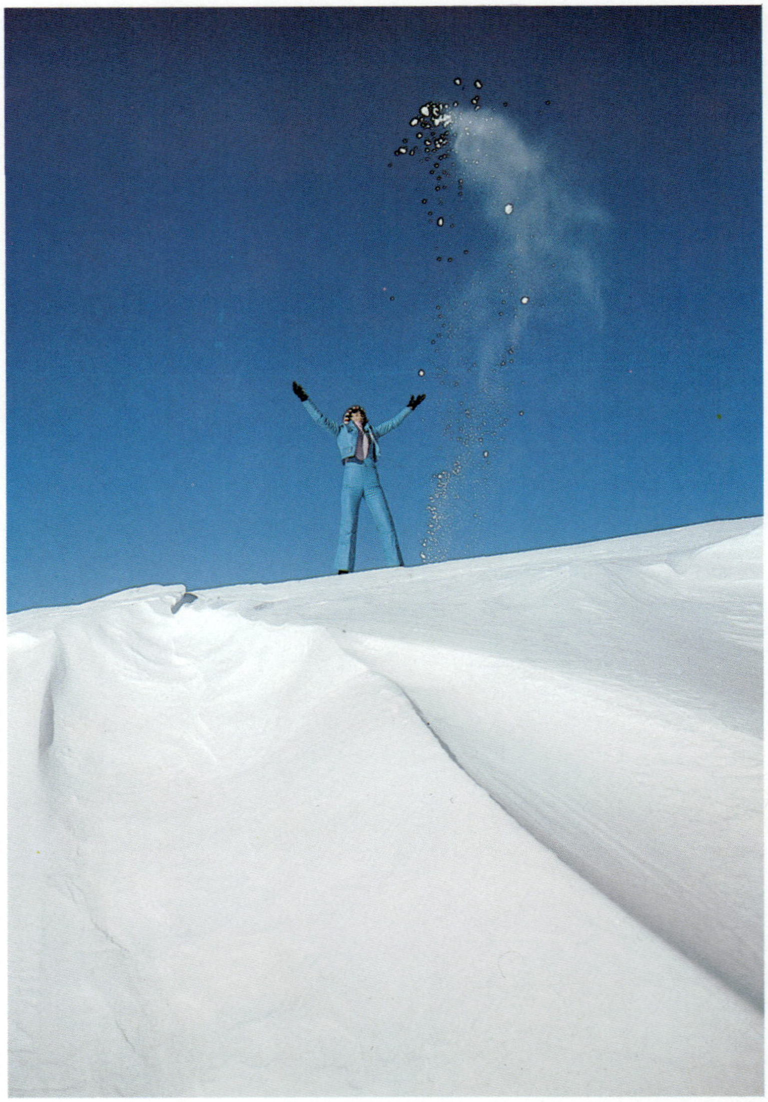

ACTION AND COMPOSITION

Although the old-fashioned 'rules of composition' are now rightly regarded as useful generalisations rather than rigid rules, there is no doubt that some compositions are more dynamic than others. To take a very simple example, let us return to our skier. If he is just entering the picture, there is a feeling (no matter how irrational) that he has the rest of the frame to ski across; whereas if he is at the other side of the picture there is a feeling of tension, as if he is about to burst through the border.

There are a number of tricks like this, though purists object to some of them. One is the choice of lens; a long lens will 'stack up' the action in a way familiar from coverage of motor races, whilst a wide angle will stretch or accentuate perspective – for example, a wide-angle lens mounted in an aeroplane, and so positioned as to show a part of the aeroplane, will dramatically emphasise the isolation of a skydiver. Another is tilting the camera; we are conscious that mountains have steep slopes, so if the camera is tilted slightly to emphasise the slope we accept this as natural. It is possible to overdo this; there is one otherwise excellent publicity picture of a four-wheel-drive vehicle fording a stream – but if the hill were as steep as the picture shows, the stream would be more like a waterfall than the brook it appears to be in the picture! It is hard to criticise them too much, though, because anyone who has ever tried to show the steepness of a hill (in San Francisco, for example) will realise just how tame it can appear in the final image. It is interesting to speculate how much of this is due to our acclimatisation to exaggerated photography.

Even the time-worn concepts of 'balance' and the 'S curve' can be applied. According to classical theory, a composition had to be 'balanced' with a primary subject and a secondary; if we omit the balancing secondary, there is a certain tension in the picture. Similarly, the old 'S curve' leading into the picture can be used to convey the idea of rapid movement along that curve.

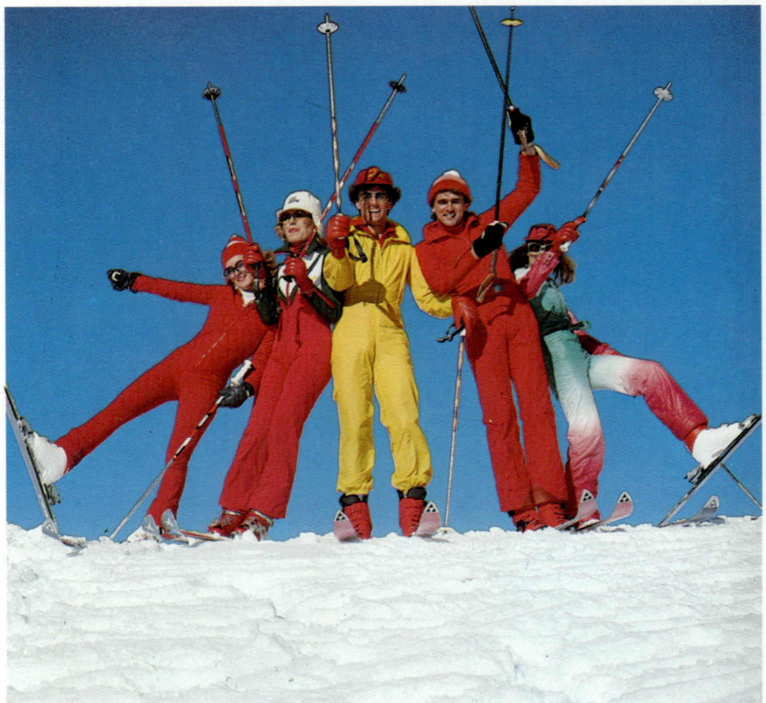

ACTION AND COLOUR

The feeling of action in a picture can, as already mentioned, be influenced by colour. Reds and yellows are considered to be 'advancing' colours – and certainly, small areas of these in otherwise subdued pictures fairly leap out at you. Other colours,

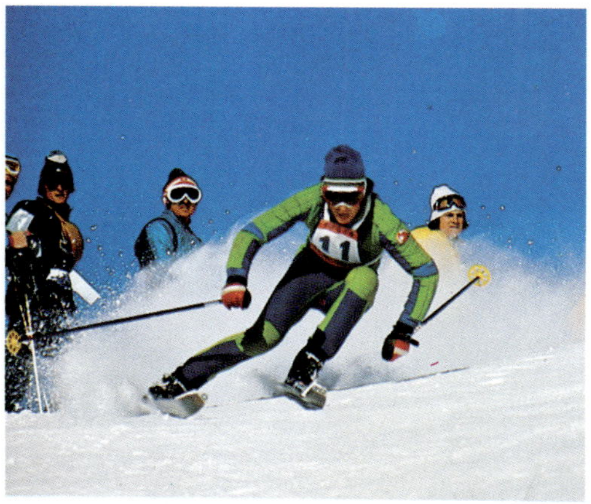

Exposures for lights and other night subjects with some 'Kodak' Colour Films

Film	Subject		
	Lights at night (no shadow detail)	Subjects lit by lights at night (some shadow detail)	Moonlit landscapes
KODACHROME 25 (Daylight)	1/15 sec at f/2.8	1/15 sec at f/2	45 sec at f/2
KODACHROME 64 (Daylight) EKTACHROME 64 Professional 6117 (Daylight) EKTACHROME 64 and 64 Professional (Daylight)	1/15 sec at f/4	1/30 sec at f/2	35 sec at f/2.8
EKTACHROME Professional 6118 (Tungsten) EKTACHROME 50 Professional (Tungsten)	1/15 sec at f/2.8	1/15 sec at f/2.8	20 sec at f/2
EKTACHROME 200 and 200 Professional (Daylight)	1/15 sec at f/5.6	1/30 sec at f/4	10 sec at f/2.8
EKTACHROME 160 and 160 Professional (Tungsten)	1/15 sec at f/5.6	1/30 sec at f/3.5	15 sec at f/2.8
EKTACHROME 400 (Daylight) KODACOLOR 400	1/15 sec at f/8	1/30 sec at f/4.5	12 sec at f/4
VERICOLOR II Professional, Type S and Professional 4107, Type S	1/15 sec at f/4.5	1/30 sec at f/2.8	Not recommended, but try 20 sec at f/2.8
VERICOLOR II Professional, Type L and Professional 4108, Type L VERICOLOR II Commercial, Type S and Commercial 4119, Type S KODACOLOR II	1/15 sec at f/4	1/15 sec at f/2.8	12 sec at f/2

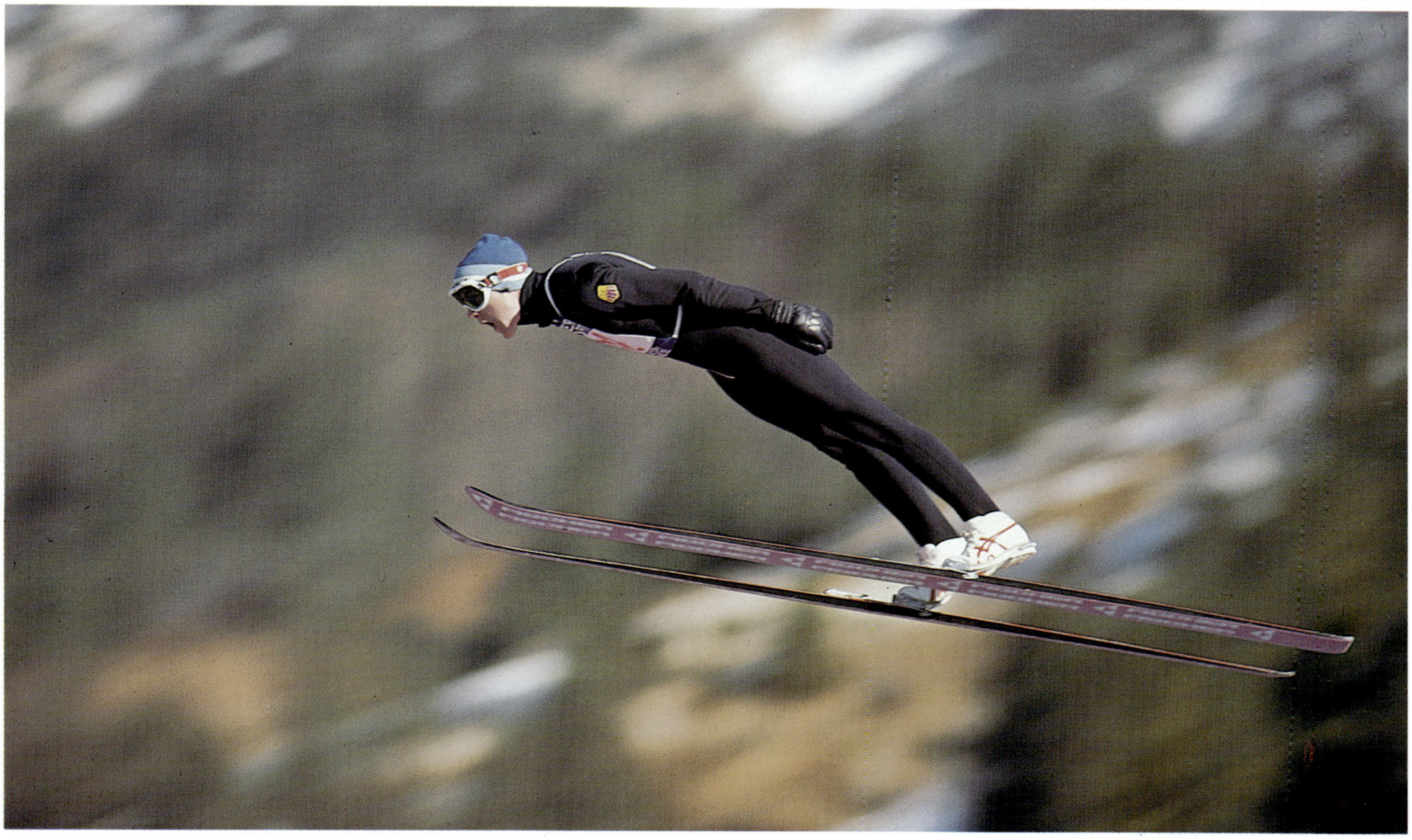

Above: Panning techniques *may require a little practice, but once mastered they can be used to considerable creative effect in the sports or action shot.* ***Top and facing page:*** *Polarising filters penetrate haze, reduce reflections and lead to strong, saturated colour.*

such as blue and green, are 'retreating' colours, and lack the psychological impact of the advancing ones. Ideally, the active part of the picture should be in an advancing colour; this is one of the reasons why red ski clothing is standard for photography.

Two other key points are simplicity and contrast. When something really grabs our attention, we are aware of it almost to the exclusion of all else. A successful action picture duplicates this in two ways. First, it uses a few bright simple colours – or at least, it manages to contrast the principal subject with its background. It is, for example, extremely difficult to make an effective picture of a number of soldiers in camouflage, no matter how dramatic their exploits. The vast majority of successful war pictures are either close-ups of one man, or at most a few, or they use dramatically the colours of war – the red of fire and blood, or the monochrome brown of the trenches.

Of course, it is not necessary to rely exclusively on colour. The famous raising of the flag on Mount Suribachi is a classic example of a composition which works as well in black-and-white as in colour (or indeed when cast in bronze); but such a combination of dramatic events, a penetrating eye, and sheer luck does not often come anyone's way.

In conclusion, it may seem that I have emphasised the calculating aspect of action photography too much; but for every picture which is attained by sheer luck in the heat of the event, there are ten which are achieved by mastery of the craft – and a thousand which are abject failures.

NATURAL HISTORY PHOTOGRAPHY

There are those who wince whenever creativity and natural history photography are mentioned in the same breath: their view is that a natural history photograph exists solely to record its subject as accurately as possible, and that there is therefore no room for creativity.

This argument can be attacked on three grounds. First, to obtain an accurate picture may require a great deal of creativity, albeit not necessarily of the artistic kind: surely Steven Dalton's masterful pictures of insects in flight involved a great deal of creativity in simply working out how to take them. He had to devise special shutters, flashguns, and methods of triggering them both, and then had to persuade his subjects to fly or hop in the right directions.

Secondly, there is no particular reason why a picture should not be both biologically accurate and aesthetically pleasing. It may be unusual, or even accidental, but when it does happen, the result can be doubly pleasing.

Finally, there is no reason why a photograph 'should' be an accurate biological record. Whilst no-one would condone an insensitive photographer who upset the animal and damaged its habitat, why should anyone condemn a photographer for taking an attractive picture even if it does not clearly show the diagnostic features for identifying the species?

Because the field of natural history photography is so vast, it embraces many different kinds of photographer and many different kinds of equipment. There are certain ground rules, though, which are true for all types of natural history photography: these are covered first, after which we take a brief look at different specialised fields.

The first thing is equipment. Whatever your equipment – and it will vary considerably according to your chosen field – you must be totally familiar with it, and able to operate any control at

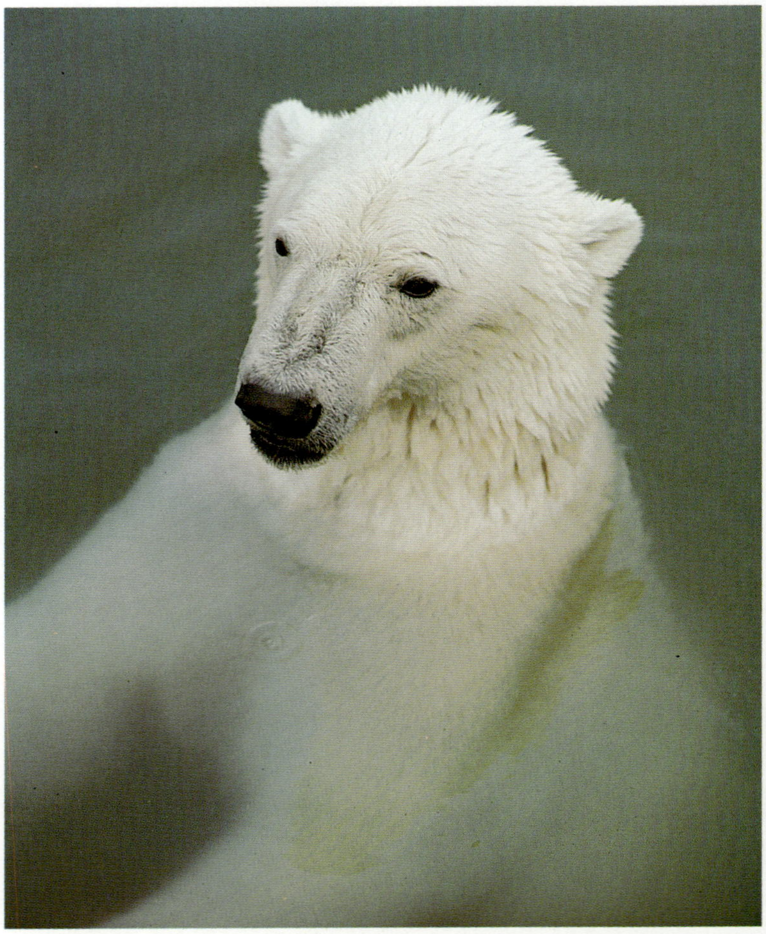

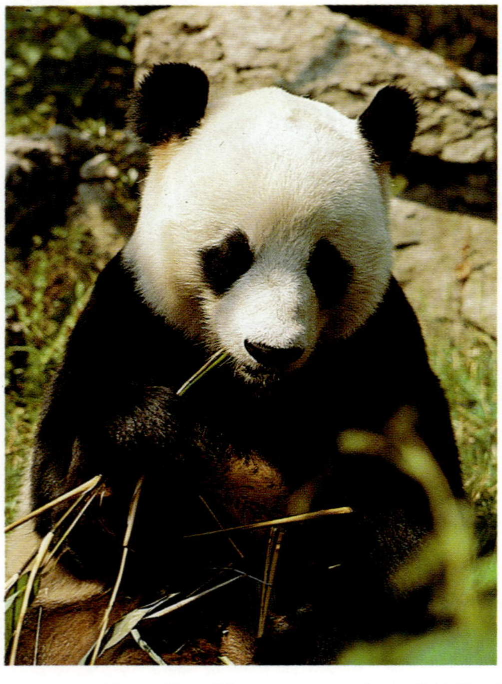

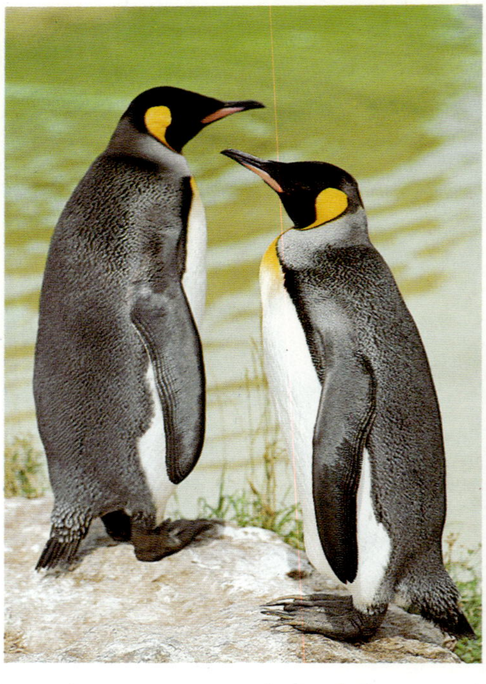

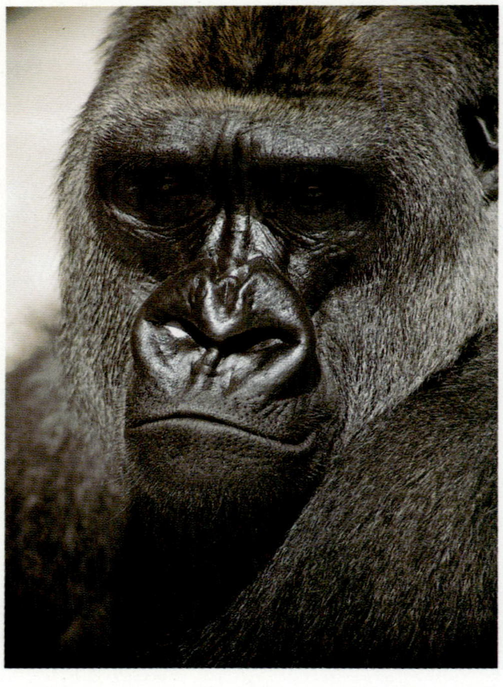

a moment's notice. Many successful wildlife photographers use automatic cameras to free them from many of the mechanical concerns of photography; the concentration required is (or should be) so great that you have no attention left to spare for the mechanics of operating the camera.

Secondly, you need to be dedicated. Whilst there is a place for anyone with a good eye for a picture to take the occasional

Animals have expressions too. *How closely these equate to our interpretation of them is a matter for debate, but there is no doubt that they can look reflective, intelligent, and happy as well as the more usual amusing or alarming. As in many other branches of photography, the secret is often patience – that, and shooting for the percentages.*

lucky shot, the person who knows all about his subject obviously has a very much better chance. If you know the habits of the species in general, and (preferably) of your own individual specimen, life will be very much easier. For example, a cat almost invariably stretches on waking up naturally; so if you want a cat stretching (whether a domestic moggie or a lioness), just wait around until a sleeping one wakes up. Furthermore, a cat normally sleeps after eating; so, for the stretching shot, feed the cat – and wait!

This points up the third necessity: patience. Although animals are far more perverse and infuriating than plants, it is

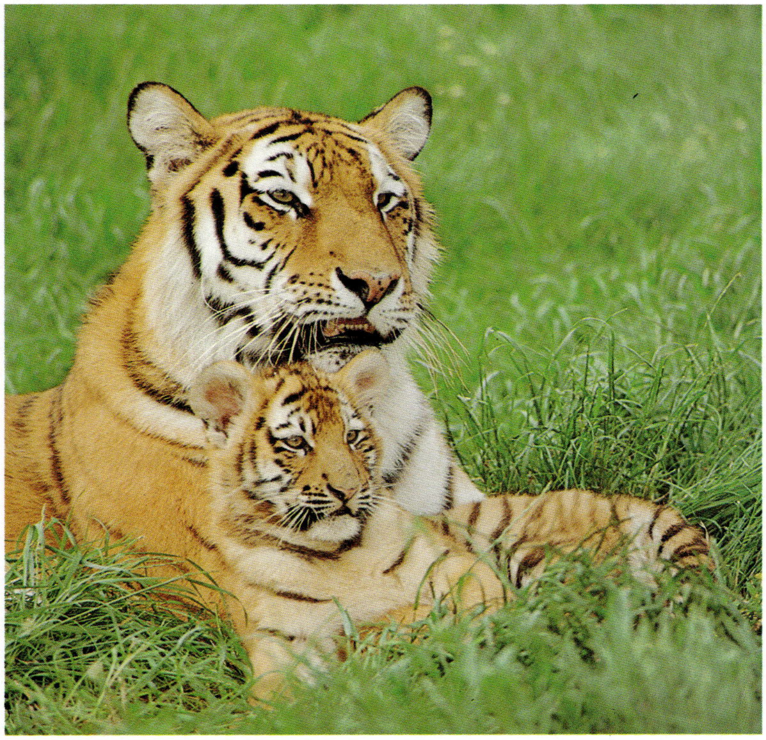

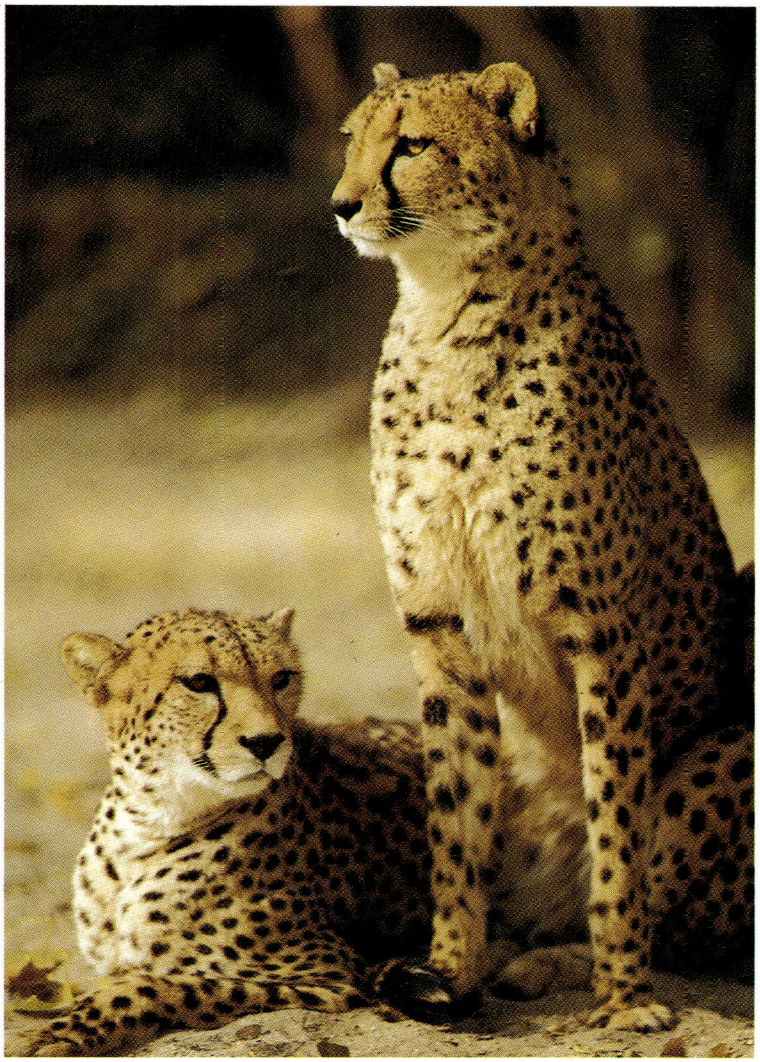

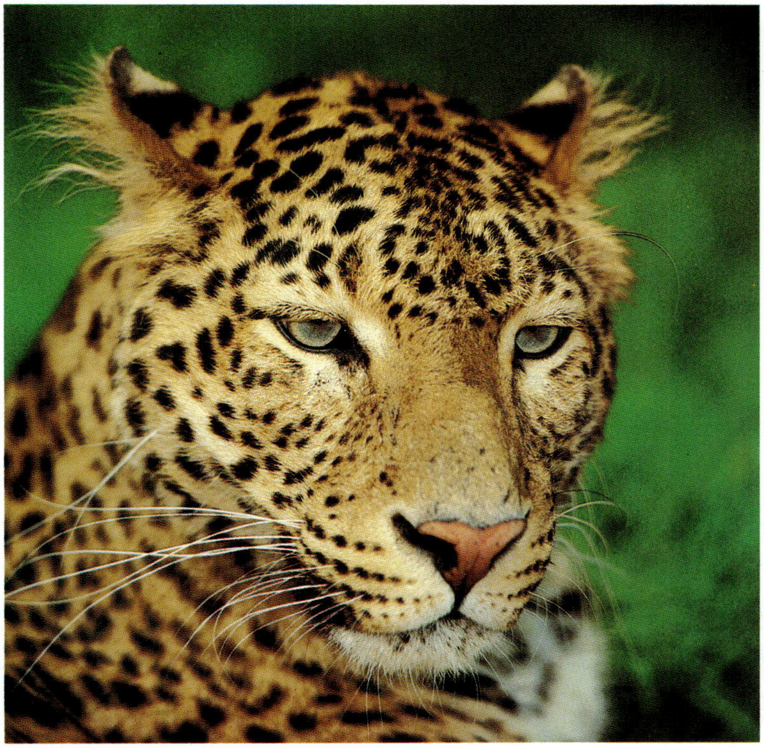

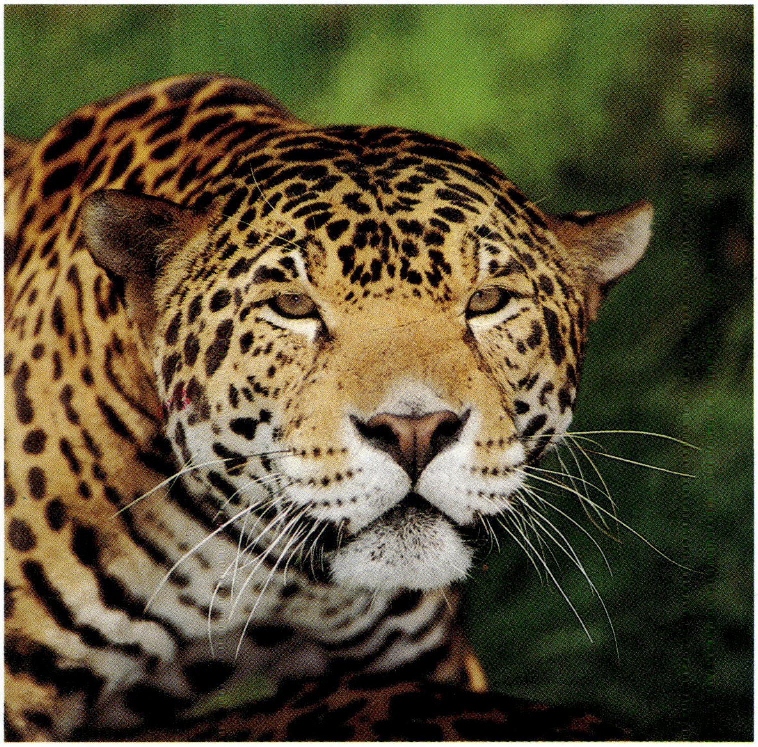

NATURAL HISTORY PHOTOGRAPHY

A good way to gain expertise *is to specialise in one animal – such as the big cats, here. After a while, you begin to learn their habits: when they sleep, how they eat and play, the relationship between adults and cubs. Although most of this information is specific, the habit and means of observing can be carried across to other species.*

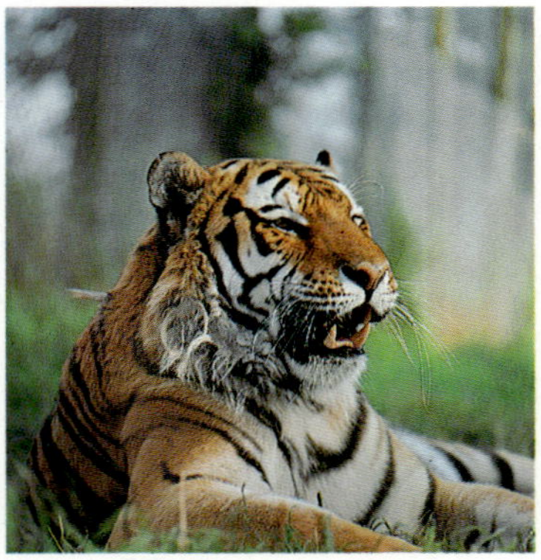

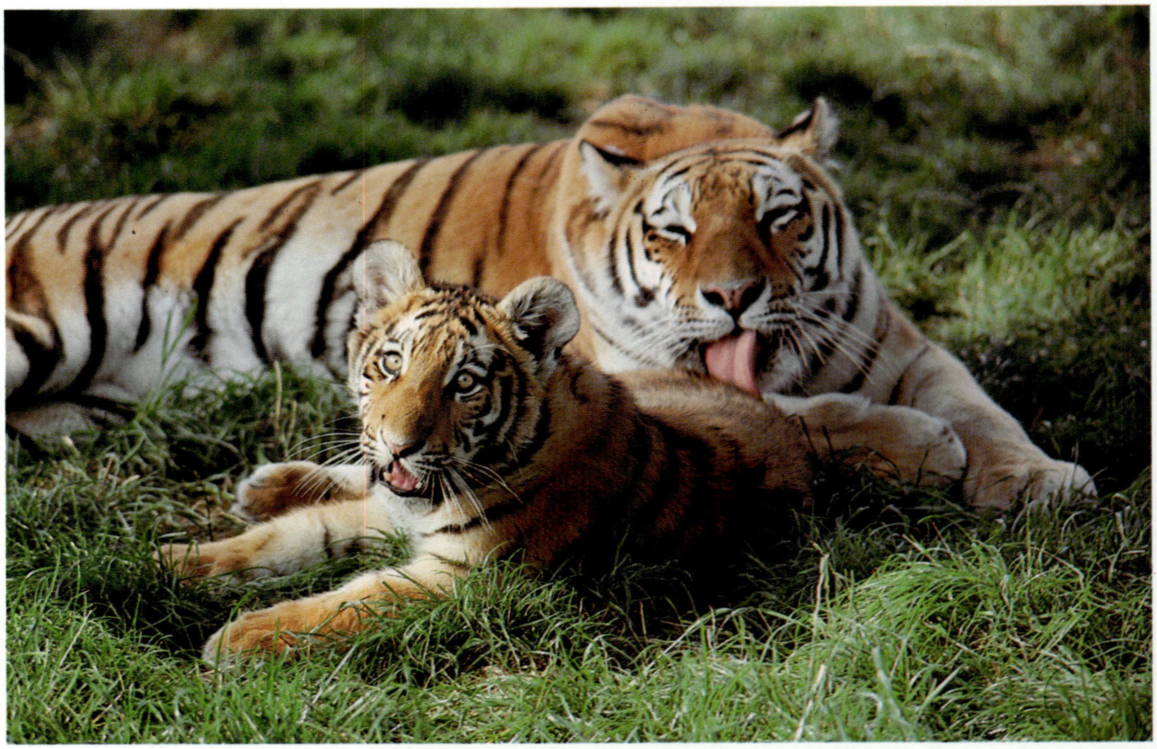

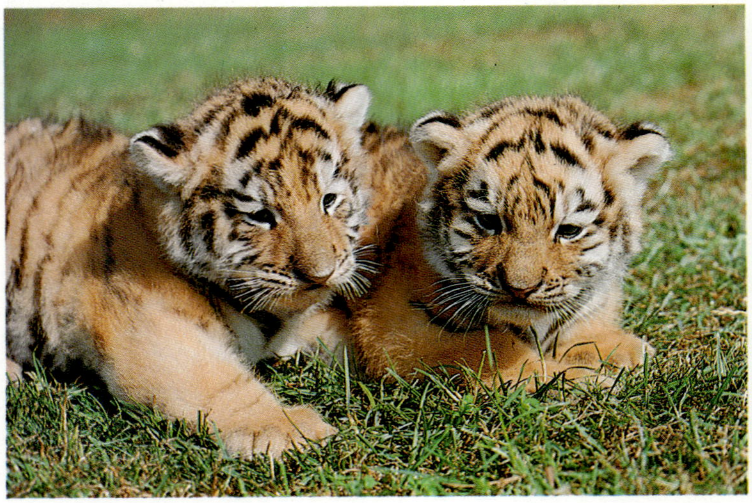

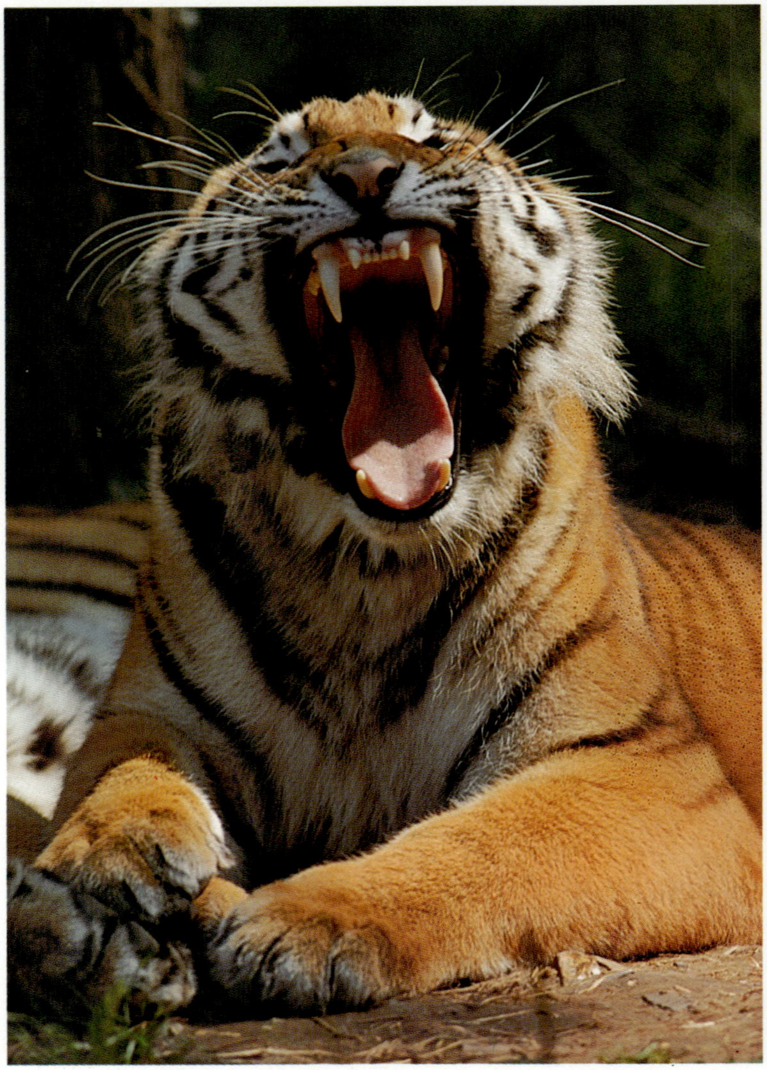

surprising just how difficult it can be to find a perfect specimen of a plant . . . in the right lighting . . . in the right surroundings . . . with a flower open and the dew fresh on it . . . not waving in the breeze . . . The impatient photographer will be content simply to get an image: the good photographer will wait for the right image, though he may expose a lot of film whilst waiting.

Finally, you need to be alert. The difference between a mediocre picture (or no picture at all) and a great picture may be how fast you can spot the subject, get the camera to your eye, and take the picture. Physical fitness helps; ideally, you should pursue a sport such as fencing, which exercises both body and mind.

BIRDS AND LARGE ANIMALS

Most people start in natural history photography in this way, often as an extension of an existing interest. The big problem is that almost all wildlife is wary, and some of it is dangerous too. For the dangerous variety, you should never expose yourself to even the slightest danger without having someone else around to

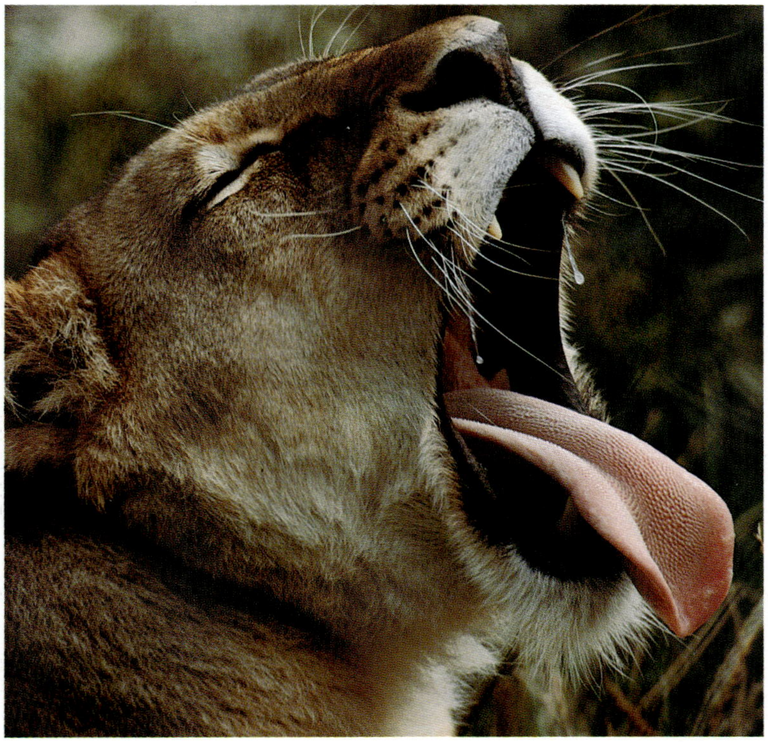

act as lookout. It is all too easy to become so obsessed with getting a picture that you fail to notice the tiger's mate that is stalking you: it may sound melodramatic, but it does happen, especially with scorpions and snakes.

As for combatting the wariness, there are three possible solutions. One is to cultivate the Red Indian skills of tracking and moving noiselessly; it is not as difficult to do this as you might think. Consider camouflage, too: streaks of greasepaint or cocoa powder on the face, drab, ragged clothing – real Commando stuff. Secondly, you can use hides. Some of these are quite elaborate, and the photographer can live in them for days if necessary, but others are no more than stones, branches, and a bit of green tarpaulin. After establishing the hide, you may need to wait for quite some time for the animals to regain confidence, but quite a useful trick is to have someone else come to the hide with you; he then leaves, with you inside, and since very few animals seem to be able to count, they may well assume that the danger has gone away. The third trick is to use long lenses.

Whilst it is quite possible to get very good pictures using lenses of up to 200mm or so, it is difficult: far more usual are 400, 500, 600, 800, and 1000mm lenses on 35mm. This, incidentally, is one of the several reasons why 35mm is popular with natural history photographers: the longest lenses available for larger formats are often shorter in absolute terms, and certainly far shorter in relative terms. A 500mm lens on a Hasselblad (the longest easily available) is roughly equivalent to 300mm on

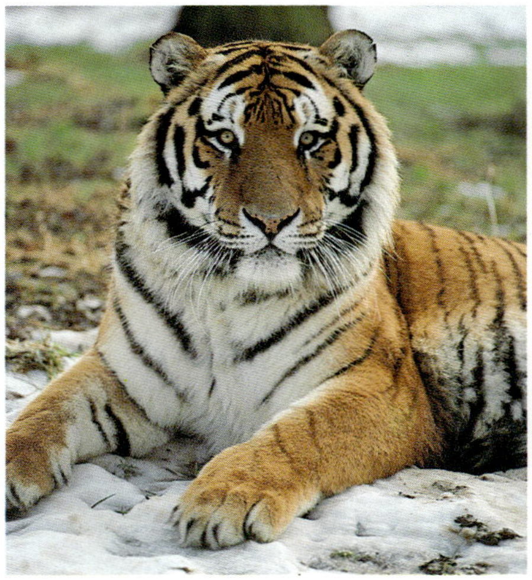

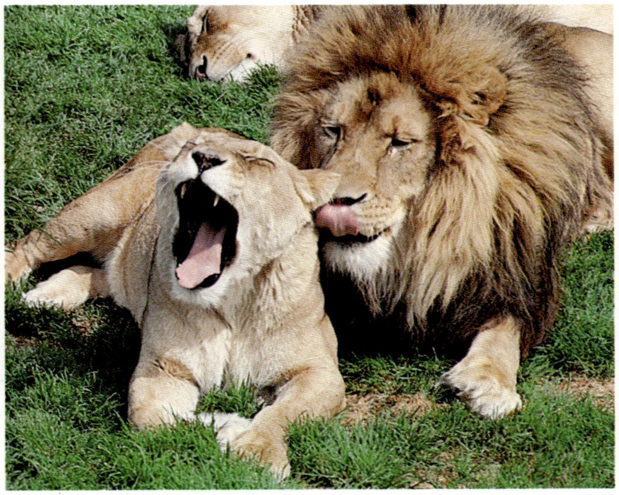

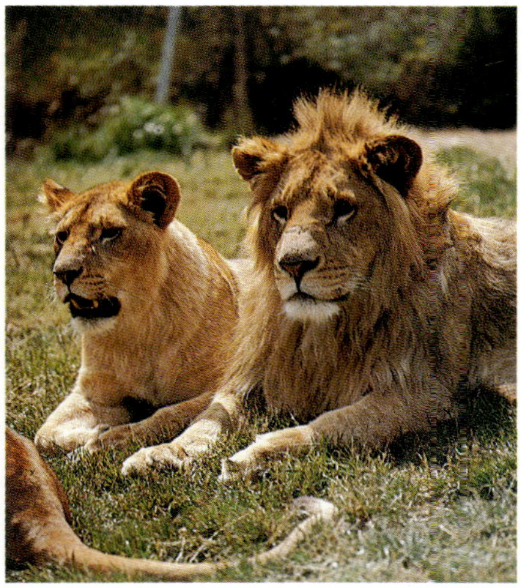

When photographing any *animal big enough to be dangerous, always remember that no matter how lazy and cuddly it may look, it can probably move with lightning speed and it may well be able to kill you. This does not only apply to the more obvious animals: a domestic sow, with piglets, can kill in their defence. In European and American wildlife parks, always keep windows closed: in the wild, listen to the advice of your guide, never work alone; always have someone to guard your back. Try to keep calm, and avoid excessive exercise; too fast a heartbeat means camera shake.*

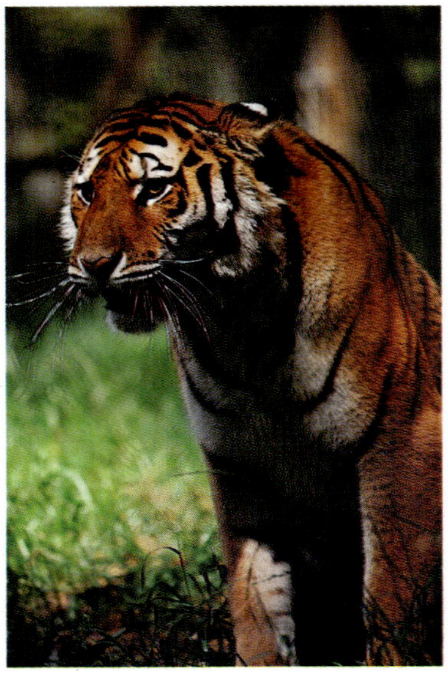

35mm: a 1000mm lens on 35mm could roughly be matched for magnification by a 1600mm on a Hasselblad.

The problems with these very long lenses, though, is that they are large, heavy, expensive, of limited maximum aperture, and require <u>very</u> substantial tripods if camera shake is to be avoided. They also need very clean air: any haze will show up as a degradation of image quality and colour. Many excellent long-focus lenses are quite unfairly accused of poor definition because of this. The rule, then, is to use the shortest focal length you can get away with, as close as possible.

Of course, there are animals sufficiently sure of themselves that you can use lenses of 135mm or even less: with the pigeons in Trafalgar Square, for instance, a 24mm lens is fine. The rules about not startling the animal still apply, and plenty of patience is still needed; a good way to sharpen your stalking skills is to try to photograph a domestic cat. Remember two things, though. With a few domestic exceptions, the only animals which do not fear man are those which can easily take him to pieces: rhinos are a good example. The other thing is that almost any animal

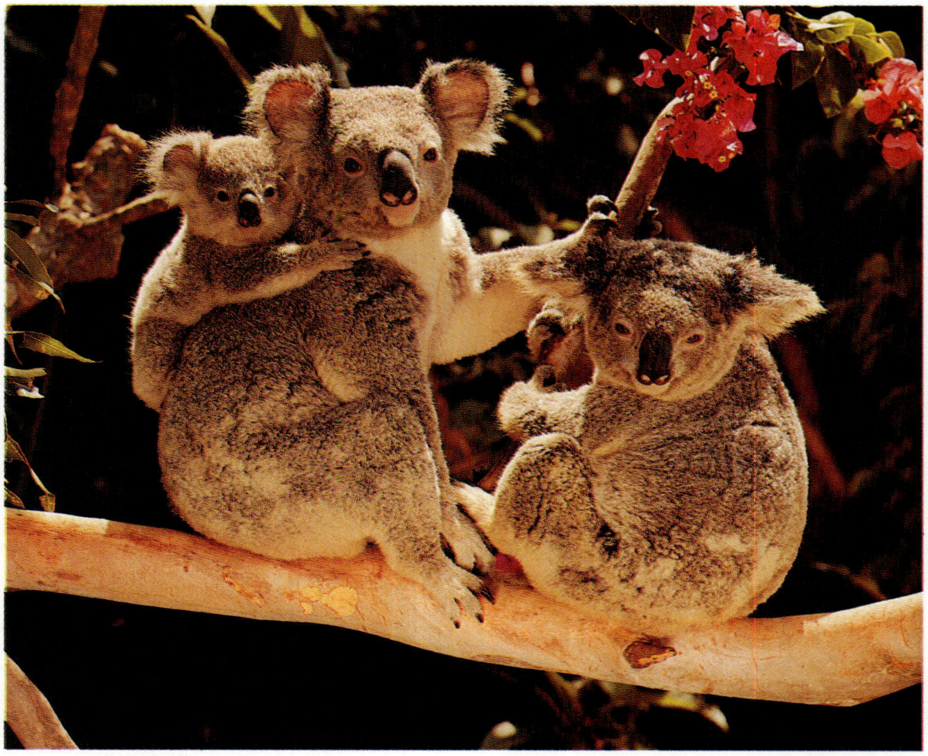

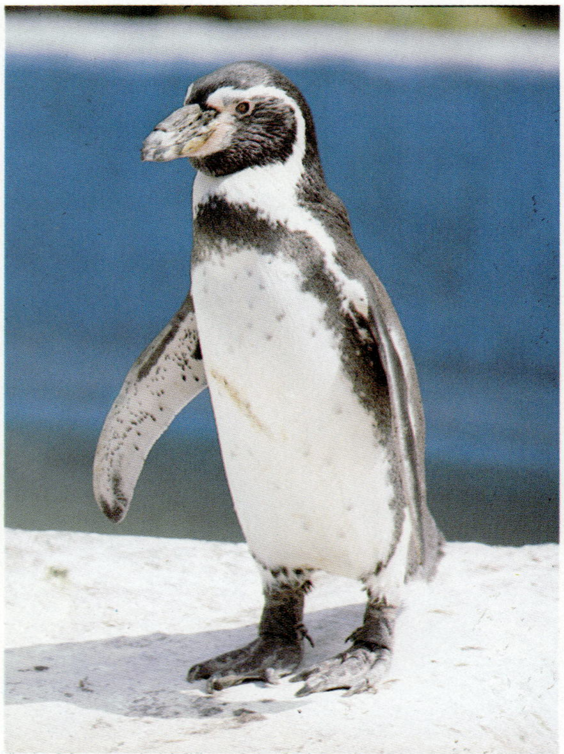

can and will move surprisingly quickly, so alertness is essential. If the animal is harmless, you will only lose the picture, but if it is dangerous, you can lose a lot more.

To return to equipment, there is no doubt that 35mm is overwhelmingly the most popular. It is relatively cheap, a vast array of lenses is available, the camera is not too heavy to carry for long distances, and you get 36 pictures from a roll. This not only cuts down the amount of film you have to carry about: it also reduces the number of times you have to reload (and the best action always seems to take place during reloading), and it means that you can shoot more pictures. In wildlife photography you are almost always shooting for the percentages, and plenty of relatively cheap film means that you can increase your chances enormously.

ZOOS

It may seem a little odd to consider zoo photography separately, but there are many differences between photographing an animal in captivity and photographing it in the wild. First, you can usually get much closer with far less trouble (and danger). Any good medium telephoto is suitable, with something like a top-flight 70-210mm zoom as the very best option. The flexibility and speed of operation outweighs the slight loss of image quality, which will in any case be invisible on the kinds of subjects you are tackling.

Secondly, the animals are relatively tame; a good deal less patience is required in the average zoo than in the average jungle or other natural habitat.

Thirdly, the environment itself introduces problems. Bars are there for a reason: poking the camera through them is not a good idea, though you may sometimes be able to persuade a keeper to cover you whilst you do so. Obviously, it is better to go along at less busy times if you want to talk to the keepers, who are also likely to be very knowledgeable about the animals in their care. Watch out for obtrusive backgrounds, too; a neutral concrete wall (provided the join between floor and wall is not an obvious straight line) is not too bad, but often there are man-

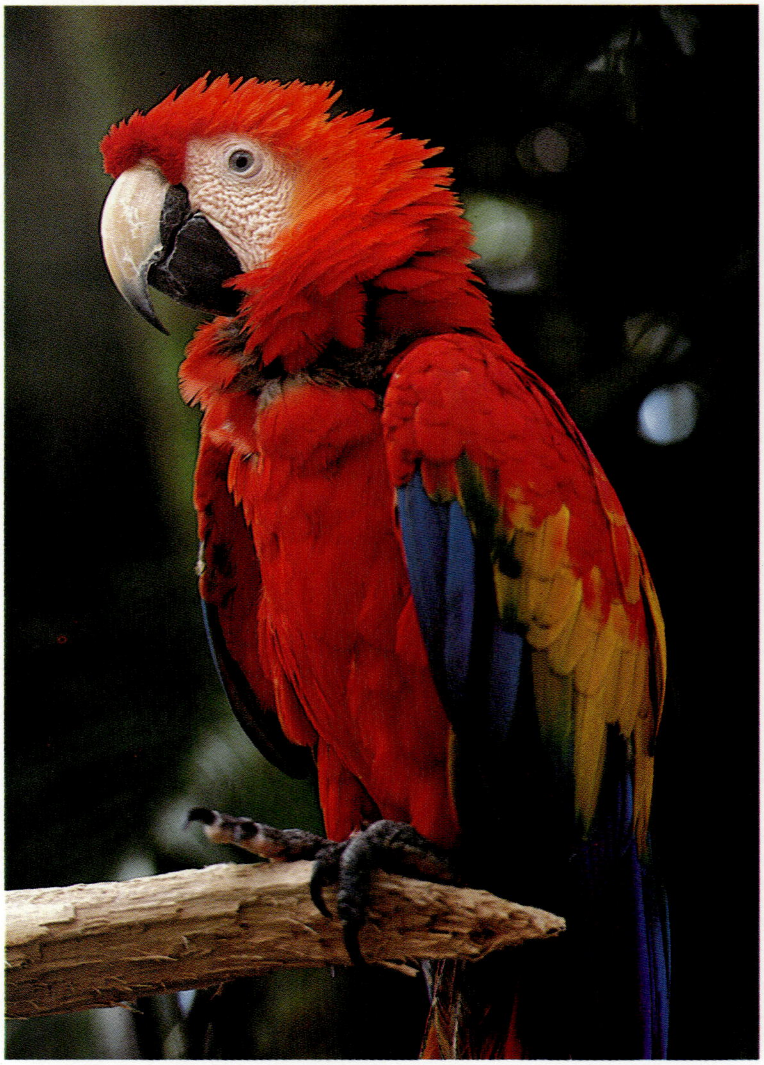

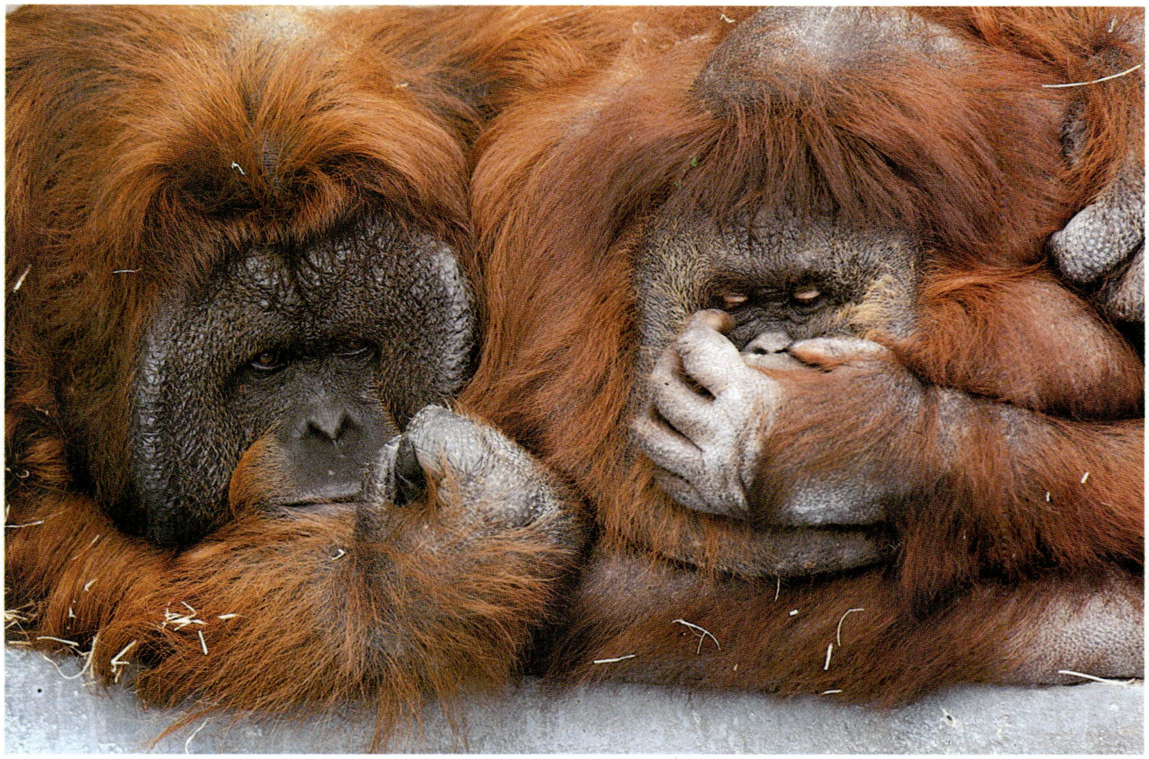

Never dismiss the amusing, the brightly coloured, or the simply unusual as fit only for snapshots; if you don't get any fun out of your photography, why do you do it? Zoom lenses are ideal for such pictures – apart from their inherent flexibility, they can also be used to accurately crop the image in the viewfinder.

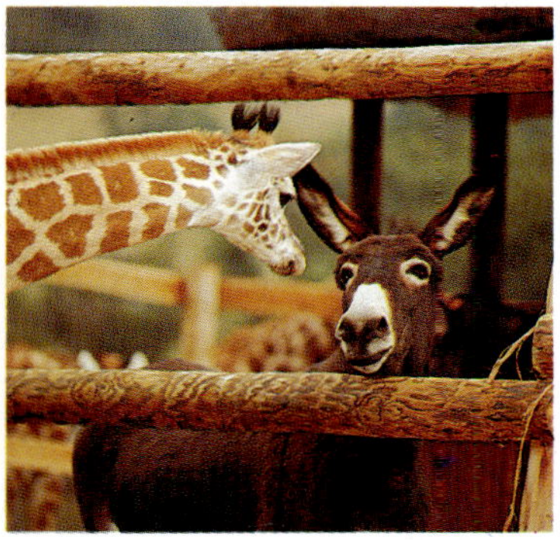

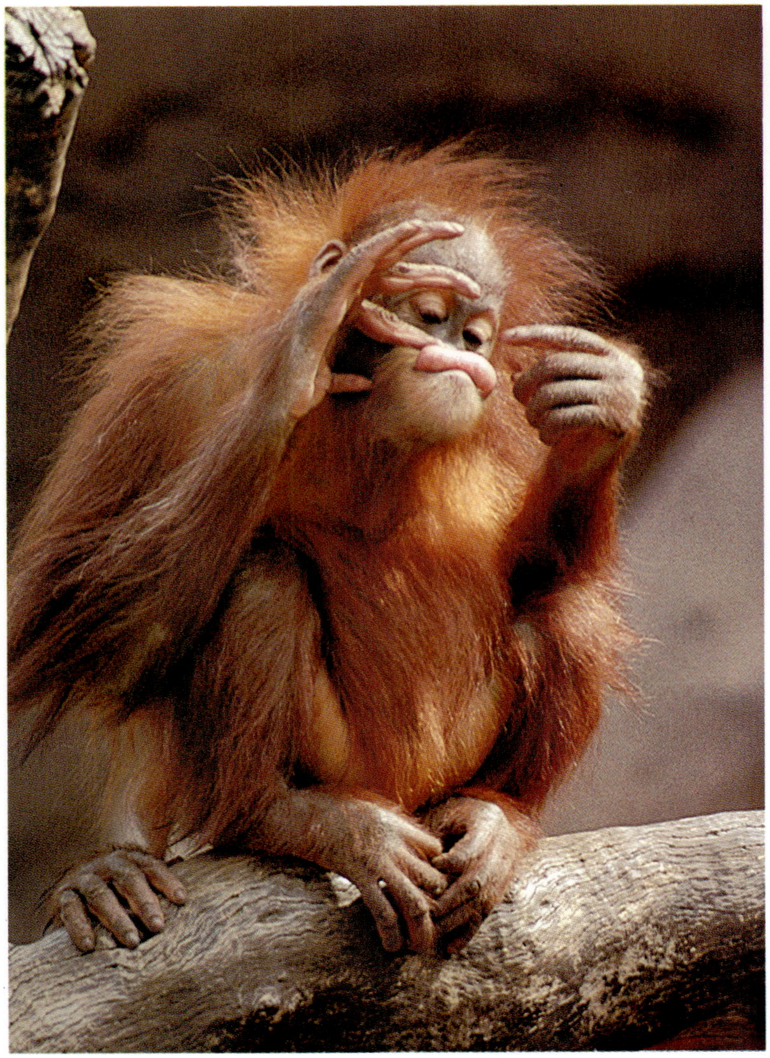

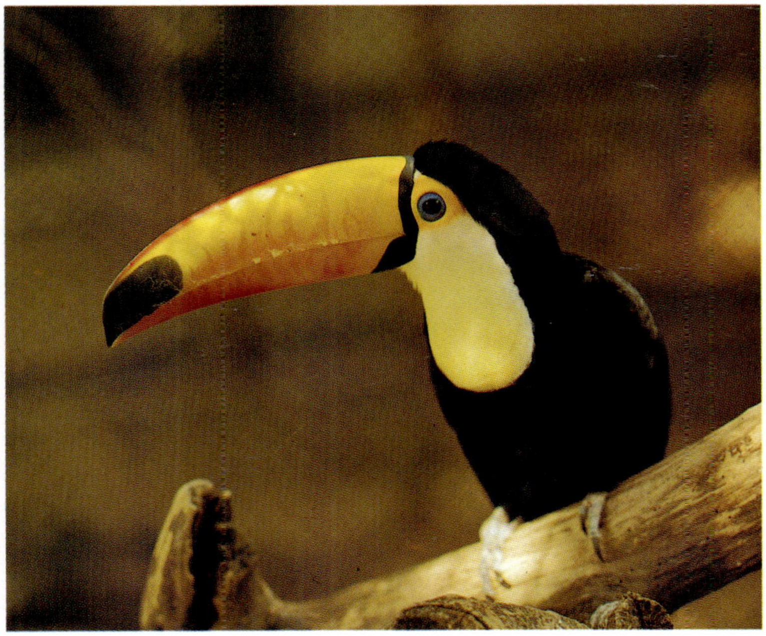

made structures at the back of the cage. A very useful trick is differential focus, with the lens used as wide open as possible; a 135/2.8 is ideal. If the bars are close enough, you may be able to 'lose' those, and if you can throw the background out of focus as well you may be able to achieve remarkably natural-looking pictures. Try to suit the weather to the animal, though: lions look very depressed on a rainy day, but sun can cheer them up considerably.

The last big difference about the zoo is that it is a lot more available than some exotic location in Africa or India, and so affords an excellent opportunity to try your hand at animal photography. The price of admission is usually a good deal less than the price of a single film, so it is an option well worth exploring.

CLOSE-UP AND MACROPHOTOGRAPHY

This is the other type of photography which most people automatically think of when natural history photography is mentioned. It embodies all the difficulties of conventional wildlife photography, with the additional problem that you have to get very close indeed to your subject, you are working with virtually no depth of field, and normally you will be running out of light as well.

Here more than anywhere you have to know the habits of your subject, and here more than anywhere you have to have the right equipment. The former can only be acquired by study of your chosen animal (insect or whatever), but the latter allows a few general rules.

35mm is the usual format, for the reasons already stated and especially because you are shooting for the percentages: with a really difficult subject, one frame out of thirty six might not be a bad success rate. It is also far easier to get close-up gear for 35mm cameras, than for other formats. This falls into two general groups: methods of increasing extension, and special lenses.

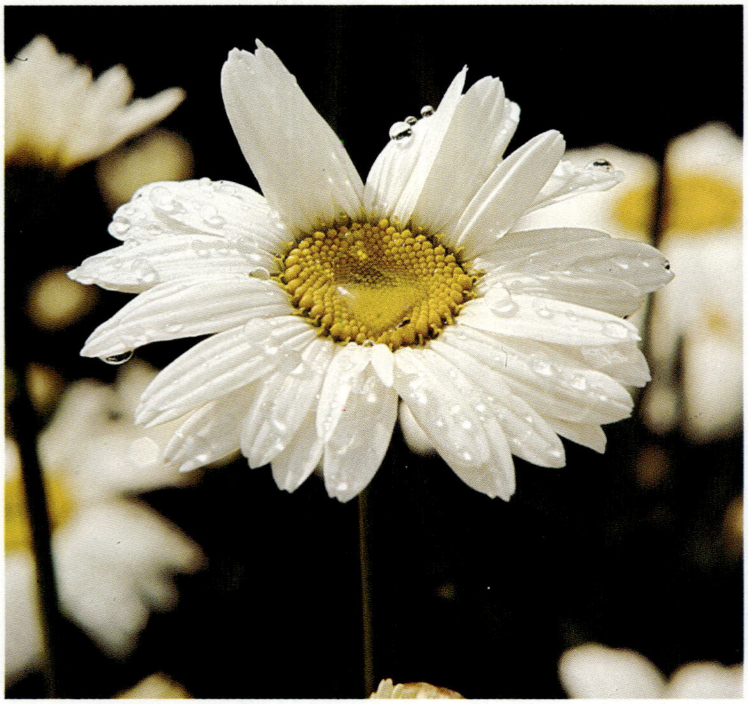

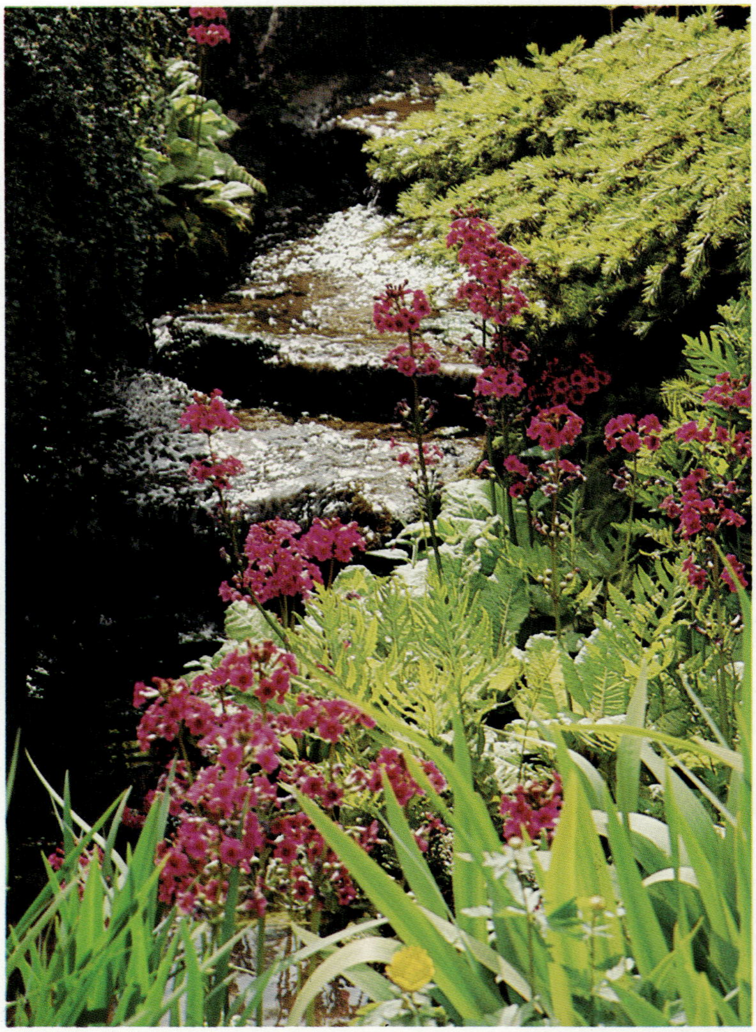

In general, flowers are best *shown either in close-up, like the daisy* ***above,*** *or in small groups. What very seldom works is the long shot, where each flower is reduced to a pin-prick of colour among the green. Incidentally, many photographers carry a small atomiser or spray-gun to get the dewy effect in close-ups.*

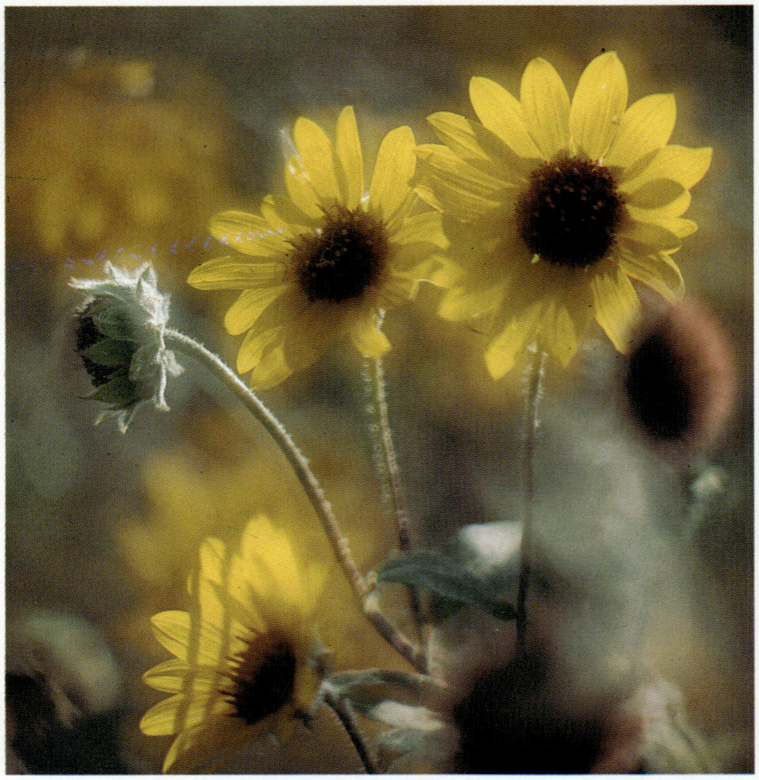

The normal lens on a 35mm camera can be focused down to about 45cm. There are three reasons for this. The first is that lens mounts to focus closer are considerably bulkier and more expensive than ordinary ones. The second is that the performance of many lenses (especially fast ones) deteriorates dramatically at very close distances. The third is that the marked f/stops no longer hold good, and the lens must be opened up if underexposure is to be avoided.

Extension tubes and bellows get around the first problem, but leave the other two. In practice, many lenses of around f/2 are quite acceptable even when used close up, especially if they

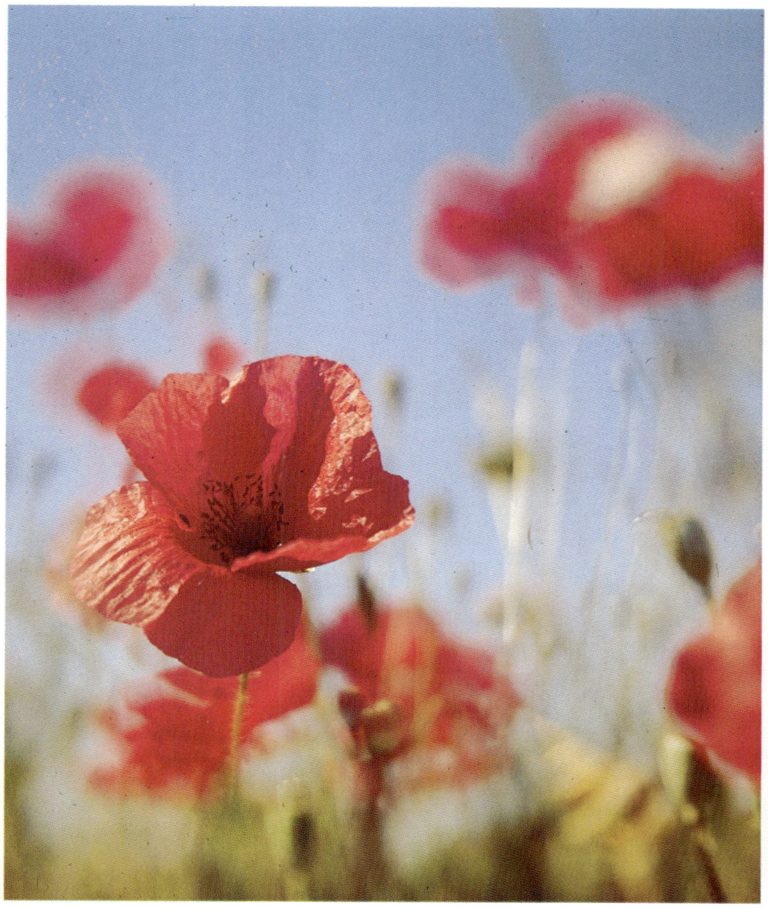

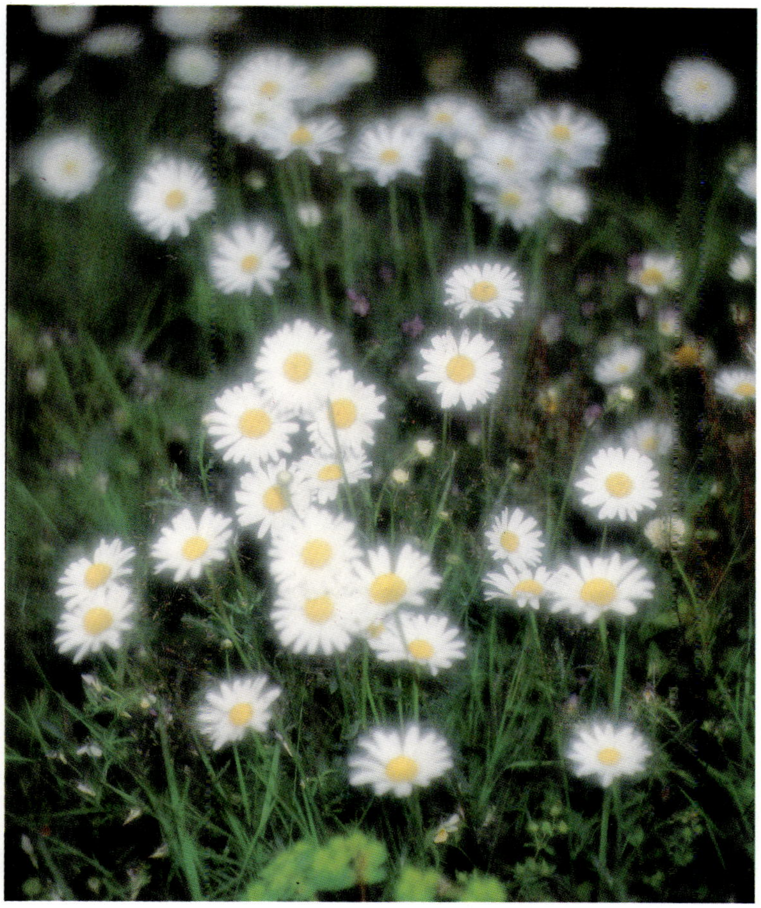

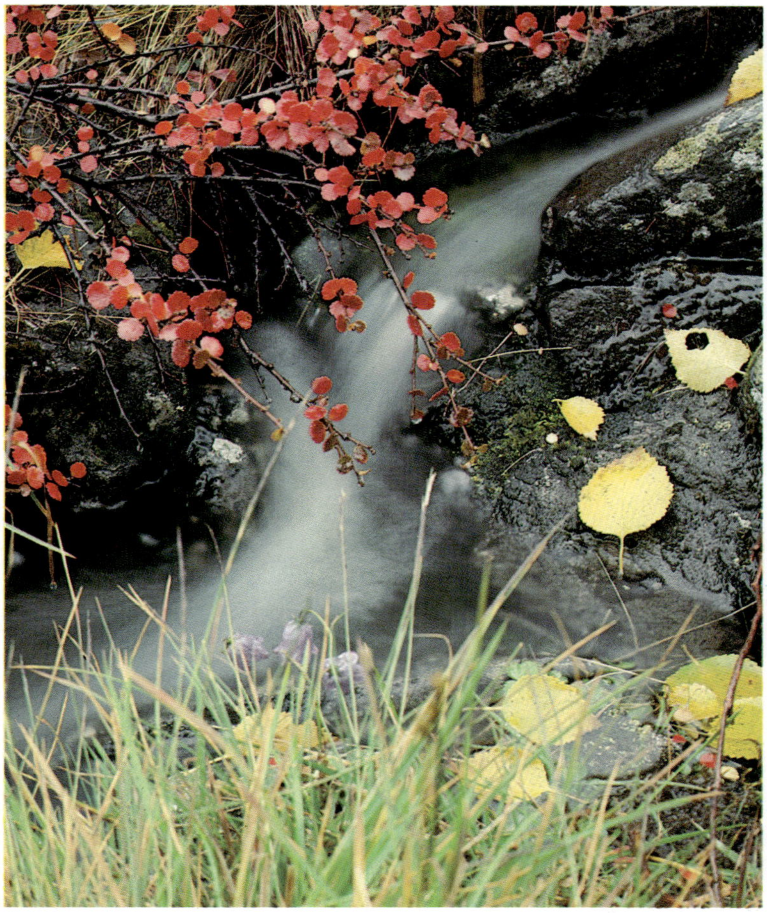

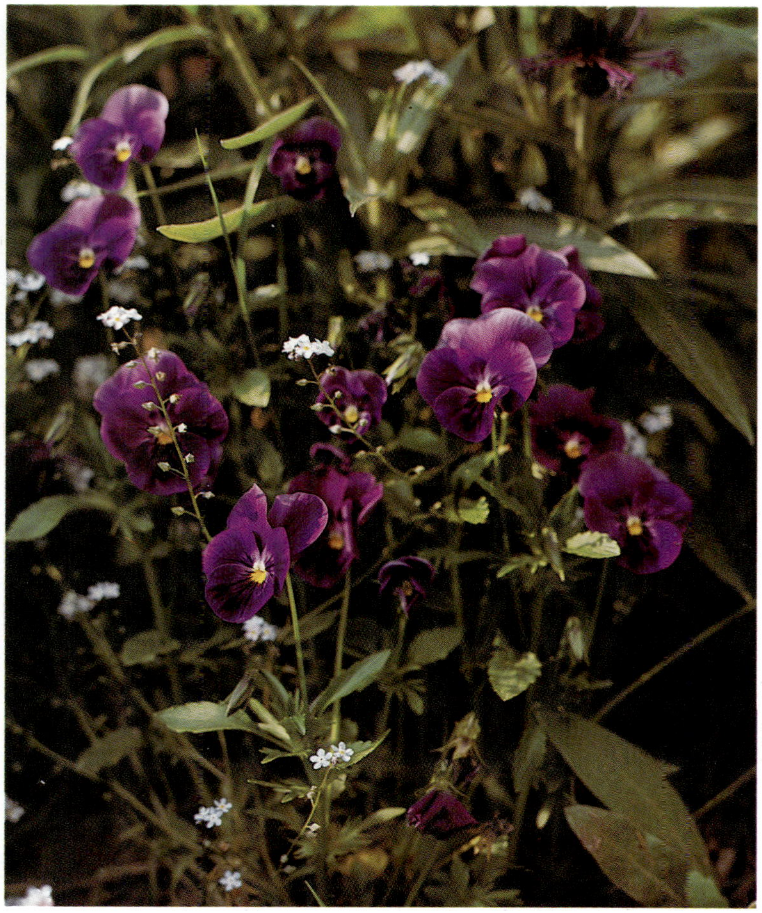

NATURAL HISTORY PHOTOGRAPHY

***Flower photography – and** indeed any form of close-up – is a field where the relative merits of 35mm and rollfilm are about equal. One offers better image quality; the other, greater depth of field, easier handling, and shorter exposures.*

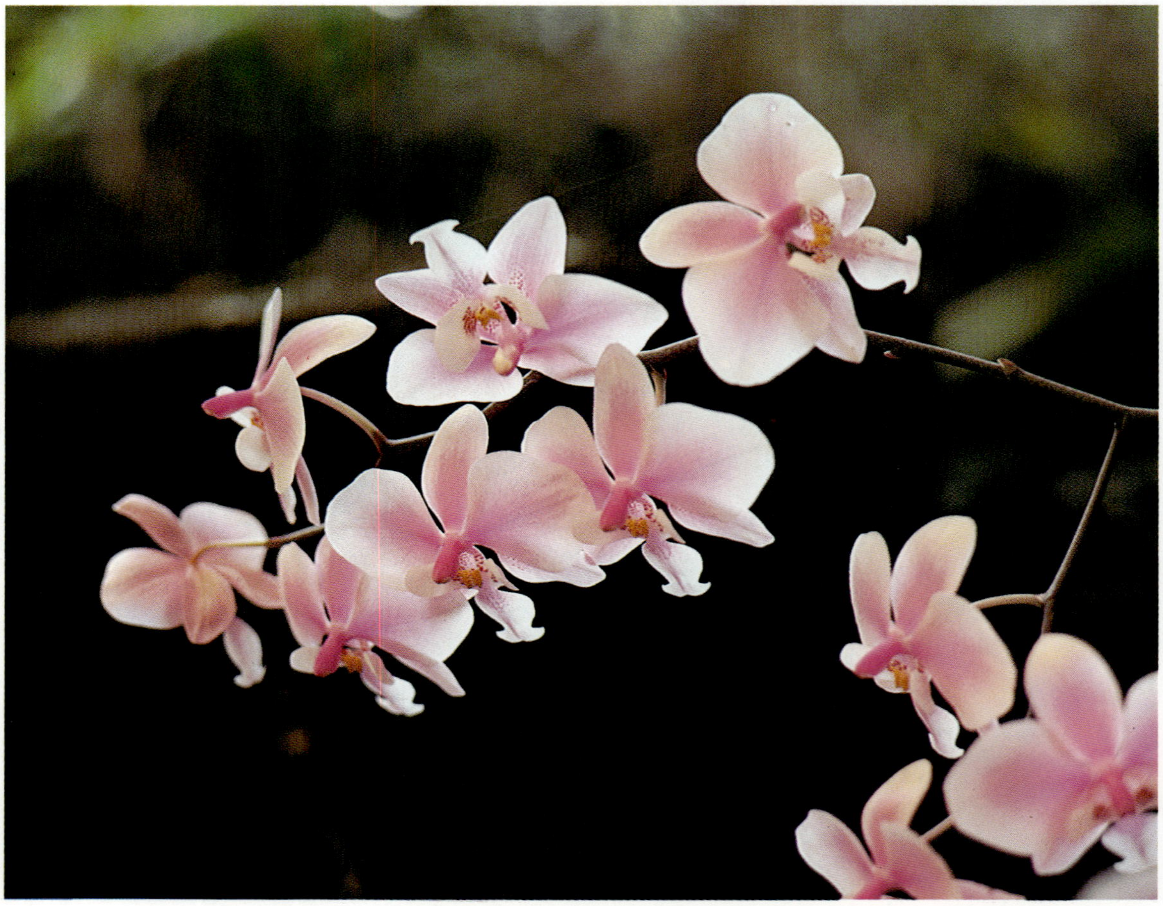

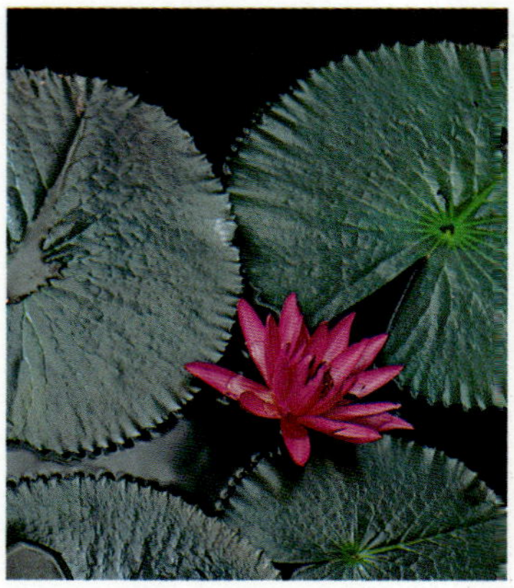

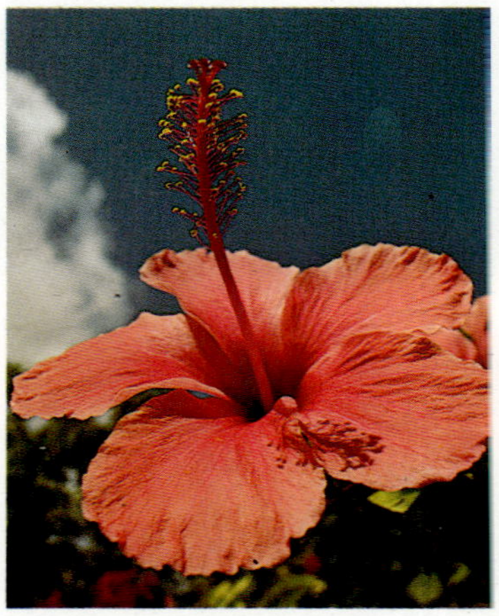

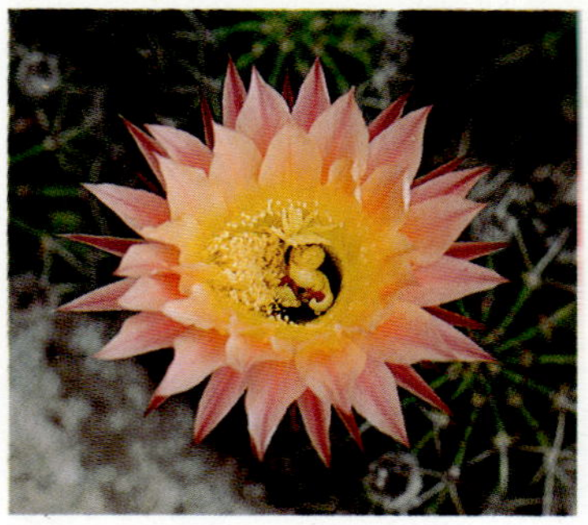

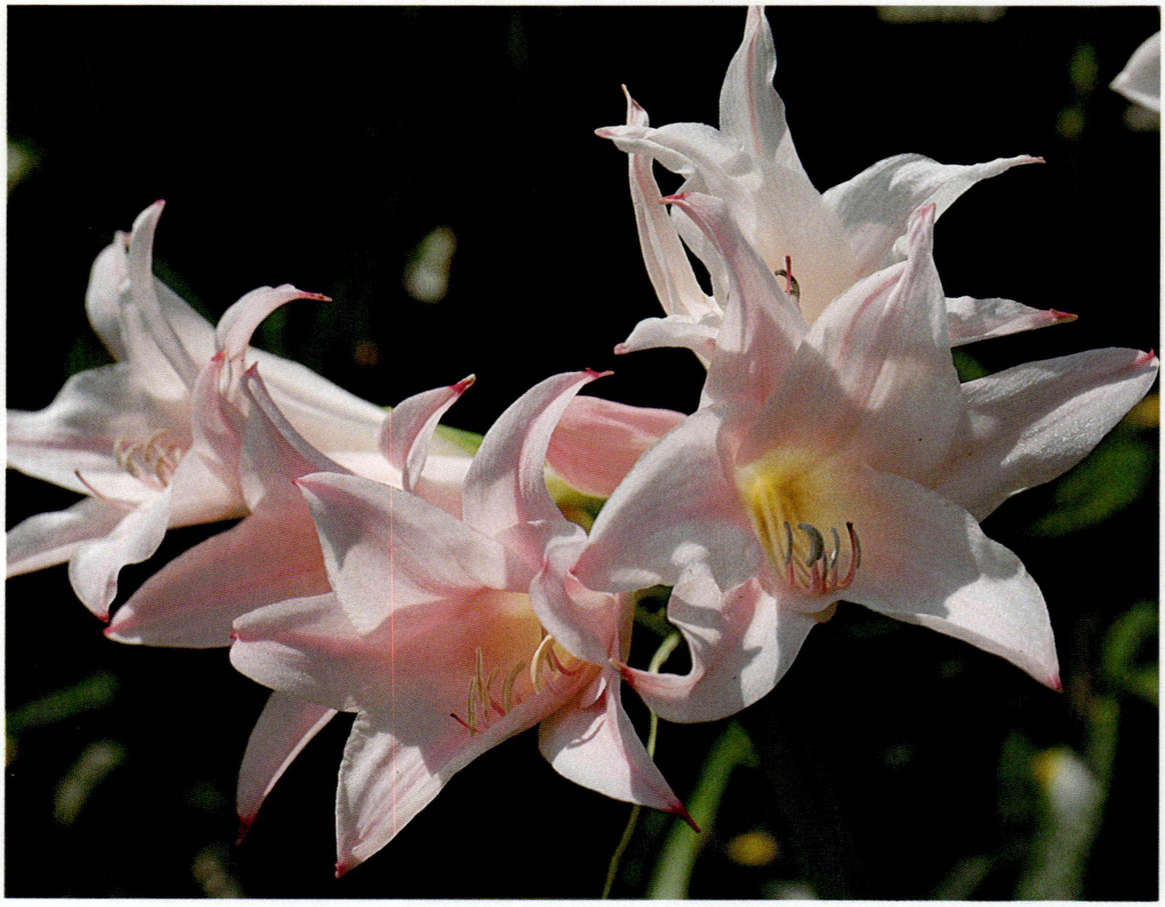

***In general, 35mm is best for** broad areas of colour and graphic shapes, as in the two pictures **right and top right.** Rollfilm scores where very fine detail is paramount, as on the **facing page, top left.** Many serious natural history photographers own both 35mm and rollfilm systems; 35mm is indisputably best to start with.*

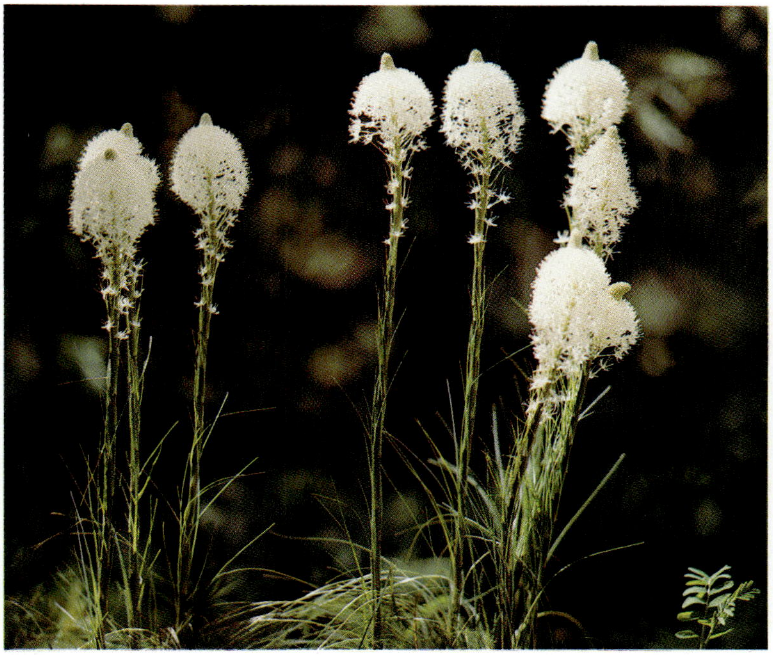
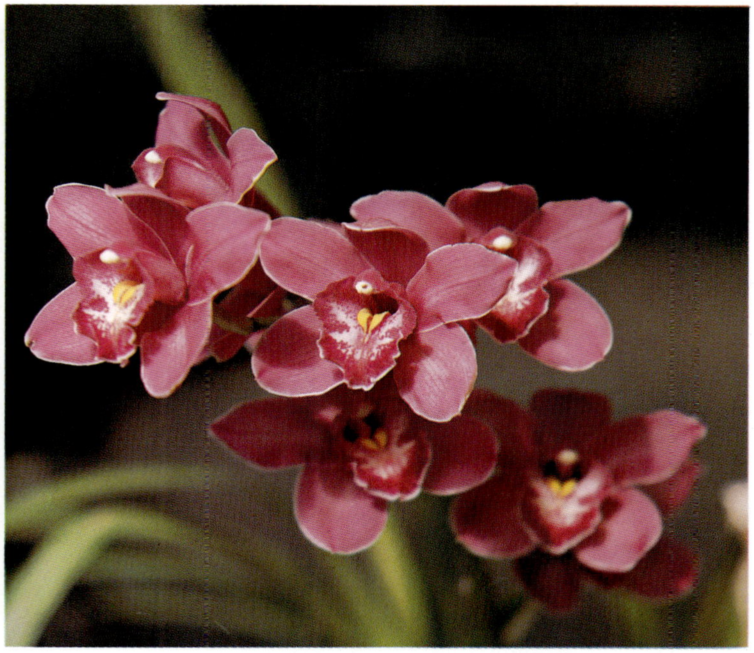
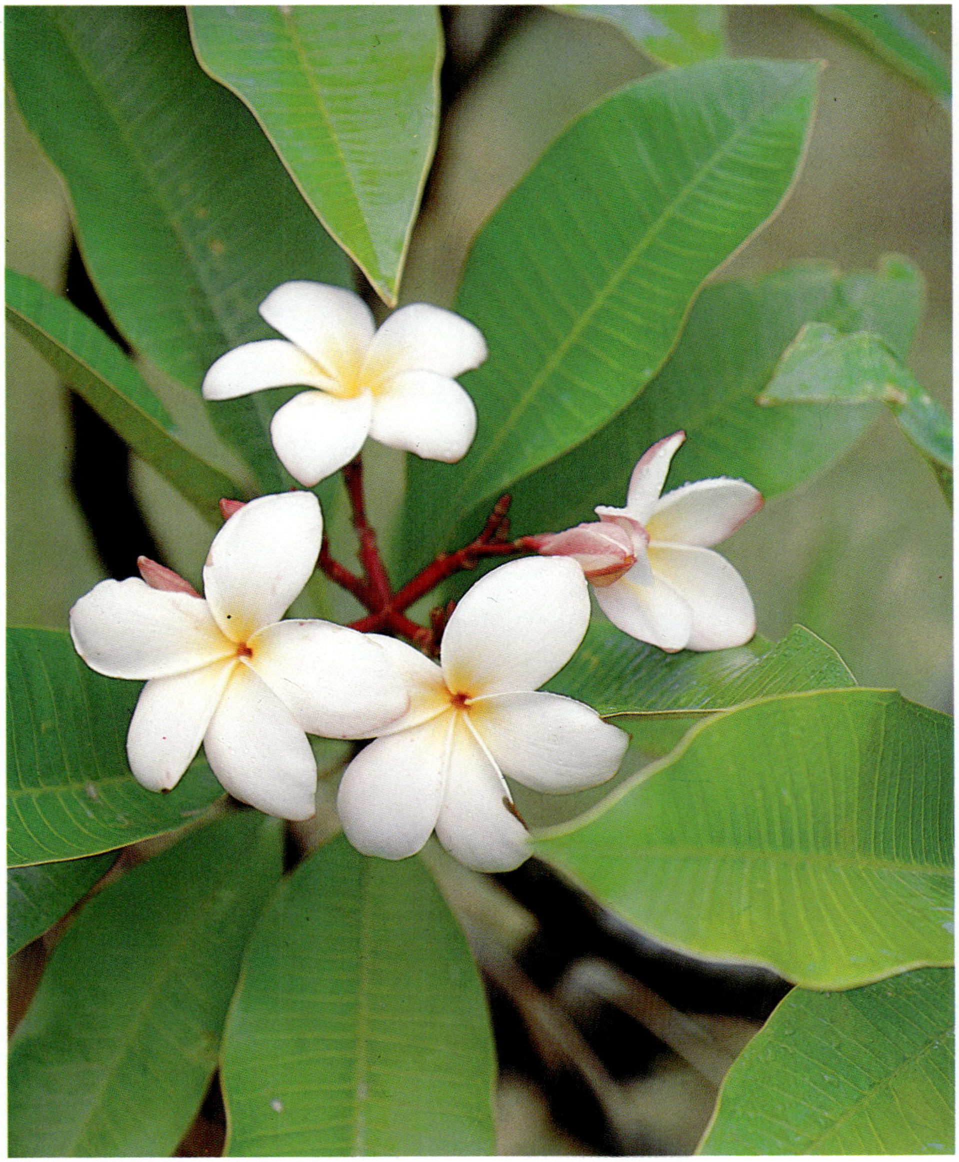
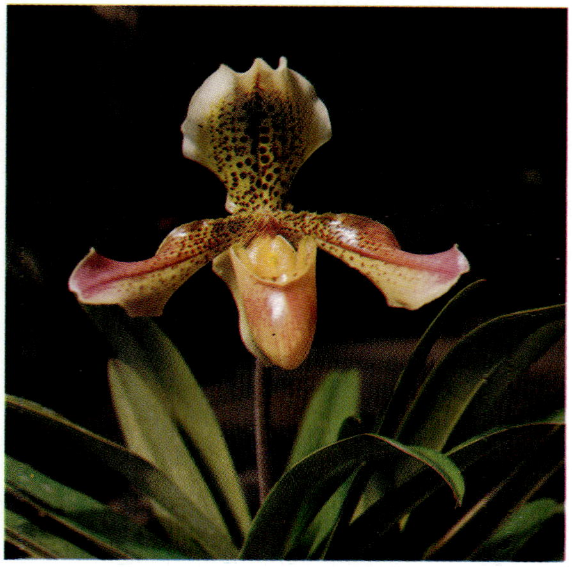
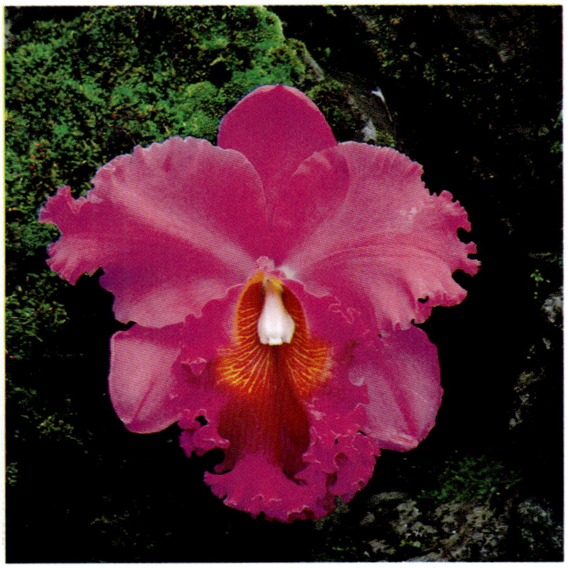

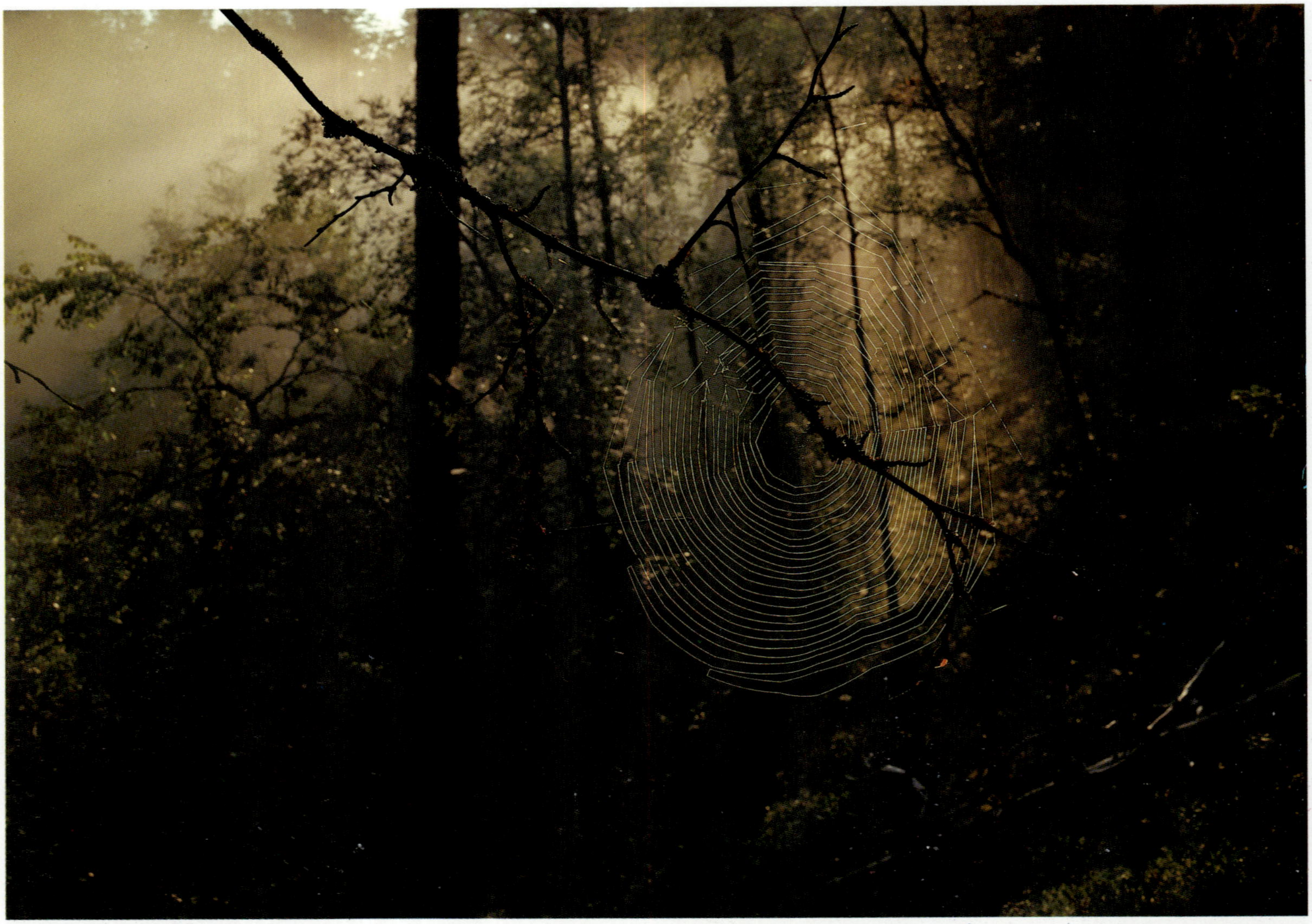

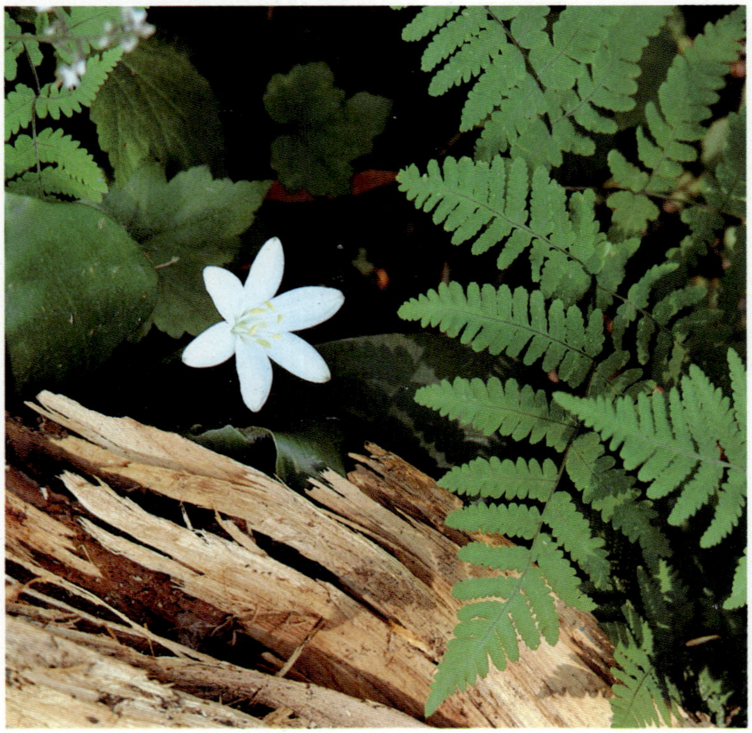

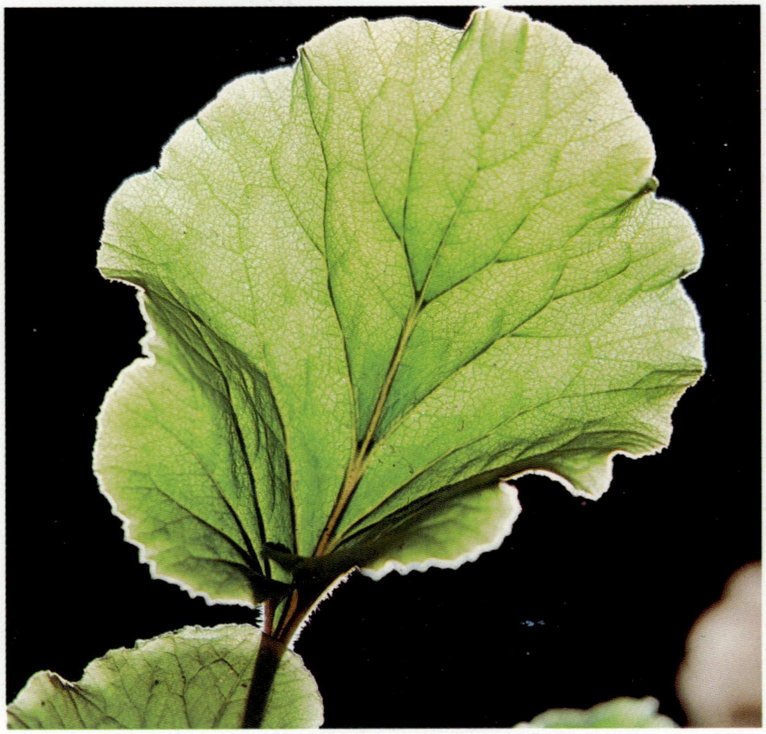

as 'f/8½'. At 150mm, the factor would be 1.5, so if you set f/8 you would get f/12 – effectively f/11 (the difference is about −10%, less than the variation between film batches).

Going on to special lenses, the cheapest is simply a positive close-up lens, which screws onto the camera lens in the same way as a filter and effectively shortens its focal length, so that the standard extension is enough for a closest focusing distance of (say) 20cm instead of 45cm. With a simple Tessar-type lens, and working at a modest aperture (f/8 or less), these can be very good; the best of them are cemented and corrected doublets in their own right, but no manufacturers commonly encountered (except Leitz) still follow this path. With the wrong lens, or at wide apertures, results can be disastrous: the best way to find out is to check a close-up lens on your camera.

Much more expensive are lenses specially designed to focus very close. The best known and most widely used of these is the Micro Nikkor for the Nikon, which used to be f/3.5 and is now f/2.8. The relatively low speed allows the designer to correct the lens very highly, and in addition he optimises the corrections for a rather nearer subject than a normal lens: at around 1/10 life size (subject distance about 30cm) is best, but performance is still superb at infinity or at 10x life size – though a bellows or extension tube is needed to get this close. Like most similar lenses, the Micro Nikkor focuses continuously down to ½ life size, then uses an extension ring for 1:1 reproduction.

Such 'macro' lenses are available in a number of focal lengths, from around 40mm to 90mm, 105mm, and even 200mm; the longer focal lengths give more 'stand off', which is useful when photographing (for example) insects, but are bulkier, slower, and more expensive than the shorter ones. Incidentally, the Micro Nikkor is so good that many people who own one use it in place of a faster standard lens.

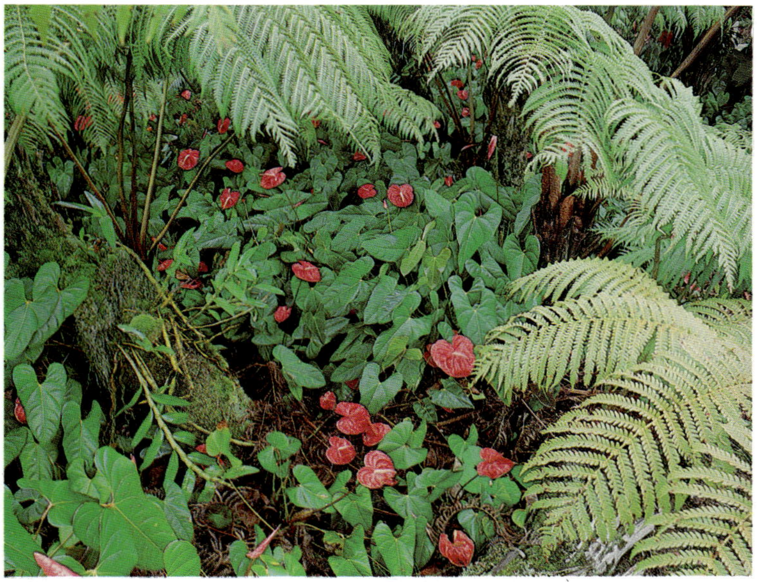

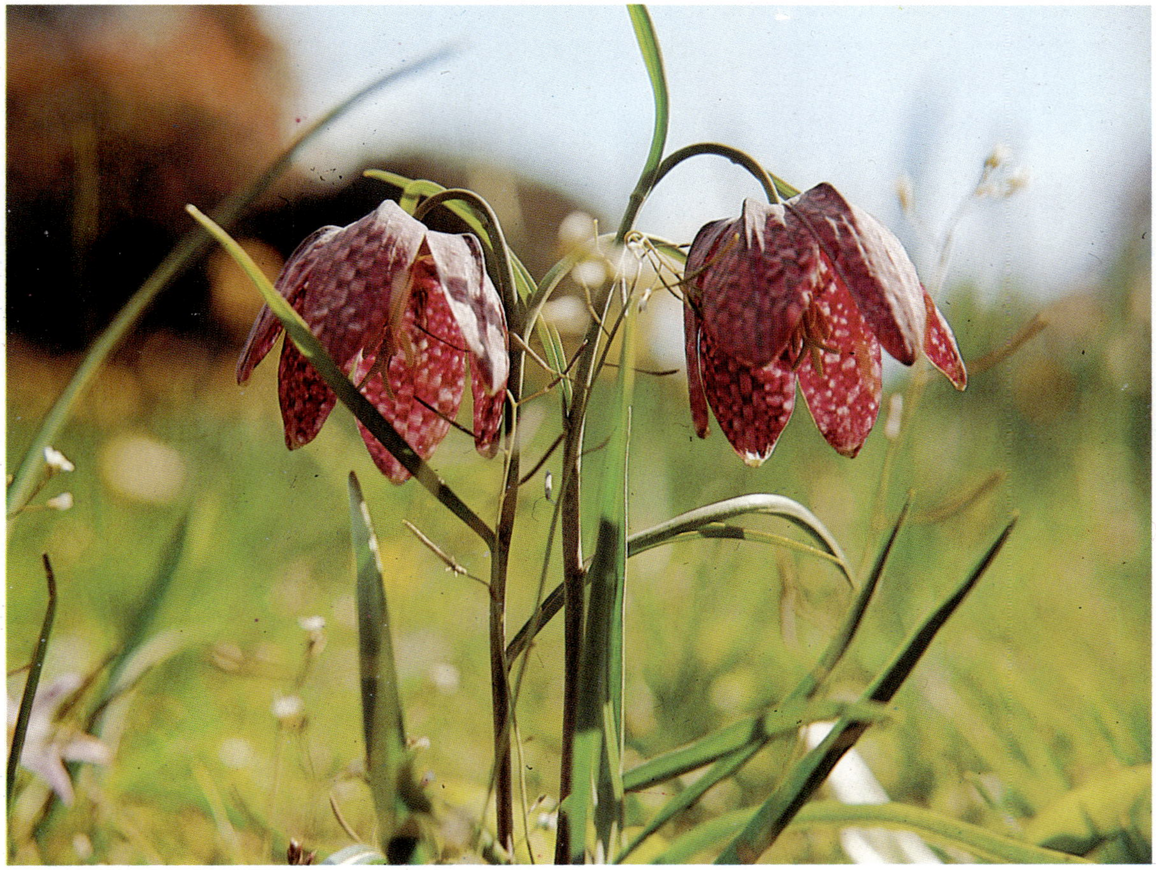

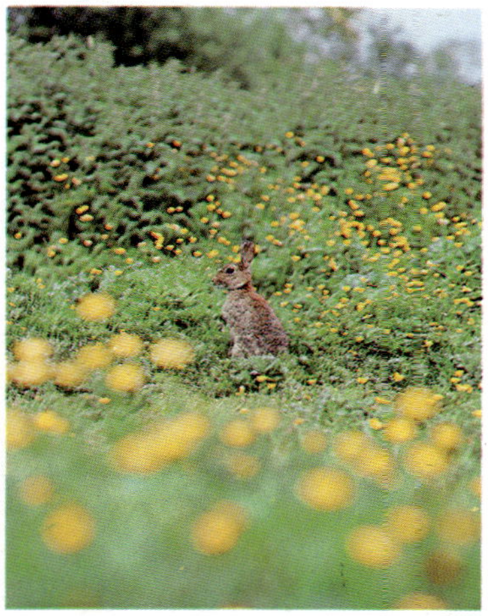

Specially computed macro *lenses are often slower than their general-purpose counterparts, but offer superb contrast and resolution in addition to their close-focusing ability. The spider web* ***facing page top*** *is one of the most difficult subjects to expose correctly; ideally, the web itself should catch the light, with a dark background. Bracketing is usually essential, as metering the web itself is next to impossible.*

are reversed (so that the back of the lens faces towards the subject). Faster lenses, or lenses of poorer quality, may vary from the acceptable to the useless.

The increase in exposure can be handled by most TTL meters, but in their absence quite awkward calculations are required. The most convenient is probably $F' = F\left(\frac{N}{N-1}\right)$, where N is the subject distance expressed as a multiple of the focal length of the lens (measure from the middle of the lens). For example, at one foot (300mm), using a 50mm (2″) lens, $\left(\frac{N}{N-1}\right)$ is 6/5. Multiply F (the metered exposure using a non-TTL meter) by 6/5 to get F,' the effective aperture when F is set. For example, if you set f/8 you get f/9.6, commonly expressed in photographic terms

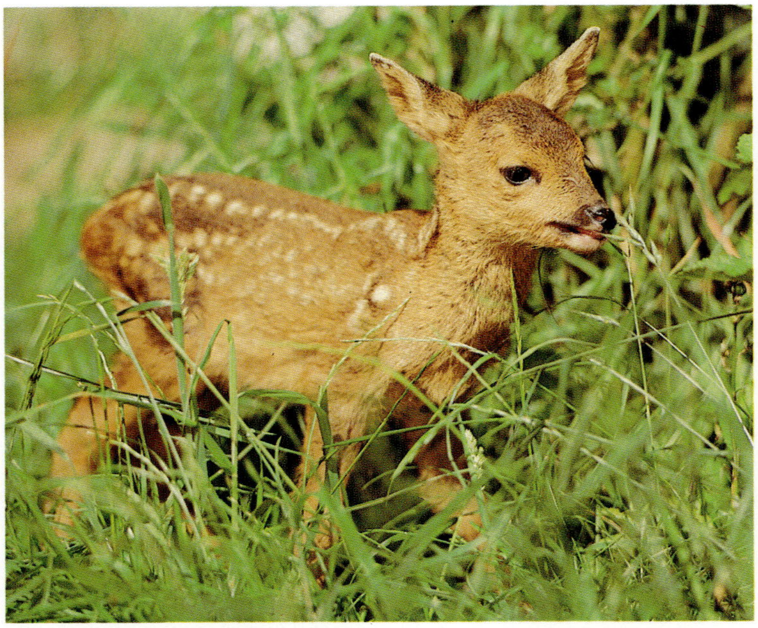

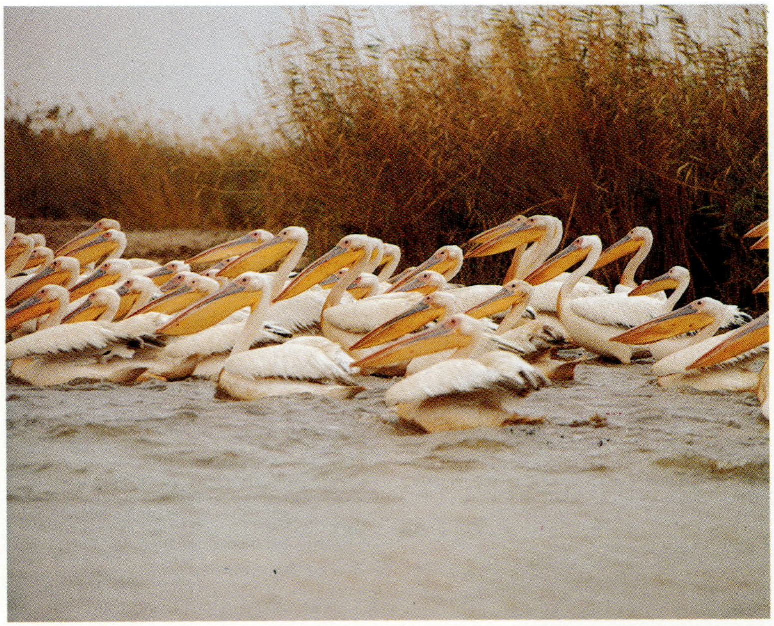

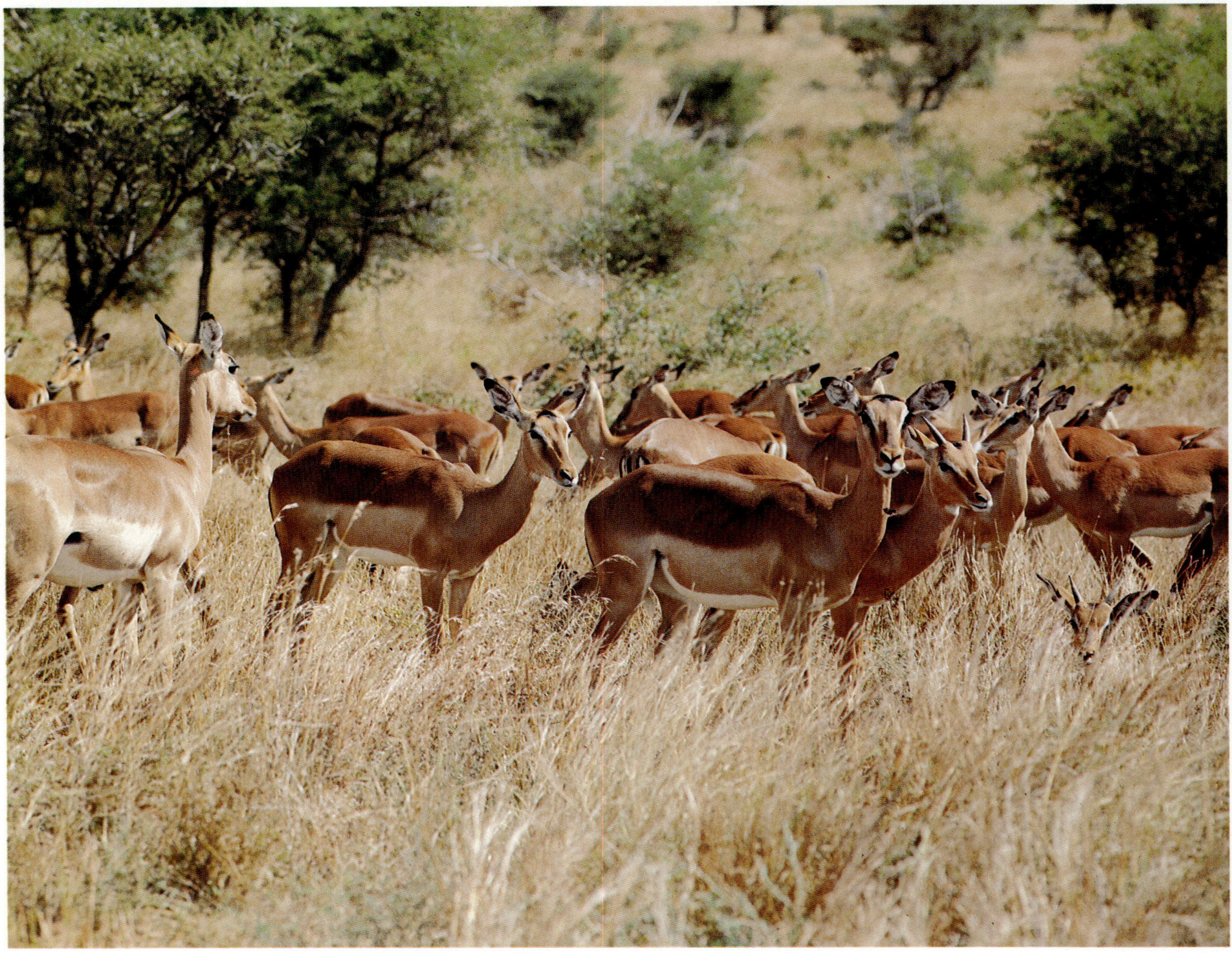

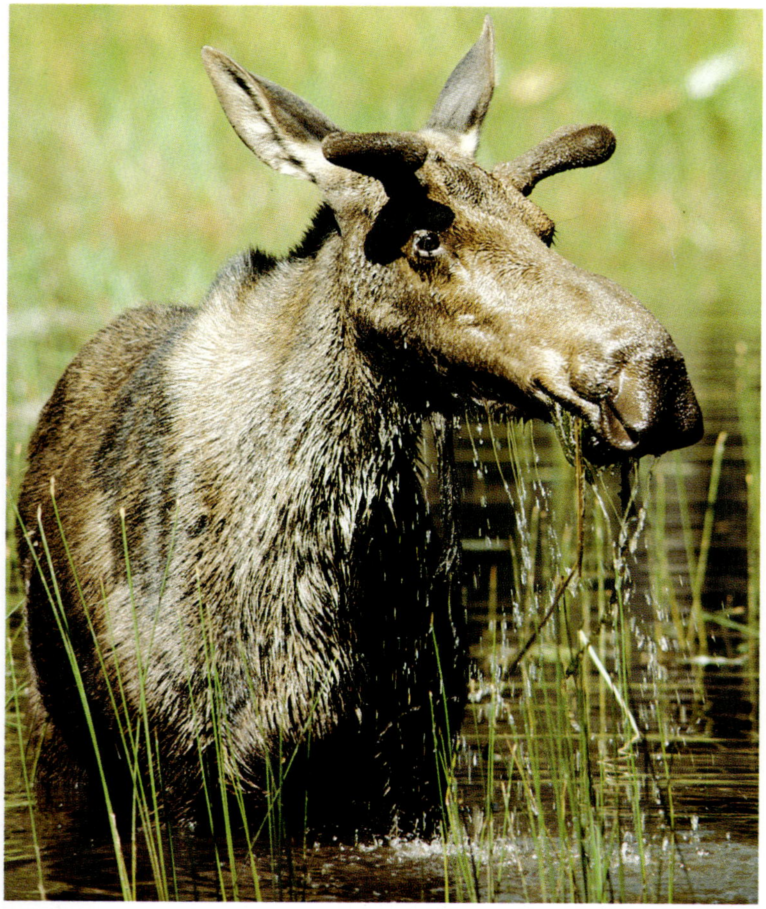

The so-called 'macro zooms' are not always such a good bet: in fact, with few exceptions, their performance close-up is horrible. The best of them all is arguably the 90-180mm Flat Field Series 1 Vivitar, a massive, expensive, slow (f/4.5) lens which was discontinued some time ago, but is in great demand among the *cognoscenti*. The advantage of the zooms, though, is that the diaphragm is normally mechanically compensated to ensure a constant aperture even in the macro mode. This is rather more convenient than the fixed-length lenses, which require either TTL metering or the same sort of calculations as described previously – though for obvious reasons, the longer lenses can achieve a given reproduction ratio with less diaphragm adjustment.

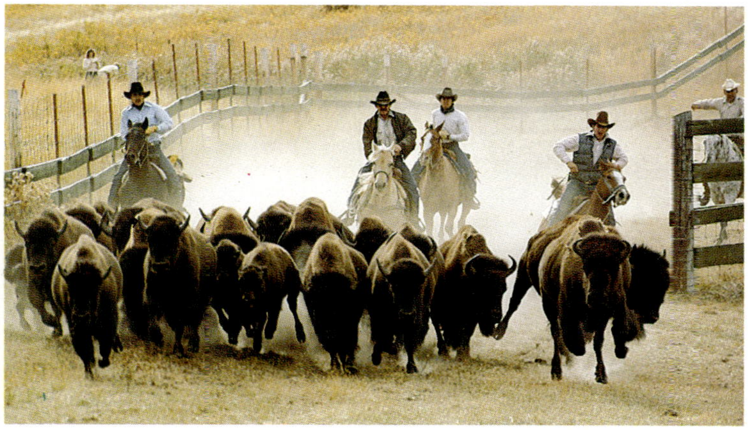

Although forethought is an *important element in creativity, many shots require a snap decision and response, as the opportunity to capture the sight can vanish as suddenly as it appeared. Animals in the wild are a case in point, where just a simple record may be the major consideration.*

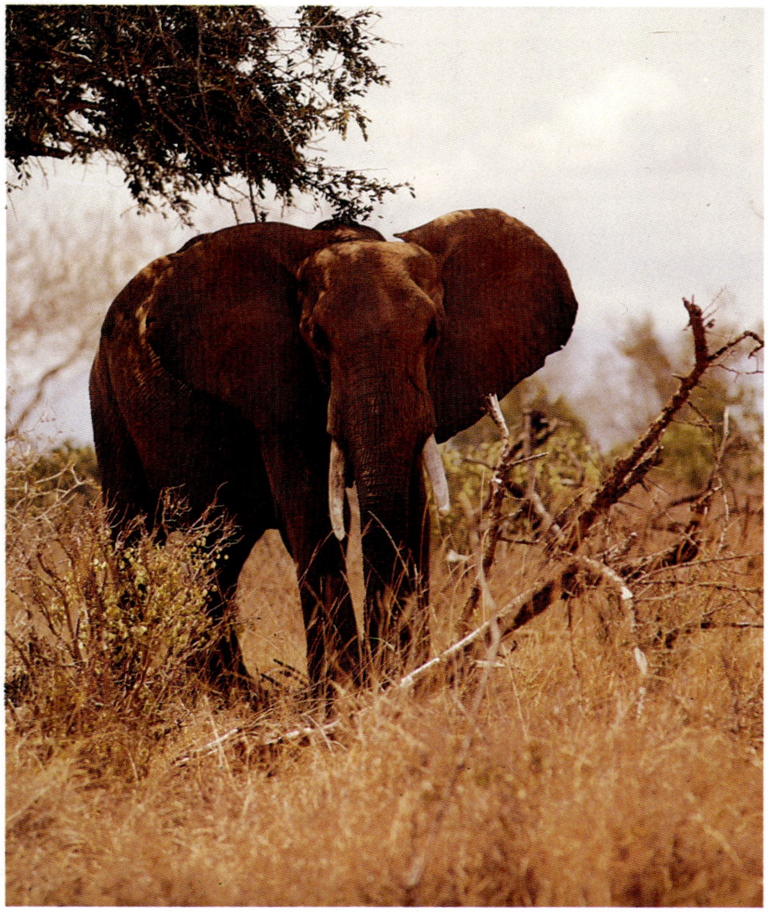

With any close-up system, though, a major problem is depth-of-field. Depth of field is constant for any given reproduction ratio no matter how it is achieved, and in extreme close-ups it is shallow. Add to this the need to open up to get a reasonable amount of light on the film, and you have a major problem. The only effective answer is to have lots of light to start with, and the discussions of the best way to light macro subjects can fill whole chapters. The easiest (but most expensive) way is with a ringlight, a circular flash tube around the lens, but others involve the use of large soft reflectors or even a 'Pepper's Ghost' system with a sheet of plane parallel glass at 45° in front of the lens and a flash fired from the side.

Regardless of all the drawbacks of macro photography, though, it is always worth trying to get a picture. At the very worst, you will fail; at the best, you may be handsomely rewarded. Even such theoretically disastrous combinations as a macro zoom and a teleconverter used together have been known to bring home the bacon!

SPECIALISED NATURAL HISTORY PHOTOGRAPHY

There are many fields so specialised that only an active practitioner can know much about them: examples include underwater photography, photography in caves (potholes), the photography of insects in flight, and so forth. As it is impossible in a single book, let alone a single chapter, to explain all the ramifications of the different kinds of specialisation, all I can suggest is that you look at the pictures in this book and elsewhere; if they inspire you to try something of your own, get hold of a specialised book on the subject and use that as a starting point.

REPORTAGE

Reportage, also known as photojournalism, is traditionally concerned with 'telling it like it is'. The classic image of the newspaper photographer is of a hard-bitten type carrying a Speed Graphic; his trendier replacement, the photojournalist, is visualised as being hung about with battered Leicas or Nikons, jetting to far-flung parts of the world and photographing wars and insurrections.

Whilst there is considerably more than a grain of truth in both these stereotypes, there is a lot more to it than that. Photojournalism also embraces the photographers of the Farm Security Administration recording the dire plight of sharecroppers in the 1930s; Jill Freedman's essays, 'Circus Days' and 'Firehouse'; Lartigue's 'Diary of a Century'; Cartier-Bresson's innumerable works; Bert Hardy's sensitive investigations; Gene Smith's hard-hitting 'Minamata'; even (arguably) Bailey's 'Goodbye Baby and Amen' or Diane Arbus's freak shows. Yet each of these is very different in approach, intent, and technique: Lartigue was an inspired snapshotter, the FSA was a Government-sponsored project involving many photographers over a long period of time, and 'Minamata' was the result of one man's obsession.

The attentive reader will have noticed that the works referred to above are primarily (in some cases exclusively) in black-and-white. This is because that has historically tended to be the appropriate medium for reportage, for two reasons. The first is that most periodicals use far more black-and-white than colour; this is especially true in the case of newspapers, although a surprising number of magazines are still a very long way from being all (or even mostly) in colour. Because the pictures were (and often still are) reproduced in black-and-white, it made sense to shoot them in black-and-white.

The second reason is that black-and-white is more tolerant of exposure errors, quicker and less critical to process, and faster. Although photographers like McCullin take careful meter readings under fire and expose their pictures perfectly, most are not made of such stern stuff and correct exposure is the exception rather than the norm. On some papers, this even applies to such dangerous circumstances as mayoral receptions and church tea-parties; the technical skill and knowledge of some newsmen is unbelievably low. Speed of processing is an obvious advantage, as is in-the-field processing and transmission of pictures by wire machine. Sheer film speed is useful, too: although 3M's tungsten-light film is rated at 640 and can be pushed a stop or so without serious quality loss, black-and-white films are still acceptable at 3200 ASA or more: if highlight detail is all you need, effective ratings of 10,000 ASA and more are possible, especially with such gems as 2475 and 2485 Kodak recording films.

Nevertheless, there is still a place – and an honourable place – for colour in reportage. It is not widely known that there are extant some colour pictures from the FSA programme in the 1930s, and now, of course, there is a great deal of colour reportage in the colour supplements of newspapers and in such magazines as Paris Match, Stern, Geo, etc.

The problem with colour reportage is that it is still a relatively new medium. Whilst this may be a source of delight to the innovator, it does make life a little difficult both commercially and from the point of view of reader acceptance. In addition to the technical difficulties outlined above, picture editors are not sure what they are looking for in colour reportage (and may have limited colour budgets anyway) and the person who looks at the photograph may find that it jars with his preconceptions of how a news picture 'should' look.

Because most of us get our knowledge of reportage

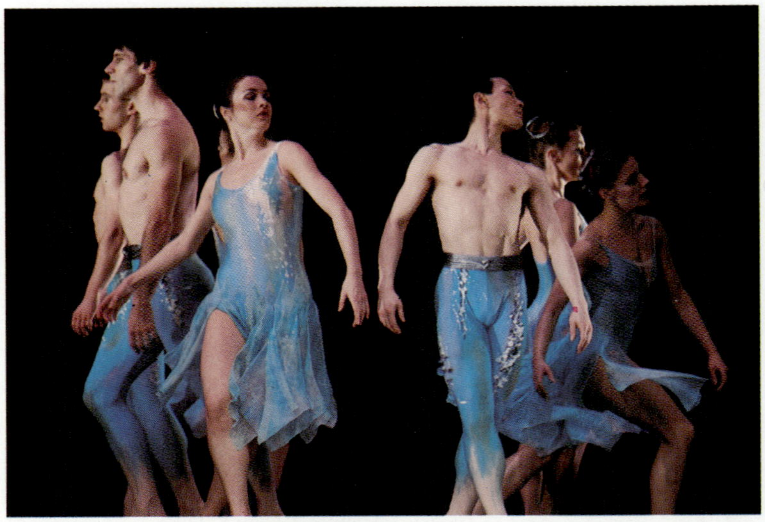
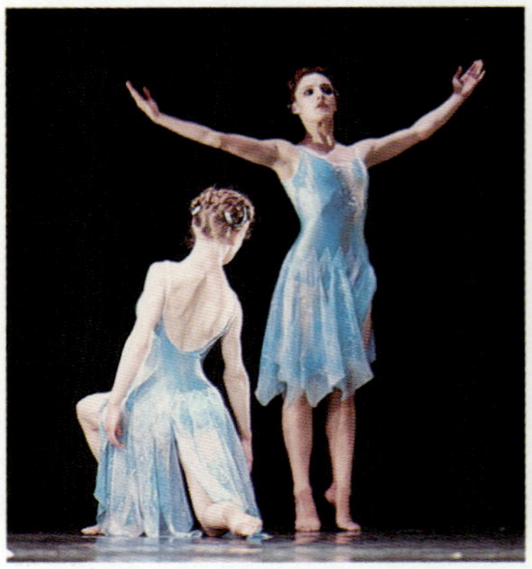
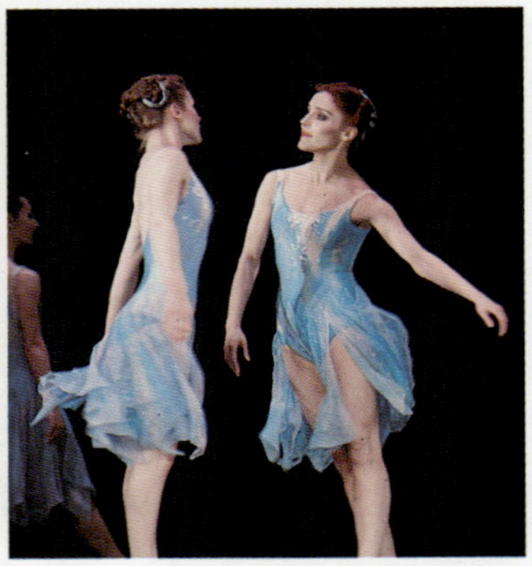
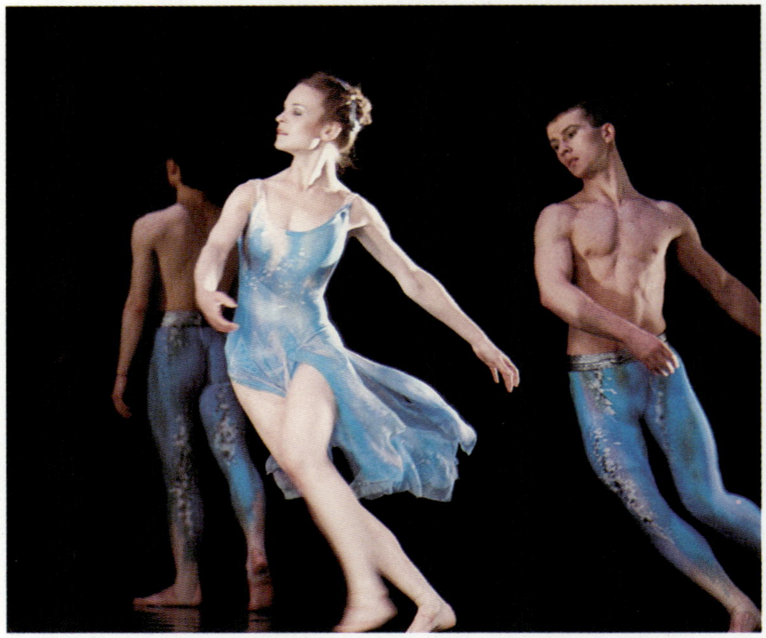

Dance studios are an excellent *place to practice your reportage techniques. You have to be able to focus rapidly and accurately; to compose almost automatically; to compensate for rapidly changing lighting as the dancers move across the stage; and (perhaps most important of all) to select the best pictures afterwards. These thirteen pictures come from a single 36-exposure roll; the errors have already been weeded out. Put yourself in the place of a picture editor – which* ***three*** *pictures would you select?*

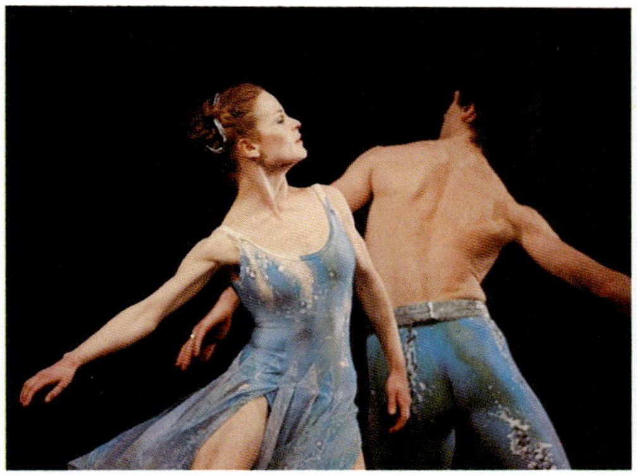
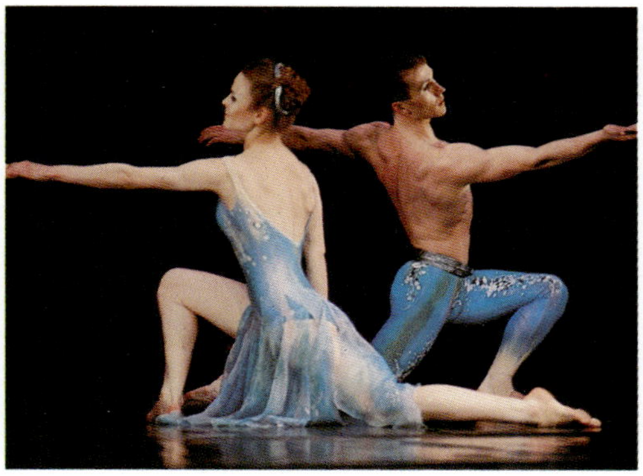
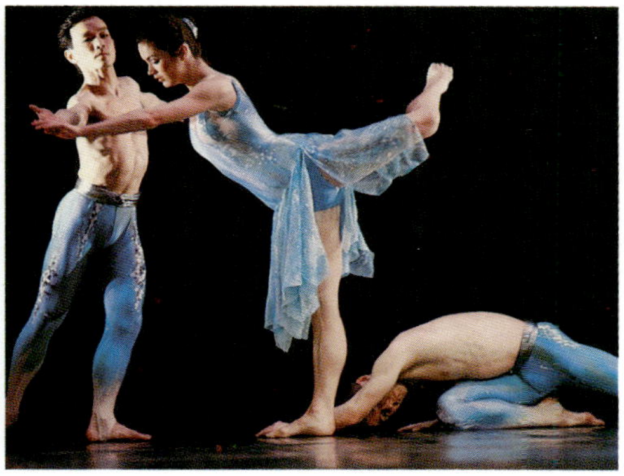
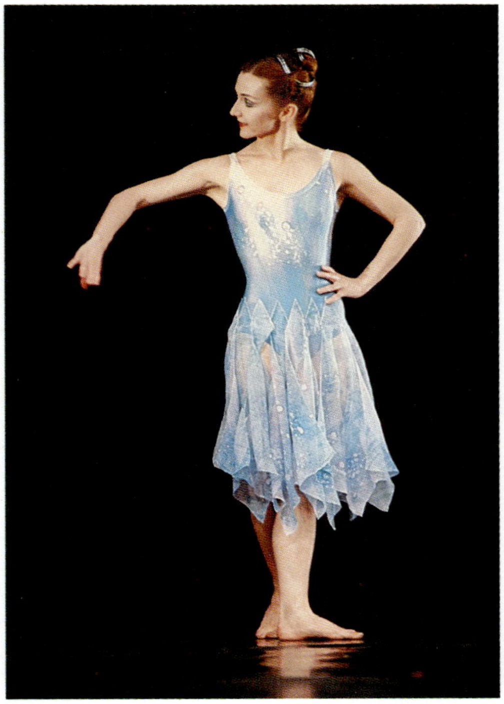
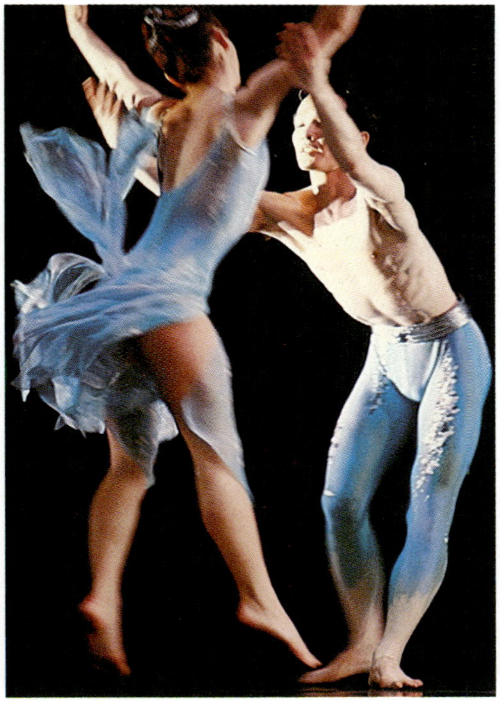
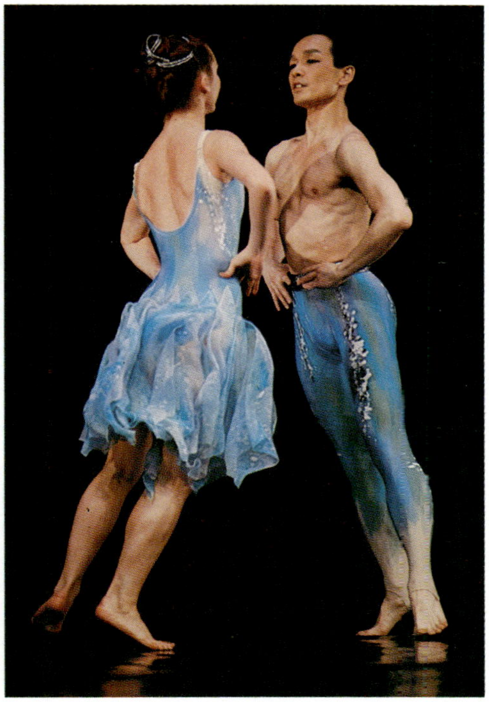
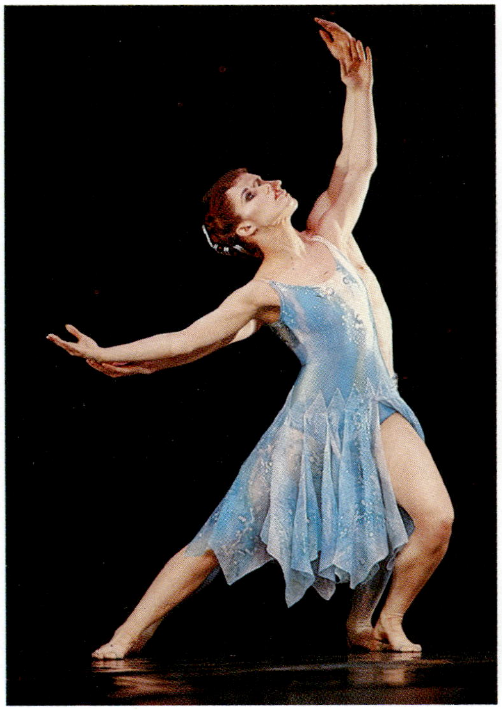
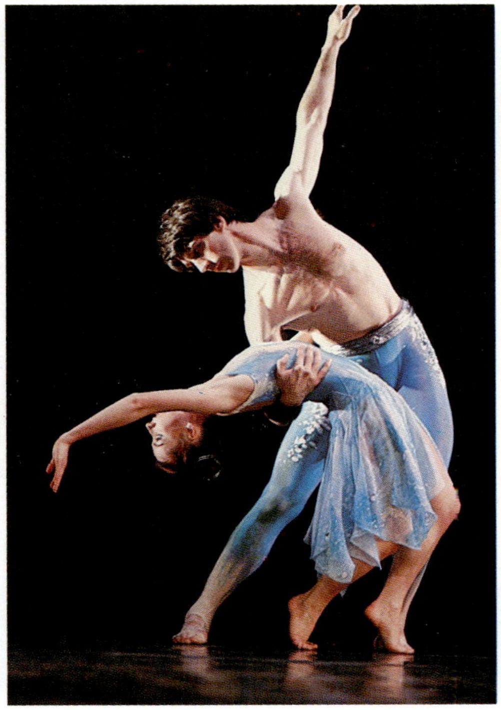
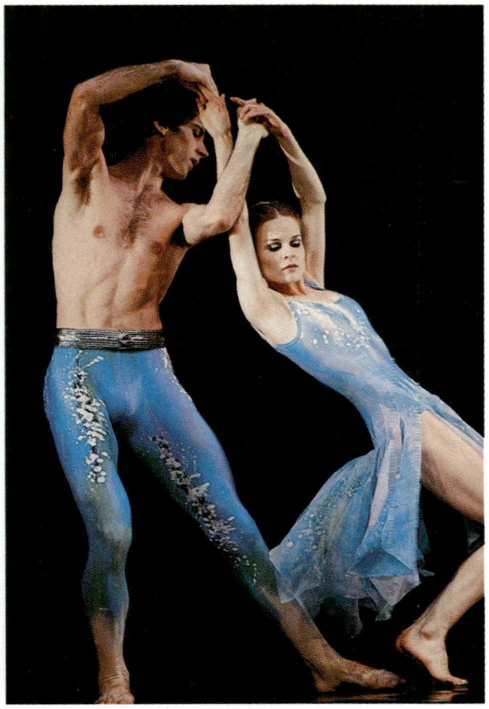

***Colour is being used more and** more for 'hard' news, but it is much more usual to find it in 'soft' stories in magazines – pictures which can be set up in advance, rather than snatched in the heat of the moment. Many of these pictures can be extremely beautiful, and they are normally taken with fairly simple 35mm equipment, such as any amateur might have.*

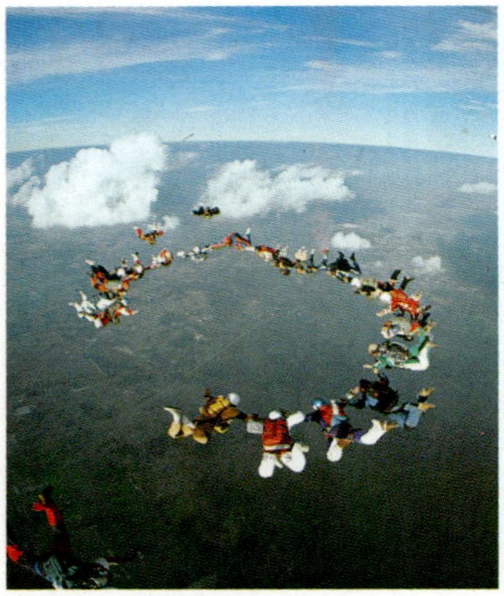

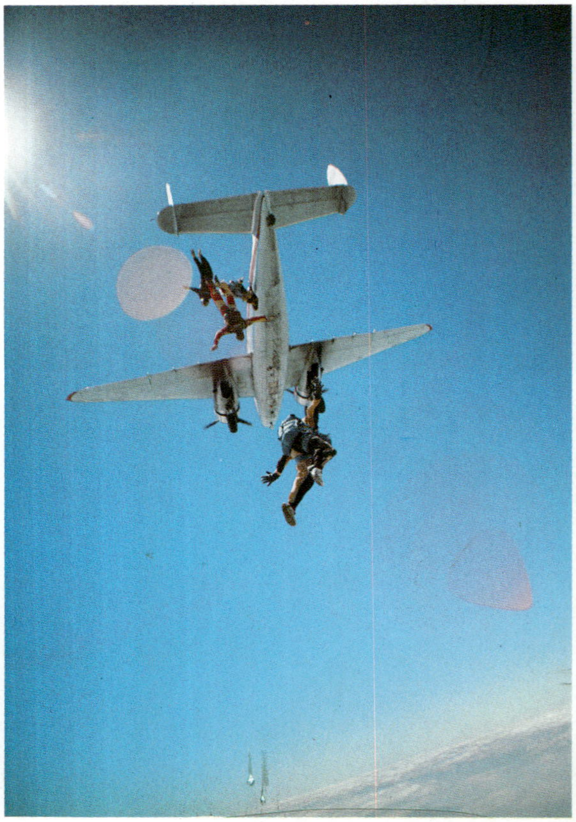

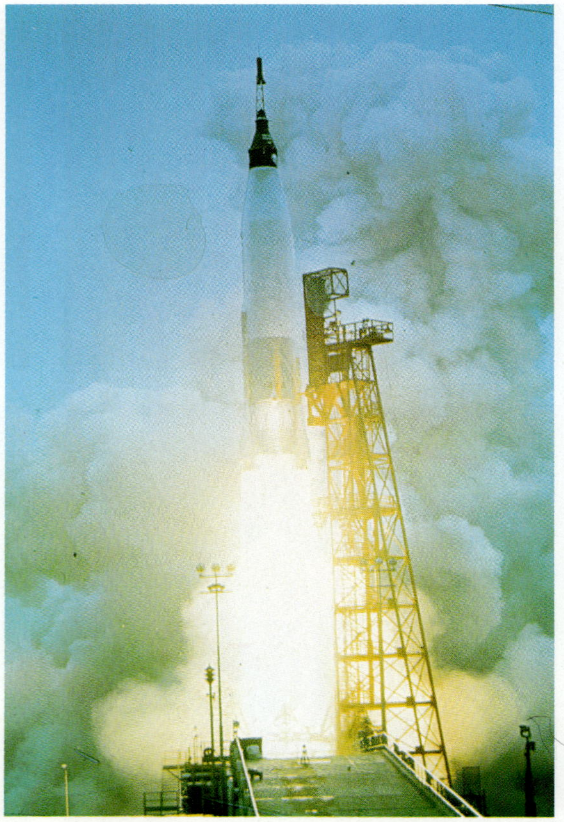

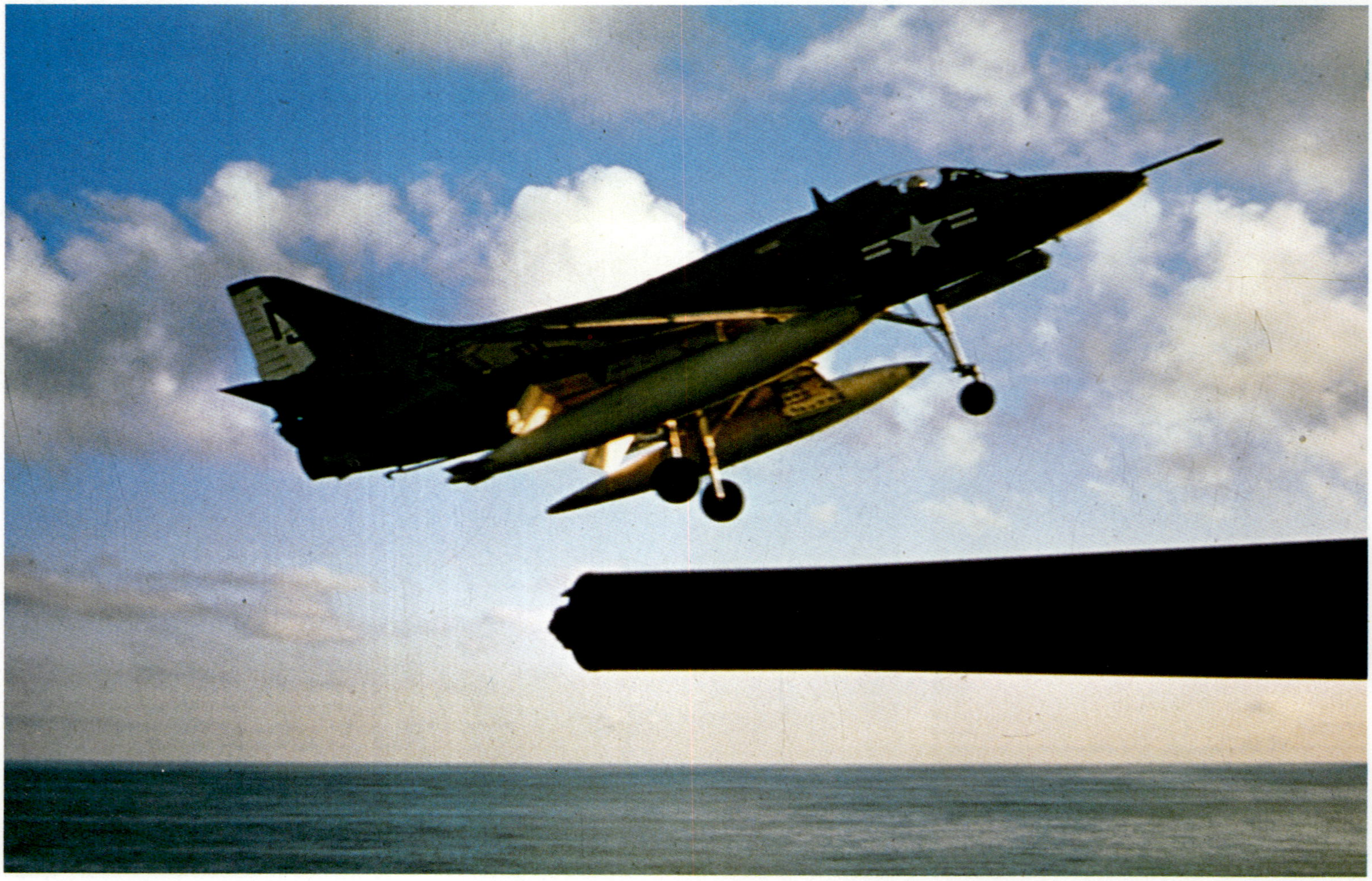

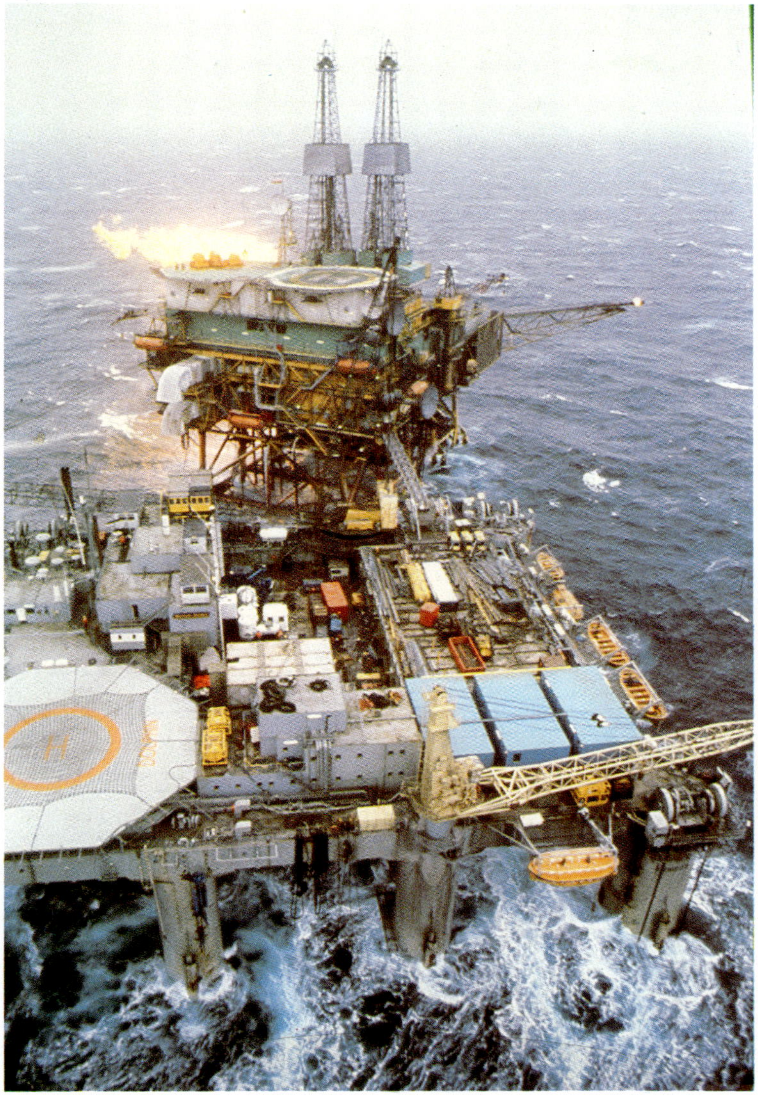

photography from newspapers, we are quite happy to see a grainy picture of limited tonal range under the label 'reportage'; the grain corresponds to the half-tone screen used for newspaper reproduction, and the limited tonal range to the quality of newspaper printing. On the other hand, we derive our understanding of colour photography from advertising (where technical quality is usually impeccable) and from our own pictures, wherein the quality is usually surprisingly good. Grain and a general flatness of colour is quite acceptable in a news picture, because we mentally equate it with black-and-white; but colour casts are much less acceptable. It is in the nature of colour film to give colour casts when mistreated during processing, overheated in the camera, or used in lighting for which it was not designed – and as all of these circumstances can arise very easily in certain types of reportage, colour is little used in (for example) war photography.

Even if we could get impeccable colour (and McCullin seems to manage it pretty well), it would still jar upon some sensibilities because it 'prettifies' some subjects to an intolerable

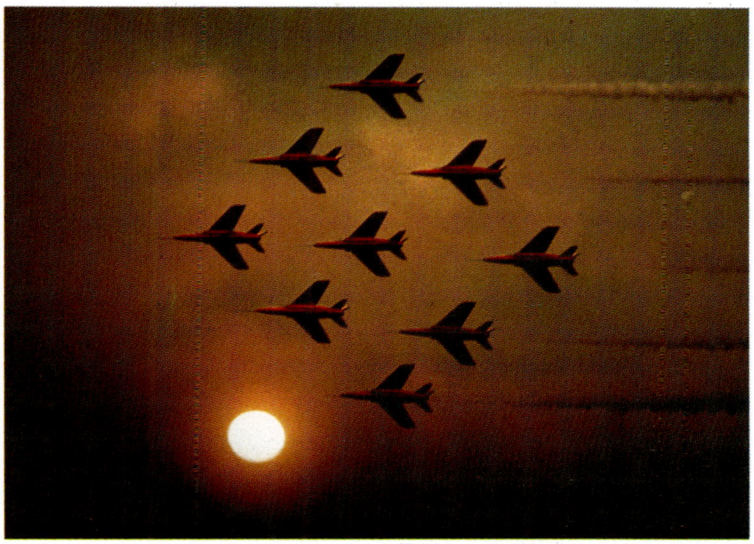

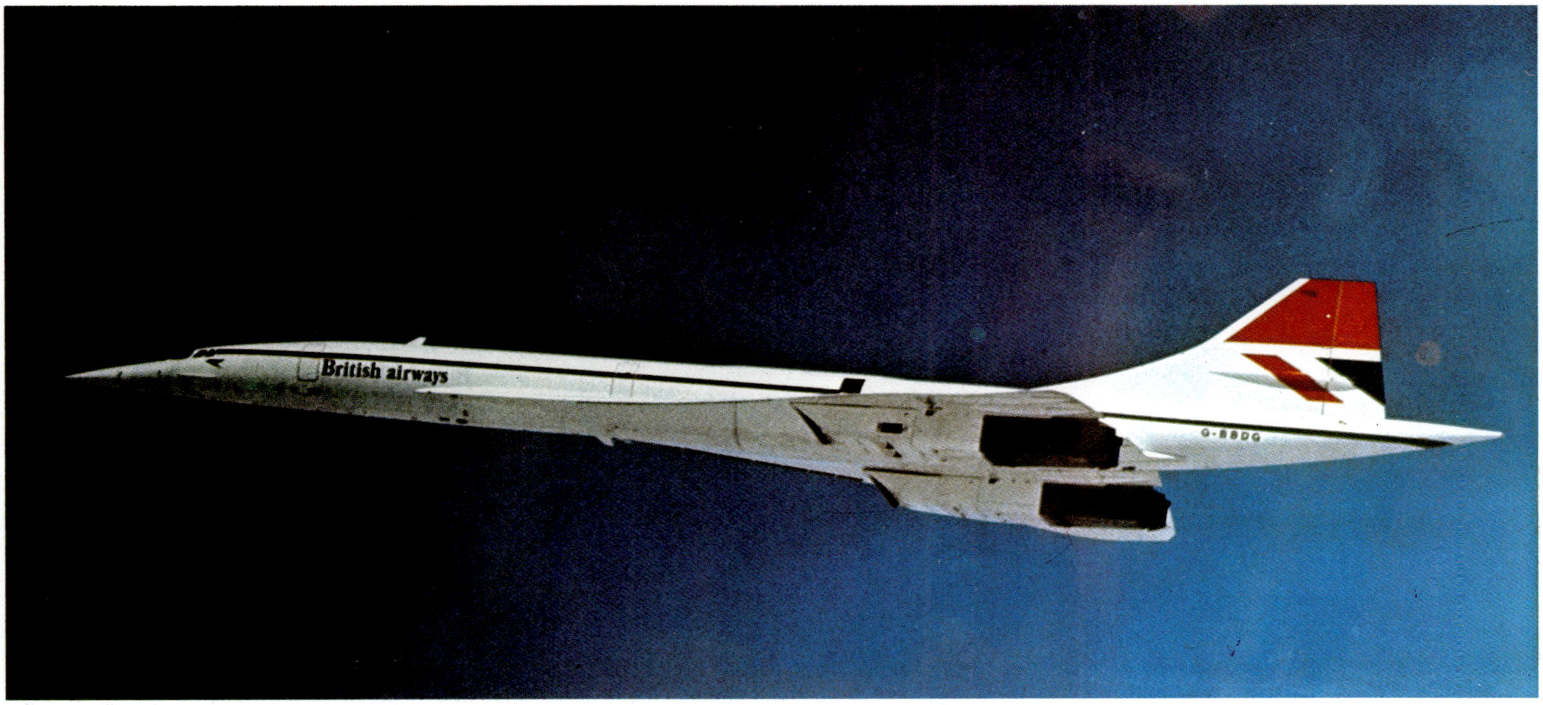

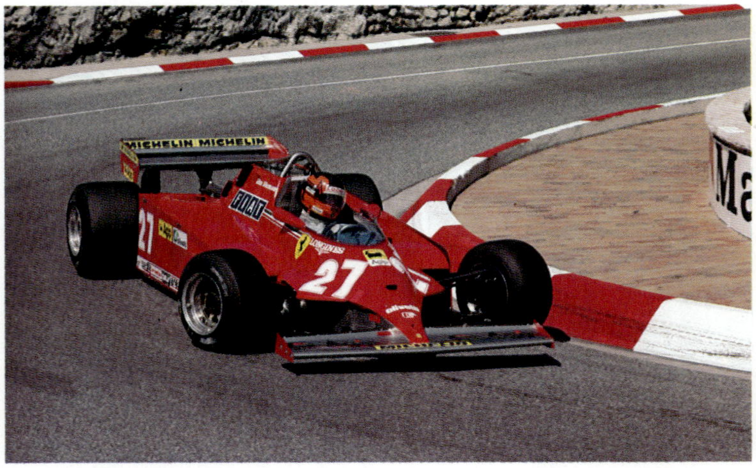

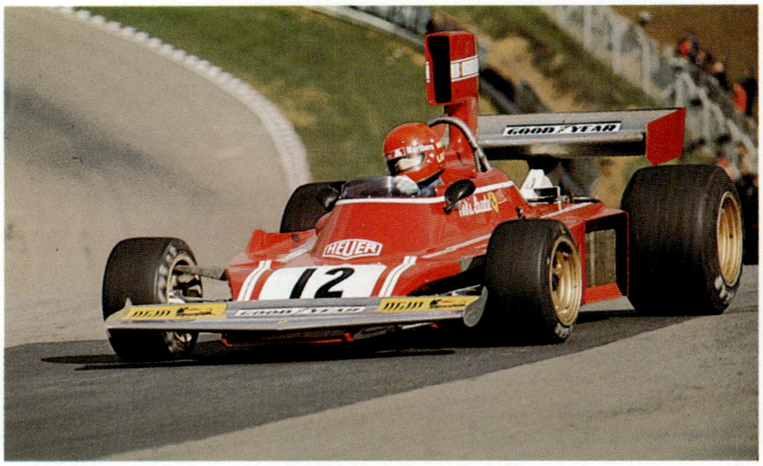

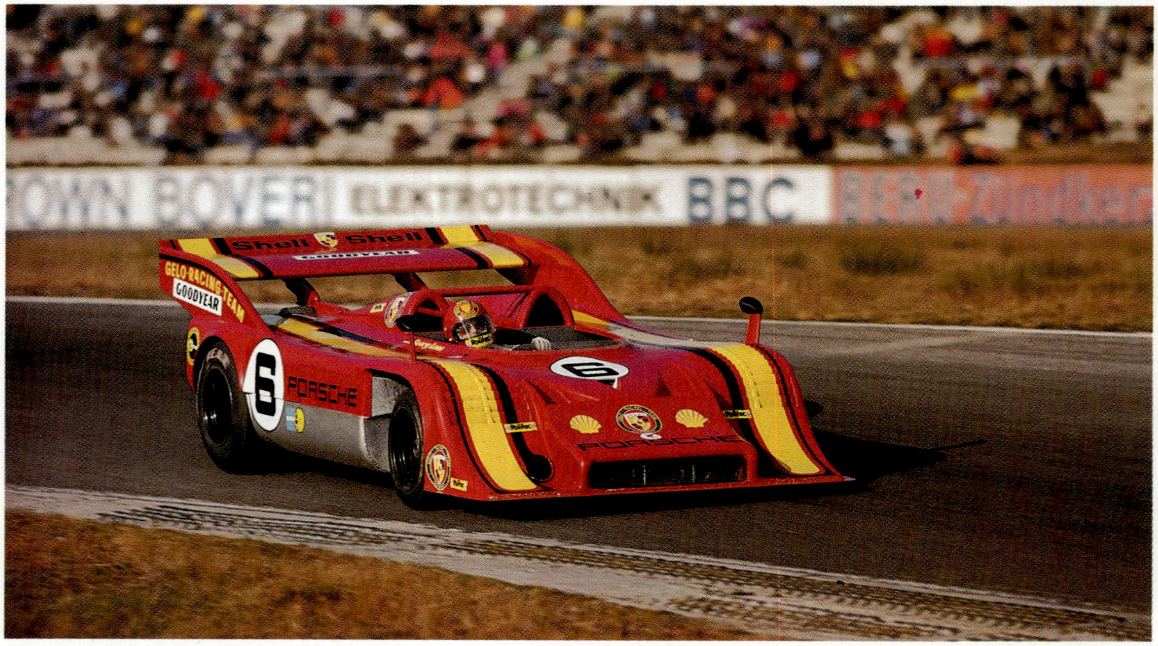

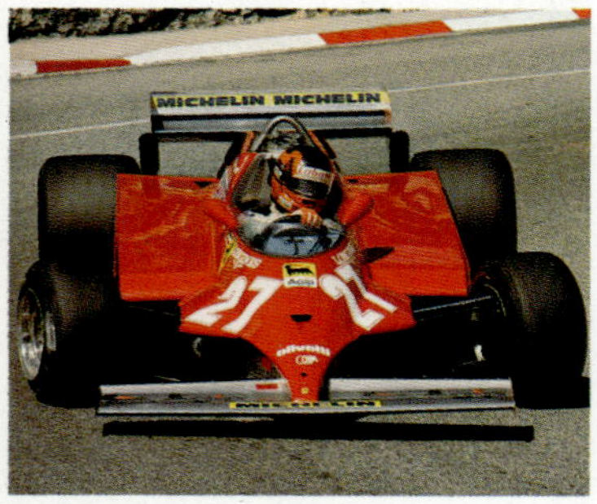

Another good way to practice *your reportage skills is on racing cars; at the big professional events, there is little room for the amateur in the best places, but at vintage and 'club' meets you can often get in among the action. Ensure preferential treatment next time with complimentary prints.*

extent. This is once again a consequence of our preconceptions; we are accustomed to cooing over a successful snapshot, 'Didn't it come out well?' We expect pleasant subjects in a colour picture – and when we do not get them, we may not be well pleased. Whilst this means that a really good picture can derive extra impact from its reversal of our expectations, it also means that anything less may be diminished or even demeaned by the use of colour: in simple terms, a war can look too much like a vacation.

Of course, this may be used to good effect when the subject is inherently an agreeable or enjoyable one. A fine example of this is any great State occasion, with a royal wedding or investiture a prime example. All the pomp and glory looks well in colour, because (after all) it was designed to. It was meant to be an occasion for public rejoicing, a holiday, a break from routine – and this fits in well with our preconceptions about colour pictures.

In practice, this effect extends also to several occasions which are not ostensibly purely for the fun of it. A military parade is an excellent example, because once again the intention of the organisers is to stir and enthuse the populace; they want you to forget that the purpose of an army – any army – is to kill people. By extension, State funerals are highly suitable subjects for colour photography; the fact of death is subjugated to the achievements of the dead person in life.

Having thus established that some subjects are more suitable than others for reportage in colour, there are two things to consider. The first is the choice of equipment, and the second is the style or technique.

Equipment is (as ever) a matter of personal choice, but there are two groups of equipment which are widely used. The first is the simple, strong, fast-handling 35mm camera with standard or wide-angle lens. The traditional choice was always the Leica, though the reflex Nikon has supplanted it to a great extent. With a fast standard or 35mm lens, this type of gear is favoured by the photographer who likes to get in among the action. The alternative is the SLR equipped with a moderately long lens – 135-200mm, with the 180/2.8 a long-time favourite – used at a distance to pick out colourful details. Some photographers favour even longer lenses, but the trouble with these is that they are heavy and have limited maximum apertures, though the latter has now been remedied with the 300/2.8 lenses from Nikon and Canon; the drawbacks are now weight and price, instead.

The standard/wide approach is considerably more difficult to handle in colour than in black-and-white, principally because of the extra variable introduced in the form of colour. The black-and-white user can compose his picture so that the principal interest is highlighted, and the rest played down; if need be, an

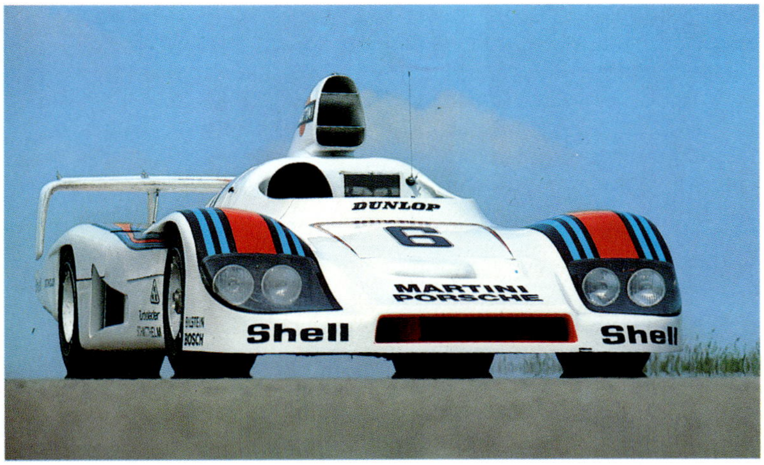

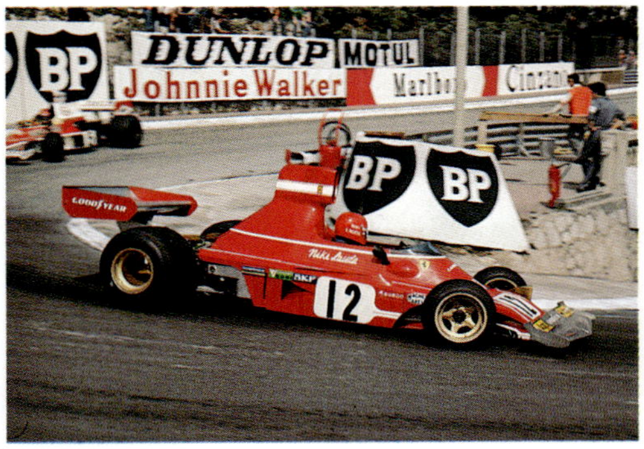

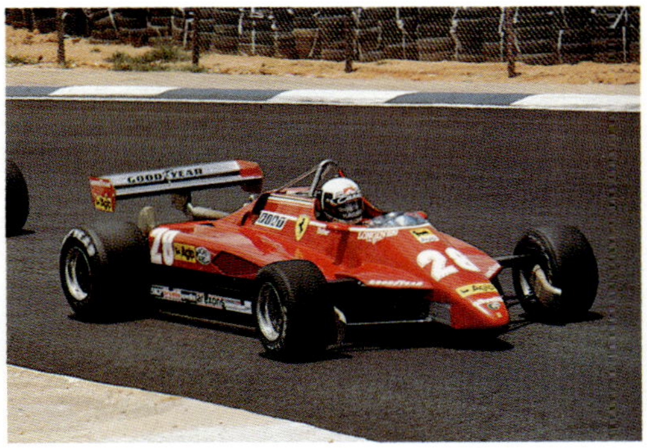

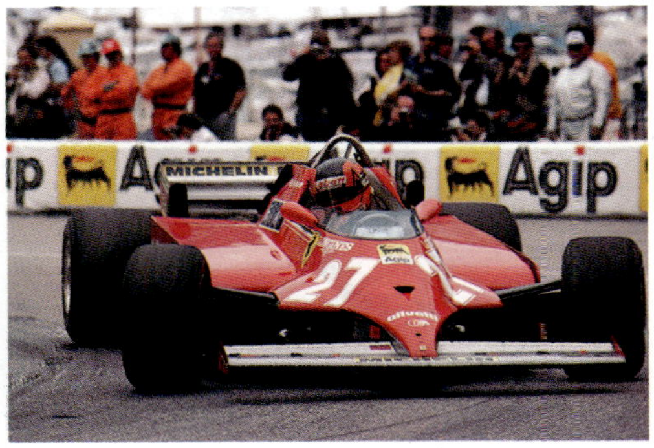

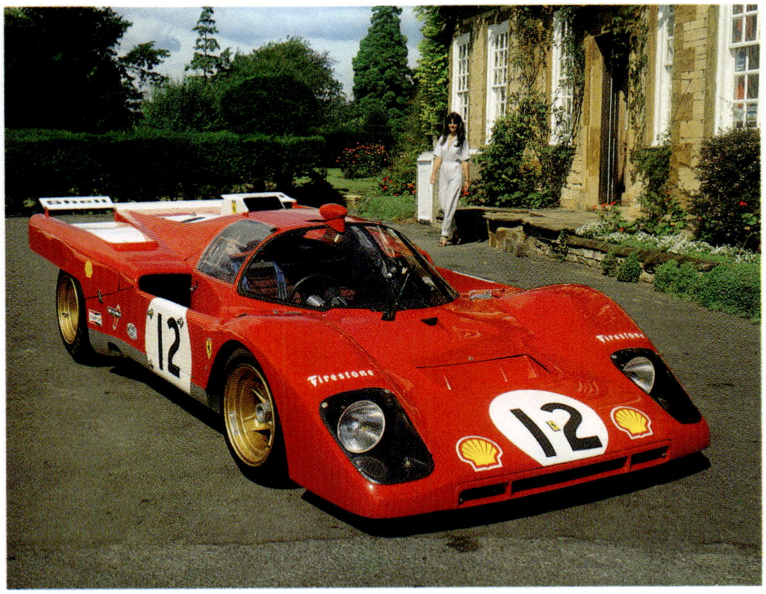

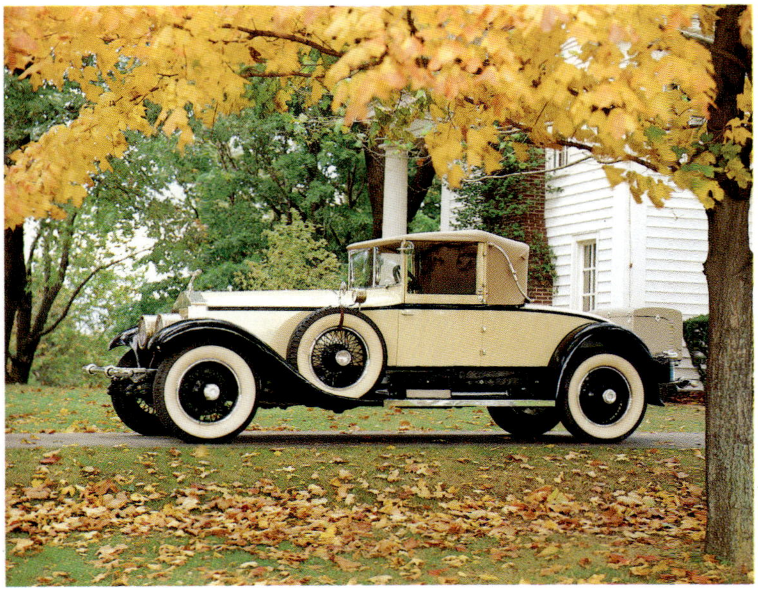

unnecessarily bright patch near the edge can be darkened during printing to make sure that it does not draw the eye away from the main subject. With colour, instead of tone, this is very much more difficult: there is no intermediate printing process (though darkening can be effected in the final printing process, if the image is to be printed), and whilst an area of red may reproduce on black-and-white as an unobtrusive <u>tone</u>, as a <u>colour</u> it can be all too obvious.

Given that in colour reportage both this and the technical difficulties already mentioned must be mastered, it is scarcely surprising that so little reportage is in colour or that so few photographers are famed for their colour reportage. In practice, therefore, it tends to be fairly 'soft' news that is covered in colour – sports, games, parades, etc., where it does not really matter all that much if the picture is not particularly good and where in any case the pressure is nothing like as great as it might be whilst covering a war. The other thing which can be covered in colour is 'semi-soft' news, the kind of thing that drags on and on and in which the pictures are not particularly dated: in Vietnam or Afghanistan, for example, it did not much matter whether a picture was a day old or a month old – as long as it was a good enough picture.

Within this framework, there is the question of the attitude adopted by the photographer – what I earlier called the 'political' aspect. In the nature of reportage, what is being photographed is likely to arouse strong emotions. To take the example of Vietnam, the photographer could choose to show the undoubted heroism of many of those fighting there; the equally undoubted cowardice of others; the repulsive conditions in which the fighting was actually done; what happens to a man (American or Viet Cong) when he steps on an anti-personnel mine; the bars and whorehouses of Hanoi; or any of a hundred other things. Having photographed them, the use to which the pictures are put is another major consideration. Taking the bars and whorehouses, for example, he could portray them as a well-deserved rest for men on (or beyond) the limits of endurance or as a vile sink of iniquity sapping the spirits of innocent young men. Little though I love politics and the mouthings of extremists, I am forced to agree with the oft-repeated sentiment of some Marxist photographers, at least with respect to reportage: every act of taking a photograph is a political act. After that . . . it's your politics.

WE DO THE REST

At the very beginning of this book, I quoted the old Kodak slogan: "You press the button and we do the rest."

So far, we have looked mostly at the button-pushing side; indeed, as stated at the beginning, there is little reason (except, perhaps, in colour printing) not to let someone else do the rest. On the other hand, it is unrealistic to pretend that the photographer's involvement with the picture ends at the moment of pressing the button.

There is simply no space here to discuss at length the creative techniques possible in the darkroom; the afterwork you can perform on the print; the possibilities of hand-colouring, retouching, or mixing photography and artwork; or the best way to present a picture. The creative photographer must, however, be aware of all of this and more besides. The rest of this chapter explores, in no particular order, a number of other possibilities which you may care to follow up.

INFRA-RED AND ULTRA-VIOLET

In colour photography, there are two kinds of infra-red equipment. The first uses conventional cameras and special 'false colour' film. This is a normal integral tripack, but one layer is sensitised to green, one to red, and one to infra-red. All are sensitive to blue, so a blue-absorbing (= yellow) filter is always necessary. Alternatively, filters of other colours may be used: Kodak recommend light green, orange, red, and amber, but you may also care to experiment with 'effects' filters, just to see what happens. The false-colour IR films are very sensitive to heat, and should be refrigerated before use (as well as between exposure and development if much time elapses). Exposure is critical; bracketing is essential. Finally, not all cloth focal-plane shutter blinds are totally IR opaque, so keep the lens cap on between exposures unless you have a metal focal-plane (or leaf) shutter.

The other kind of IR photography records much longer waves, beyond about 14000Å, and requires special 'thermographic' cameras equipped with IR sensors; these are more electronic than conventionally photographic, and are responsible for 'heat trace photographs' showing phantom vehicles in car parks, phantom bodies in beds, etc. They are also staggeringly expensive, and are normally the preserve of government agencies and the like.

There are also two kinds of ultra-violet (UV) photography. The first uses UV 'light' directly, with a filter which is visually opaque. Only the UV wavelengths very close to the visible spectrum can pass through ordinary glass; for shorter

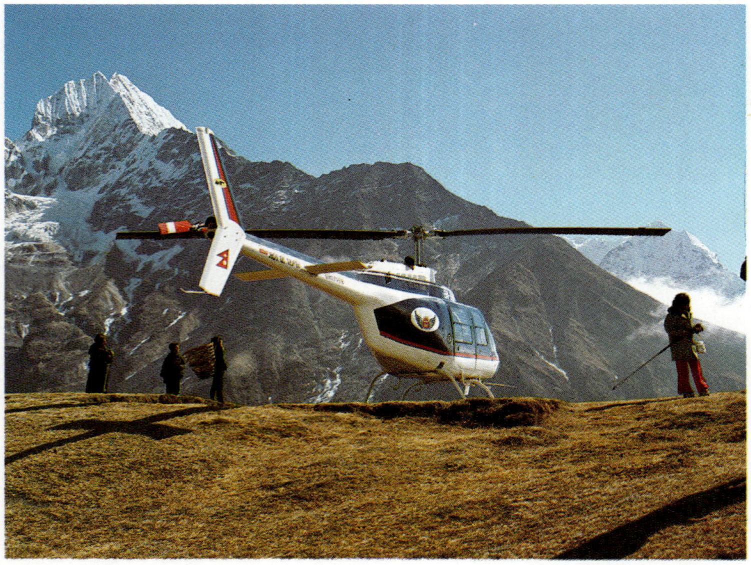

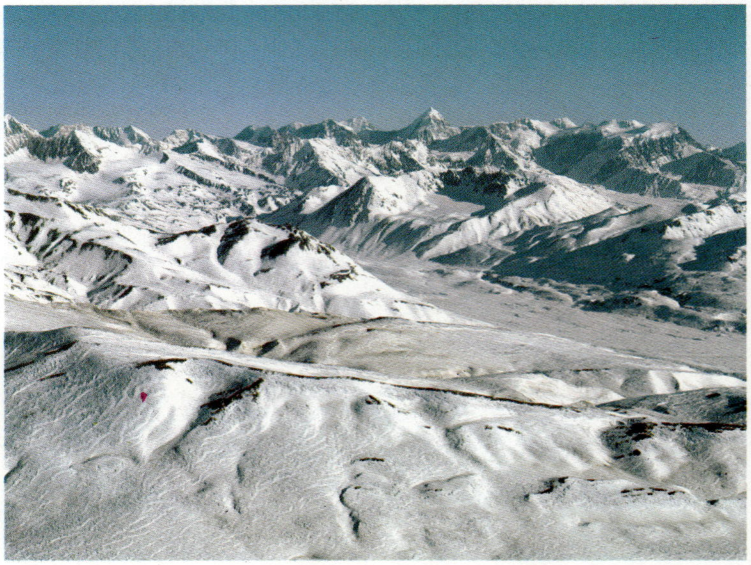

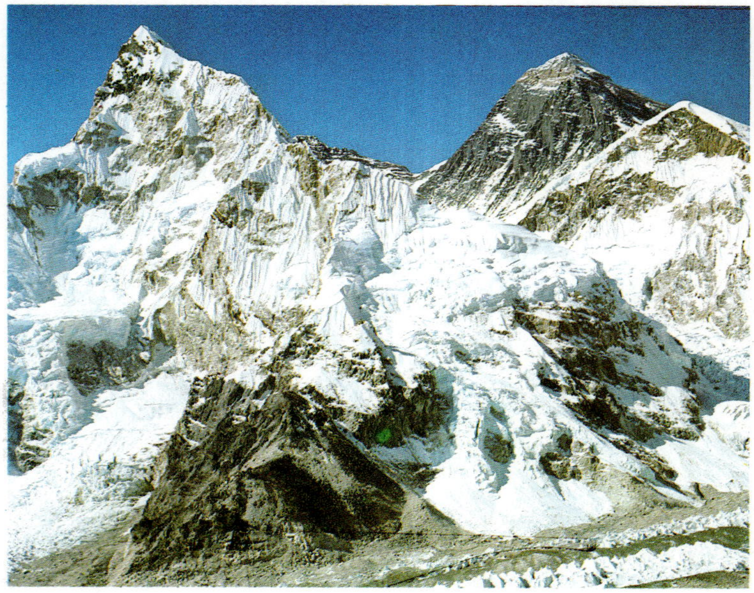

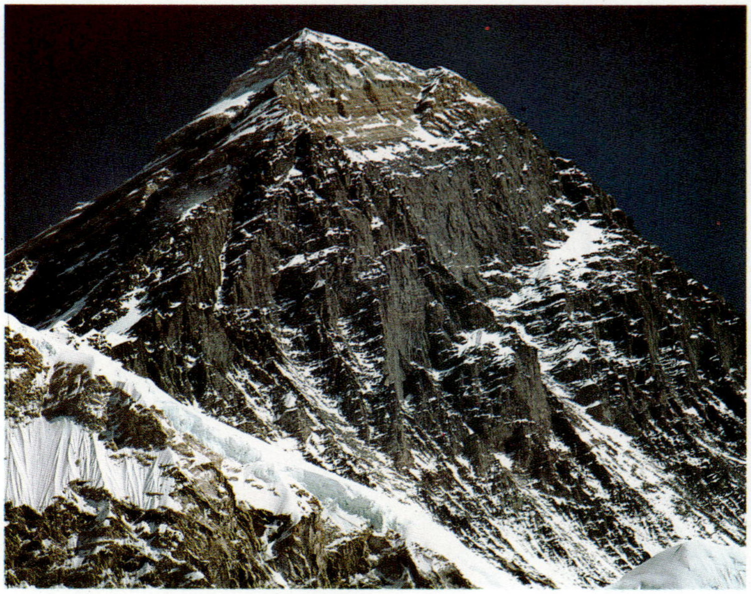

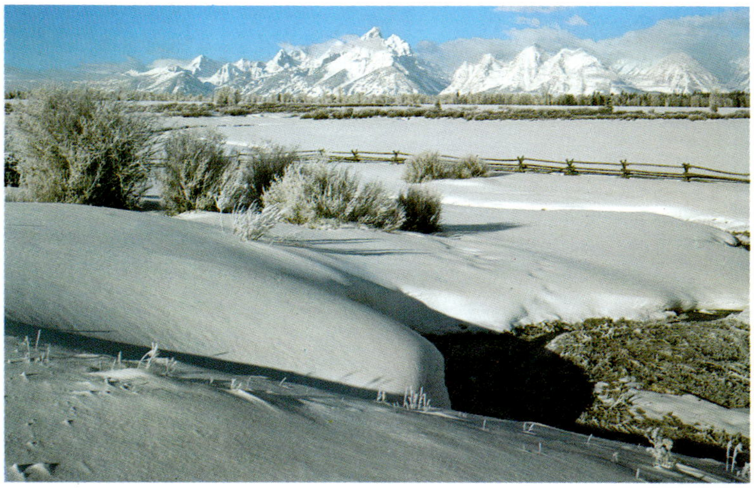

wavelengths, special quartz lenses are used. Much more interesting for the creative photographer is ultra-violet fluorescence photography.

This makes use of the fact that many materials fluoresce, or glow, when UV light shines upon them. The glow is quite faint, so it is usual to take such photographs in a darkened room with the only 'light source' being a UV fluorescent tube (obtainable from many electronics hobby stockists). The light recorded on the film comes from the fluorescent sample itself – which can be something as unusual as a starched shirt, a piece of plastic, a pile of laboratory chemicals, or many common minerals!

When using UV light you should ALWAYS wear goggles and take care to avoid undue exposure to the UV, which can otherwise produce painful conjunctivitis and artificial (but convincing) sunburn. You will not be aware of the adverse effects until an hour or two after excessive exposure, so it is all too easy to forget.

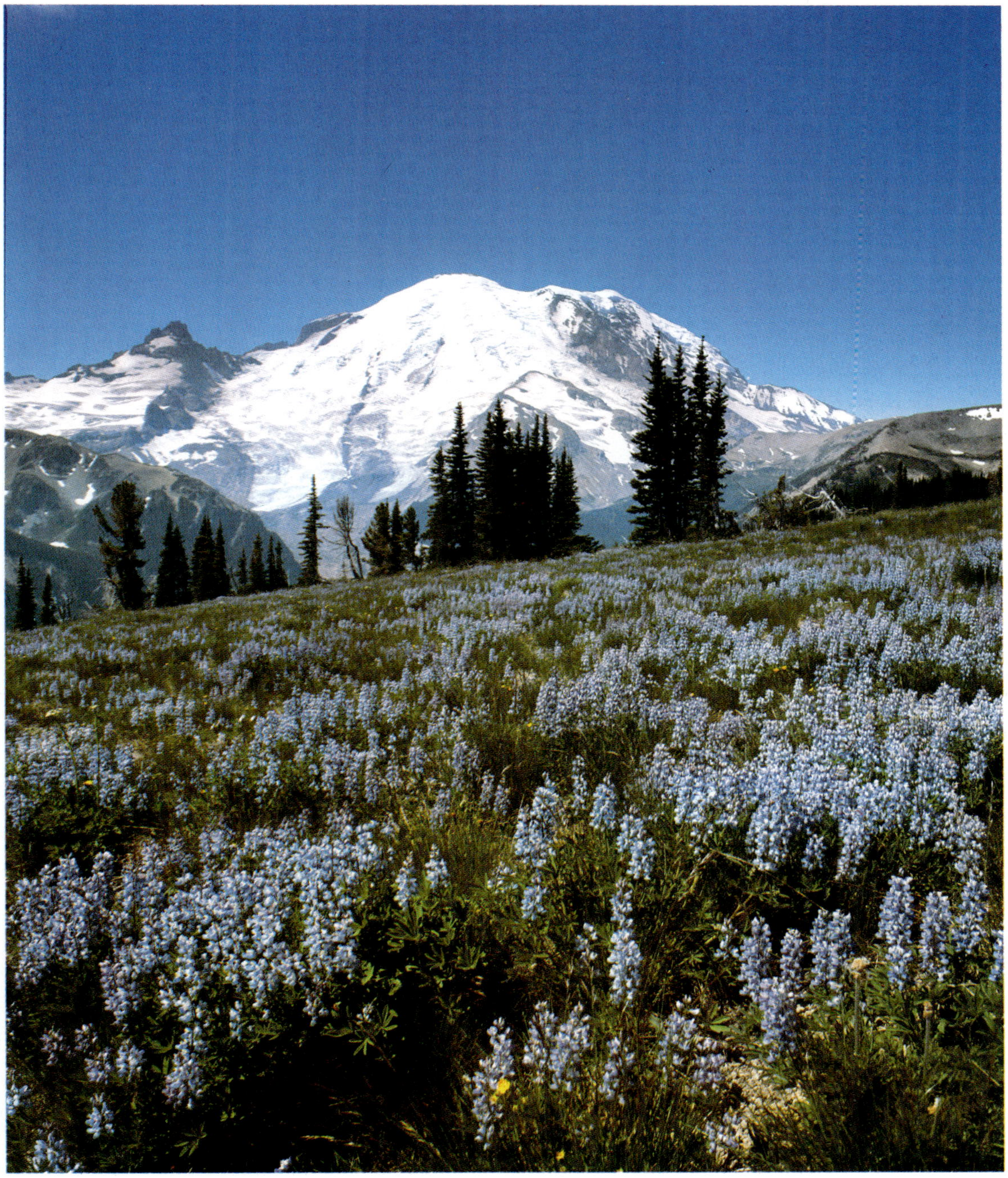

One of the great advantages of *modern slide films is that once you have taken the picture, the processing laboratory really does do the rest. This frees the photographer to concentrate on two things; taking the picture, and selling it. An insight into the commercial world often leaves amateurs feeling that perhaps they would do better not to sell their pictures. A typical art-director's reaction, on looking over the mountain pictures on this page, would be 'where can I put the text?' The flawless azure sky and the wildflowers on the grassy slopes are nothing to him: he just sees it in terms of so many ems in twelve point on fourteen, left justified, and wonders whether he can get all his text in. He will cheerfully chop about a carefully composed picture, and then wonder why the photographer looks pained: 'He's getting paid, isn't he?' This does not mean, though, that anything less than the best is good enough: the picture is* ***selected*** *on its merit, no matter how it may be violated later. Furthermore, as explained in the text, the larger-format picture has an additional and quite unfair advantage: when you are going through five hundred pictures, it is easier to see. Nevertheless, professional photographers can and do take beautiful pictures, just for their own amusement; much as they prize some of their commercial shots, their favourites were taken for love, not money. Every photograph must be taken as if it were the only one.*

WE DO THE REST

FILM PROCESSING

Standard processing (including speed adjustment) is best left to processing labs. There is, however, a variety of non-standard processing which can be interesting. This is processing positive (reversal) film as a negative. The alternative, processing negative as positive, is not always effective, as most colour negative films have a heavy orange cast to make printing easier. With some films this will decolourise during (reversal) processing, but you cannot rely on this.

The effects are weird and fascinating, especially if you choose your subjects carefully, and the only drawback is that some negative processing solutions will be contaminated if positive film is processed in them – so warn the lab first.

OTHER DARKROOM TECHNIQUES

In conventional colour printing (whether neg/pos or pos/pos) you can of course vary colour by varying filtration; you can also try out 'effects' filters, including 'action makers', starbursts, multi-image, etc.

In a less conventional field you can try tone separation; this involves making three separation negatives (by contact is easiest) from a black-and-white negative (in which case you have one for the highlights, one for the mid-tones, and one for the shadows) or from a colour slide (using whatever effects filters take your fancy). You then print through each of these in turn, using magenta for one, cyan for the next, and yellow for the third.

Very strange and wonderful effects are obtainable with this technique; those who get really hooked start evolving all sorts of variations of their own.

SLIDE COPYING

There is more to this apparently simple operation than meets the eye. The most important thing is that your light source must be consistent both in intensity and colour temperature; most people use electronic flash, though some use photo-floods. To avoid hot-spots, either bounce the light off a plain white card or use thick opal glass or Perspex (Lucite – methyl methacrylate) diffusers.

A good slow standard lens plus extension rings (or better still a bellows) will allow you to get close enough. Faster lenses than f/1.8, or wide-angles for reflexes, or worse still zooms, will give horrible results. Many professionals use an enlarger lens on the bellows for best results.

A problem in straight copying is contrast control; second generation pictures tend to be of higher contrast than originals. If you want the higher contrast (which you may do in creative work), fine. Otherwise, there are three solutions. One is to use special duplicating stock, only available in bulk. The second is to buy an Illumitran or similar with contrast control unit. The third is far cheaper and only slightly behind the Illumitran in convenience; leave some white background around the slide, so that some of the light from the copying table spills and flattens contrast – remember to leave off the lens hood. You can also try using a dirty UV filter.

When you introduce filters, the fun really starts. You can correct off colours, or add colour casts; you can use effects filters (including soft focus, action maker, etc.); and with a little care you can try partial filtering effects – the square 'system' filters are useful for this, and gel filters are even better.

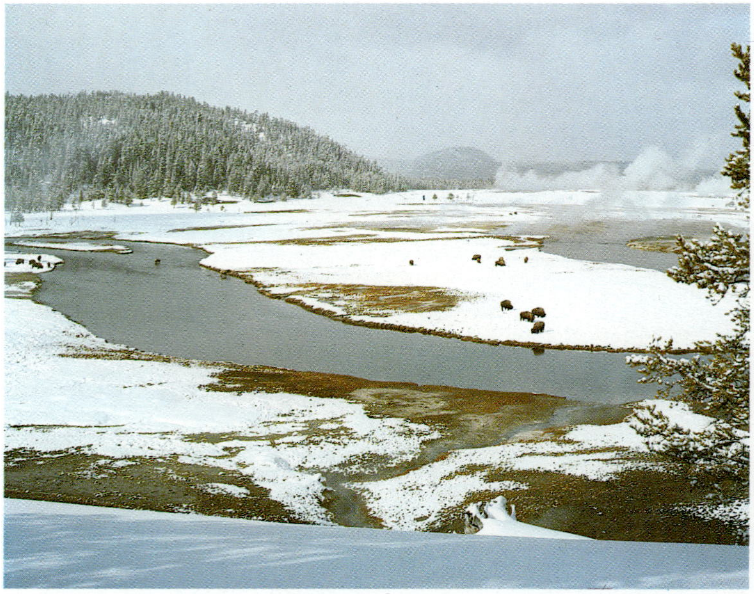

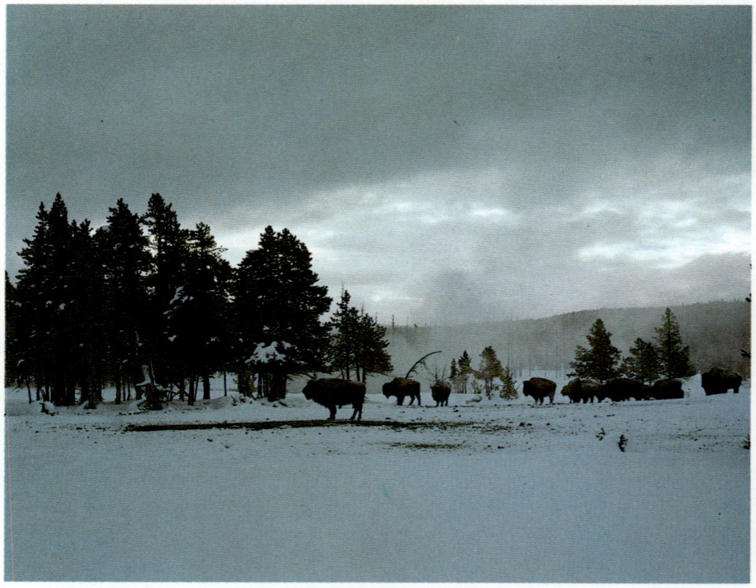

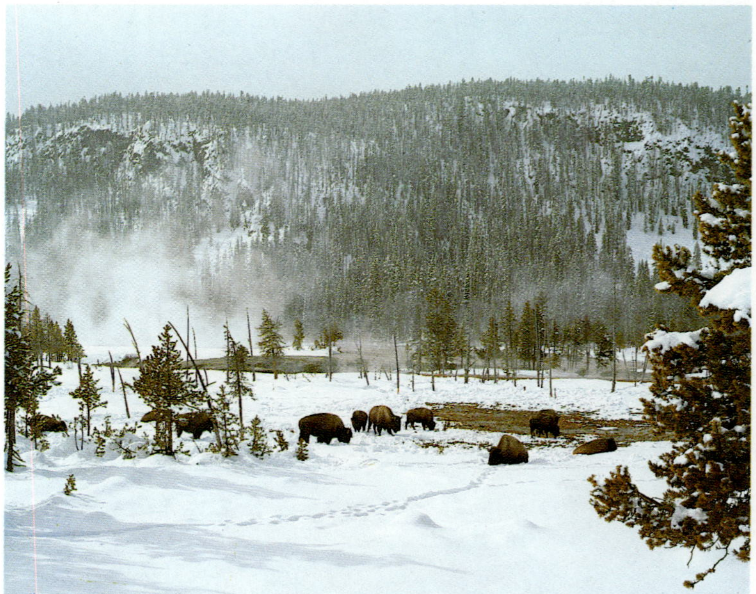

Whenever you shoot for *publication, always bear in mind how the pictures are to be used – how many, how big, and what sort of layout. The five pictures on these two pages would be a fine illustration for an article if used together; but which one sums the story up?*

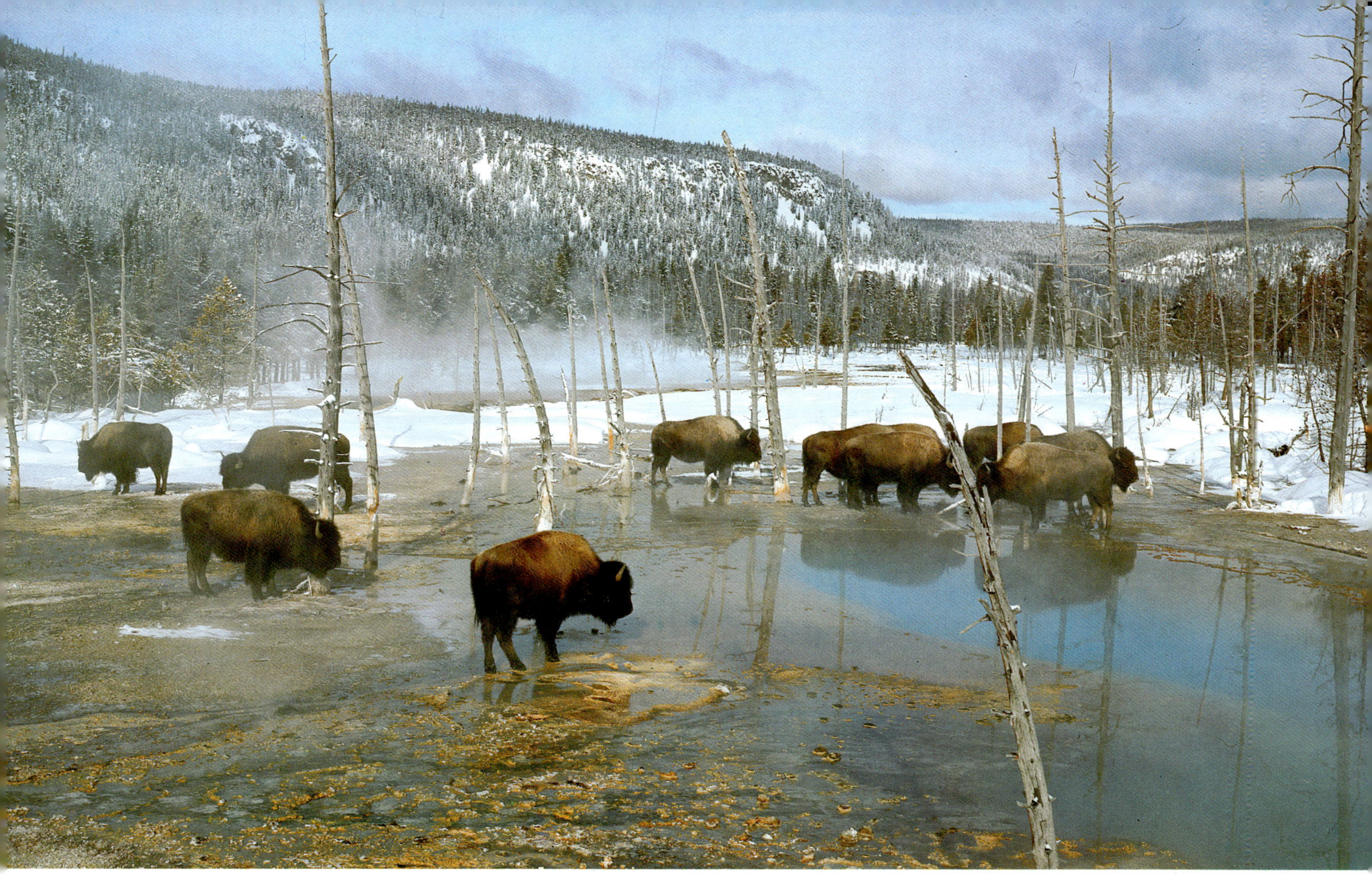
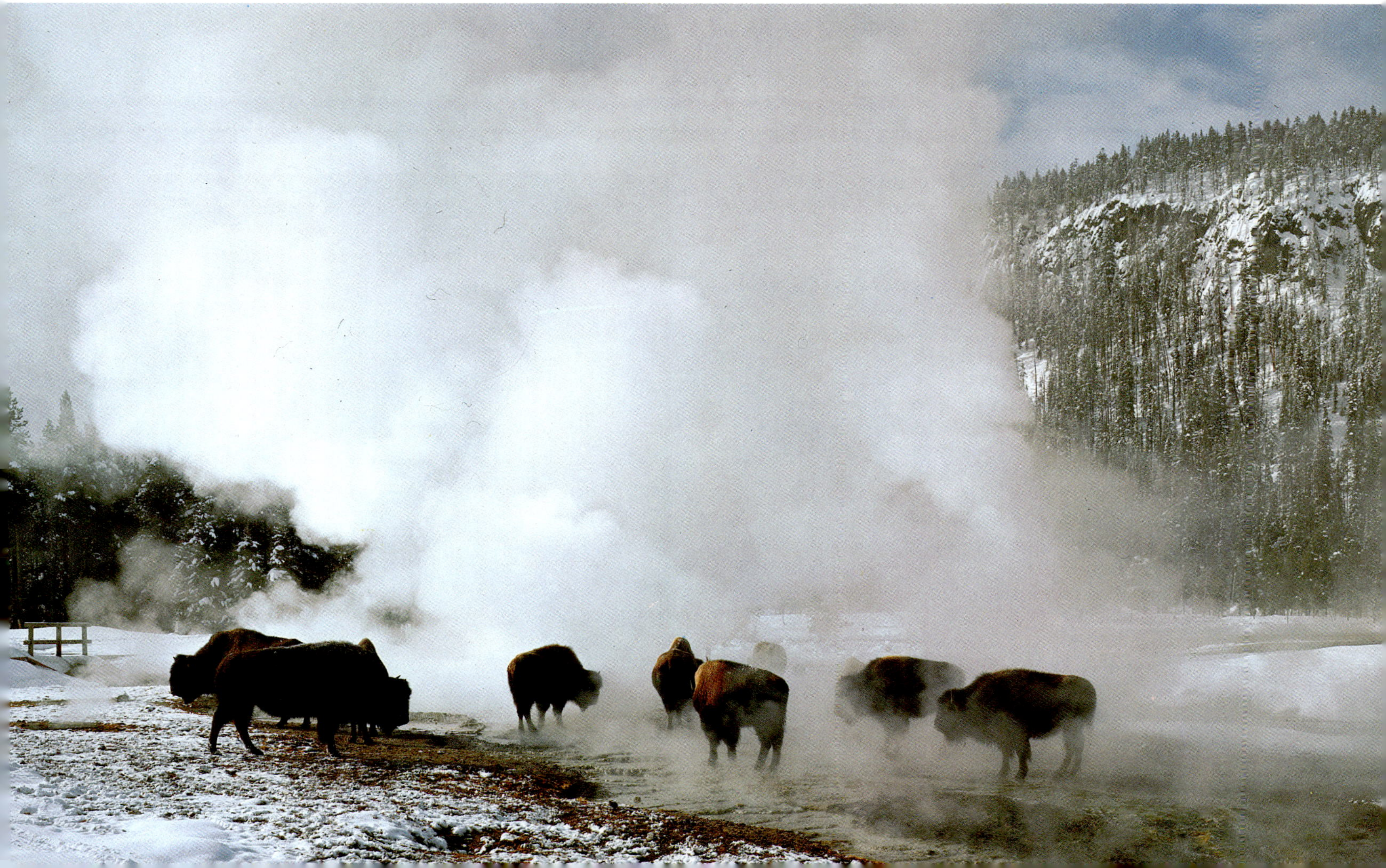

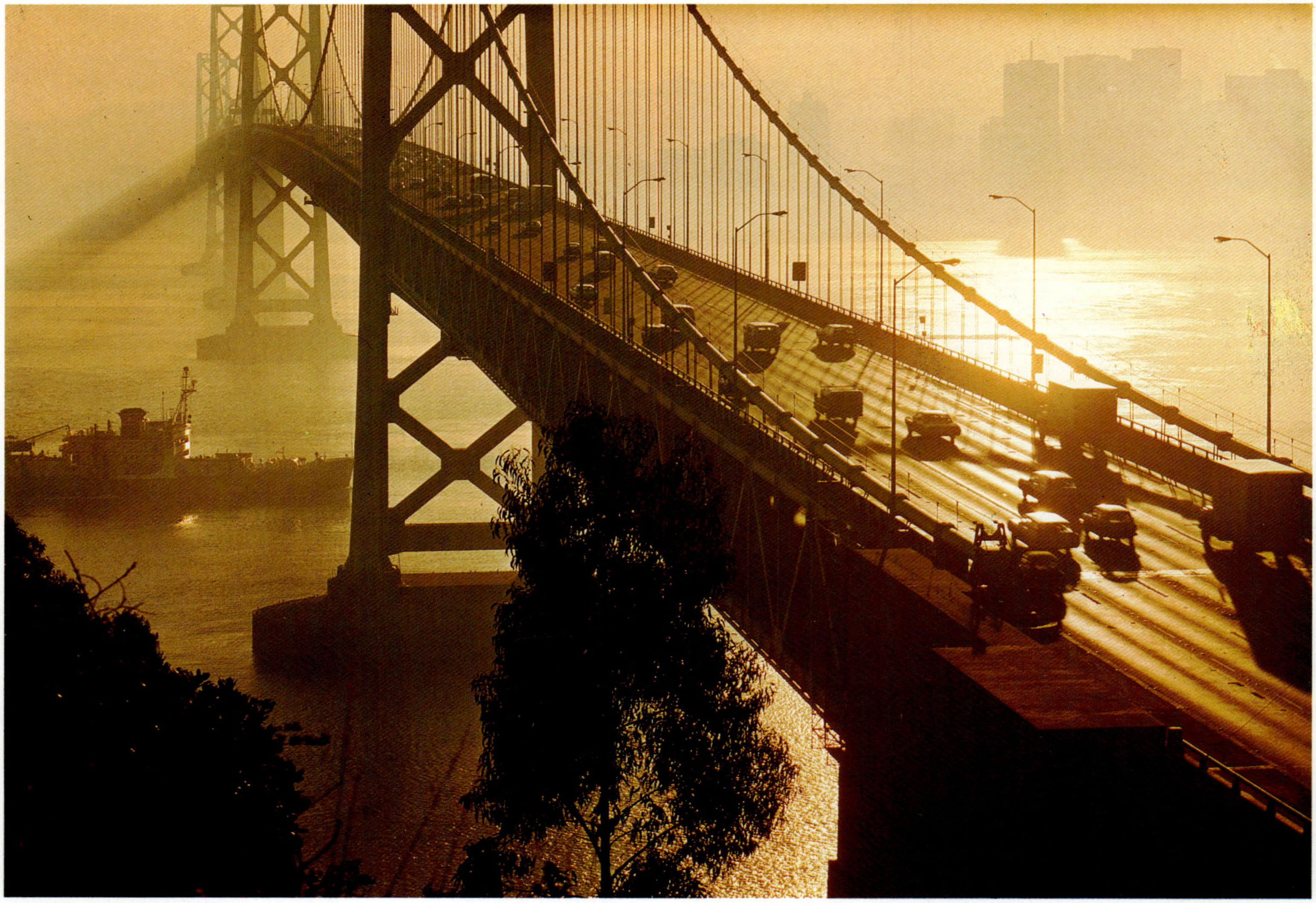

Even the most hackneyed *subjects can be photographed creatively. Two lighting effects which are always useful are shooting into the sun and underexposing, which gives the golden/silhouette effect above, and waiting until nightfall.*

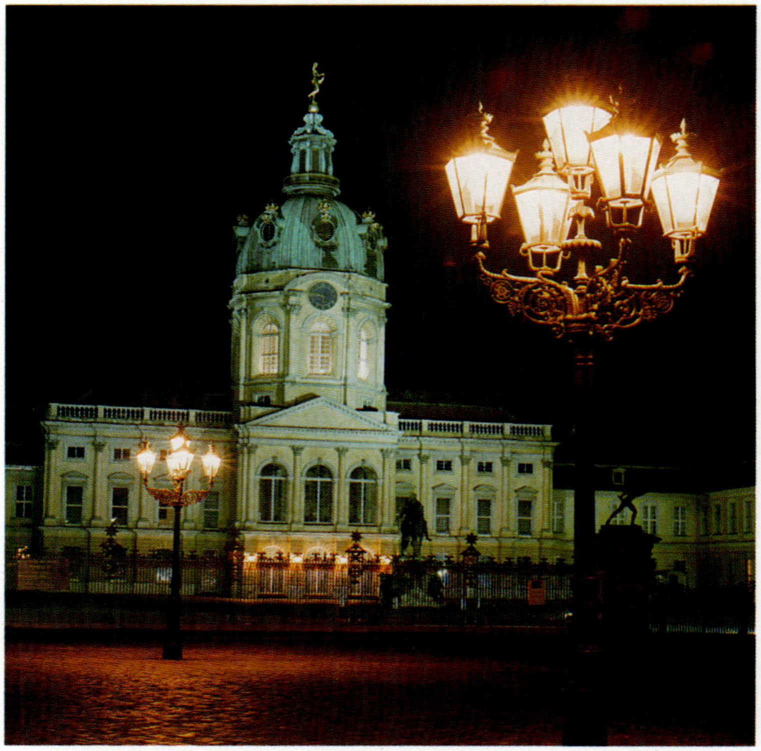

You can also try lightening underexposed slides (darkening overexposed ones is usually less successful), and cropping. Slight cropping can often improve composition, and in exteme cases you can 'pull up' a tiny fraction of a picture so that the dye structure of the film shows up, as described earlier.

You can also 'dupe up' from 35mm to larger formats or 'dupe down' from larger formats to smaller; make 'sandwiches' or double exposures; and make colour negatives (or black-and-white negatives) from colour slides. Incidentally, the effects obtainable with a sandwich and a double exposure are not the same. In a sandwich, the dark part of one slide will obscure anything on the other but the light part will allow detail to show through. In a double exposure, the dark part of one slide will allow the other slide to be recorded, but the light parts will burn out any detail in the other.

Another method of slide copying is to copy the projected image. This is not suitable for high-quality duplicates, indistinguishable from the originals, but it does allow you to experiment with all kinds of projection surfaces. Patterns projected onto nudes are now almost hackneyed, but there is still plenty of scope for experiment; imagine projecting a scorpion or a centipede onto a nude.

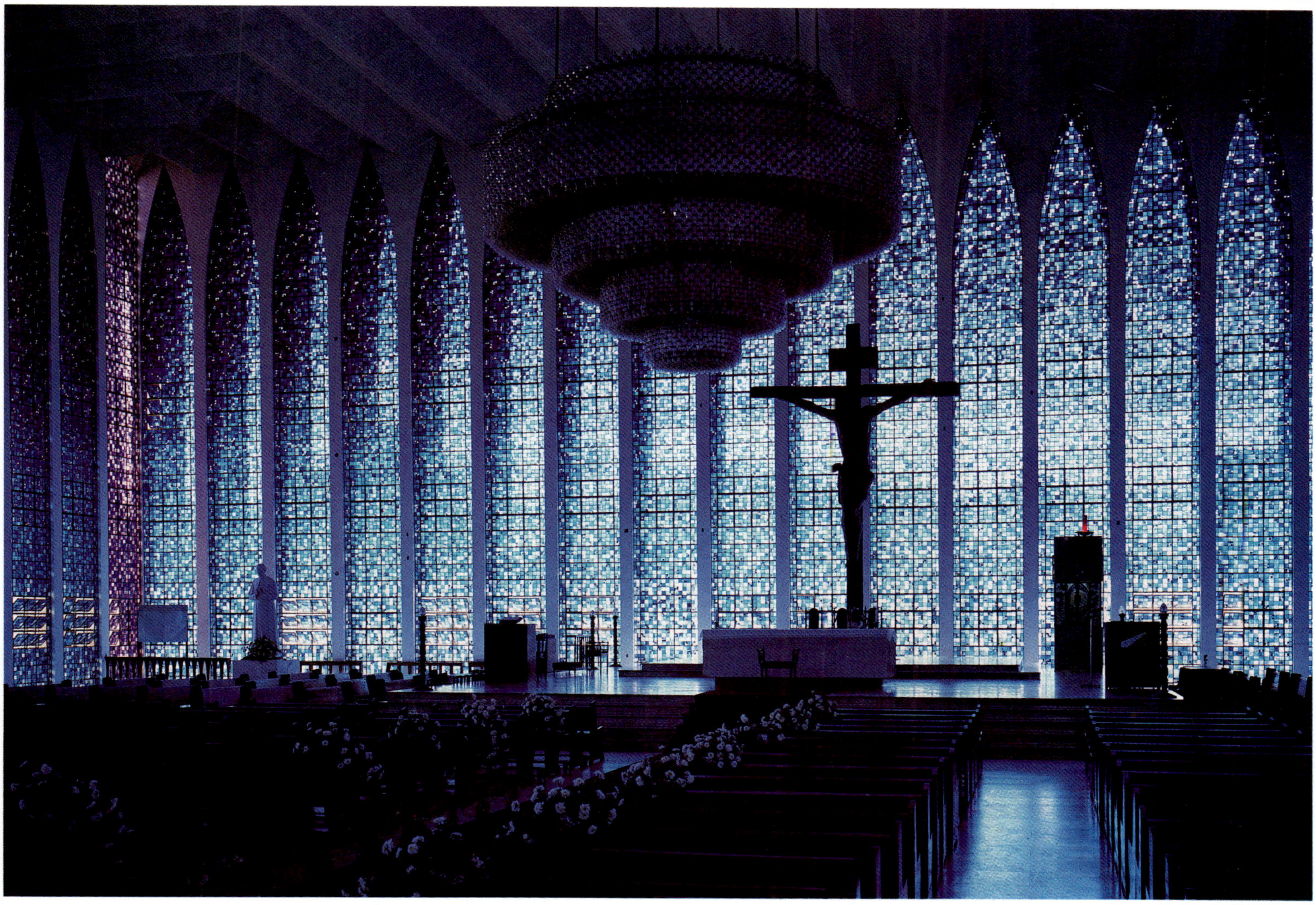

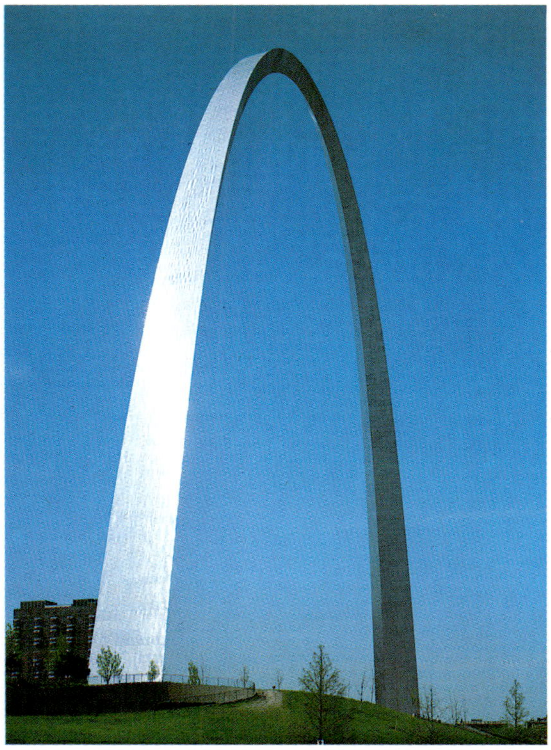

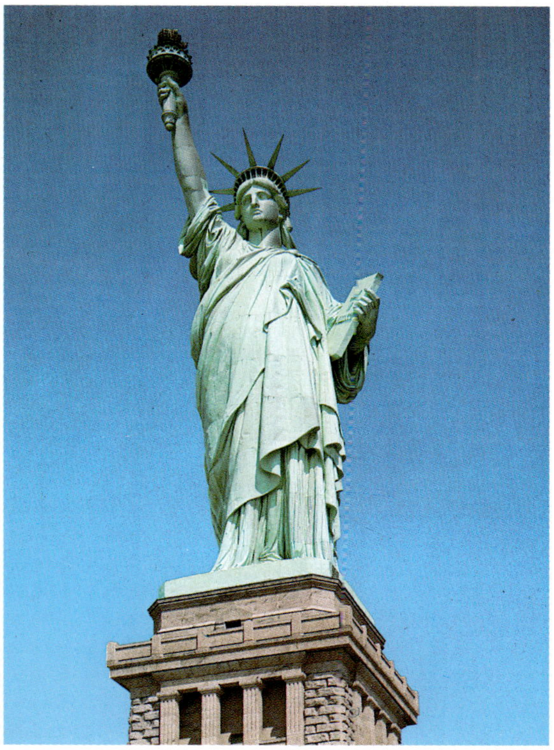

The cathedral interior, above, *is a prime example of technique in the service of creativity. The rising and swing front of a technical camera were used to preserve the soaring verticals; the high viewpoint and wide-angle lens (90mm on 5 x 4") convey the airy spaciousness; and the blue light filtering through the stained-glass windows gives the right feeling of coolness and quiet. When you see a picture which really impresses you, always try to work out how it was taken. Do not neglect the everyday, though. Technically excellent pictures, even if they have appeared a hundred times before, are always in demand. Even quite ordinary 'stock shots,' taken with care, can be both attractive and saleable. The pictures on the left, from rollfilm transparencies, are a good example.*

WE DO THE REST

Some places are so beautiful *that it seems virtually impossible not to take a good picture; but when you look closely at the pictures on these two pages, you begin to see just how much artlessness is the result of art. The picture of Mount Fuji is a particularly fine example. The colours are what first catch the eye, with the blue of the sky, the white and purple of the mountain, and the red-gold of the paddy. Then you see the little figures, and last of all you realise that the white streak across the middle is the famous 'bullet train.' Everything – even down to the cloud beside the mountain – is just right. The photographer just mounted his camera on a tripod . . . and waited. The colours in the lakeside scene, and in the picture of Schloss Neuschwanstein, are the colours of autumn. It was not by chance that the photographer was there on that morning. The same goes for the other two pictures: the sun striking the church balances the dark mass of the mountain; the late summer haze on the steep cobbled streets reinforces the weariness of the cyclists. Nothing is left to chance.*

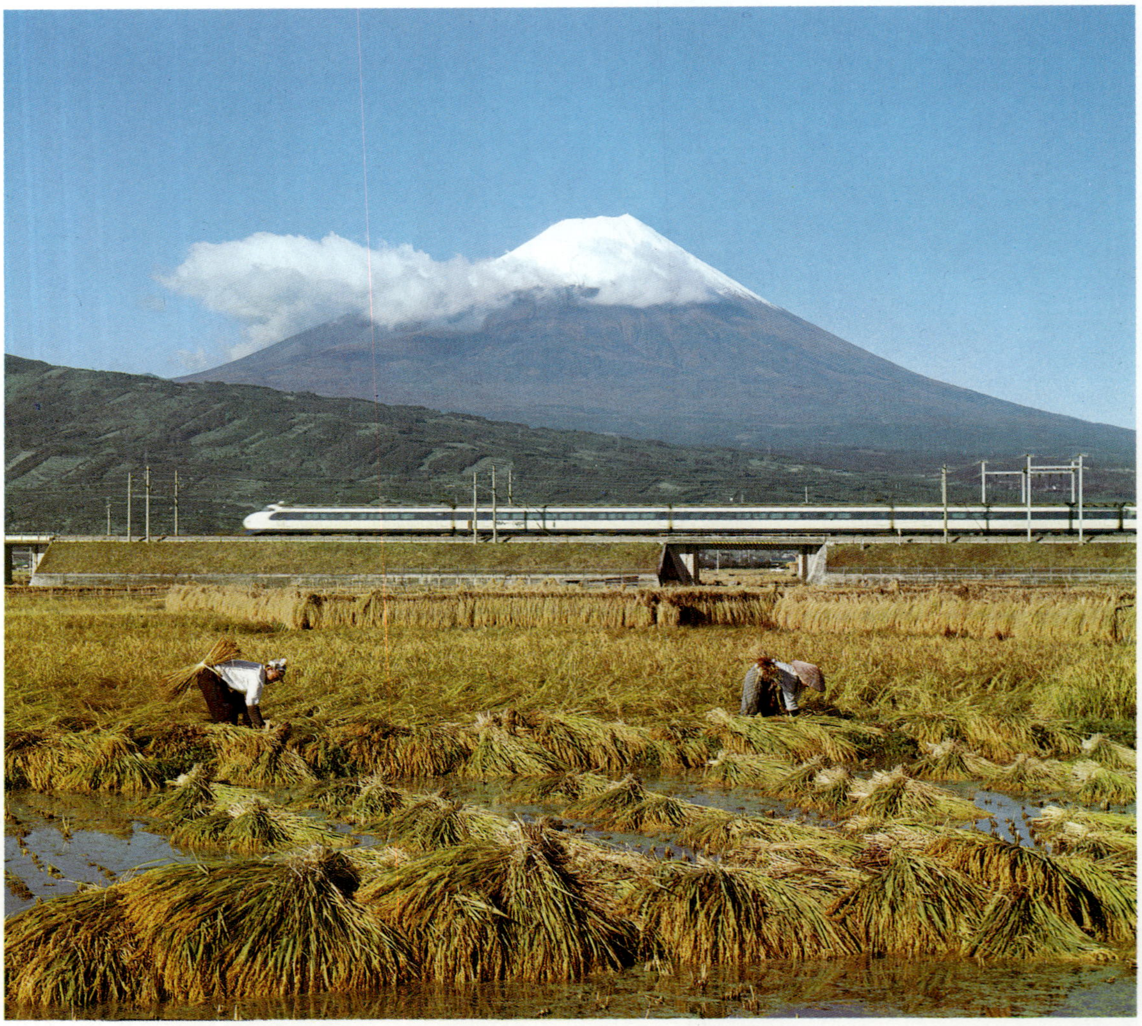

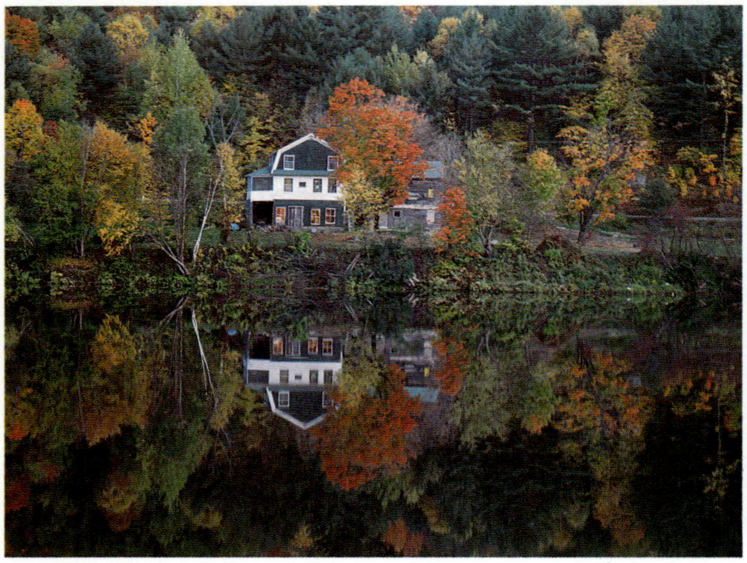

AFTERWORK ON PRINTS

Straightforward spotting of prints should be routine; black spots are not usually too bad, but white ones can easily be filled in with retouching dyes. A few people can even do this on transparencies (large format, of course), but this requires skill bordering on the supernatural.

Retouching is another matter. Whilst the sable-hair brush and the knife come immediately to mind, professional retouchers make heavy use of the airbrush – a sort of miniature spraygun, resembling a fountain pen, which can be used to apply dye or pigment to the picture.

Airbrushing is widely used to enhance colours. The beautiful green eyes seen on the covers of many glossy magazines, for example, owe more to De Vilbiss (the airbrush manufacturers) than to nature or photography. White pigments allow too-bright colours to be 'knocked back,' or alternatively they can be 'shadowed' with black. It is also possible to block out unwanted areas: many of the pictures of immaculate machinery to be seen in manufacturers' catalogues started out as ordinary oily greasy machines against a working factory background, but the airbrush has removed the background and repainted the machine so that it appears pristine and as if photographed in a 'cove' with white floor, walls, and ceiling.

Although the airbrush is much employed in what might be called 'straight' retouching, there are also many creative uses which can be found for it. The first is adding colour to black-and-white pictures; the black-and-white face with red lips is maybe a cliché, but similar tricks can be employed to great effect. Secondly, the airbrush leaves no brush-strokes, and may be made to give a very 'photographic' effect. Many of the so-called 'photo-realist' painters employ the airbrush extensively, and among photographers Peter Barry is famous for his melding of photography and airbrush work to create strange and often surreal

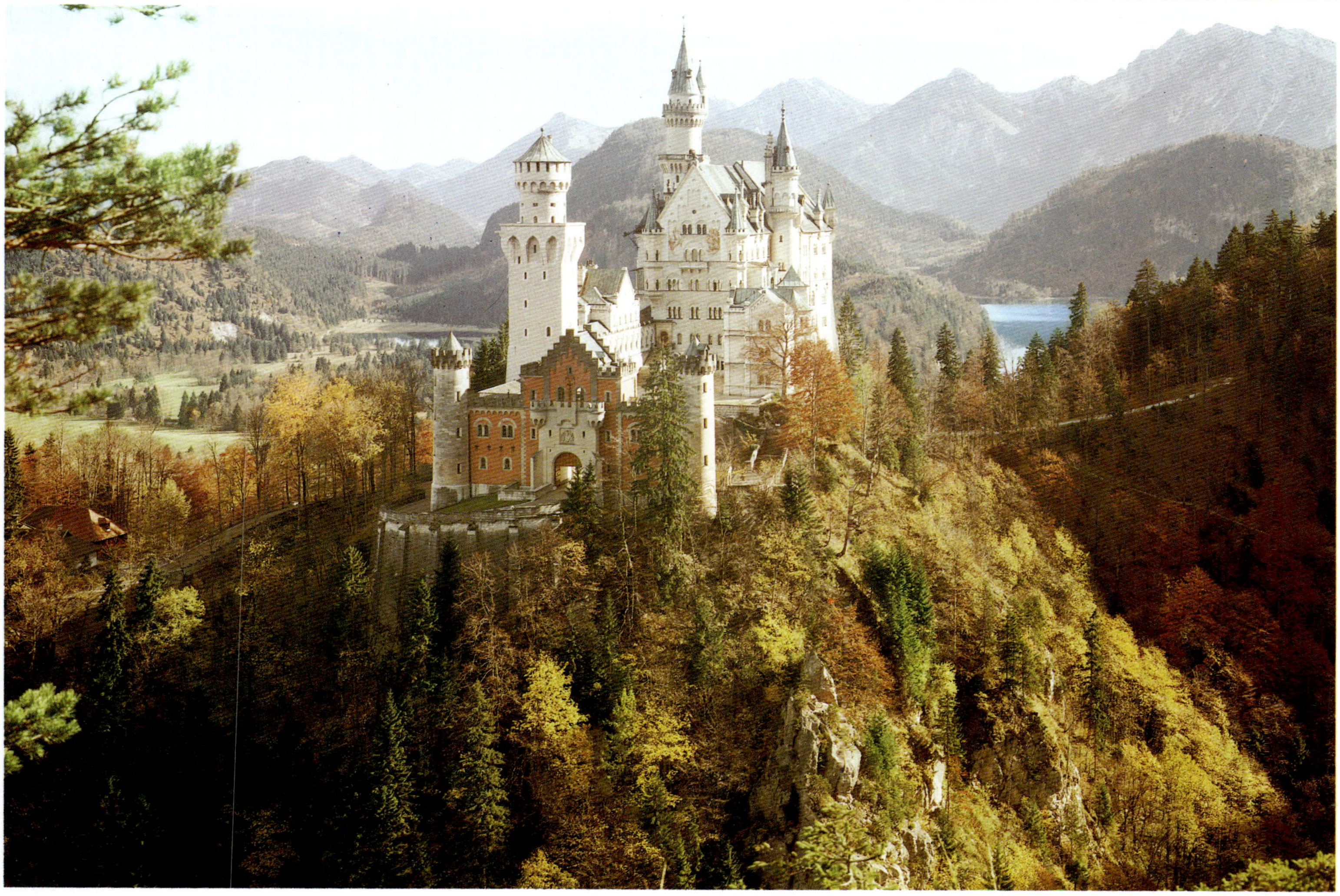

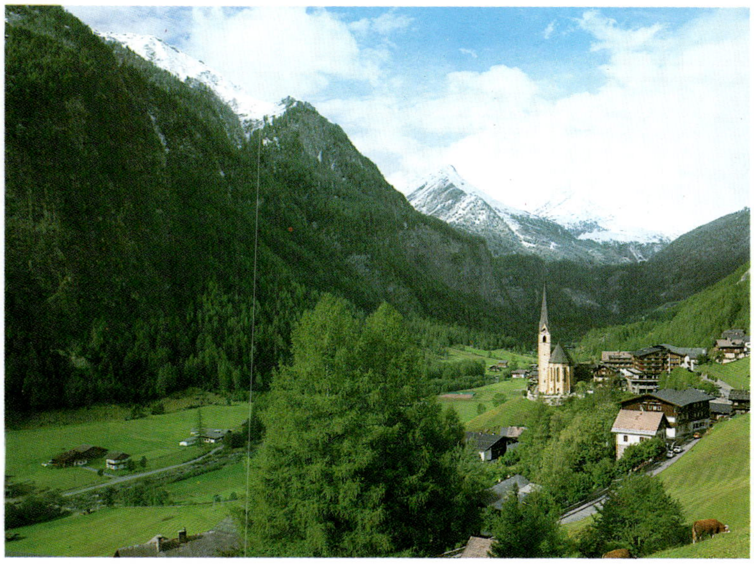

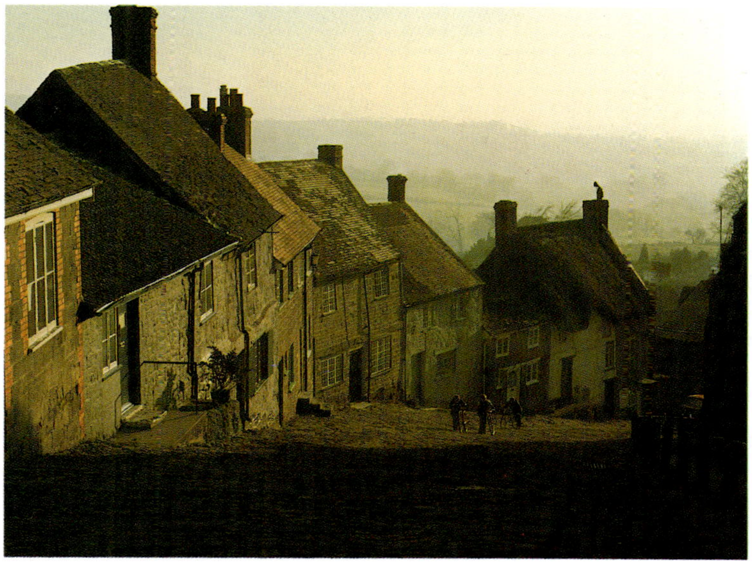

images. Thirdly, it may be used in collage.

Collage literally means 'glueing', and the essence of collage and montage is that the photograph is physically cut up and then glued back together. Parts can be omitted or repeated, and you can incorporate other photographs (or artwork or anything else) as you feel inclined.

When you want the handiwork to be obvious, you can exhibit the work itself; otherwise, you can copy it onto a new piece of film to present a 'seamless' new picture. If you are going to do this, it is best to work on a larger scale than the intended final result: for example, if you want a 10 x 8″ final print, make a work print at least 11 x 14″ and preferably even bigger, so that your handiwork is scaled down in the final picture.

There is also a sort of 'punk' school which tears, burns,

WE DO THE REST

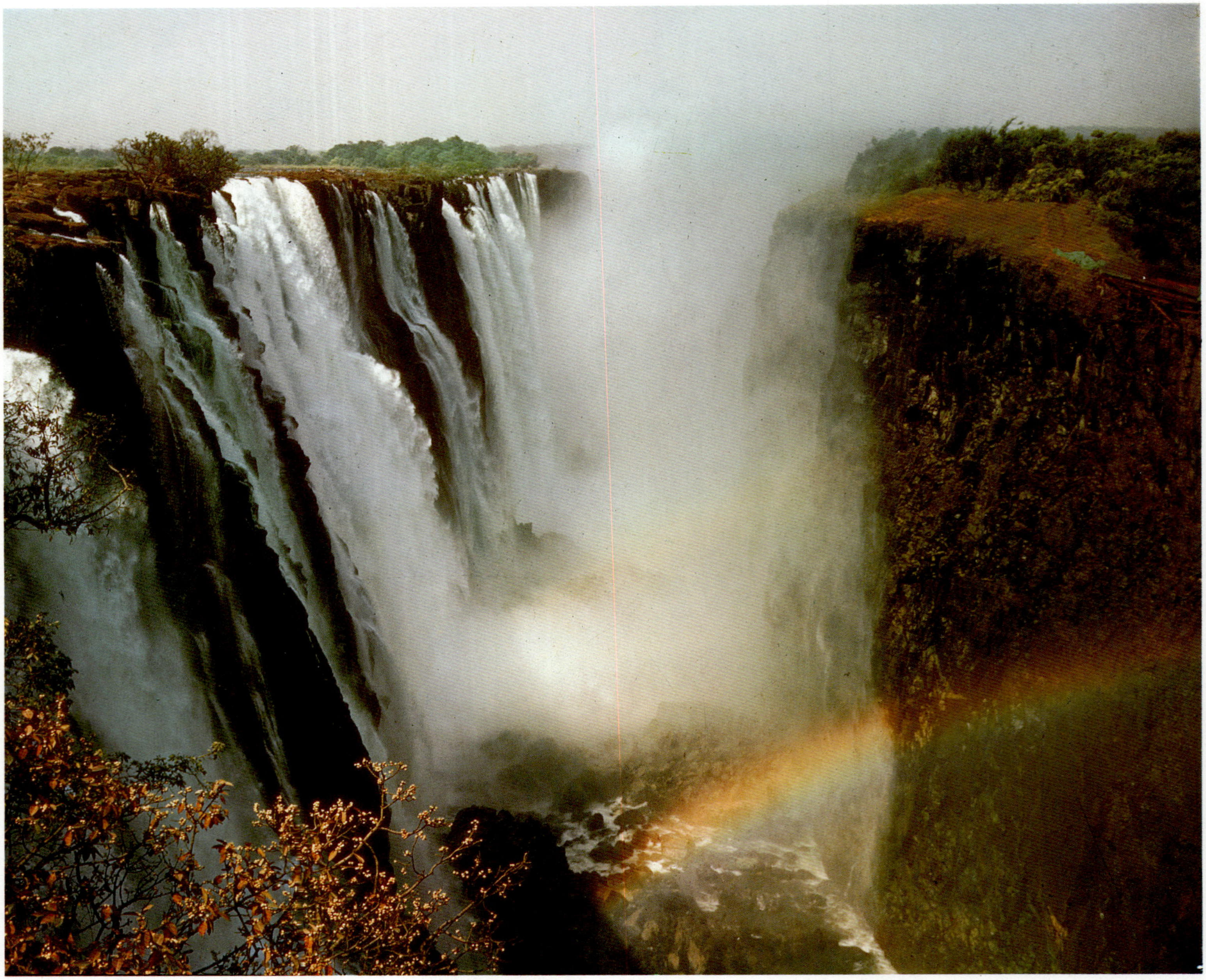

mangles, stains, and otherwise physically attacks prints or even slides. Whilst this can be very effective, one cannot help feeling that it is often done for effect – effect which, when the picture is displayed, turns out to be lacking.

CREATIVE PRESENTATION

Too many photographers lavish great time and effort on making a really superb image, and then file it away and forget about it. If a picture is worth spending time on – either in the taking or in the darkroom – it should also be worth displaying.

For a picture which is in itself a strong image, a plain frame is best; anything too ornate will only attract attention away from the picture. Personal tastes will vary, but a good choice is the modern brushed aluminium for a 'gallery' look, or plain light wood for more homely pictures such as landscapes or portraits.

On the other hand, it is perfectly possible to use a frame as a part of the picture: a heavy ornate gilt frame might suit a portrait, especially one in a deliberately old-fashioned style, and a heavy oak frame might go well with a rich blue sky.

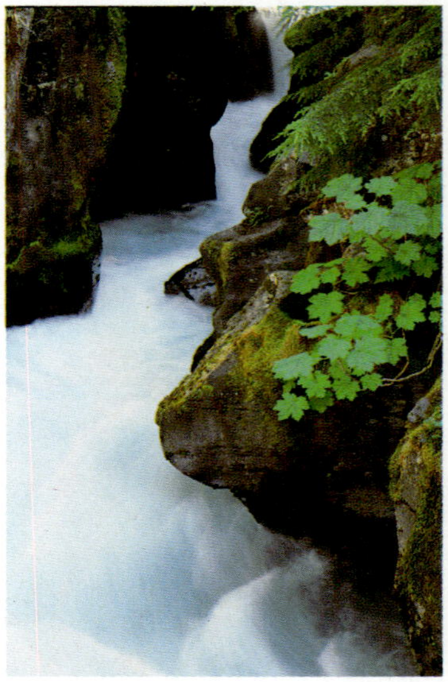

Is there any way to improve *your creativity? Yes. For a start, look at every picture you can. Analyse what you like about it, and what is wrong with it. But there is a more active way than that. Set yourself a theme. Before you start to photograph it, think about it: explore all its connotations in your mind. Go through your own picture files, imagining you are a picture editor – that should get you going. Then – and only then – get out and start taking pictures. The theme here is water. There is a lot more that can be said. Why not try to say it?*

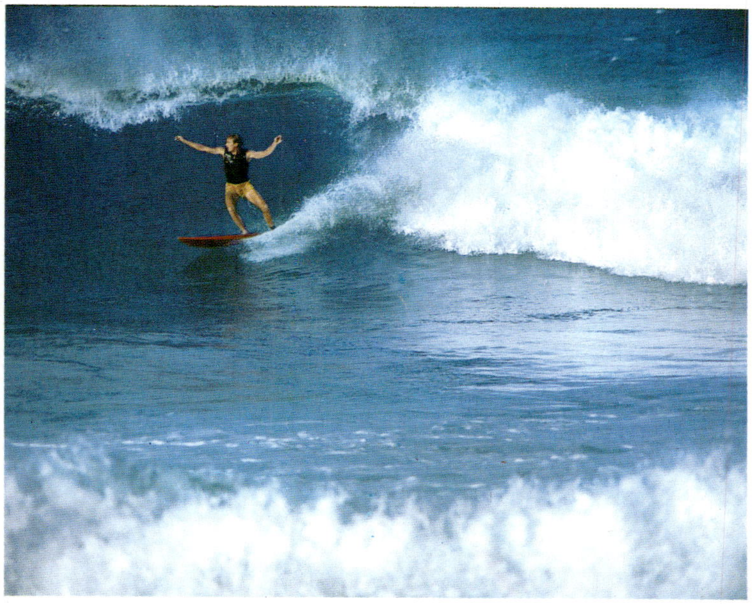

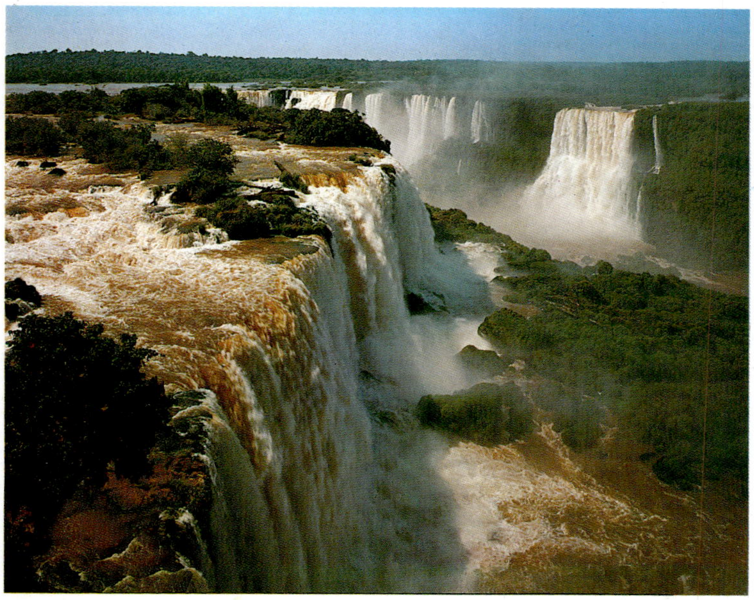

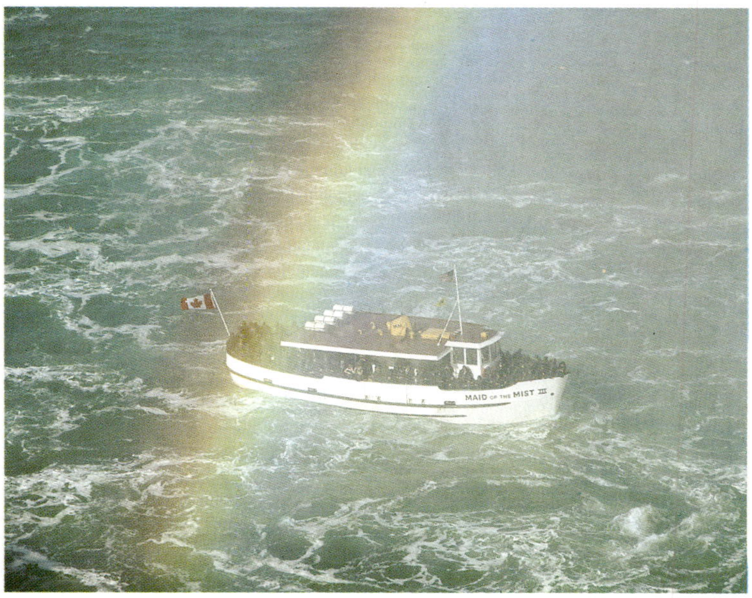

If you want to sell your pictures, you must also present them well. Transparencies, as already explained, are the only possible medium, and the usual method of presentation is the black card cut-out frame. The transparency (in or out of a projection frame in the case of 35mm) is taped inside the frame, and the whole thing is protected with an acetate envelope, clear on one side and frosted (to act as a diffuser) on the back. The normal size for 35mm and all rollfilm formats is a mask about 9 x 12 cm; this makes them a convenient size for handling and leaves space for any information needed to be typed on a plain white label and stuck to the mount. A typical caption might include place, date, and a brief description of what is going on, such as "Buddhist monastery, Rewalsar (Northern India) 1982." Few people are remotely interested in exposure details, films etc., but don't forget your name, address, and telephone number!

POSTSCRIPT

This book is ended: we have come to the end of the road as far as words and pictures are concerned. I have tried to do three things.

First, I have tried to explain as many tricks of the trade as possible, so that you will not be at a loss when it comes to bending the photographic process to suit your personal vision.

Secondly, I have tried to spark as many ideas as possible. You may not like some of the pictures in this book; you may disagree with some of the text; but the mere fact that you have reacted shows that your critical faculties are in some kind of working order.

Thirdly, I have tried to include a wide selection of work from some of the finest photographers around today. Do not be ashamed to copy them; copying is a traditional way of learning. On the other hand, do not copy them forever. Once you have mastered a technique – try to take it in a new direction. You will have to be pretty original, because many of the photographers featured in this book are very inventive, very versatile, and very creative; and for that very reason, none of them would pretend that he had done all there was to be done in a particular field.

You are not alone, though. This book is over, but every day there is a stream of new images to look at: on advertising hoardings, in magazines, in other books. Learn to look critically at everything you see. In pictures, try to work out what pleases you (or displeases you) about a particular image: is it the colour, the subject matter, the shape, the memories it evokes? Do not be too impressed by the arguments of others: of more than one critic it may fairly be said 'he writes a very fine picture,' and in his excellent book The Painted Word Tom Wolfe exposes the absurdity of an art establishment which hides ever-diminishing creativity behind ever-expanding clouds of (nigh-meaningless) words.

Try to apply what you learn from the pictures to what you see around you in real life. You are impressed by a landscape: how could you best express that landscape, compressing a hundred square miles of land into a piece of coloured plastic 24 x 36mm? Would it look best in the evening, with lowering clouds; fresh and bright, in the dawn; sunbaked at noon; grey with rain? The picture you want may not be the easy one: you may have to come back day after day, perhaps year after year if you visit the place seldom, until you can match your vision. By all means take a reference picture, but do not confuse it with the picture in your mind: keep that pristine until you can get it down on film.

Finally, remember that creativity isn't easy; anyone who tells you it is must be lying. It can be frustrating; it can be heartbreaking; it can make you wonder why on earth you don't take up some easier hobby, like lion taming or brain surgery; but when it all goes right, you know why you do it.